The Internet of Things in the Defence Industry

The Internet of Things in the Defence Industry: Challenges and Solutions for Military Security

EDITED BY

KAVITA SAHU

Dr. Harisingh Gour Vishwavidyalaya, India

AND

RAJEEV KUMAR

Shri Ramswaroop Memorial University, India

emerald PUBLISHING

United Kingdom – North America – Japan – India – Malaysia – China

Emerald Publishing Limited
Emerald Publishing, Floor 5, Northspring, 21-23 Wellington Street, Leeds LS1 4DL.

First edition 2026

British Library Cataloguing in Publication Data
A catalogue record for this book is available from the British Library

ISBN: 978-1-83549-199-7 (Print)
ISBN: 978-1-83549-198-0 (Online)
ISBN: 978-1-83549-200-0 (Epub)

Printed and bound by CPI Group (UK) Ltd, Croydon, CR0 4YY

*To my beloved parents, **Mrs Shanti Sahu** and **Mr Suresh Sahu**, whose unconditional love, strength, and sacrifices have been the foundation of all my journeys.*

Kavita Sahu

Contents

About the Editors

Kavita Sahu holds PhD in Computer Science and is currently working as an Assistant Professor in the Department of Computer Science and Applications at the Dr. Harisingh Gour Vishwavidyalaya (A Central University), Madhya Pradesh, India.

Rajeev Kumar holds PhD in Information Technology and is currently working as a Deputy Director (Research) & an Associate Professor in the Department of Computer Science and Engineering at the Shri Ramswaroop Memorial University, Uttar Pradesh, India.

List of Contributors

Anurag A. S.	Central University of Kerala, India
Alka Agrawal	Babasaheb Bhimrao Ambedkar University, India
Katyayani Akella	Symbiosis International (Deemed University), India
V. P. Arun	JKKN College of Engineering and Technology, India
Naimisha Awasthi	Centre for Advanced Studies, India
Anirban Bhowmik	M.U.C. Women's College, India
Tarun Biswas	Indian Institute of Information Technology Ranchi, India
Dukuru Chiranjevi	Indian Institute of Information Technology Ranchi, India
R. Dhaya	PNG University of Technology, Papua New Guinea
R. Adline Freeda	KCG College of Technology, India
Anindya Ghatak	Bennett University, India
Prateek Raj Gautam	UPES, India
Omprakash Kaiwartya	Nottingham Trent University, UK
R. Kanthavel	PNG University of Technology, Papua New Guinea
Sunil Karforma	The University of Burdwan, India
Atul B. Kathole	Dr. D. Y. Patil Institute of Technology, India
Neha Katiyar	Bennett University, India
Suhel Ahmad Khan	Indira Gandhi National Tribal University, India
Raees Ahamd Khan	Babasaheb Bhimrao Ambedkar University, India
Kritika Khandelwal	Manipal University Jaipur, India
Abhishek Kumar	University of Agder, Norway
Sarang Kumar	University of Agder, Norway
Snehlata Kumari	University of Hertfordshire, UK
Johnpaul M.	Central University of Kerala, India
R. Maheswari	Kongu Engineering College, India
Amita Sanjiv Mirge	Pimpri Chinchwad College of Engineering, India
Mohd Nadeem	Shri Ramswaroop Memorial University, India
Satyanarayana Nandury	GITAM (Deemed University), India
Suvarna Ganesh Patil	Dr. D. Y. Patil Institute of Technology, India
Abhishek Kumar Pandey	Center for Security, Theory and Algorithmic Research, India

Karuna Sahu	Accenture, India
T. P. Saravanan	Nandha Engineering College, India
Amal Krishna Sarkar	Sanjay Gandhi Postgraduate Institute of Medical Sciences, India
A. K. Singh	Shri Ramswaroop Memorial University, India
Inderjeet Singh	Vara Technology, India
Kushal Pal Singh	Malviya National Institute of Technology, India
Vijayanand Srinivasan	Sri Venkateswara College of Engineering, India
R. K. Srivastava	Dr. Shakuntala Misra National Rehabilitation University, India
Hardeo Kumar Thakur	Bennett University, India
S. C. Vetrivel	Kongu Engineering College, India

Preface

The rapid evolution of the Internet of Things (IoT) is fundamentally reshaping the global defence landscape, presenting both unprecedented opportunities and critical challenges. As military systems become more interconnected, intelligent, and data-driven, the integration of IoT technologies into defence infrastructures has emerged as a strategic imperative. This edited volume brings together diverse perspectives and research contributions that explore the multifaceted role of IoT in enhancing military security, operational efficiency, and resilience.

This book opens with an in-depth overview of the challenges and solutions related to deploying IoT in the defence industry, setting the tone for subsequent discussions on data protection, privacy concerns, and the ethical and legal implications of such technological transformations. The integration of soft computing approaches and cryptographic mechanisms for secure data transmission reflects the necessity of safeguarding sensitive military information in an increasingly connected environment.

With the advent of quantum computing, the cybersecurity paradigm is undergoing a transformation. This volume delves into how the convergence of quantum technologies with IoT can redefine threat mitigation strategies in defence contexts. Additionally, it explores real-world applications of IoT, such as battlefield surveillance, logistics optimization, intrusion detection systems, and adaptive security frameworks – highlighting the tangible impact of smart systems on mission readiness and tactical operations.

Chapters dedicated to next-generation network infrastructures, such as 5G and 6G, emphasize the challenges of virtualized environments and IoT device integration in high-stakes scenarios. The book also explores cutting-edge applications including, malware detection techniques, and artificial intelligence-driven decision systems – all tailored for defence environments.

By presenting comprehensive insights across technical, operational, and strategic dimensions, this volume serves as a valuable resource for researchers, practitioners, defence technologists, and policymakers. It aims to inspire future innovations and foster a secure, ethical, and efficient implementation of IoT technologies in defence sectors worldwide.

As defence ecosystems continue to evolve, this book invites readers to engage critically with emerging innovations while being mindful of the complex ethical, legal, and infrastructural challenges that accompany such rapid transformation.

Acknowledgements

We extend our heartfelt gratitude to all the scholars, researchers, and contributors who have played a significant role in shaping this edited volume, *The Internet of Things in the Defence Industry: Challenges and Solutions for Military Security*. Your dedication, expertise, and commitment to advancing research in this critical domain have made this work possible.

We express our sincere appreciation to **Prof R. K. Srivastava**, Professor and Head, Department of Computer Science, Dr Shakuntala Mishra National Rehabilitation University, Lucknow, Uttar Pradesh, India, for his constant support, insightful suggestions, and academic mentorship throughout the development of this volume.

We are equally thankful to **Prof Raees Ahmad Khan**, Professor of Information Technology, Babasaheb Bhimrao Ambedkar University, Lucknow, Uttar Pradesh, India, whose guidance, insightful suggestions, academic mentorship, and domain expertise in cybersecurity and IoT have been instrumental in shaping the structure and thematic relevance of several chapters in this book.

We also extend our gratitude to **Dr Suhel Ahmad Khan**, Assistant Professor, Department of Computer Science, Indira Gandhi National Tribal University, Madhya Pradesh, India, and **Dr Saswat Kishore Mishra**, Associate Professor of Economics, KIIT Deemed University, Bhubaneswar, Odisha, India, for their interdisciplinary inputs that enriched the depth and breadth of the discussion across technological, ethical, and economic dimensions.

Our special thanks to **Prof (Col.) A. K. Singh**, Advisor and Former Vice Chancellor, Shri Ramswaroop Memorial University, Barabanki, Uttar Pradesh, India, for his strategic vision and valuable feedback on defence-oriented research directions and practical applications.

We further acknowledge the exceptional efforts of all contributing authors across the 14 chapters of this volume. Their original research, diverse perspectives, and collaborative spirit have led to a rich compendium of knowledge exploring the intersection of IoT, cybersecurity, policy, ethics, and defence technologies. Your commitment to scholarly excellence is truly commendable.

This book stands as a testament to the power of collaborative and cross-institutional research, and we remain indebted to each contributor and mentor whose support made this possible.

Thank you all for your valuable contributions.

Chapter 1

The Internet of Things in the Defence Industry: Challenges and Solutions for Military Security

R. Kanthavel[a], *R. Adline Freeda*[b] *and R. Dhaya*[a]

[a]*School of Electrical and Communication Engineering, PNG University of Technology, Papua New Guinea*
[b]*Department of Information Technology, KCG College of Technology, India*

Abstract

IoT applications have become so indispensable in the modern digital world; in the sphere of modern warfare, Internet of Medical Things (IoMT) or Internet of Battlefield Things (IoBT) is growing. The technology is based on equipping military-grade physical objects with advanced software and sensors in order to set up an exchange of data and execution of tasks with higher accuracy and speed. IoMT and IoBT enable soldiers to make use of several devices, combat equipment with embedded sensors capturing biometrics, among others. Given the rising complexity and unpredictability of military operations, IoT presents a strategic advantage in supporting the defence personnel to respond appropriately under intense pressure. However, security of the IoT applications has been a concern, more so in the defence sector, where breaches could cost not just revenue but even client trust. The security lapses in IoT applications may have disastrous consequences of the potentially causing sensitive data disclosure or erosion of stakeholder confidence.

Keywords: Internet of Medical Things (IoMT); Internet of Battlefield Things (IoBT); physical objects; sensor; exchange of data; sensitive data

---

The Internet of Things in the Defence Industry:
Challenges and Solutions for Military Security, 1–22

Published under exclusive licence by Emerald Publishing Limited
doi:10.1108/978-1-83549-198-020261001

1. Introduction

IoT integration into the defence sector is changing the character of military operations due to its wide span of systems and equipment connections. In this area, IoT technology allows never-before-seen levels of data collection, connectivity, and automation in such a diversity of applications as smart weaponry, drones, enhanced surveillance systems, and logistics management. Though there are many strategic benefits to these developments, there are also new risks and challenges that come along with them, especially in terms of security. There are several concerns in this respect that the implementation of IoT presents in the context of military security. Among the most important is the susceptibility of IoT devices to hacking. Therefore, the number of interconnected devices rises, increasing the attack surface for the attacker to exploit vulnerabilities and hence put sensitive information or systems into jeopardy (Burmaoglu et al., 2019). Therefore, the risks for manipulation of military equipment, data breach, and possible leakage of intelligence or disruption of operations exist.

The complexity of management and protection for the large and heterogeneous network of IoT devices also raises huge logistical challenges. Ensuring interoperability, resilience, and dependability of these systems in difficult and changing contexts is paramount. Despite all this, the defence sector is trying hard to make IoT systems more secure. This is to be done by creating the latest state-of-the-art cyber security defences, based on machine learning (ML) algorithms for anomaly detection, blockchain technology for secure data transmission, and artificial intelligence (AI) for predictive maintenance. Moreover, best practices in cyber security coupled with stringent rules and standards on makers of IoT devices could significantly reduce the risks (Ferrag et al., 2021).

The other difficult task, other than these potential risks to cyber security, is the management and protection of such a large Internet of Things (IoT) network of devices. The ability needed to be sure that every device is hardened, reliable, and interoperable – much more so under the challenging, varying conditions that are often encountered in military operations – is fully respected. Keeping these systems operational and intact would need robust encryption, secure protocols for communication, and frequent software updates. In consideration of extracting meaningful insights from this humongous amount of data created by IoT devices, sophisticated data analytics and processing capabilities are required (Blanco-Novoa et al., 2020). Although presupposed to revolutionize the defence domain, the ability to handle the security threats thereby associated requires a great mind and planning. In this regard, state-of-the-art technologies coupled with the implementation of comprehensive security procedures will ensure that the military will fully reap the benefits associated with IoT without threats.

2. Security Vulnerabilities in IoT Devices and Networks

The security vulnerabilities in IoT devices and networks are a serious issue because dependence on IoT technology is increasing in many sectors like defence, healthcare, and smart infrastructures. Among these very reasons come multifarious

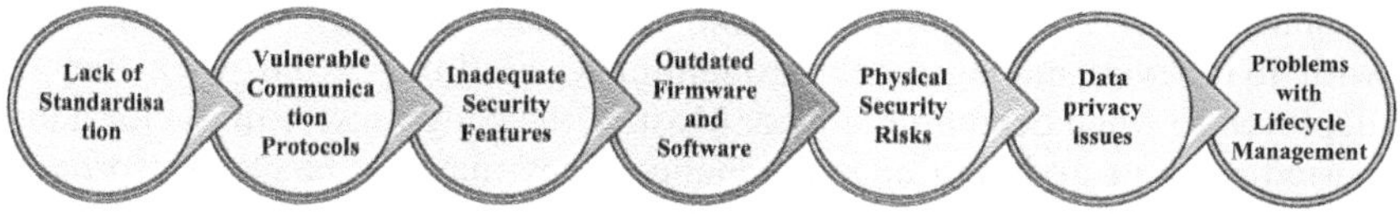

Fig. 1.1. Security Vulnerabilities in IoT Devices.

factors that cause these weaknesses. These security vulnerabilities are shown in Fig. 1.1 and explained as follows:

- **Lack of Standardization**: IoT consists of a very fragmented ecosystem, where devices from different manufacturers often run diverse platforms and communication protocols. The lack of standardization in these devices makes it difficult to implement security measures with uniformity throughout devices and networks. As there are no standardized guidelines on the security of devices, each device is not easily made to comply with best practices, thereby rendering the whole network susceptible to attacks.
- **Vulnerable Communication Protocols:** Popular communication protocols were initially designed with security not necessarily as the number one priority, and these are very often utilized by any IoT device. Widely used protocols, such as HTTP, MQTT, and CoAP, are useful but very vulnerable to attacks like data spoofing, eavesdropping, and man-in-the-middle. Moreover, many IoT devices are too resource-constrained to use secure communication routes and robust encryption (Dhaya et al., 2022).
- **Inadequate Security Features:** Most of the IoT devices are designed considering cost-effectiveness and user-friendliness rather than robust security features. As such, they may miss out on core security features, including strong authentication procedures, encryption, and secure firmware upgrades expected to be available in the devices. Because of this, they face numerous kinds of attacks, such as device manipulation, unauthorized access, and data leakage.
- **Outdated Firmware and Software:** IoT devices often have outdated firmware and software, probably with numerous unpatched vulnerabilities. Periodic patches and updates are needed in order to close these security holes; however, the way most of them are designed makes them very hard to update, and some even go without updates. They thus become susceptible to known weaknesses that attackers may perhaps exploit.
- **Physical Security Risks:** Unlike most conventional IT systems, the majority of IoT devices are deployed in physically accessible environments. The risk of physical attacks, theft, or tampering is therefore heightened, and this reduces the integrity of the device. For instance, an attacker who has physically accessed the device could extract sensitive information or even reprogram it for malicious purposes.
- **Data Privacy Issues**: IoT devices often collect and transfer sensitive data, such as personal information, medical records, and operational data. If adequate security measures are not in place, this could result in a violation of privacy in the event that interception or exposure of such data takes place. These risks can still be increased by the poor encryption of data and bad practices in data management.

- **Problems with Lifecycle Management:** Additional security risks come along with IoT device management throughout its lifetime – from when they are deployed to when decommissioned. Most of the gadgets were in use for a long period without updating or maintenance. They may not be cleaned properly while ultimately being decommissioned that would result in residual data, which might turn out to be potentially exploitable.

The exploitation of these vulnerabilities calls for a multifaceted strategy that will incorporate the safe design of devices, creation, and implementation of industry-wide security standards, frequent software and firmware updates, strong techniques of encryption, and appropriate lifecycle management. Security in IoT devices is crucial to ensure that sensitive data remains safe and vital systems' integrity is maintained as their deployment increases.

3. Threats Posed by Cyber-physical Attacks on Military IoT Systems

- **Critical Operations Interruption:** For example, weapon systems, communication networks, surveillance equipment, or other instrumentation are often part of the critical operations that military IoT systems are. These systems could be the subject of a cyber-physical attack that would block operation, delay responses, or even endanger critical missions. For example, the loss of coordination among forces due to the disabling or manipulation of their communication networks can have an impact on the ability to exercise command and control.
- **Sabotage of Military Equipment:** Military equipment integrated with an IoT system may be compromised, such as vehicles, drones, or weapons, to alter functions. Attackers can cause equipment failure, make it unavailable, or even turn it against employers. For example, a hacker-reprogrammed drone could be made to misdirect and crash or undertake some other activities that suddenly lead to collateral damage or mission failure.
- **Data Manipulation and Misinformation:** Data gathered or transmitted from IoT systems can be manipulated by adversaries to deceive military decision-makers. This can result in misleading readings that either mask real threats or indicate that there are threats where none exist through the falsification of sensor data. Should this happen, it opens a door to responses that will be insufficient, resources being inefficiently allocated, and strategic decisions based on bad premises; all of this could endanger lives (Madakam et al., 2015).
- **Sabotage of Military Equipment**: IoT devices in military vehicles, drones, weapons, and many other forms of military equipment, including defaulted IoT systems of control and regulation, have reprogrammable logic. Such equipment can be compromised in an attack in order to be made available for a certain set

of uses only, cause malfunctions that would make the equipment inoperable, or even initiate the equipment to turn on its operators.

- **Espionage and Intelligence Gathering**: Through cyber-physical attacks, adversaries can gather intelligence by compromising IoT devices that collect and transmit sensitive data. Once access is gained to communication equipment, sensors, or surveillance systems, attackers can observe troop movements, monitor conversations, and intercept classified information. Such breaches can provide a significant tactical advantage to enemies and endanger ongoing military operations.
- **Data Manipulation and Misinformation:** Attackers can manipulate information that is either broadcast to or captured by IoT systems to mislead military decision-making. For example, if the data collected by sensors is tampered with, a wrong statistic may be developed which, to a military decision-maker, either hides the real risks or exposes the existence of a non-risk. This, therefore, results in unsuitable reactions, inefficient use of resources, and poor strategic judgements, not least of which could endanger lives.
- **Compromise of Supply Chains and Logistics:** Military logistics relies upon IoT technologies in the tracking and management of the supply of ammunition, equipment, and other resources. Such cyber physical attacks could therefore compromise the logistics of supply chains, which would lead critical supplies to either be rationed or come to a complete halt. Even the manipulation of inventory data, especially through the introduction of faulty or counterfeit equipment into the supply chain, could lead to sabotage or misdeliveries.
- **Compromise of Autonomous Systems:** The military highly depends on autonomous systems, controlled by IoT networks, such as robotic platforms or unmanned aerial vehicle (UAVs). Cyber-physical attacks on such systems can take control, make them dysfunctional, or change their behaviour. This may lead to unintentional conflicts or the loss of valuable assets (Chui et al., 2021).
- **Strategic and Psychological Effects:** In addition to direct operational and physical damage, cyber-physical attacks can have psychological and strategic effects. The ability to breach systems could weaken the defence capacity and technological infrastructure of a country. This might affect international relations and broader questions of national security.

Cyber-physical attacks on the military IoT systems are very complex and multi-dimensional, which can also cause damage to the intelligence, disruption in the operations, and may even cause bodily harm. Due to this fact, strong cybersecurity protection is needed where IoT technology is incorporated into the military system for assurance of resilience and integrity in operations.

4. Privacy Concerns and Data Protection in IoT-Driven Defence Environments

The integration of IoT devices in defence operations enhances efficiency and connectivity but also introduces significant privacy and data protection concerns (Bandyopadhyay et al., 2013; Dhaya & Kanthavel, 2022a; Jacobsson &

Rickhammar, 2022). These challenges arise due to the extensive collection, storage, and processing of sensitive military and personal data. To address these issues effectively, we can categorize them into the following sub-sections.

4.1. Risks of Data Breaches and Unauthorized Access

IoT devices in defence settings are interconnected, creating a vast network where a single vulnerability can compromise an entire system. This poses a severe threat, as unauthorized access to sensitive military data can have catastrophic consequences for national security.

a) Vulnerabilities in IoT Devices and Networks
   - Many IoT devices used in defence lack robust security features, such as multi-factor authentication, advanced encryption, or firmware updates.
   - A breach in one device can act as a gateway to infiltrate a larger military network, exposing crucial information such as troop movements, operational plans, and strategic decisions.
   - Cybercriminals or hostile entities can exploit weak encryption mechanisms, leading to espionage or cyber warfare threats.

b) Consequences of Data Breaches
   - Leaked sensitive military information can be used for surveillance, blackmail, or strategic manipulation by adversaries.
   - Exposure of personal data of military personnel (e.g. location, medical records, and communication logs) can put them at risk of targeted attacks.
   - Insider threats can also arise when individuals within the system misuse their access privileges.

To mitigate these risks, defence organizations must adopt advanced cybersecurity measures such as network segmentation, AI-driven threat detection, and end-to-end encryption protocols.

4.2. Handling of Personally Identifiable Information and Data Sovereignty

Beyond operational data, IoT devices also collect and store Personally Identifiable Information (PII), which includes details about military personnel, their geolocation, and sensitive communications. Mishandling such data can lead to privacy violations and security risks.

a) Challenges in Protecting PII
   - IoT devices inadvertently collect large amounts of PII, including biometric data, movement patterns, and personal communication records.
   - Improper access controls or inadequate anonymization can lead to unauthorized tracking of military personnel.
   - Inadequate data retention policies may result in unnecessary storage of outdated or irrelevant sensitive information, increasing exposure risks.

b) Data Sovereignty and Cross-Border Data Transfers
   - Military IoT data may be processed or stored on cloud servers located in foreign countries, leading to jurisdictional conflicts.
   - Variations in international data protection laws can expose critical information to foreign intelligence agencies.
   - Defence organizations need to establish strict policies ensuring data localization and compliance with national security regulations.

To safeguard PII and maintain data sovereignty, organizations should implement strict access control mechanisms, anonymization techniques, and secure data transfer protocols. Additionally, encryption policies should align with national defence standards to prevent unauthorized foreign access.

Privacy concerns and data protection in IoT-driven defence environments require a multi-layered security approach. Addressing vulnerabilities in IoT networks, enhancing security mechanisms, implementing strict PII management policies, and ensuring data sovereignty are essential to mitigating risks. By integrating advanced cybersecurity strategies and regulatory compliance measures, defence organizations can enhance operational security while protecting sensitive information from adversarial threats.

5. Authentication and Access Control Mechanisms for Secure Military IoT Deployments

This will become seriously relevant; there has to be authentication and gain access to manipulate approaches for army IoT deployments to ensure that sensitive statistics and systems are stable. Such strategies ought to be stable, scalable, and durable with a view to prevent unwanted entry and deliver a guarantee that the most effective legal people and gadgets can communicate with military IoT networks; in any other case, this would come at a high cost. Fig. 1.2 shows the authentication and access control mechanisms that this work will consider. The following key factors in the direction of establishing successful authentication and get right of entry to manipulate in army IoT environments.

- **Multi-Factor Authentication (MFA):** Making a person provide numerous forms of authentication before gaining admission to, MFA strengthens protection. This typically takes the shape of three things: something a person is, something the person has – as an example, a smart card or security token, and something the user knows – as an example, a password or PIN; for example, biometric statistics, which accommodates fingerprints and face recognition. Indeed, even in the event that one of the factors – a password, say – is compromised; MFA radically reduces the risk of unwanted access. MFA can protect military IoT systems from unauthorized access to critical infrastructures, control systems, and sensitive data.
- **Role-Based Access Control (RBAC):** Role-based access is a method that simplifies access control to several resources, based on the roles users are placed in an organization. RBAC can reduce the probability of unauthorized access in

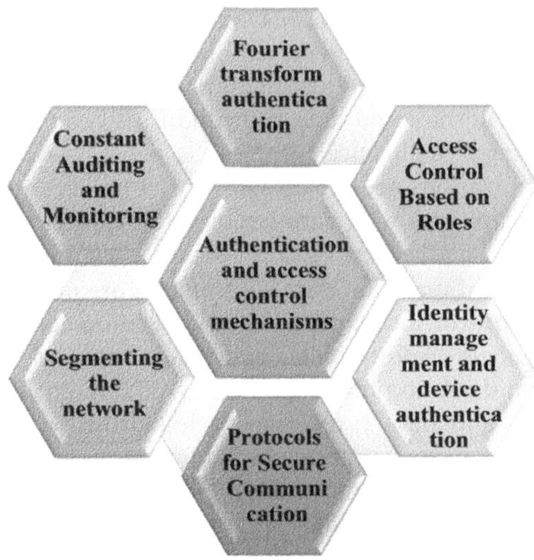

Fig. 1.2. Authentication and Access Control Mechanisms.

a military organization by providing roles to people for accessing the specific information and tools required to complete this task. The roles can be customized based on the level of the department, position, or level of their functions. This process makes it quite simple to administer the access rights, especially within large and complex organizations.

- **Identity Management and Device Authentication:** This makes device authentication within a military IoT network just as important as the authentication of users. Device authentication will therefore ensure that only devices considered trustworthy can establish a connection across the network and communicate with other systems or devices. This can be done through cryptographic keys, digital certificates, or secure hardware modules. The identity management system can be used to store records of activities carried by authorized devices, credential management, and inventory. This is of key importance in military settings in which the integrity and reliability of IoT devices are pivotal (Bandyopadhyay et al., 2013).
- **Protocols for Secure Communication:** Data exchanged between IoT devices and systems should be secure; therefore, communication must be carried out through secure methods. During transmission, protocols like DTLS (Datagram Transport Layer Security) and TLS (Transport Layer Security) guarantee encryption and data integrity. For added security, they can be used in combination with mutual authentication; this means that the client authenticates the server, and the server also authenticates the client. Secure communication channels will prevent data from being read, altered, or eavesdropped during the operation in military deployment where the information is highly sensitive.
- **Segmenting the Network:** A network can be fragmented into small, isolated portions or segments. This process is called network segmentation. This form of segregation of sensitive systems and data from the least critical part of the network will allow a military entity to better manage and monitor access.

Access control lists can be used to specify rules relating to network segments or resources that particular devices or people may access. In case there is a security crisis, this finer control will help in containing the damage and avoiding unauthorized access.

- **Constant Auditing and Monitoring:** To ensure military IoT deployments are safe, ongoing auditing and monitoring needs to be done. Monitoring device interactions, user activities, and access attempts can be done to identify and respond to questionable activity in near real-time. Logging and auditing provide a record of the access and actions. Log data could be used for forensic analysis in case of security breaches. Apart from just raising alarms, an automated monitoring system can trigger automated responses such as revoking access or isolation of compromised devices.

Any IoT-enabled military installation should be made secure through the integration of effective authentication and access control mechanisms. These protections will maintain operational integrity, safeguard sensitive information, and prevent illegal access to critical systems. Security and resilience in IoT infrastructure can be enhanced by best practices and the newest technologies from the military.

6. Encryption and Cryptographic Techniques for Safeguarding IoT Communications

Cryptography and encryption form the base of secure communications in the IoT, especially in military installations. Such techniques guarantee the authenticity, confidentiality, and integrity of the data exchanged between devices, systems, and networks in the IoT. Given the heterogeneity of IoT devices, which are mostly resource-constrained, appropriate cryptographic defences should be in place against a wide range of cyber threats. Here are some of the imperative cryptographic and encryption techniques in IoT contexts:

- **Symmetric Key Encryption:** When the same key is used for the encryption of data and the same key is used for its decryption, it is said to be symmetric key encryption. It is well-suited for processing and energy-constrained IoT devices since symmetric encryption tends to be faster and less resource-intensive than asymmetric encryption. Triple Data Encryption Standard and Advanced Encryption Standard are two of the most common symmetric encryption methods. Symmetric key encryption can be implemented into the military IoT systems to ensure fast, secure connectivity, and protect data while at rest.
- **Public Key Cryptography with Asymmetric Key Encryption:** In asymmetric key encryption, a pair of keys is utilized: a private key is used for decryption and a public key is used for encryption. This enables secure communication without parties exchanging a secret key in advance. Public-key cryptography, more precisely, is helpful for setting up secure channels over untrusted networks (Hoffman, 2006). Among the common algorithms are Elliptic Curve Cryptography and Rivest-Shamir-Adleman. Even though asymmetric encryption consumes more processing power than symmetric encryption under most

scenarios, it can still turn out to be beneficial in secure device authentication and key exchange within the IoT.
- **Hybrid Encryption:** Hybrid encryption provides the benefits of both symmetric and asymmetric cryptography. A symmetric key is securely transmitted using asymmetric encryption, and such a symmetric key is then used for actual data encryption and decryption. The hybrid algorithm thus exploits the strengths of asymmetric encryption for key management and symmetric encryption for large data volumes. This will be used in most secure communication protocols, like TLS, as it provides a requisite security component when IoT data is being secured in transit.

Definition and Functions of Hashing: Hashing may be defined as cryptographic method that includes a hash function – a cryptographic routine that takes an arbitrary-size input and produces a fixed-size output called a hash. They help in ensuring data integrity since modification of the input data would result in a different hash value by providing every source of information with a unique representation. Some of the standard forms of hash function algorithms include Secure Hash Algorithm, SHA-256, and SHA-3. Hashing functions are a useful tool in IoT systems in that they may confirm the integrity of software updates and transferred data, thus preventing their manipulation (Rodosek & Golling, 2013).

- **Digital Signatures:** Digital signatures are a technique that could be used to verify the integrity and validity of digital messages or documents. They are a combination of asymmetric encryption and hash functions. By using the sender's private key, the recipient might check the material with the signature using their public key. Digital signatures could also be employed in verifying data transmissions, firmware updates, command messages, and other military IoT applications similar in nature to prove that information from these sources is credible.
- **Safeguarding Key Administration:** A prerequisite for security in cryptographic systems is adequate key management, including the generation, distribution, storage, and finally, rotation of cryptographic keys. The IoT comes with a high level of dispersion and diversity of devices, making key management complex. Key storage technologies that ensure security include hardware security modules or secure elements, which protect keys against undesired access. Long-term security maintenance is guaranteed by the possibility of revocation and automated key rotation.
- **Minor Cryptography:** Since the majority of IoT devices have low processing power and memory, such devices cannot utilize the classic cryptographic techniques. Lightweight cryptography attempts to achieve enough security using only a few computational and energy resources. A few examples of lightweight encryption algorithms are the SIMON and SPECK algorithms that were proposed by the NSA. Lightweight cryptography is, hence, significant for resource-constrained scenarios of applications of IoT, like in wearables or remote sensors (Devi et al., 2020).
- **Cryptography End to End:** By making sure that data is encrypted at the sending device itself and can only be decoded at the receiving device, End-to-End Encryption (E2EE) prevents middlemen from viewing the content. Data confidentiality

during transmission across probably unsafe networks relies heavily on E2EE. Even in the event that channels of communication get hacked, E2EE would prevent the capture of critical data during transmission in military IoT systems.

- **Post-Quantum Cryptography (PQC):** The development of quantum computing could render most conventional encryption techniques vulnerable to quantum attacks. The aim of PQC is to develop algorithms resistant to attack by quantum computers. In the defence industry, where long-term data security is paramount, deploying PQC is viewed as a strategy to future-proof IoT security, even while remaining in its research stages of development.

The military and other critical settings have always been especially dependent on encryption and cryptographic techniques to ensure the security of IoT links. Such strategies ensure protection against cyber threats in terms of maintaining data confidentiality, integrity, and authenticity. With regard to proper mixes of cryptographic techniques that are implemented to keep IoT systems secure and reliable, several considerations in this relationship should be actualized, bearing in mind the specific requirements and limitations of IoT devices (Kimani et al., 2019; Wheelus & Zhu, 2020). This Table 1.1 summarizes some of the cryptographic techniques, along with their key features, strengths, weaknesses, and typical uses. The trade-offs with every technique differ, and the choice of which one to use normally depends on specific security requirements and resource constraints of an IoT deployment.

Table 1.1. Comparative Study on Encryption and Cryptographic Techniques.

Technique	Description	Strengths	Limitations	Use Cases in IoT
Symmetric Key Encryption	Uses the same key for both encryption and decryption	Fast and efficient Less computationally intensive	Key distribution is challenging Less secure if the key is compromised	Secure data transmission Encrypting data at rest
Asymmetric Key Encryption	Uses a pair of public and private keys for encryption and decryption	Secure key distribution No need for pre-shared keys	Computationally intensive Slower than symmetric encryption	Secure device authentication Key exchange
Hybrid Encryption	Combines symmetric and asymmetric encryption for enhanced security and efficiency	Combines security and efficiency Secure key management	Complexity in implementation	Secure communications (e.g. TLS)

(*Continued*)

Table 1.1. (*Continued*)

Technique	Description	Strengths	Limitations	Use Cases in IoT
Hash Functions	Generates a fixed-size hash from variable input data for integrity checks	Fast and efficient Ensures data integrity	Does not provide confidentiality Vulnerable to hash collisions (depends on the algorithm)	Data integrity verification Password hashing
Digital Signatures	Provides authenticity and integrity using asymmetric encryption and hash functions	Ensures authenticity and integrity Non-repudiation	Requires a reliable public key infrastructure (PKI)	Authenticating software updates Signing sensitive data
Secure Key Management	Involves secure generation, distribution, storage, and rotation of cryptographic keys	Protects key confidentiality Automated key lifecycle management	Complexity in management Potential for key compromise if not properly secured	Managing keys for IoT devices
Lightweight Cryptography	Designed for resource-constrained devices with limited computational power and memory	Low resource consumption Suitable for low-power devices	May offer a lower security margin than traditional algorithms	Wearable devices Remote sensors
E2EE	Encrypts data on the sending device and decrypts it on the receiving device, preventing intermediary access	High data confidentiality Protects data even in transit	Complex to implement May require additional computational resources	Secure messaging Protecting sensitive communications
PQC	Develops algorithms resistant to quantum computing attacks	Future-proof against quantum attacks	Still in the research phase Computationally intensive	Long-term data security High-security environments

7. Intrusion Detection and Prevention Systems for Military IoT Networks

7.1. Role and Importance of IDPS in Military IoT Networks

Intrusion Detection and Prevention Systems (IDPS) play a crucial role in military IoT networks, which integrate a wide range of devices, from basic sensors to advanced communication systems and unmanned drones (Fei et al., 2023; Kanthavel et al., 2021; Manyika et al., 2013; Narang et al., 2018). These networks operate in highly sensitive environments where security breaches can have severe consequences, including compromised intelligence, disrupted operations, and potential loss of life.

IDPS is designed to monitor and analyze network traffic in real-time, detecting and neutralizing threats with minimal delay. Given the diversity of devices and the necessity for real-time decision-making, IDPS solutions must balance high-performance threat detection with low latency to ensure mission-critical operations are not disrupted. Additionally, IDPS must uphold stringent security standards to preserve the confidentiality and integrity of military data.

A fundamental aspect of military IDPS deployment is the distinction between Host-based IDPS (HIDPS) and Network-based IDPS (NIDPS).

- HIDPS secures individual devices, protecting endpoints such as command terminals, drones, or soldier-worn sensors from internal or external threats.
- NIDPS, on the other hand, monitors device-to-device activity across the network, identifying and mitigating threats at the communication level.

The choice between HIDPS and NIDPS depends on the specific security requirements of the military operation and the nature of threats that need to be addressed.

7.2. Detection Techniques and Challenges in Military IDPS

Military IDPS solutions typically employ a combination of signature-based and anomaly-based detection techniques (Fei et al., 2023; Kanthavel et al., 2021; Manyika et al., 2013; Narang et al., 2018):

- Signature-based detection identifies known threats by matching traffic patterns against a database of pre-recorded attack signatures. This method is effective for recognizing established threats but struggles against novel or evolving attacks.
- Anomaly-based detection, in contrast, builds a profile of normal system behaviour and flags deviations that may indicate suspicious activity. This technique is more effective in detecting zero-day attacks and new cyber threats that do not have predefined signatures.

The integration of ML and AI has significantly enhanced IDPS capabilities, allowing them to analyze large volumes of data and adapt to emerging threats.

However, challenges remain, particularly with encrypted traffic, which is a standard feature in military networks. Encryption complicates threat detection, as traditional IDPS methods cannot inspect encrypted data payloads directly. To overcome this, some IDPS solutions analyze traffic metadata or employ specialized decryption techniques that enable threat detection without compromising security.

Another significant challenge is the reduction of false positives. Excessive false alarms can lead to operational delays and resource wastage. Modern IDPS solutions implement advanced filtering mechanisms and ML-driven refinement techniques to minimize false positives, ensuring only genuine threats are prioritized for response.

7.3. Integration, Maintenance, and Future Enhancements of Military IDPS

For comprehensive protection, IDPS should not function in isolation but must integrate with other cybersecurity measures such as firewalls, antivirus software, and threat intelligence platforms (Fei et al., 2023; Kanthavel et al., 2021; Manyika et al., 2013; Narang et al., 2018). A well-coordinated defense strategy enables faster threat identification and response, reinforcing network resilience against sophisticated cyberattacks.

Continuous testing, assessment, and updates are essential to maintaining the effectiveness of military IDPS. As cyber threats evolve, IDPS solutions must adapt accordingly by updating detection algorithms, refining behavioural analysis models, and incorporating new threat intelligence data. To future-proof IDPS solutions, the following advancements should be prioritized:

- Scalability and flexibility to accommodate the growing complexity of military IoT networks.
- Real-time threat intelligence sharing to facilitate rapid responses to cyber incidents.
- Automated response mechanisms powered by AI to counteract threats without human intervention.

8. Resilience and Reliability of IoT-Enabled Defence Systems

The efficacy and protection of military operations rely heavily on the robustness and dependability of IoT-enabled defence systems. These systems must be resilient enough to tolerate and recover from disruptions while maintaining operational performance. Given that these systems integrate multiple IoT devices – such as sensors, communication networks, and automated systems – it is crucial to ensure both resilience and reliability. This section explores how to enhance resilience and reliability in IoT-enabled defence systems and why these factors are essential in defence operations (Kanthavel et al., 2021; 2022; Kavak et al., 2021; Sangeetha et al., 2021).

8.1. Resilience of IoT-Enabled Defence Systems

Resilience in IoT-enabled defence systems refers to their ability to withstand and recover from disruptions while continuing to function effectively. Achieving resilience requires several key strategies:

- **Design for Failure:** IoT-enabled defence systems must be designed with the assumption that failures are inevitable. Implementing graceful failure handling ensures that the system remains operational even when individual components fail. Redundancy is a critical technique, where essential components are duplicated so that backup systems can take over when primary ones fail.
- **Robust Security Measures:** Given the increasing cyber threats to military IoT infrastructure, implementing strong access control, authentication mechanisms, and encryption for data and communications is essential. This prevents unauthorized access, tampering, and potential system compromise.
- **Adaptive Response Mechanisms:** A truly resilient system can dynamically adjust to new threats and operational changes. This includes modifying security configurations, deploying additional protective measures, and reconfiguring networks in real time to mitigate emerging risks.
- **Regular Software Updates and Patch Management:** Keeping IoT devices and systems up to date with frequent security patches and software updates is crucial for resilience. This practice ensures that known vulnerabilities are addressed before adversaries can exploit them.
- **Fault Tolerant Architecture:** Fault tolerance ensures that systems can detect, isolate, and recover from failures without significant operational disruption. Automated failover mechanisms help redirect operations to backup systems or alternative communication channels in case of failures.
- **Resilient Communication Networks:** Defence IoT systems require robust communication networks that can sustain disruptions. Techniques such as error correction, redundant communication paths, and decentralized network architecture enhance network reliability, ensuring seamless communication even in contested environments.
- **Continuous Testing and Simulation:** Conducting regular stress testing, penetration testing, and failure mode simulations helps identify vulnerabilities and improve system resilience. Simulating real-world disruptions prepares defence IoT systems for unexpected challenges.

By focusing on these resilience-enhancing strategies, defence organizations can build IoT-enabled systems that withstand cyber threats, hardware malfunctions, and operational stress while maintaining continuous functionality.

8.2. Reliability of IoT-Enabled Defence Systems

While resilience focuses on withstanding and recovering from disruptions, reliability ensures that IoT-enabled defence systems consistently perform their intended functions without failure. A reliable system is one that provides continuous availability, predictable performance, and accuracy under all conditions. Key factors influencing reliability include:

- **Predictive Maintenance and Self-Healing Capabilities:** Advanced predictive maintenance techniques, using ML and IoT sensors, help identify potential failures before they occur. Self-healing capabilities enable systems to automatically detect, diagnose, and resolve issues without human intervention, improving overall reliability.
- **System Redundancy and Backup Protocols:** Implementing redundant hardware and backup systems ensures operational continuity. If a primary system component fails, an identical backup can immediately take over, minimizing downtime and maintaining reliability in critical missions.
- **High-Quality Components and Manufacturing Standards:** Defence IoT systems should use military-grade components and stringent manufacturing standards to withstand harsh environments, such as extreme temperatures, vibrations, and electromagnetic interference. Using high-quality components reduces the risk of failures and extends system longevity.
- **Real-Time Data Integrity and Accuracy:** IoT-enabled defence systems rely on real-time data to make strategic decisions. Ensuring data accuracy through robust data validation mechanisms, encryption, and secure transmission protocols prevents errors and misinformation that could compromise operations.
- **Network Stability and Low Latency Communication:** Reliable IoT systems require low-latency, high-bandwidth communication networks to ensure timely data transmission. 5G-enabled networks, satellite-based communication, and dedicated military-grade infrastructure improve connectivity in diverse operational scenarios.
- **Scalability and Interoperability:** As defence systems evolve, IoT-enabled architectures must be scalable to integrate new technologies without compromising reliability. Interoperability across different military branches, allied forces, and command structures ensures seamless collaboration and information sharing.

Resilience and reliability are fundamental for maintaining the effectiveness and security of IoT-enabled defence systems. Resilience ensures that systems can endure disruptions and recover swiftly, while reliability guarantees continuous and predictable operation. Military organizations must adopt a multi-layered approach involving redundancy, robust security, predictive maintenance, and advanced communication technologies to optimize these systems. By prioritizing resilience and reliability, defence forces can enhance mission success, reduce system vulnerabilities, and maintain operational superiority in complex and evolving environments.

9. Case Studies and Best Practices in Securing Military IoT Infrastructures

Fig. 1.3 shows the case studies on military IoT infrastructures which include US Department of Defence (DoD) Initiative for IoT Security, The IoT Defence

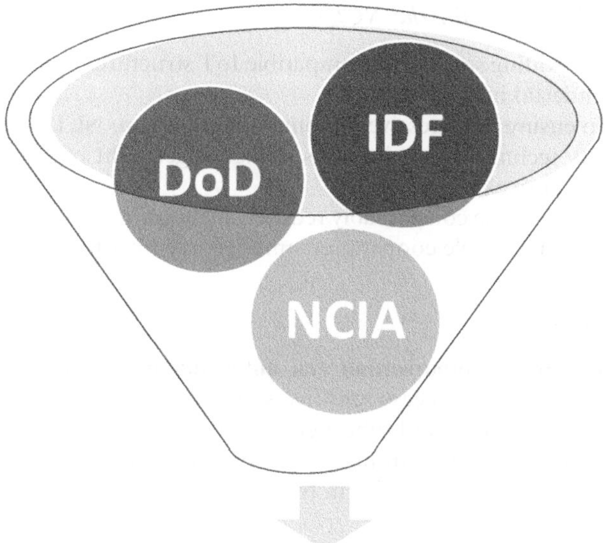

Fig. 1.3. Case Studies on Military IoT Infrastructures.

Strategy of the Israel Defence Forces (IDF) and Security protocols for the NATO Communications and Information Agency (NCIA):

9.1. US Department of Defence (DoD) Initiative for IoT Security

- **Challenge:** A huge network of IoT gadgets utilized in several navy packages requires to be secured through the DoD.
- **Solution:** To find anomalies and threats in real time, the DoD deployed a multi-layered protection device with robust encryption, strict tool authentication, and on-going monitoring.
- **Result**: As a give up end result of this approach, army networks in the mean-time are far more regular, and important systems are less liable to cyberattacks (Tonge et al., 2013).

9.2. The IoT Defence Strategy of the IDF

- **Challenge:** The IDF's IoT infrastructure turns out to be the victim of ultra-modern cyberattacks.
- **Solution**: They created an intensive defence plan with steady verbal exchange routes, state-of-the-art encryption techniques, and real-time hazard detection.
- **Result:** By successfully thwarting a couple of tried breaches, the technique multiplied the overall resilience in their IoT structures.

9.3. Security Protocols for the NCIA

- **Challenge**: Providing secure and compatible IoT structures for all NATO members is an undertaking.
- **Solution:** To ensure an excessive diploma of protection, NCIA implemented a unified safety technique that includes stringent get right of entry to controls and regular security checks.
- **Result:** This technique considerably reduced the hazard of protection breaches even as facilitating stable cooperation amongst member nations.

9.4. Best Practices

- **Put in place strong authorization and authentication:** Permit only accepted humans and devices to access sensitive statistics and systems through multi-challenge authentication and robust credential management.
- **Encrypt Facts:** To save you from unwanted access and manipulation, be sure that facts are encrypted when it's in transit and at relaxation (Sathyaraj et al., 2022).
- **Continuous Patching and Updating:** Keeping IoT structures and devices on top of things with the latest security updates will be very beneficial in reinstating known vulnerabilities and decreasing the danger of exploits.
- **Segmentation of a network:** To reduce the viable impact of any safety breaches, phase networks to split essential structures from much less sensitive IoT devices.
- **Constant Watching and Identifying Threats:** To unexpectedly discover and address suspicious interest, put in region threat detection and real-time monitoring technology (Ullah et al., 2019).
- **Regularly perform security audits:** To locate such vulnerabilities and connect them before they may be exploited, conduct regular security checks.
- **Employee Education and Training:** To make certain they may be nicely-organized, provide military employees everyday training on emerging risks and exceptional practices for IoT protection.

Military organizations might also enhance the safety in their IoT infrastructures and support their defences against the constantly converting cyber chance panorama by means of the usage of these best practices and gaining knowledge of from that case research.

10. Regulatory and Policy Considerations for IoT Security in the Defence Sector

10.1. Compliance with International and National Security Frameworks

Ensuring regulatory and policy adherence for IoT security in the defence sector requires alignment with both international cybersecurity standards and national security regulations. Given the highly sensitive nature of defence operations, compliance frameworks such as the General Data Protection Regulation (GDPR) play a crucial role in safeguarding classified and personal data (Dhaya & Kanthavel, 2022b; Kaur & Ramkumar, 2022; Radhakrishnan et al., 2022). Under GDPR, any IoT devices handling sensitive information must comply with strict data privacy and protection laws, ensuring that data transmission and storage mechanisms uphold confidentiality, integrity, and availability. Additionally, adherence to globally recognized cybersecurity frameworks, such as:

- **NIST Cybersecurity Framework**: A comprehensive guideline offering a structured approach to risk management, threat mitigation, and incident response in IoT environments.
- **ISO/IEC 27001:** A widely accepted standard that provides best practices for implementing, managing, and continually improving an organization's information security management system (ISMS).

Beyond international standards, specific national security laws also dictate cybersecurity practices in the defence sector. For example:

- **Defence Federal Acquisition Regulation Supplement (DFARS)**: Defines strict cybersecurity requirements for defence contractors handling Controlled Unclassified Information (CUI).
- **Federal Information Security Management Act (FISMA)**: Mandates federal agencies to implement robust security controls to protect their information systems, including IoT infrastructures used in defence applications.

By conforming to these regulatory frameworks, defence organizations can establish robust security protocols that fortify IoT ecosystems against cyber threats while maintaining operational reliability and national security integrity.

10.2. Risk Mitigation Strategies and Secure Supply Chain Management

Regulatory policies in the defence sector emphasize the implementation of comprehensive risk mitigation measures tailored to IoT security challenges (Dhaya & Kanthavel, 2022b; Kaur & Ramkumar, 2022; Radhakrishnan et al., 2022). This involves:

- **Access Control Mechanisms**: Implementing stringent authentication and authorization protocols to ensure that only authorized personnel can access critical IoT systems.
- **Incident Response and Recovery Policies**: Regularly updating security response frameworks to detect, mitigate, and recover from cyber incidents efficiently.
- **Secure Vendor Vetting**: Ensuring that third-party vendors comply with stringent security guidelines before integrating their IoT devices into the defence infrastructure.

A major component of security regulation also involves supply chain protection. Ensuring end-to-end security across the supply chain is vital, as compromised IoT components can introduce vulnerabilities that adversaries may exploit. Defence agencies must:

- **Enforce Strict Compliance for Suppliers**: Mandating security compliance audits for all third-party vendors handling IoT components.
- **Adopt Encryption Mechanisms**: Deploying robust encryption techniques to secure communication channels and prevent unauthorized interception of critical defence data.
- **Regular Cybersecurity Training**: Ensuring that personnel handling IoT systems receive continuous training on evolving cybersecurity threats and best practices.

To maintain the highest security standards, defence agencies should conduct regular security audits and compliance assessments to verify adherence to IoT security policies. Proactive monitoring and updating of cybersecurity frameworks will enable defence organizations to effectively counter emerging cyber threats and ensure long-term security resilience.

11. Conclusion

The protection of IoT infrastructures within the defence industry presents a complex problem that calls for the following strict regulations and policies. Conformance to data protection legislation like GDPR, and national security rules like FISMA or DFARS, will enable the defence organizations to achieve high protection of sensitive data and assurance of compliance with mandatory standards. The ISO/IEC 27001 and the NIST Cyber-security Framework provide a structured approach towards handling security threats related to IoT devices. Foundational policies related to supply chain security, incident response, risk management, and access control should be designed and updated effectively. This is augmented by staff training, encryption, and continuous monitoring to enhance defences against new threats. Taken together, these precautions are the context for protection of the vital resources and preservation of operational integrity against an ever-increasing intricacy in the area of military IoT systems.

References

Bandyopadhyay, S., Balamuralidhar, P., & Pal, A. (2013). Interoperation among IoT standards. *Journal of ICT Standardization*, *1*(2), 253–270.

Blanco-Novoa, Ó., Fraga-Lamas, P. A., Vilar-Montesinos, M., & Fernández-Caramés, T. M. (2020). Creating the internet of augmented things: An open-source framework to make IoT devices and augmented and mixed reality systems talk to each other. *Sensors*, *20*(11), 3328.

Burmaoglu, S., Saritas, O., & Yalcin, H. (2019). Defence 4.0: Internet of Things in military. In D. Meissner, L. Gokhberg, & O. Saritas (Eds.), *Emerging technologies for economic development*. Science, Technology and Innovation Studies. Springer. https://doi.org/10.1007/978-3-030-04370-4_14

Chui, M., Collins, M., & Patel, M. (2021). *IoT value set to accelerate through 2030: Where and how to capture it*. https://www.mckinsey.com/business-functions/mckinsey-digital/our-insights/iot-value-set-to-accelerate-through-2030-where-and-how-tocapture-it

Daim, T. U., Chiavetta, D., Porter, A. L., & Saritas, O. (Eds.). (2016). *Anticipating future innovation pathways through large data analysis*. Springer.

Devi, M., Dhaya, R., Kanthavel, R., Algarni, F., & Dixikha, P. (2020). Data Science for Internet of Things (IoT). In *Second international conference on computer networks and communication technologies: ICCNCT 2019* (pp. 60–70). Springer International Publishing.

Dhaya, R., & Kanthavel, R. (2022a). Energy efficient resource allocation algorithm for agriculture IoT. *Wireless Personal Communications*, *125*(2), 1361–1383.

Dhaya, R., & Kanthavel, R. (2022b). Futuristic research perspectives of IoT platforms. In D. J. Mala (Ed.), *Integrating AI in IoT analytics on the cloud for healthcare applications* (pp. 258–275).

Dhaya, R., Kanthavel, R., & Bangali, H. (2022). Perspectives on deep learning techniques for industrial IoT. In R. Raut, S. Krit, & P. Chatterjee (Eds.), *Machine vision for Industry 4.0* (pp. 79–100). CRC Press.

Fei, W., Ohno, H., & Sampalli, S. (2023). A systematic review of IoT Security: Research potential, challenges, and future directions. *ACM Computing Surveys*, *56*, 5, Article 111 (May 2024), 40 pages. https://doi.org/10.1145/3625094

Ferrag, M. A., Friha, O., Maglaras, L., Janicke, H., & Shu, L. (2021). Federated deep learning for cyber security in the internet of things: Concepts, applications, and experimental analysis. *IEEE Access*, *9*, 138509–138542.

Hoffman, F. G. (2006). Complex irregular warfare: The next revolution in military affairs. *Orbis*, *50*(3), 395–411.

Jacobsson, M., & Rickhammar, O. (2022). Recent M&A in the telecom industry: Industrial wireless networks. (Master's thesis, KTH Industrial Engineering and Management, TRITA-ITM-EX 2022:443). KTH Royal Institute of Technology

Kanthavel, R., Indra Priyadharshini, S., Sudha, D., Sundara Velrani, K., & Dhaya, R. (2022). Multi-hoped cooperative communication-based wireless underground sensor network design. *International Journal of Communication Systems*, *35*(10), e5174.

Kanthavel, D., Sangeetha, S. K. B., & Keerthana, K. P. (2021). An empirical study of vehicle to infrastructure communications-an intense learning of smart infrastructure for safety and mobility. *International Journal of Intelligent Networks*, *2*, 77–82.

Kaur, J., & Ramkumar, K. R. (2022). The recent trends in cyber security: A review. *Journal of King Saud University-Computer and Information Sciences*, *34*(8), 5766–5781.

Kavak, H., Padilla, J. J., Vernon-Bido, D., Diallo, S. Y., Gore, R., & Shetty, S. (2021). Simulation for cybersecurity: State of the art and future directions. *Journal of Cybersecurity*, *7*(1), tyab005.

Kimani, K., Oduol, V., & Langat, K. (2019). Cyber security challenges for IoT-based smart grid networks. *International Journal of Critical Infrastructure Protection*, *25*, 36–49.

Madakam, S., Ramaswamy, R., & Tripathi, S. (2015). Internet of Things (IoT): A literature review. *Journal of Computer and Communications*, *3*(5), 164–173.

Manyika, J., Chui, M., Bughin, J., Dobbs, R., Bisson, P., & Marrs, A. (2013). *Disruptive technologies: Advances that will transform life, business, and the global economy* (Vol. 180, pp. 17–21). Mckinsey global institute.

Narang, S., Nalwa, T., Choudhury, T., & Kashyap, N. (2018, February). An efficient method for security measurement in internet of things. In *2018 international conference on communication, computing and internet of things (IC3IoT)* (pp. 319–323). IEEE.

Radhakrishnan, K., Ramakrishnan, D., Khalaf, O. I., Uddin, M., Chen, C. L., & Wu, C. M. (2022). A novel deep learning-based cooperative communication channel model for wireless underground sensor networks. *Sensors*, *22*(12), 4475.

Rodosek, G. D., & Golling, M. (2013). Cyber security: Challenges and application areas. In M. Essig, M. Hülsmann, E.-M. Kern, & S. Klein-Schmeink (Eds.), *Supply chain safety management: Security and robustness in logistics* (pp. 179–197). Springer Berlin Heidelberg.

Sangeetha, S. K. B., Dhaya, R., Shah, D. T., Dharanidharan, R., & Reddy, K. P. S. (2021, February). An empirical analysis of machine learning frameworks for digital pathology in medical science. *Journal of Physics: Conference Series*, *1767*(1), 012031.

Sathyaraj, R., Kanthavel, R., Cavaliere, L. P. L., Vyas, S., Maheswari, S., Gupta, R. K., & Sengan, S. (2022). Analysis on prediction of COVID-19 with machine learning algorithms. *International Journal of Uncertainty, Fuzziness and Knowledge-Based Systems*, *30*(Supp01), 67–82.

Tonge, A. M., Kasture, S. S., & Chaudhari, S. R. (2013). Cyber security: Challenges for society-literature review. *IOSR Journal of Computer Engineering*, 2(12), 67–75.

Ullah, F., Naeem, H., Jabbar, S., Khalid, S., Latif, M. A., Al-Turjman, F., & Mostarda, L. (2019). Cyber security threats detection in internet of things using deep learning approach. *IEEE Access*, *7*, 124379–124389.

Wheelus, C., & Zhu, X. (2020). IoT network security: Threats, risks, and a data-driven defence framework. *IoT*, *1*(2), 259–285.

Chapter 2

Privacy Concerns and Data Protection in IoT-Driven Defence Environments

S. C. Vetrivel[a], V. P. Arun[b], T. P. Saravanan[a] and R. Maheswari[a]

[a]*Kongu Engineering College, India*
[b]*JKKN College of Engineering and Technology, India*

Abstract

The integration of Internet of Things (IoT) technologies in defense environments has significantly enhanced operational capabilities, situational awareness, and decision-making processes. However, the proliferation of interconnected devices and the vast amounts of data generated pose substantial privacy concerns and data protection challenges. This chapter examines the privacy risks associated with IoT in defense settings, including unauthorized data access, surveillance, and cyber-attacks. It also explores the complexities of safeguarding sensitive information in an ecosystem where devices often have varying security protocols and vulnerabilities. The chapter emphasizes the importance of implementing robust encryption methods, advanced authentication mechanisms, and comprehensive regulatory frameworks to ensure data integrity and confidentiality. Additionally, it highlights the need for continuous monitoring and adaptive security strategies to address emerging threats in real-time. By balancing technological advancements with stringent privacy and data protection measures, defense organizations can leverage IoT innovations while mitigating potential risks.

Keywords: Internet of Things (IoT); defence environments; privacy concerns; data protection; cybersecurity; data encryption

The Internet of Things in the Defence Industry:
Challenges and Solutions for Military Security, 23–58

Published under exclusive licence by Emerald Publishing Limited
doi:10.1108/978-1-83549-198-020261002

1. Introduction

1.1. Overview of IoT in Defence Environments

The IoT represents a significant technological advancement that has found substantial applications in defence environments. IoT in defence involves the integration of interconnected devices, sensors, and systems that communicate and exchange data to enhance situational awareness, operational efficiency, and decision-making processes. These IoT-enabled devices can range from wearable gadgets for soldiers, unmanned aerial vehicles (UAVs), surveillance systems, and smart weapons to logistics and supply chain management tools. In modern defence settings, IoT facilitates real-time monitoring and data collection from various sources, providing a comprehensive view of the battlefield and operational environments. This real-time data is crucial for commanders and decision-makers to make informed decisions quickly, improving the agility and responsiveness of military operations (Ahmi et al., 2019). For instance, wearable sensors can track the health and vitals of soldiers, UAVs can provide aerial surveillance and reconnaissance, and smart munitions can be guided with pinpoint accuracy to their targets.

Moreover, IoT systems enhance the automation of routine tasks and maintenance processes, reducing human error and increasing efficiency. Predictive maintenance, powered by IoT sensors, ensures that equipment and vehicles are serviced before failures occur, thus maintaining operational readiness and reducing downtime (Al Shuhaimi et al., 2016). Logistics and supply chains are also optimized through IoT, ensuring the timely delivery of supplies and equipment to the frontline. The integration of IoT in defence environments promises enhanced operational capabilities, but it also introduces complexities and vulnerabilities that need to be addressed. The interconnected nature of IoT systems makes them susceptible to cyber threats, necessitating robust security measures to protect sensitive military data and maintain the integrity of operations.

1.2. Importance of Privacy and Data Protection

Privacy and data protection are critical concerns in the deployment of IoT in defence environments due to the sensitive nature of military operations and the potential risks associated with data breaches. In the context of defence, the stakes are exceptionally high, as compromised data can lead to severe consequences, including loss of life, compromised missions, and national security threats (Alaba et al., 2017). The importance of privacy in defence IoT systems cannot be overstated. Military operations often involve classified information that, if intercepted or exposed, could provide adversaries with critical intelligence. For instance, the location data of troops, strategic plans, and real-time surveillance feeds must be protected to prevent enemy forces from gaining an advantage. Ensuring the confidentiality of such data is paramount to safeguarding national security and maintaining the element of surprise in military strategies. Data protection is equally vital, as IoT devices in defence environments collect and transmit vast amounts of data. This data includes not only strategic and operational information but also personal data of military personnel, such as health records and biometric data. Protecting this data from unauthorized access, tampering, or theft is crucial to maintaining the integrity and trustworthiness of defence operations. Moreover, the interconnected nature of IoT devices means that a vulnerability in one device can potentially compromise the entire network. Implementing robust data protection measures, such as encryption, secure communication protocols, and stringent access controls, is essential to mitigate these risks (Ali et al., 2018). Additionally, compliance with international and national data protection regulations is necessary to ensure that defence IoT systems adhere to legal standards and best practices.

1.3. Objectives of the Study

The study aims to explore and address the critical aspects of privacy concerns and data protection in IoT-driven defence environments. To achieve this overarching goal, the study sets forth the following specific objectives:

1. **Analyze the Current State of IoT Integration in Defence Environments:**
   - To examine the extent and manner in which IoT technologies are currently being implemented in various defence operations.
   - To identify the key applications, benefits, and challenges associated with IoT deployment in military contexts.
2. **Identify and Categorize Privacy Concerns:**
   - To identify the different types of privacy risks and concerns that arise from the use of IoT devices and systems in defence environments.
   - To categorize these privacy concerns based on their potential impact on national security, operational integrity, and individual privacy of military personnel.
3. **Evaluate Data Protection Strategies and Technologies:**
   - To evaluate existing data protection strategies and technologies used in IoT systems within defence environments.
   - To assess the effectiveness of encryption techniques, access control mechanisms, data anonymization methods, and secure communication protocols in safeguarding sensitive military data.
4. **Assess Regulatory Frameworks and Compliance Challenges:**
   - To review international and national data protection regulations relevant to IoT applications in defence.
   - To identify the compliance challenges faced by defence organizations in adhering to these regulations and propose solutions to overcome these challenges.
5. **Investigate Technological Solutions for Enhanced Security:**
   - To explore advanced technological solutions that can enhance privacy and data protection in IoT-driven defence environments.
   - To examine the potential of emerging technologies such as blockchain, artificial intelligence (AI), and machine learning (ML) in mitigating privacy and security risks.

6. **Develop a Risk Management Framework:**
   - To develop a comprehensive risk management framework that identifies, assesses, and mitigates the risks associated with IoT implementation in defence.
   - To propose best practices and guidelines for incident response, recovery, and continuous monitoring of IoT systems in defence contexts.
7. **Conduct Case Studies and Comparative Analysis:**
   - To conduct detailed case studies of successful and failed IoT implementations in defence environments to derive lessons learned.
   - To perform a comparative analysis of different defence organizations' approaches to privacy and data protection in IoT deployments.
8. **Explore Ethical Considerations and Societal Implications:**
   - To investigate the ethical issues related to privacy and data protection in IoT-driven defence environments.
   - To assess the broader societal implications of privacy breaches and propose ethical guidelines for the development and deployment of IoT systems in defence.

2. IoT in Defence: An Overview

2.1. Evolution of IoT in Defence

The evolution of the IoT in defence has been driven by the rapid advancements in technology and the increasing need for enhanced situational awareness, operational efficiency, and decision-making capabilities in military operations (Boyack, 2004). The concept of interconnected devices communicating and sharing data to perform coordinated tasks has been a transformative force in modern warfare.

2.1.1. Early Beginnings

The early integration of IoT concepts in defence can be traced back to the use of basic sensors and telemetry systems. These systems were primarily used for tracking and monitoring purposes, such as in missile guidance systems and reconnaissance missions (Bugeja et al., 2016). The initial focus was on enhancing the accuracy and reliability of data collected from the battlefield, enabling better-informed decisions.

2.1.2. Technological Advancements

The development of advanced communication technologies, such as satellite communications and wireless networks, significantly accelerated the evolution of IoT in defence. The ability to transmit data in real-time over long distances allowed for more dynamic and responsive military operations (Checkland, 1999). The miniaturization of sensors and improvements in battery technology further expanded the range of IoT applications, making it feasible to deploy sensors in various environments and on different platforms, including soldiers, vehicles, and unmanned systems.

2.1.3. Integration with Emerging Technologies

The integration of IoT with emerging technologies such as AI, ML, and big data analytics marked a significant milestone in its evolution (Conti et al., 2018). AI and ML algorithms enabled the analysis of vast amounts of data collected by IoT devices, providing actionable insights and predictive capabilities (Conti et al., 2016). For example, predictive maintenance systems use data from IoT sensors to anticipate equipment failures and schedule timely repairs, thereby reducing downtime and enhancing operational readiness.

2.1.4. Modern IoT-Driven Defence Systems

Today, IoT is deeply embedded in defence systems, supporting a wide array of applications that enhance situational awareness, operational efficiency, and decision-making. Modern IoT-driven defence systems are characterized by their ability to collect, process, and analyze data in real-time, providing a comprehensive and dynamic picture of the operational environment. These systems are highly interconnected, often leveraging cloud computing and edge computing to handle the large volumes of data generated by IoT devices (Culbert, 2020). The continuous evolution of IoT in defence is driven by ongoing technological advancements and the increasing complexity of modern warfare. The future of IoT in defence promises further integration with cutting-edge technologies such as quantum computing and advanced robotics, potentially revolutionizing military operations and strategy.

2.2. Applications of IoT in Military Operations

The applications of IoT in military operations are diverse and far-reaching, offering significant enhancements in terms of efficiency, effectiveness, and safety (Dalipi & Yayilgan, 2016). The interconnected nature of IoT devices allows for seamless communication and coordination across different aspects of military operations, from logistics and supply chain management to battlefield awareness and soldier health monitoring.

2.2.1. Enhanced Situational Awareness

One of the primary applications of IoT in military operations is the enhancement of situational awareness. IoT devices, such as surveillance cameras, drones, and sensors, continuously collect data from the battlefield, providing real-time intelligence on enemy movements, environmental conditions, and potential threats (Donthu et al., 2021). This data is transmitted to command centres, where it is analyzed to generate actionable insights, enabling military commanders to make informed decisions quickly.

2.2.2. Smart Weaponry and Munitions

IoT has revolutionized the development and deployment of smart weaponry and munitions. These advanced weapons systems are equipped with sensors and connectivity features that allow for precision targeting and real-time adjustments based on battlefield conditions (Estrada et al., 2020). For example, smart missiles can adjust their trajectory mid-flight to hit moving targets accurately, while IoT-enabled artillery systems can coordinate fire missions with high precision, reducing collateral damage and enhancing mission effectiveness.

2.2.3. Soldier Health and Performance Monitoring

Wearable IoT devices are increasingly being used to monitor the health and performance of soldiers in real-time. These devices track vital signs, physical activity, and environmental conditions, providing valuable data on soldier readiness and well-being. In critical situations, health data can be transmitted to medical teams for rapid response and intervention, potentially saving lives (Gemalto, 2020). Additionally, performance data can be used to optimize training programs and ensure that soldiers are in peak physical condition.

2.2.4. Logistics and Supply Chain Management

IoT plays a crucial role in optimizing logistics and supply chain management in military operations. IoT sensors and tracking devices monitor the movement and condition of supplies, equipment, and vehicles, ensuring that they reach their destinations on time and in optimal condition (Hassan, 2019). Real-time tracking of inventory levels allows for better resource allocation and reduces the risk of shortages or overstocking. Predictive analytics, powered by IoT data, can forecast supply needs based on mission requirements, further enhancing logistical efficiency.

2.2.5. Autonomous and Unmanned Systems

The use of autonomous and unmanned systems, such as drones, unmanned ground vehicles, and autonomous underwater vehicles, is a prominent application of IoT in military operations (He et al., 2016). These systems are equipped with IoT sensors and connectivity features that enable them to perform a variety of tasks, including surveillance, reconnaissance, logistics support, and combat operations. Autonomous systems can operate in hazardous environments without risking human lives, providing a significant tactical advantage.

2.2.6. Cybersecurity and Threat Detection

IoT devices also play a vital role in enhancing cybersecurity and threat detection in military operations. Networked sensors and monitoring systems detect unusual activities and potential cyber threats in real-time, allowing for rapid response and mitigation. IoT-enabled cybersecurity solutions leverage AI and ML to identify and counteract sophisticated cyberattacks, protecting critical military infrastructure and data from adversaries.

2.3. Benefits of IoT in Defence

The integration of IoT in defence environments brings a multitude of benefits that enhance operational efficiency, situational awareness, and strategic capabilities.

These benefits contribute significantly to the effectiveness and readiness of military forces, providing them with a technological edge in modern warfare.

2.3.1. Enhanced Situational Awareness

IoT-enabled devices and sensors provide real-time data collection and transmission from various sources on the battlefield. This comprehensive and continuous flow of information enhances situational awareness, allowing military commanders to monitor troop movements, enemy activities, and environmental conditions in real-time (Hosseini et al., 2018). Enhanced situational awareness leads to more informed decision-making and a more agile response to dynamic battlefield scenarios.

2.3.2. Improved Operational Efficiency

IoT technologies streamline and automate numerous processes within military operations, leading to improved efficiency. For example, predictive maintenance systems use IoT sensors to monitor the condition of equipment and vehicles, predicting when maintenance is required to prevent failures. This proactive approach reduces downtime and extends the lifespan of critical assets, ensuring they are always mission-ready. IoT-enabled logistics systems optimize the supply chain by tracking inventory levels and the movement of supplies, ensuring that resources are available when and where they are needed.

2.3.3. Precision and Accuracy in Combat

IoT contributes to the development and deployment of smart weapons and munitions that can be precisely guided and controlled. These systems utilize real-time data to adjust their trajectory and targeting, increasing accuracy and reducing collateral damage. Precision-guided munitions enhance the effectiveness of combat operations by ensuring that targets are accurately hit, even in complex and dynamic environments.

2.3.4. Health and Safety Monitoring

Wearable IoT devices monitor the health and vitals of soldiers in real-time, providing critical data on their physical condition. This information is invaluable for medical teams, enabling rapid response to injuries or health issues on the battlefield. Additionally, IoT devices can monitor environmental conditions, such as temperature and air quality, alerting soldiers to potential hazards and improving their overall safety.

2.3.5. Enhanced Communication and Coordination

IoT facilitates seamless communication and coordination among various military units and command centres. Networked IoT devices enable real-time sharing of information, ensuring that all units are synchronized and operating with the latest data. This enhanced communication capability is crucial for coordinating complex operations and maintaining a unified strategic approach.

2.3.6. Cost Savings and Resource Optimization

The efficiency and automation provided by IoT technologies lead to significant cost savings and resource optimization. By reducing equipment downtime through predictive maintenance and optimizing logistics and supply chains, military organizations can allocate resources more effectively and reduce unnecessary expenditures (Izzat et al., 2020). The long-term cost benefits of IoT adoption contribute to more sustainable and efficient military operations.

2.4. Challenges in Implementing IoT in Defence

While the benefits of IoT in defence are substantial, implementing these technologies also presents several challenges that need to be addressed to ensure successful deployment and operation. These challenges encompass technical, operational, and security-related aspects. Fig. 2.1 shows the graphical representation of the challenges faced by different industries in implementing IoT in defence.

2.4.1. Cybersecurity Risks

One of the most significant challenges in implementing IoT in defence is ensuring robust cybersecurity. The interconnected nature of IoT devices creates numerous entry points for cyber threats, making the entire system vulnerable to attacks. Cybersecurity breaches can lead to data theft, unauthorized access, and manipulation of critical systems, potentially compromising military operations. Ensuring

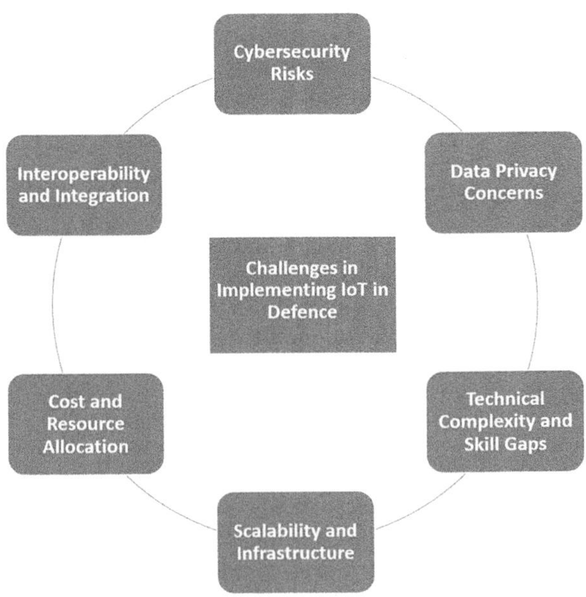

Fig. 2.1. Challenges in Implementing IoT in Defence.

the security of IoT devices and networks requires comprehensive and continuously updated cybersecurity measures, including encryption, secure communication protocols, and intrusion detection systems.

2.4.2. Data Privacy Concerns

IoT devices in defence environments collect vast amounts of data, including sensitive and classified information. Protecting the privacy of this data is crucial to prevent it from falling into the wrong hands. Ensuring data privacy involves implementing strict access controls, data anonymization techniques, and secure storage solutions (Jiang et al., 2022). Compliance with national and international data protection regulations adds an additional layer of complexity to managing data privacy in IoT-driven defence systems.

2.4.3. Interoperability and Integration

Defence environments often involve a wide range of systems and technologies from different vendors and generations. Ensuring that new IoT devices can seamlessly integrate and communicate with existing systems is a significant challenge. Interoperability issues can hinder the effective deployment of IoT solutions, leading to inefficiencies and operational disruptions. Developing standardized protocols and interfaces is essential to facilitate the smooth integration and interoperability of IoT devices in defence.

2.4.4. Scalability and Infrastructure

Deploying IoT systems on a large scale in defence environments requires substantial infrastructure investment. This includes establishing reliable communication networks, data storage solutions, and processing capabilities. Ensuring that the infrastructure can support the scale and complexity of IoT deployments is critical for their successful implementation. Additionally, scalability issues need to be addressed to accommodate the growing number of IoT devices and the increasing volume of data they generate.

2.4.5. Technical Complexity and Skill Gaps

The technical complexity of IoT systems presents a challenge in terms of implementation and maintenance. Defence organizations need skilled personnel who are proficient in IoT technologies, cybersecurity, data analytics, and system integration (Khan & Salah, 2018). Addressing skill gaps and providing adequate training for military and technical staff is essential to ensure the effective operation and management of IoT systems.

2.4.6. Cost and Resource Allocation

Implementing IoT in defence environments requires significant investment in technology, infrastructure, and personnel. Budget constraints and competing priorities can pose challenges in allocating the necessary resources for IoT projects.

Ensuring that the benefits of IoT adoption justify the costs and that resources are allocated efficiently is crucial for the successful deployment of IoT technologies in defence.

3. Privacy Concerns in IoT-Driven Defence Environments

3.1. Definition and Scope of Privacy Concerns

Privacy concerns in the context of IoT-driven defence environments refer to the potential risks and threats to the confidentiality, integrity, and availability of sensitive information that IoT devices and systems collect, store, process, and transmit. The scope of these concerns is broad, encompassing various aspects of military operations, personnel data, and national security.

3.1.1. Definition of Privacy Concerns

In defence environments, privacy concerns revolve around the protection of classified information, operational data, and personal information of military personnel. This includes:

- **Confidentiality:** Ensuring that sensitive information is accessible only to authorized individuals and entities. Unauthorized access or disclosure of this information can compromise military operations and national security.
- **Integrity:** Maintaining the accuracy and completeness of data throughout its lifecycle. Any alteration or tampering with data can lead to misinformation and potentially disastrous consequences.
- **Availability:** Ensuring that information and systems are accessible when needed for operational purposes. Denial of access due to cyberattacks or system failures can hinder military effectiveness.

3.1.2. Scope of Privacy Concerns

The scope of privacy concerns in IoT-driven defence environments covers various dimensions:

- **Operational Data:** This includes real-time data collected from IoT devices used in the field, such as surveillance footage, troop movements, and environmental conditions. Unauthorized access to this data can reveal strategic information to adversaries.
- **Personal Data:** IoT devices often collect personal information about military personnel, such as health records, biometric data, and location data. Protecting this information is crucial to safeguarding the privacy and security of individuals.
- **Communication Networks:** The interconnected nature of IoT devices relies on robust communication networks. Securing these networks from eavesdropping, interception, and disruption is essential to maintain the confidentiality and integrity of transmitted data.

- **Stored Data:** Data stored in IoT devices, databases, and cloud systems must be protected from unauthorized access and breaches. This includes implementing strong encryption and access control measures.
- **Data Processing:** IoT systems often involve complex data processing and analytics to derive actionable insights. Ensuring that data processing mechanisms are secure and comply with privacy regulations is vital.
- **Interoperability:** IoT systems in defence environments often interact with other systems and platforms. Ensuring that these interactions do not compromise privacy is a critical aspect of the scope.

3.2. Types of Privacy Risks in Defence IoT

The deployment of IoT in defence environments introduces various privacy risks that can potentially compromise the security and effectiveness of military operations. These risks can be categorized based on their nature and impact.

Data Breach Risks: Data breaches occur when unauthorized individuals or entities gain access to sensitive information. In defence IoT systems, data breaches can result from weak security protocols, inadequate encryption, or vulnerabilities in IoT devices and networks. The consequences of data breaches in defence environments are severe, as they can lead to the exposure of classified information, operational plans, and personal data of military personnel.

Location Tracking and Surveillance Risks: IoT devices often collect and transmit location data, which can be exploited by adversaries for tracking and surveillance purposes. Unauthorized access to location data can reveal the movements and positions of military units, compromising operational security. Additionally, constant surveillance can infringe on the privacy of military personnel, affecting their morale and well-being.

Interception and Eavesdropping Risks: The communication networks used by IoT devices in defence are susceptible to interception and eavesdropping attacks. Adversaries can intercept data transmissions to gain access to sensitive information or manipulate data for malicious purposes. Securing communication channels through encryption and secure protocols is essential to mitigate these risks.

Data Manipulation and Integrity Risks: IoT devices collect and process vast amounts of data, which must remain accurate and reliable. Data manipulation attacks involve altering or tampering with data to mislead decision-makers or disrupt operations. Ensuring the integrity of data through validation and verification mechanisms is crucial to prevent such attacks.

Unauthorized Access and Control Risks: Unauthorized access to IoT devices and systems can allow adversaries to take control of critical assets, such as surveillance systems, drones, or smart weaponry (Khvoynitskaya, 2020). This can lead to the manipulation of these assets for malicious purposes, posing a significant threat to military operations and personnel safety. Implementing strong access control measures and authentication mechanisms is vital to prevent unauthorized access.

Privacy Risks from Data Aggregation: IoT devices collect diverse types of data, which can be aggregated to create detailed profiles of military operations and personnel. This aggregated data, if accessed by adversaries, can provide comprehensive insights into military strategies, capabilities, and weaknesses. Ensuring that data aggregation processes are secure and comply with privacy regulations is essential to mitigate these risks.

Supply Chain and Third-Party Risks: IoT devices and systems in defence environments often rely on components and services from third-party vendors. Supply chain vulnerabilities can introduce privacy risks, as compromised components or services can be exploited by adversaries to gain access to sensitive information. Ensuring the security and integrity of the supply chain through rigorous vetting and monitoring of vendors is crucial.

Insider Threats: Insider threats involve individuals within the defence organization who have access to IoT systems and data. These individuals may intentionally or unintentionally compromise privacy by leaking sensitive information or exploiting system vulnerabilities (Klarin, 2019). Implementing strict access controls, monitoring, and awareness programs can help mitigate insider threats.

3.3. Case Studies of Privacy Breaches in Defence IoT

The implementation of IoT in defence environments, while offering significant operational advantages, has also led to several high-profile privacy breaches. These case studies illustrate the vulnerabilities and consequences of such breaches, highlighting the importance of robust security measures.

1. **Compromised Military Drone Footage**
   In 2011, it was reported that insurgents in Iraq and Afghanistan had intercepted live video feeds from US military drones. Using inexpensive software, they were able to view unencrypted footage, gaining valuable intelligence on US military operations and targets. This breach exposed critical operational data, compromised missions, and put soldiers' lives at risk. The incident underscored the necessity of encrypting all data transmissions from IoT devices in defence environments to prevent unauthorized access and interception (https://www.theguardian.com/world/2009/dec/17/skygrabber-american-drones-hacked).
2. **Cyber Attack on US Central Command**
   In 2015, the social media accounts of US Central Command (CENTCOM) were hacked by a group claiming allegiance to ISIS. While this attack did not involve direct IoT systems, it demonstrated the potential for social engineering attacks to gain access to sensitive information. The hackers posted documents that appeared to contain information on military operations, potentially sourced from compromised IoT systems or other digital channels. This case highlighted the need for comprehensive cybersecurity strategies that include both technical measures and user awareness to protect against multifaceted threats (https://www.trendmicro.com/vinfo/in/security/news/cyber-attacks/us-central-command-hack-a-warning-for-high-profile-accounts).

3. **Stuxnet and Industrial Control Systems (ICS)**
The Stuxnet worm, uncovered in 2010, struck industrial control systems and is widely regarded as a tool deployed to disrupt Iran's nuclear efforts. While not a traditional IoT breach, Stuxnet demonstrated how malware could infiltrate and manipulate automated systems (Klarin & Suseno, 2023). Defence environments, which increasingly rely on IoT for various automated functions, are similarly vulnerable to such attacks. The incident emphasized the importance of securing both software and hardware components of IoT systems against sophisticated cyber threats.
4. **Hacking of US Army Wearables**
In 2018, it was revealed that data from fitness trackers used by military personnel could be accessed to reveal sensitive information about troop movements and base locations. The incident involved the aggregation of GPS data from wearable devices, which was then inadvertently made public through a fitness tracking app. This breach highlighted the risks associated with the use of commercial IoT devices in military environments and the need for stringent data privacy measures, including disabling location tracking features when they are not necessary for operational purposes (https://fieldeffect.com/blog/soldiers-receive-unsolicited-smartwatches-malware).

3.4. Impact of Privacy Breaches on National Security

Privacy breaches in IoT-driven defence environments can have far-reaching and severe consequences for national security. The impacts can be immediate and long-lasting, affecting various aspects of military operations and strategic capabilities.

3.4.1. Compromise of Strategic Operations

Privacy breaches can result in the unauthorized disclosure of sensitive operational data, compromising strategic military operations. Adversaries gaining access to real-time intelligence, troop movements, and mission plans can disrupt or sabotage military efforts, leading to mission failures and increased casualties (Ad et al., 2006). Such breaches undermine the effectiveness of military strategies and diminish the element of surprise, which is often crucial in combat situations.

3.4.2. Loss of Technological Advantage

IoT systems in defence often incorporate cutting-edge technologies that provide a strategic advantage over adversaries. Breaches that expose the technical details of these systems can erode this advantage, allowing adversaries to reverse-engineer or counteract the technology. This loss of technological superiority can shift the balance of power, making it more challenging for military forces to maintain an edge in conflicts.

3.4.3. Threats to Personnel Safety

Breaches involving the personal data of military personnel, such as health records, biometric data, and location information, pose significant risks to their safety and security. Adversaries can use this information to target individuals, orchestrate kidnappings, or launch personalized attacks. Protecting the privacy of personnel data is crucial to ensuring their safety and maintaining morale within the military.

3.4.4. Damage to National Reputation and Alliances

Significant privacy breaches can damage the reputation of a nation and its defence capabilities on the global stage. Allies may lose confidence in the nation's ability to secure sensitive information, leading to strained diplomatic and military relationships (Leloglu, 2016). This erosion of trust can impact international collaborations, intelligence sharing, and joint military operations, ultimately weakening collective security efforts.

3.4.5. Economic and Resource Implications

Addressing the aftermath of privacy breaches can be costly and resource-intensive. The financial burden of mitigating breaches includes investing in advanced cybersecurity measures, conducting thorough investigations, and rectifying compromised systems. Additionally, breaches can lead to the loss of critical intellectual property and technological innovations, which can have long-term economic repercussions for the defence industry.

3.4.6. Legal and Regulatory Consequences

Privacy breaches can result in legal and regulatory consequences, especially if they involve the mishandling of personal data. Defence organizations may face lawsuits, fines, and penalties for failing to comply with data protection regulations. The legal implications extend to potential restrictions on the deployment and use of IoT technologies in defence, impacting operational capabilities.

3.4.7. Psychological Impact

The psychological impact of privacy breaches on military personnel and the public cannot be underestimated. Breaches that expose sensitive information can lead to a loss of confidence in the security measures employed by defence organizations. This erosion of trust can affect the morale of military personnel, leading to decreased operational effectiveness and increased stress levels.

4. Data Protection Strategies in IoT-Driven Defence Environments

4.1. Overview of Data Protection in IoT

Data protection in IoT, especially within defence environments, is critical due to the sensitive nature of the information involved and the significant consequences of potential breaches. It encompasses various practices, technologies, and policies aimed at securing data from unauthorized access, alteration, or destruction throughout its lifecycle. Key elements include data encryption, which transforms information into a secure format, ensuring that even if intercepted, it remains unreadable. Implementing stringent access control mechanisms, such as multi-factor authentication (MFA) and role-based access control (RBAC), is essential to limit data access to authorized personnel only (Li et al., 2022). Anonymization and masking techniques reduce the risk of exposing personally identifiable information, while secure communication protocols, such as TLS and SSL, protect data transmitted between IoT devices and central systems. Intrusion detection and prevention systems (IDPS) play a vital role in monitoring network traffic for suspicious activities, enabling timely intervention. Additionally, ensuring data integrity through checksums, hashes, and digital signatures verifies that data remains unaltered during transmission and storage. Compliance with data protection regulations, conducting regular audits, and addressing challenges such as the complexity of IoT ecosystems and evolving cyber threats are crucial for maintaining robust data protection measures in defence settings.

4.2. Encryption Techniques for Defence IoT

Encryption is fundamental to data protection in IoT environments, particularly in defence, where safeguarding sensitive information is essential. Symmetric encryption, notably the Advanced Encryption Standard (AES), employs the same key for both encryption and decryption, making it efficient for environments where secure key management is feasible. AES is widely adopted due to its strong security and ability to encrypt substantial data efficiently (Liu et al., 2017). Asymmetric encryption, or public-key encryption, utilizes a pair of keys – one public for encryption and one private for decryption – offering a secure means of communication and key exchange. Prominent asymmetric algorithms include Rivest-Shamir-Adleman (RSA), which provides robust security with large key sizes, and Elliptic Curve Cryptography (ECC), which offers comparable security with shorter key lengths, making it particularly suitable for IoT devices with limited resources. These encryption techniques are essential in protecting data integrity and confidentiality, ensuring that defence IoT systems remain resilient against unauthorized access and cyber threats.

4.3. Access Control Mechanisms

Access control mechanisms are vital in safeguarding sensitive data within IoT-driven defence environments. These mechanisms ensure that only authorized personnel and systems can access critical information, thereby mitigating the risk of unauthorized access and data breaches. Various approaches to access control can be implemented, including mandatory access control (MAC), discretionary access control (DAC), and RBAC. MAC restricts access based on predefined policies set by system administrators, making it suitable for highly sensitive defence applications (Liyanage et al., 2020). In contrast, DAC allows users to control access to their resources, offering flexibility but requiring vigilant management to prevent misuse. RBAC, one of the most widely used models, assigns permissions based on user roles, streamlining access management while ensuring that individuals only have access to the data necessary for their specific job functions. Implementing MFA adds an additional layer of security, requiring users to provide multiple forms of identification before gaining access to sensitive information (Makhdoom et al., 2018). This is particularly crucial in defence environments, where the cost of a breach can be significant. Continuous monitoring and auditing of access logs further enhances security by identifying and responding to suspicious access attempts, ensuring that access control mechanisms remain effective and adaptive to emerging threats.

4.4. Data Anonymization and Masking Techniques

Data anonymization and masking techniques are essential for protecting sensitive information in IoT-driven defence environments, particularly when sharing or processing data that includes personally identifiable information (PII) or classified details. Data anonymization involves altering data in such a way that it cannot be traced back to an individual or entity, thus preserving privacy while allowing for valuable data analysis. Techniques such as k-anonymity and differential privacy are commonly used; k-anonymity ensures that data cannot be uniquely identified among a group of at least k individuals, while differential privacy adds randomness to data queries to prevent the identification of individuals even when multiple data sources are combined (Meng et al., 2018). Data masking, on the other hand, modifies data in a reversible manner, allowing authorized users to access masked data while keeping sensitive information hidden. Common masking techniques include substitution, shuffling, and encryption of specific data fields, which maintain data utility for testing and development purposes without exposing sensitive details. These techniques are critical in defence settings where operational data needs to be shared with external partners or during training exercises, as they help maintain confidentiality while still enabling analytical insights.

4.5. Secure Communication Protocols

Secure communication protocols are fundamental for protecting data in transit within IoT-driven defence environments, where the integrity and confidentiality of information are paramount. These protocols ensure that data exchanged between IoT devices and central systems is encrypted and safeguarded against interception or tampering. Transport Layer Security (TLS) is one of the most widely used protocols, providing a secure channel over a computer network by encrypting the data being transmitted and ensuring authentication between communicating parties. Another important protocol is Datagram Transport Layer Security (DTLS), which is designed for securing datagram-based applications, such as IoT devices, ensuring low-latency communication while maintaining security. Additionally, secure messaging protocols like Message Queuing Telemetry Transport (MQTT) and Constrained Application Protocol (CoAP) are specifically tailored for IoT environments, enabling efficient communication while incorporating security features such as authentication and encryption. Implementing these secure communication protocols is essential for mitigating risks associated with eavesdropping, man-in-the-middle attacks, and data breaches, ensuring that sensitive information remains confidential and secure throughout its transmission (Monther & Tawalbeh, 2020). As the landscape of cyber threats evolves, continuously updating and adapting these protocols to incorporate the latest security advancements is critical for maintaining a resilient defence infrastructure.

5. Regulatory Frameworks and Compliance

5.1. International Data Protection Regulations

International data protection regulations play a crucial role in governing the handling of personal and sensitive data across borders, particularly in the context of IoT-driven defence environments where data security is paramount. One of the most comprehensive frameworks is the General Data Protection Regulation (GDPR), enacted by the European Union (EU) in 2018. GDPR sets strict guidelines on data processing, emphasizing principles such as data minimization, consent, transparency, and the right to access and erase personal data (Nazarov & Klarin, 2020). It mandates organizations to implement appropriate technical and organizational measures to protect data, with penalties for non-compliance reaching up to 4% of annual global turnover. Another significant regulation is the California Consumer Privacy Act (CCPA), which enhances privacy rights and consumer protection for residents of California. CCPA empowers individuals to know what personal data is being collected about them, allows them to request the deletion of their data, and gives them the right to opt-out of the sale of their data to third parties.

In addition to these regulations, international frameworks such as the Asia-Pacific Economic Cooperation (APEC) Privacy Framework and the OECD Privacy Guidelines provide guidance for data protection practices in member countries. The APEC framework promotes data protection while facilitating cross-border trade and information flows, recognizing the need for cooperation among economies in a digital landscape. Furthermore, the Council of Europe's Convention 108 is another landmark treaty focusing on the protection of individuals regarding automated processing of personal data (Rafols et al., 2012). These international regulations highlight the growing recognition of the need for robust data protection measures, particularly in contexts where sensitive information is handled, such as in defence IoT applications. Compliance with these regulations not only ensures legal adherence but also fosters trust among stakeholders, including military personnel and citizens, in the handling of their personal and sensitive data.

5.2. National Regulations on Defence Data Protection

National regulations on defence data protection are designed to address the unique challenges associated with safeguarding sensitive military information and operational data within a country's jurisdiction. These regulations are crucial in establishing frameworks that dictate how defence organizations handle data, ensuring that national security is upheld while complying with broader data protection standards. In the United States, the Federal Information Security Management Act (FISMA) mandates that federal agencies, including those in the defence sector, implement information security programs to protect sensitive data. FISMA emphasizes risk management and requires agencies to develop, document, and implement information security policies and procedures to safeguard data integrity, confidentiality, and availability.

Similarly, the Department of Defense (DoD) has established specific guidelines and regulations, such as the DoD Instruction 8500.01, which provides a framework for cybersecurity and the protection of information systems within the defence domain (Rossetto et al., 2018). These guidelines emphasize a risk-based approach to security, requiring the identification and management of risks associated with data protection. The DoD also implements the Cybersecurity Maturity Model Certification (CMMC), which sets cybersecurity standards for contractors and suppliers working with the defence sector, ensuring that sensitive information is adequately protected throughout the supply chain.

In the United Kingdom, the Defence and Security Industrial Strategy (DSIS) outlines the government's approach to data protection within the defence sector, emphasizing the need for robust cybersecurity measures to safeguard sensitive information. The UK's Data Protection Act 2018, which incorporates GDPR principles, establishes the legal framework for data protection across various sectors, including defence, ensuring that personal and sensitive data is handled in compliance with established standards. These national regulations are complemented by collaborative efforts among allied nations to enhance data protection in defence contexts, recognizing that the interconnected nature of modern military operations necessitates a coordinated approach to data security. By adhering to these regulations, defence organizations can ensure that they not only protect sensitive information effectively but also maintain operational integrity and trust within the military and among the public.

5.3. Compliance Requirements for Defence IoT Systems

Compliance requirements for defence IoT systems are critical for ensuring the secure handling of sensitive data and maintaining national security. These requirements stem from a combination of international regulations, national laws, and specific military guidelines that govern how data must be processed, stored, and transmitted within defence environments. One of the primary compliance frameworks applicable to defence IoT systems is the Federal Risk and Authorization Management Program (FedRAMP) in the United States, which establishes standardized security requirements for cloud services used by federal agencies (Ryan, 2019). For defence contractors, adhering to the Cybersecurity Maturity Model Certification (CMMC) is essential, as it sets forth specific practices and processes that contractors must implement to ensure adequate cybersecurity measures are in place to protect sensitive data.

In addition to these frameworks, defence IoT systems must comply with regulations such as the General Data Protection Regulation (GDPR) and the National Institute of Standards and Technology (NIST) Special Publication 800-171, which provides guidelines for protecting controlled unclassified information

(CUI) in non-federal systems. These regulations emphasize principles like data minimization, access control, encryption, and incident response, ensuring that sensitive data is protected throughout its lifecycle. Furthermore, regular audits and assessments are often mandated to verify compliance with established standards and identify any areas needing improvement. Defence organizations must also ensure that their personnel are adequately trained in data protection protocols and that robust incident response plans are in place to address potential data breaches or security incidents. By adhering to these compliance requirements, defence IoT systems can effectively mitigate risks associated with data security and maintain operational integrity.

5.4. Challenges in Regulatory Compliance

Regulatory compliance presents several challenges for defence IoT systems, primarily due to the complexity of the regulatory landscape and the rapidly evolving nature of technology. One significant challenge is the diversity of regulations across jurisdictions, which can create confusion for defence organizations operating internationally. Navigating the varying requirements of different countries or regions can complicate compliance efforts, leading to potential gaps in data protection and security.

Another challenge is the inherent complexity of IoT ecosystems, which consist of numerous interconnected devices, sensors, and applications. Ensuring that all components comply with stringent regulatory requirements can be a daunting task, particularly when devices are manufactured by different vendors with varying security standards. Moreover, the dynamic nature of IoT environments, where devices are frequently added, updated, or replaced, necessitates continuous monitoring and adaptation of compliance strategies, which can strain resources (Seet et al., 2018). Resource constraints often hinder effective compliance. Many defence organizations may lack the necessary personnel, expertise, or budget to implement and maintain comprehensive compliance programs. This can lead to insufficient training and awareness among staff regarding data protection protocols, increasing the risk of non-compliance. Technological challenges also play a significant role, as outdated systems and legacy infrastructure may not be equipped to meet current regulatory standards. Upgrading these systems can be costly and time-consuming, further complicating compliance efforts. Finally, the growing threat landscape, characterized by sophisticated cyberattacks and data breaches, necessitates constant vigilance and adaptation of compliance measures, requiring organizations to invest in advanced security technologies and practices to safeguard sensitive data.

6. Technological Solutions for Enhancing Privacy and Data Protection

6.1. Advanced Encryption Standards

Advanced Encryption Standards (AES) are widely recognized as one of the most secure encryption algorithms used to protect sensitive data, particularly in

IoT-driven defence environments. Established by the National Institute of Standards and Technology (NIST) in 2001, AES was designed to replace the older Data Encryption Standard (DES) due to its vulnerabilities to brute-force attacks (Sethi & Sarangi, 2017). AES operates on fixed block sizes of 128 bits and supports key lengths of 128, 192, and 256 bits, allowing for varying levels of security. The algorithm employs a symmetric encryption method, meaning the same key is used for both encryption and decryption, which facilitates efficient processing – an essential factor for devices with limited computational resources typically found in IoT applications.

AES is characterized by its resistance to known cryptographic attacks, including linear and differential cryptanalysis, making it suitable for securing data at rest and in transit within defence systems. Its implementation in various security protocols, such as TLS and IPsec, underscores its significance in establishing secure communications across networks. Moreover, AES can be effectively integrated into IoT devices to protect sensitive information, such as classified military communications or personal data of service members (Siby et al., 2017). However, the challenge lies in secure key management, as the effectiveness of AES depends heavily on the secrecy of the encryption key. Therefore, employing robust key management practices, such as periodic key rotation and secure key storage, is critical to maximizing the effectiveness of AES in protecting defence data. Overall, AES serves as a cornerstone in the framework of data protection, enabling defence organizations to secure their critical information against unauthorized access and cyber threats.

6.2. Blockchain Technology for Data Integrity

Blockchain technology offers a revolutionary approach to ensuring data integrity in IoT-driven defence environments by providing a decentralized and tamper-resistant method for recording and verifying transactions. At its core, blockchain consists of a distributed ledger that records data across multiple nodes in a network, making it nearly impossible for any single entity to alter the information without consensus from the majority of participants. This feature is particularly valuable in defence settings, where maintaining the accuracy and authenticity of data is crucial for operational success and national security. One of the primary applications of blockchain in defence is in the management of supply chains, where it can be used to track the provenance and movement of critical materials and equipment (Simms, 2019). By recording each transaction on a blockchain, defence organizations can ensure transparency and accountability, making it easier to verify the integrity of supplies and reduce the risk of fraud or counterfeiting. Additionally, blockchain can enhance the security of IoT devices by enabling secure communication and data sharing among interconnected devices. Smart contracts – self-executing contracts with the terms of the agreement directly written into code – can automate processes while ensuring compliance with predefined rules, further enhancing operational efficiency.

Fig. 2.2 shows the data integrity for blockchain and the attributes affecting it. Moreover, the immutability of blockchain records provides a reliable audit

Fig. 2.2. Blockchain technology for Data Integrity (Image Reference: https://www.dataexpertise.in/blockchain-technology-data-integrity-security/).

trail, allowing defence organizations to track access and modifications to sensitive data. This feature is particularly important for ensuring compliance with regulations and standards governing data protection. However, while blockchain technology holds significant promise for enhancing data integrity, challenges such as scalability, interoperability with existing systems, and energy consumption must be addressed to realize its full potential in defence applications. As defence organizations increasingly adopt blockchain solutions, ongoing research and collaboration will be essential to overcoming these challenges and harnessing the benefits of this transformative technology.

6.3. AI and ML for Threat Detection

AI and ML are transforming threat detection in IoT-driven defence environments by providing advanced capabilities for identifying, analyzing, and responding to potential security threats. The sheer volume of data generated by IoT devices presents significant challenges for traditional security measures, making AI and ML essential for enhancing cybersecurity. These technologies leverage algorithms and models that can learn from data patterns and adapt to new threats in real time.

AI and ML enable proactive threat detection by analyzing vast amounts of data to identify anomalies that may indicate malicious activity. For example, unsupervised learning techniques can detect unusual patterns in network traffic, user behaviour, or device interactions, flagging activities that deviate from established baselines. This capability is particularly crucial in defence settings, where early detection of threats can prevent unauthorized access to sensitive information or compromise of critical systems. AI-driven systems can automate the analysis of security incidents, significantly reducing response times. By correlating data from multiple sources, these systems can provide security analysts with actionable insights and recommendations, allowing for quicker decision-making. Furthermore, natural language processing (NLP) can be utilized to analyze unstructured data, such as reports and social media feeds, to gather intelligence on emerging threats and trends that may impact defence operations.

The deployment of AI and ML technologies also allows for continuous improvement of threat detection systems through adaptive learning. As new threats emerge, these systems can update their models based on new data, ensuring that detection mechanisms remain effective against evolving tactics employed by cyber adversaries. However, integrating AI and ML into defence cybersecurity frameworks requires addressing challenges such as data privacy, the potential for biased algorithms, and the need for robust training datasets to ensure the accuracy and reliability of threat detection capabilities.

6.4. Intrusion Detection and Prevention Systems

Intrusion Detection and Prevention Systems (IDPS) are critical components of cybersecurity in IoT-driven defence environments, designed to monitor network traffic and identify potential security breaches. These systems can be categorized into two primary types: intrusion detection systems (IDS), which focus on identifying and alerting administrators to suspicious activities, and intrusion prevention systems (IPS), which take proactive measures to block or mitigate threats in real time.

IDPS solutions utilize various techniques for threat detection, including signature-based detection, which identifies known threats by comparing incoming traffic against a database of known attack signatures. While effective for recognizing established threats, this approach may not detect new or evolving attacks. In contrast, anomaly-based detection employs statistical analysis and ML techniques to establish baselines of normal network behaviour and flag deviations that may indicate a potential intrusion (Dalipi & Yayilgan 2016). This dual approach enables defence organizations to identify both known and unknown threats, providing a comprehensive security posture (Singh et al., 2016). Moreover, IDPS can be integrated with other security measures, such as firewalls and security information and event management (SIEM) systems, to create a layered defense strategy. By correlating alerts from IDPS with data from other security solutions, organizations can enhance their situational awareness and improve incident response capabilities. Advanced IDPS solutions may also incorporate

AI and ML technologies to automate threat detection and response, allowing for faster identification and mitigation of potential breaches.

However, implementing IDPS in defence environments comes with challenges. The high volume of data generated by IoT devices can lead to a significant number of false positives, overwhelming security personnel and potentially leading to alert fatigue. To address this, organizations must fine-tune their detection rules and leverage advanced analytics to reduce noise while maintaining sensitivity to genuine threats. Ensuring that IDPS can effectively monitor encrypted traffic is crucial, as a growing portion of network communications is secured, making it difficult to analyze for potential threats without proper decryption methods.

7. Risk Management and Mitigation Strategies

7.1. Identifying and Assessing Risks

Identifying and assessing risks in IoT-driven defence environments is a fundamental process for ensuring the security and integrity of sensitive data and operational systems. This process begins with a thorough understanding of the specific assets, technologies, and information systems that are part of the IoT ecosystem. A comprehensive risk assessment involves several steps: asset identification, threat identification, vulnerability assessment, and impact analysis.

Asset identification involves cataloging all critical assets, including IoT devices, data repositories, and communication channels, to understand their role and value within the defence framework. Once assets are identified, organizations can move to threat identification, which involves recognizing potential threats that could exploit vulnerabilities within these assets. Threats can range from cyberattacks, such as malware or denial-of-service attacks, to physical threats like unauthorized access to facilities housing IoT devices.

The next step is vulnerability assessment, where organizations evaluate the weaknesses within their systems that could be exploited by identified threats. This assessment includes reviewing existing security measures, outdated software, and configuration errors. The results of this evaluation help in understanding the level of risk associated with each vulnerability.

Following the assessment, organizations conduct impact analysis to determine the potential consequences of successful attacks or breaches. This analysis considers the impact on operational capabilities, data integrity, financial costs, and reputational damage. By evaluating both the likelihood of occurrence and the potential impact of various threats, organizations can prioritize risks and develop strategies for mitigation (Sohal et al., 2018). A risk matrix may be employed to visually represent risks, categorizing them based on their likelihood and severity. This systematic approach ensures that defence organizations can effectively allocate resources and implement security measures tailored to the identified risks.

7.2. Risk Management Frameworks

Risk management frameworks provide structured methodologies for identifying, assessing, and mitigating risks within IoT-driven defence environments. These frameworks offer guidance on best practices, processes, and standards for managing cybersecurity risks effectively. Several widely recognized frameworks can be adopted by defence organizations, each with its unique focus and applicability. One prominent framework is the NIST Risk Management Framework (RMF), which outlines a structured process for integrating security and risk management into the system development lifecycle. The NIST RMF consists of several key steps: categorizing information systems, selecting security controls, implementing those controls, assessing their effectiveness, authorizing system operation, and continuously monitoring security posture. This framework emphasizes a risk-based approach, allowing organizations to tailor their security measures based on the specific risks they face, which is especially pertinent in the dynamic landscape of IoT security.

Another widely used framework is the ISO/IEC 27001, which provides a comprehensive approach to managing information security risks. It focuses on establishing, implementing, maintaining, and continually improving an information security management system (ISMS). ISO/IEC 27001 emphasizes risk assessment and treatment, allowing organizations to identify and mitigate risks based on their specific operational context (Sun et al., 2016). This framework is particularly valuable for defense organizations aiming to achieve international standards in data protection and cybersecurity.

The CIS Controls is another practical framework that outlines a set of best practices for cybersecurity defense. It comprises a prioritized list of actions that organizations can take to improve their security posture, focusing on actionable steps that provide the most significant risk reduction. This framework is beneficial for defence organizations looking for a straightforward, implementation-oriented approach to risk management. Frameworks such as the COBIT (Control Objectives for Information and Related Technologies) and the FAIR (Factor Analysis of Information Risk) model provide further methodologies for aligning risk management with business objectives and quantifying risk, respectively (Ad et al., 2006). Each of these frameworks can be adapted to suit the specific needs of IoT-driven defence environments, allowing organizations to create a robust risk management strategy that enhances their overall cybersecurity resilience. By implementing an appropriate risk management framework, defence organizations can systematically identify vulnerabilities, assess potential impacts, and develop effective mitigation strategies, ultimately safeguarding critical assets and ensuring operational continuity.

7.3. Incident Response and Recovery Plans

Incident response and recovery plans are essential components of an effective cybersecurity strategy in IoT-driven defence environments. These plans outline the processes and procedures that organizations must follow in the event of a security incident, enabling them to respond swiftly and effectively to minimize damage and restore normal operations. A well-structured incident response plan typically consists of several key phases: preparation, detection and analysis, containment, eradication, recovery, and post-incident review.

Preparation involves establishing an incident response team, developing communication protocols, and providing training to ensure all personnel are aware of their roles during an incident. This phase may also include the implementation of monitoring tools and technologies to facilitate early detection of potential security breaches (Tawalbeh & Somani, 2016). During the detection and analysis phase, organizations must identify and assess incidents as they occur. This involves monitoring alerts, analyzing logs, and correlating data from various sources to determine the nature and scope of the incident. Rapid identification is crucial to limit the potential impact on critical systems and data.

Once an incident is confirmed, the containment phase begins. This step aims to prevent further damage by isolating affected systems and stopping the spread of the incident. Depending on the severity of the threat, containment strategies may include taking systems offline or blocking malicious traffic at the network level. Following containment, the eradication phase focuses on identifying the root cause of the incident and removing any malicious elements from the environment. This may involve applying patches, removing malware, or addressing vulnerabilities that were exploited during the incident.

The recovery phase is dedicated to restoring affected systems to normal operation and ensuring that they are secure before bringing them back online. This often involves restoring data from backups, reconfiguring systems, and conducting thorough testing to confirm that all security measures are in place. Finally, the post-incident review allows organizations to analyze the incident's impact, assess the effectiveness of the response, and identify areas for improvement. This review is critical for refining incident response plans and enhancing overall cybersecurity posture. By conducting regular drills and tabletop exercises, defence organizations can ensure that their incident response plans remain effective and up-to-date, enabling them to respond to incidents swiftly and efficiently.

7.4. Best Practices for Risk Mitigation

Implementing best practices for risk mitigation is essential for enhancing the security posture of IoT-driven defence environments. These practices provide a framework for organizations to identify, assess, and address potential security threats proactively. Some key best practices include:

Comprehensive Risk Assessment: Conduct regular risk assessments to identify vulnerabilities and threats specific to the IoT landscape. This involves not only assessing the technology but also considering human factors, such as employee training and awareness.

Robust Access Controls: Implement strict access control measures, ensuring that only authorized personnel have access to sensitive data and systems. RBACs can help minimize risks by granting users permissions based on their specific job functions.

Regular Software Updates and Patching: Keeping IoT devices and systems up to date with the latest security patches is crucial for mitigating vulnerabilities.

Establish a routine process for monitoring and applying updates to ensure all devices are protected against known threats.

Encryption and Secure Communication: Utilize strong encryption techniques for data at rest and in transit to safeguard sensitive information from unauthorized access. Employing secure communication protocols, such as HTTPS, TLS, and VPNs, helps protect data integrity and confidentiality.

Network Segmentation: Segmenting the network into isolated zones can help limit the spread of potential attacks. By creating separate environments for different IoT devices and systems, organizations can enhance security and contain threats more effectively.

Monitoring and Threat Intelligence: Continuously monitor network traffic and system activities to detect anomalies and potential threats in real time. Leveraging threat intelligence feeds can provide valuable insights into emerging threats and vulnerabilities relevant to the defence sector.

Incident Response Preparedness: Develop and regularly update incident response plans to ensure that the organization can respond effectively to security incidents. Conduct regular training and simulation exercises to prepare staff for potential threats.

Vendor Risk Management: Establish processes for evaluating and managing risks associated with third-party vendors and suppliers. Conduct thorough assessments of vendor security practices and ensure they align with the organization's security policies.

User Training and Awareness: Implement ongoing training programs for employees to raise awareness about cybersecurity best practices and potential threats, such as phishing attacks. Educating personnel on how to recognize and report suspicious activities can significantly reduce risks.

8. Case Studies and Real-World Applications

8.1. Successful Implementations of IoT in Defence

Successful implementations of IoT in defence have demonstrated the transformative potential of these technologies to enhance operational efficiency, situational awareness, and decision-making capabilities. One prominent example is the use of IoT sensors in battlefield environments, which provide real-time data on troop movements, equipment status, and environmental conditions. For instance, the US Army has integrated IoT devices into its network of drones, vehicles, and soldiers to create a cohesive information ecosystem (Ad et al., 2006). These devices collect and transmit data on various parameters, enabling commanders to make informed decisions based on accurate and timely information, thereby improving mission outcomes.

Another successful implementation is the use of IoT for predictive maintenance in military equipment. By equipping vehicles and machinery with sensors that monitor their operational status, defence organizations can identify potential failures before they occur. This proactive approach not only reduces downtime and maintenance costs but also enhances the overall reliability of critical assets.

The US Navy has adopted this strategy in its fleet, utilizing IoT data analytics to optimize maintenance schedules and ensure that vessels are always mission-ready.

Moreover, IoT technologies have proven beneficial in supply chain management within defence operations. By employing IoT devices to track the movement of supplies and equipment, organizations can gain real-time visibility into their logistics operations. This capability enhances inventory management, reduces delays, and minimizes the risk of supply shortages in critical situations. For example, the British Army has implemented IoT solutions to improve the tracking and management of ammunition and equipment, leading to more efficient logistics operations.

The integration of IoT with AI has opened new avenues for enhancing decision-making processes. AI algorithms analyze the vast amounts of data generated by IoT devices to provide actionable insights, identify patterns, and predict future trends. This combination has been instrumental in improving threat detection and response capabilities, enabling defence organizations to adapt to rapidly changing operational environments. These successful implementations highlight the importance of investing in IoT technologies and establishing robust cybersecurity measures to protect sensitive data. As defence organizations continue to adopt IoT solutions, the lessons learned from these implementations will be crucial in guiding future strategies and ensuring that the benefits of IoT are realized while addressing the associated challenges.

8.2. Lessons Learned from Privacy Breaches

Privacy breaches in IoT-driven defence environments have highlighted critical vulnerabilities and served as valuable learning opportunities for organizations seeking to improve their cybersecurity measures. One of the key lessons learned is the importance of robust data protection protocols. High-profile breaches, such as the unauthorized access to sensitive military data through poorly secured IoT devices, underscore the need for stringent security measures, including strong encryption, secure communication protocols, and rigorous access controls. Organizations must ensure that all devices are designed with security in mind from the outset, employing best practices in IoT device management and data protection.

Another crucial lesson is the significance of continuous monitoring and threat detection. Many breaches occurred due to inadequate monitoring of IoT devices, allowing attackers to exploit vulnerabilities without detection for extended periods. Implementing real-time monitoring solutions can help organizations quickly identify anomalies and respond to potential threats before they escalate. This includes utilizing advanced analytics and AI to enhance threat detection capabilities and ensure that security teams are alerted to suspicious activities (Tawalbeh et al., 2020). Furthermore, the necessity of establishing comprehensive incident response plans cannot be overstated. Breaches often revealed the lack of preparedness among organizations to respond effectively to security incidents. A well-defined incident response plan should include clear procedures for detecting, containing, and recovering from breaches, as well as communication strategies for informing stakeholders and affected parties. Regular drills and simulations can help organizations refine their response strategies and ensure that all personnel are familiar with their roles during an incident.

Lessons learned from privacy breaches emphasize the importance of fostering a culture of cybersecurity awareness within defense organizations. Training programs should be implemented to educate personnel on the risks associated with IoT devices and the best practices for maintaining data privacy and security. Encouraging a proactive mindset towards cybersecurity can empower employees to recognize potential threats and report suspicious activities. Lastly, collaboration and information sharing among defense organizations can significantly enhance overall cybersecurity resilience. Breaches often reveal common vulnerabilities that may affect multiple organizations, highlighting the need for collective action to address these challenges. Establishing partnerships with industry leaders, cybersecurity experts, and governmental agencies can facilitate the sharing of threat intelligence and best practices, ultimately strengthening the security posture of the entire defense sector.

8.3. Comparative Analysis of Different Defence Organizations

Comparative analysis of various defence organizations reveals significant differences and similarities in how IoT technologies are adopted and integrated into military operations. Countries like the United States, China, and Israel are at the forefront of incorporating advanced IoT solutions within their defence frameworks, leveraging their technological prowess to enhance operational capabilities, see Table 2.1. The US Department of Defense, for instance, employs a comprehensive approach that includes extensive research and development, robust cybersecurity measures, and the integration of AI and autonomous systems to maintain a strategic edge. Similarly, China's People's Liberation Army focuses on utilizing IoT for real-time surveillance, data analytics, and network-centric warfare, supported by significant investments in emerging technologies. On the other hand, smaller nations such as Israel prioritize agility and innovation, often leading in the rapid deployment of cutting-edge IoT applications in defence due to their emphasis on high-tech industry collaboration and start-up culture. These organizations also vary in their approach to policy and regulatory frameworks, with some prioritizing stringent data security and privacy regulations, while others emphasize interoperability and international collaboration. By examining these diverse strategies, defence organizations can glean valuable insights into best practices and potential pitfalls, facilitating more informed decisions about their IoT adoption and implementation strategies.

8.4. Future Trends and Innovations in Defence IoT

The future of IoT in defence is poised for significant advancements, driven by technological innovations and the evolving needs of military operations. As organizations increasingly integrate IoT solutions into their frameworks, several key trends and innovations are likely to shape the landscape of defence IoT in the coming years.

Table 2.1. Comparative Analysis of Different Defence Organizations.

Defense Organization	IoT Implementation Focus	Privacy Concerns	Cybersecurity Measures	Lessons Learned
US Department of Defense	Real-time data analytics for battlefield management	High sensitivity of data; potential for breaches	Multi-layered security protocols, continuous monitoring	Importance of rapid incident response and updates
NATO	Interoperability among member nations' forces	Data sharing among nations raises privacy issues	Standardized security practices across member nations	Need for unified cybersecurity standards
Indian Armed Forces	Predictive maintenance for equipment	Risks related to unauthorized access to military data	Robust encryption and access controls	Significance of training personnel on cyber hygiene
British Army	Logistics and supply chain management	Concerns over civilian data privacy in operations	Incident response training and drills	Value of real-time threat intelligence sharing
Australian Defence Force	Enhanced situational awareness through connected systems	Balancing security with privacy of personnel data	Regular audits and compliance checks	Continuous adaptation to evolving cyber threats

Enhanced Autonomous Systems: One of the most significant trends is the growing reliance on autonomous systems powered by IoT technologies. UAVs, drones, and autonomous ground vehicles are set to become more prevalent in military operations. These systems will leverage IoT sensors to gather real-time data and make autonomous decisions, enhancing operational efficiency and reducing the risk to human personnel in combat situations.

Integration of AI: The fusion of IoT with AI will enable defence organizations to analyze vast amounts of data collected from IoT devices quickly. AI algorithms will enhance threat detection, predictive maintenance, and situational awareness by identifying patterns and anomalies in real-time. This integration will allow military forces to respond more effectively to emerging threats and improve decision-making processes.

Edge Computing: As IoT devices generate enormous volumes of data, the need for efficient data processing becomes critical. Edge computing will play a pivotal role in defence IoT by processing data closer to the source rather than relying solely on centralized cloud systems. This approach reduces latency and bandwidth usage, enabling faster response times and more efficient data management, which is essential for real-time military operations.

Advanced Security Solutions: The increasing adoption of IoT in defence also brings heightened cybersecurity concerns. Future trends will focus on developing advanced security solutions to protect IoT devices and networks from cyber threats. Innovations such as blockchain technology for secure data sharing, enhanced encryption methods, and the implementation of zero-trust architectures will be critical in ensuring the integrity and confidentiality of military data.

Interoperability and Standardization: As different military branches and allied forces adopt various IoT solutions, the need for interoperability and standardization will become paramount. Future innovations will likely focus on creating common protocols and standards that allow seamless communication and data sharing across different systems and organizations. This interoperability will enhance collaborative efforts among allied forces and streamline joint operations.

Smart Logistics and Supply Chain Management: IoT technologies will revolutionize logistics and supply chain management in defence. Future innovations will focus on creating smart supply chains that utilize real-time tracking, predictive analytics, and automated inventory management. This will enhance the efficiency of resource allocation, reduce costs, and ensure that military units have the necessary supplies when and where they are needed.

Increased Focus on Resilience and Recovery: With the growing reliance on IoT, defence organizations will prioritize resilience and recovery capabilities. Future innovations will emphasize building robust systems that can withstand cyberattacks, natural disasters, or equipment failures (Thierer, 2015). This includes developing advanced incident response plans, redundancy measures, and recovery strategies to ensure that operations can continue even in the face of significant disruptions.

Expanded Use of Wearable Technologies: Wearable IoT devices will see expanded use among military personnel, providing real-time health monitoring, location tracking, and communication capabilities. These technologies can enhance situational awareness, improve soldier safety, and facilitate better decision-making on the battlefield. Future innovations may lead to the development of more sophisticated wearable devices that integrate seamlessly with other IoT systems.

9. Ethical Considerations and Societal Implications

9.1. Ethical Issues in IoT-Driven Defence

The integration of IoT technologies into defence operations raises a multitude of ethical issues that demand careful consideration. One of the primary concerns revolves around the potential for mass surveillance. IoT devices, particularly those used for monitoring personnel and environments, can collect vast amounts of data, leading to privacy infringements. The ethical implications of surveillance become especially pronounced in military contexts, where the distinction between legitimate security measures and invasive monitoring can blur. Questions arise about how this data is collected, stored, and used, as well as who has access to it and under what circumstances.

Another significant ethical issue pertains to the use of autonomous systems and AI in military operations. As IoT devices become increasingly integrated with AI, concerns about accountability and decision-making in life-and-death situations emerge. If an autonomous drone makes a targeting decision based on IoT data, questions arise regarding who is responsible for that decision – the operator, the manufacturer, or the AI itself? The lack of transparency in AI algorithms can exacerbate these concerns, leading to potential biases and unintended consequences in operational outcomes. Data security is another critical ethical consideration. Defence organizations must ensure that the data collected by IoT devices is protected from unauthorized access and breaches. However, the ethical dilemma lies in balancing security measures with individual rights and freedoms. For example, stringent data protection measures may lead to the over-collection of personal data to ensure security, which can infringe upon individual privacy rights.

Moreover, ethical concerns also extend to the potential for misuse of IoT technologies by malicious actors. The defense sector must consider how IoT vulnerabilities could be exploited by adversaries to gather intelligence, disrupt operations, or conduct cyberattacks. This raises questions about the ethical responsibility of defense organizations to protect their systems and prevent the weaponization of IoT technologies. Finally, the environmental impact of IoT devices should not be overlooked. The production, deployment, and eventual disposal of IoT technologies contribute to electronic waste and environmental degradation. Defence organizations need to consider the sustainability of their IoT initiatives and their broader ethical implications on environmental health.

9.2. Balancing Security and Privacy

Balancing security and privacy in IoT-driven defence environments presents a complex challenge that requires careful navigation. On one hand, the need for enhanced security measures is paramount in military operations, where the stakes are high, and vulnerabilities can have dire consequences. IoT devices play a crucial role in gathering intelligence, monitoring threats, and ensuring operational readiness. However, the implementation of these devices often leads to significant concerns regarding the privacy of personnel and the public (Sadeghi et al., 2015). To achieve this balance, defence organizations must adopt a proactive approach to privacy by design. This involves integrating privacy considerations into the development and deployment of IoT technologies from the outset. By implementing data minimization practices, organizations can ensure that only the necessary data is collected, processed, and retained, reducing the risk of privacy violations. Additionally, employing strong encryption methods and secure communication protocols can protect sensitive data while allowing for effective security measures.

Transparency is also vital in balancing security and privacy. Defence organizations should communicate openly with personnel and stakeholders about how data is collected, used, and protected. Clear policies and guidelines regarding data handling and privacy rights can foster trust and ensure that individuals are aware of their rights in the context of IoT surveillance and data collection. Furthermore, establishing a robust governance framework is essential for overseeing the ethical use of IoT technologies in defence. This framework should include regular audits, assessments, and compliance checks to ensure adherence to privacy and security policies. Engaging with external stakeholders, including privacy advocates and legal experts, can provide valuable insights into best practices for maintaining this balance (Tawalbeh & Tawalbeh, 2017). Lastly, ongoing training and education for personnel are critical to cultivating a culture of awareness around privacy and security issues. By empowering individuals with the knowledge and tools to recognize and address potential privacy concerns, organizations can create a more secure environment while respecting individual rights.

9.3. Societal Impact of Privacy Breaches

Privacy breaches in IoT-driven defence environments can have profound societal impacts that extend beyond immediate security concerns. One of the most significant effects is the erosion of public trust in government institutions and military organizations. When sensitive data related to national security or personal information of service members is compromised, it can lead to public scepticism regarding the ability of these institutions to protect their citizens' privacy and security. This erosion of trust can hinder cooperation between the public and defense organizations, ultimately affecting national security efforts.

Moreover, privacy breaches can result in widespread fear and anxiety within communities. The potential misuse of personal data collected through IoT devices can lead to fears of surveillance, profiling, and discrimination. For instance, if personal data of military personnel or civilians is leaked, it could expose them to threats or targeting by adversaries, leading to a chilling effect on civil liberties and freedom of expression. This societal apprehension can foster an environment where individuals feel they are constantly monitored, stifling open discourse and dissent.

The economic impact of privacy breaches should also be considered. When breaches occur, organizations often face significant financial repercussions, including legal fees, regulatory fines, and damage to their reputation. This can divert resources away from critical defense initiatives, ultimately compromising operational readiness. Additionally, the cost of recovery and damage control can burden taxpayers, leading to calls for greater accountability and reform within defense spending. Furthermore, privacy breaches can create a ripple effect that affects other sectors beyond defense. For instance, if sensitive information from military IoT systems is leaked, it could be exploited by adversaries for cyberattacks on critical infrastructure or private sector organizations. This interconnectedness means that breaches can have far-reaching consequences, highlighting the need for robust security measures not just within defense organizations but across all sectors that may be impacted.

9.4. Ethical Guidelines for Defence IoT Systems

Establishing ethical guidelines for IoT systems in defence is essential to ensure that these technologies are used responsibly and in a manner that respects privacy, security, and human rights. These guidelines serve as a framework for defense organizations to navigate the complex ethical landscape associated with the deployment of IoT technologies. Here are some key components of these ethical guidelines:

Privacy by Design: Defence organizations should adopt a privacy-by-design approach, integrating privacy considerations into the development and deployment of IoT systems from the outset. This includes implementing data minimization practices to ensure that only necessary data is collected and processed.

Transparency and Accountability: Organizations must maintain transparency regarding their data collection practices, informing personnel and the public about how data is used and protected. Establishing clear lines of accountability for data handling and decision-making processes is crucial to building trust.

Informed Consent: Where possible, individuals should provide informed consent for the collection and use of their personal data (Tawalbeh et al., 2020). Defence organizations should clearly communicate the purpose of data collection, potential risks, and individuals' rights concerning their data.

Security Measures: Robust cybersecurity measures must be implemented to protect IoT systems and the data they collect. This includes employing strong encryption, access controls, and regular security audits to mitigate the risk of data breaches.

Ethical Use of Autonomous Systems: When deploying autonomous IoT systems, organizations should establish guidelines for their ethical use. This includes ensuring that AI algorithms are transparent and accountable, and that there are mechanisms for human oversight in critical decision-making processes.

Risk Assessment: Regular risk assessments should be conducted to evaluate the potential impacts of IoT systems on privacy, security, and human rights. Organizations should proactively address identified risks and adapt their practices accordingly.

Training and Awareness: Personnel should receive ongoing training on ethical practices related to IoT systems, including privacy rights, data protection, and cybersecurity awareness. This training should empower individuals to recognize and address potential ethical dilemmas.

Collaboration and Stakeholder Engagement: Defence organizations should engage with various stakeholders, including civil society, privacy advocates, and legal experts, to gather diverse perspectives on ethical issues related to IoT. Collaborative approaches can help shape guidelines that reflect societal values and expectations.

Continuous Review and Adaptation: Ethical guidelines should be subject to regular review and adaptation to keep pace with technological advancements and evolving societal norms. This iterative process ensures that ethical practices remain relevant and effective.

10. Conclusion

The integration of IoT technologies into defence environments has transformed military operations, enhancing capabilities such as situational awareness, logistics management, and predictive maintenance. However, this advancement comes with significant challenges, particularly concerning privacy and data protection. As IoT devices collect vast amounts of sensitive data, the potential for privacy breaches raises ethical and societal concerns that must be addressed proactively. The complexities of balancing security with privacy underscore the necessity for robust ethical guidelines and regulatory frameworks. Defence organizations must prioritize transparency, informed consent, and accountability to build trust among personnel and the public. Implementing advanced security measures and continuously assessing risks will be essential in safeguarding sensitive data from unauthorized access and cyber threats. Furthermore, emerging technologies such as AI and blockchain offer promising solutions for enhancing data integrity and threat detection in IoT-driven defence systems. However, the ethical implications of these technologies must be carefully considered to ensure responsible use. Ultimately, the future of IoT in defence will depend on the commitment of organizations to navigate these challenges thoughtfully and ethically. By embracing a proactive and collaborative approach, defence sectors can harness the benefits of IoT while safeguarding privacy and promoting the responsible use of technology, ensuring national security and public trust in an increasingly connected world.

References

Ahmi, A., Elbardan, H., & Raja Mohd Ali, R. H. (2019). Bibliometric analysis of published literature on Industry 4.0. *ICEIC 2019 - International conference on electronics, information, and communication* (pp. 1–6).

Al Shuhaimi, F., Jose, M., & Singh, A. V. (2016). Software-defined network as a solution to overcome security challenges in IoT. In *Proceedings of the reliability, infocom technologies and optimization (trends and future directions) (ICRITO)* (pp. 491–496), Noida, India.

Alaba, F. A., Othman, M., Hashem, I. A. T., & Alotaibi, F. (2017). Internet of Things security: A survey. *Journal of Network and Computer Applications*, *88*, 10–28.

Ali, S., Bosche, A., & Ford, F. (2018). *Cybersecurity is the key to unlocking demand in the Internet of Things*. Bain and Company.

Boyack, K. W. (2004). Mapping knowledge domains: Characterizing PNAS. *Proceedings of the National Academy of Sciences of the United States of America*, *101*(SUPPL. 1), 5192–5199.

Bugeja, J., Jacobsson, A., & Davidsson, P. (2016). On privacy and security challenges in smart connected homes. In *Proceedings of the European intelligence and security informatics conference (EISIC)* (pp. 172–175), Uppsala, Sweden.

Checkland, P. (1999). *Systems thinking, systems practice*. John Wiley & Sons.

Conti, M., Dehghantanha, A., Franke, K., & Watson, S. (2018). Internet of Things security and forensics: Challenges and opportunities. *Future Generation Computer Systems*, *78*, 544–546.

Conti, M., Dragoni, N., & Lesyk, V. (2016). A survey of man in the middle attacks. *IEEE Communications Surveys & Tutorials*, *18*, 2027–2051. Retrieved April 10, 2024, from https://ieeexplore.ieee.org/abstract/document/7442758

Culbert, D. (2020). *Personal data breaches and securing IoT devices*. Retrieved September 15, 2024, from https://betanews.com/2019/08/13/securing-iot-devices/

Dalipi, F., & Yayilgan, S. Y. (2016). Security and privacy considerations for IoT application on smart grids: Survey and research challenges. In *Proceedings of the Future Internet of Things and Cloud Workshops (FiCloudW)* (pp. 63–68), Vienna, Austria.

Donthu, N., Kumar, S., Mukherjee, D., Pandey, N., & Lim, W. M. (2021). How to conduct a bibliometric analysis: An overview and guidelines. *Journal of Business Research*, *133*, 285–296.

Estrada, D., Tawalbeh, L., & Vinaja, R. (2020). How secure having IoT devices in our home. *Journal of Information Security*, *11*, 81–91.

Gemalto. (2020). *Securing the IoT-Building trust in IoT devices and data*. Retrieved February 17, 2024, from https://www.gemalto.com/iot/iot-security

Hassan, W. H. (2019). Current research on Internet of Things (IoT) security: A survey. *Computer Networks*, *148*, 283–294.

He, H., Maple, C., Watson, T., Tiwari, A., Mehnen, J., Jin, Y., & Gabrys, B. (2016). The security challenges in the IoT enabled cyber-physical systems and opportunities for evolutionary computing & other computational intelligence. In *Proceedings of the Evolutionary Computation (CEC)* (pp. 1015–1021), Vancouver, BC, Canada.

Hosseini, M. R., Martek, I., Zavadskas, E. K., Aibinu, A. A., Arashpour, M., & Chileshe, N. (2018). Critical evaluation of off-site construction research: A scientometric analysis. *Automation in Construction*, *87*, 235–247. https://doi.org/10.1016/j.autcon.2017.12.002

Izzat, A., Chuck, E., & Lo'ai, T. (2020). *The NICE cyber security framework, cyber security management*. Springer.

Jiang, H., Gai, J., Zhao, S., Chaudhry, P. E., & Chaudhry, S. S. (2022). Applications and development of artificial intelligence system from the perspective of system science: A bibliometric review. *Systems Research and Behavioral Science*, *39*(3), 361–378.

Khan, M. A., & Salah, K. (2018). IoT security: Review, blockchain solutions, and open challenges. *Future Generation Computer Systems*, *82*, 395–411.

Khvoynitskaya, S. (2020). *The history and future of the Internet of Things*. Retrieved March 25, 2024, from https://www.itransition.com/blog/iot-history

Klarin, A. (2019). Mapping product and service innovation: A bibliometric analysis and a typology. *Technological Forecasting and Social Change*, *149*, 119776.

Klarin, A., & Suseno, Y. (2023). An integrative literature review of social entrepreneurship research: Mapping the literature and future research directions. *Business & Society*, *62*(3), 565–611.

Leloglu, E. (2016). A review of security concerns in Internet of Things. *Journal of Computer and Communications*, *5*, 121–136.

Li, M., Xie, Y., Gao, Y., & Zhao, Y. (2022). Organization virtualization driven by artificial intelligence. *Systems Research and Behavioral Science*, *39*(3), 633–640.

Liu, X., Zhao, M., Li, S., Zhang, F., & Trappe, W. (2017). A security framework for the Internet of Things in the future internet architecture. *Future Internet*, *9*, 27.

Liyanage, M., Braeken, A., Kumar, P., & Ylianttila, M. (2020). *IoT Security: Advances in Authentication*. John Wiley & Sons.

Makhdoom, I., Abolhasan, M., Lipman, J., Liu, R. P., & Ni, W. (2018). Anatomy of threats to the Internet of Things. *IEEE Communications Surveys & Tutorials*, *21*, 1636–1675.

Meng, Y., Zhang, W., Zhu, H., & Shen, X. S. (2018). Securing consumer IoT in the smart home: Architecture, challenges, and countermeasures. *IEEE Wireless Communications*, *25*, 53–59.

Monther, A. A., & Tawalbeh, L. (2020). Security techniques for intelligent spam sensing and anomaly detection in online social platforms. *International Journal of Electrical and Computer Engineering*, *10*, 2088–8708.

Nazarov, D., & Klarin, A. (2020). Taxonomy of Industry 4.0 research: Mapping scholarship and industry insights. *Systems Research and Behavioral Science*, *37*(4), 535–556.

Rafols, I., Leydesdorff, L., O'Hare, A., Nightingale, P., & Stirling, A. (2012). How journal rankings can suppress interdisciplinary research: A comparison between Innovation Studies and Business & Management. *Research Policy*, *41*(7), 1262–1282.

Rossetto, D. E., Bernardes, R. C., Borini, F. M., & Gattaz, C. C. (2018). Structure and evolution of innovation research in the last 60 years: Review and future trends in the field of business through the citations and co-citations analysis. *Scientometrics*, *115*(3), 1329–1363.

Ryan, M. (2019). *An Australian intellectual edge for conflict and competition in the 21st century*. Strategic & Defence Studies Centre, Australian National University.

Sadeghi, A.-R., Wachsmann, C., & Waidner, M. (2015). Security and privacy challenges in industrial internet of things. In *Proceedings of the 2015 52nd ACM/EDAC/IEEE design automation conference (DAC)* (pp. 1–6), San Francisco, CA, USA.

Seet, P.-S., Jones, J. T., Spoehr, J., & Hordacre, A.-L. (2018). *The Fourth Industrial Revolution: The implications of technological disruption for Australian VET*. NCVER.

Sethi, P., & Sarangi, S. (2017). Internet of Things: Architectures, protocols, and applications. *Journal of Electrical and Computer Engineering*, 1–25. https://doi.org/10.1155/2017/9324035

Siby, S., Maiti, R. R., & Tippenhauer, N. O. (2017). IoTscanner: Detecting privacy threats in IoT neighborhoods. In *Proceedings of the 3rd ACM international workshop on IoT privacy, trust, and security* (pp. 23–30), Abu Dhabi, United Arab Emirates.

Simms, A. (2019). Force multiplier. *Impact*, *2019*(1), 35–38.

Singh, J., Thomas, F. J.-M., Pasquier, J. B., Ko, H., & Eyers, D. M. (2016). Twenty security considerations for cloud-supported Internet of Things. *IEEE Internet of Things Journal*, *3*, 269–284.

Sohal, A. S., Sandhu, R., Sood, S. K., & Chang, V. (2018). A cybersecurity framework to identify malicious edge device in fog computing and cloud-of-things environments. *Computers & Security*, *74*, 340–354.

Sun, Y., Song, H., Jara, A. J., & Bie, R. (2016). *Internet of Things and Big Data Analytics for Smart and Connected Communities*. Retrieved April 4, 2020, from https://ieeexplore.ieee.org/stamp/stamp.jsp?tp=&arnumber=7406686

Tawalbeh, L. A., & Somani, T. F. (2016). More secure Internet of Things using robust encryption algorithms against side-channel attacks. In *Proceedings of the 2016 IEEE/ACS 13th international conference of computer systems and applications (AICCSA)* (pp. 1–6), Agadir, Morocco.

Tawalbeh, L. A., & Tawalbeh, H. (2017). Lightweight crypto and security. In H. Song, G. A. Fink & S. Jeschke (Eds.), *Security and privacy in cyber-physical systems: foundations, principles, and applications* (pp. 243–261). Wiley. https://doi.org/10.1002/9781119226079.ch12

Tawalbeh, L. A., Quwaider, M., & Tawalbeh, M. (2020). Authorization model for IoT healthcare systems: Case study. In *Proceedings of the 2020 11th international conference on information and communication systems (ICICS)* (pp. 337–342), Irbid, Jordan.

Thierer, A. D. (2015). *The Internet of Things and wearable technology: Addressing privacy and security concerns without derailing innovation*. Retrieved March 6, 2024, from http://jolt.richmond.edu/v21i2/article6.pdf

Chapter 3

Ethical and Legal Implications of IoT in Defence Operations

Abhishek Kumar[a], *Amal Krishna Sarkar*[b], *Katyayani Akella*[c] *and Satyanarayana Nandury*[d]

[a]*Department of Computer Science, University of Agder, Norway*
[b]*Sanjay Gandhi Postgraduate Institute of Medical Sciences, India*
[c]*Symbiosis International (Deemed University), India*
[d]*Research & Development, GITAM (Deemed University), India*

Abstract

The integration of the Internet of Things (IoT) into defence operations has revolutionized intelligence gathering, resource monitoring, and strategic decision-making, enhancing military efficiency and responsiveness. IoT devices, including sensors, drones, wearable technology, and connected weapon systems, offer significant advantages but also raise critical ethical and legal concerns. Ethically, the deployment of interconnected systems challenges privacy rights, accountability, and the responsible use of data, particularly in autonomous decision-making scenarios where human oversight is reduced. Legally, IoT in defence intersects with international humanitarian law (IHL), human rights regulations, and national security frameworks, creating complexities in cyber warfare, civilian protection, and responsibility attribution. The rapid pace of technological advancement often surpasses the development of regulatory mechanisms, necessitating a comprehensive framework to ensure the responsible deployment of IoT in military operations. This chapter explores these ethical and legal dimensions, addressing concerns related to autonomy, privacy, security, and compliance with international law. By proactively managing these challenges, the defence sector can establish a more accountable and secure approach to integrating IoT technologies in military operations.

The Internet of Things in the Defence Industry:
Challenges and Solutions for Military Security, 59–80

Published under exclusive licence by Emerald Publishing Limited
doi:10.1108/978-1-83549-198-020261003

Keywords: Internet of Things (IoT); military operations; ethical challenges; legal frameworks; cybersecurity

3.1. Introduction

The integration of the IoT into defence operations has significantly transformed the way military forces gather intelligence, monitor resources, and engage in tactical and strategic decision-making. IoT devices, ranging from sensors and drones to wearable technology and connected weapon systems, offer unprecedented opportunities for enhancing the efficiency, responsiveness, and effectiveness of military operations. However, this technological advancement brings with it a host of ethical and legal challenges that must be carefully considered (Santhi et al., 2024).

On the ethical front, IoT in defence raises questions about privacy, accountability, and the potential for misuse of data. The sheer volume of data generated by interconnected devices could infringe upon the privacy of individuals, whether they are soldiers, civilians, or enemy combatants. Furthermore, the automation of decision-making processes through IoT devices in critical combat scenarios challenges traditional notions of human responsibility and oversight, especially when decisions could result in loss of life or breaches of IHL.

From a legal perspective, the use of IoT in defence operations intersects with existing frameworks of international law, including the laws of armed conflict, human rights law, and national security regulations. The deployment of connected systems in warfare introduces complex issues such as the targeting of civilians, cyber-attacks, and the attribution of responsibility in the event of malfunction or failure (Taddeo et al., 2023). These legal challenges are compounded by the rapid pace of technological innovation, which often outstrips the ability of governments and international bodies to craft appropriate regulations.

As the use of IoT in defence operations continues to evolve, it is essential to establish a robust ethical and legal framework that addresses these concerns while allowing for the responsible advancement of technology. Ensuring that IoT systems are deployed in a manner that respects both human rights and the rule of law will be crucial for maintaining the legitimacy of military operations in the 21st century. This introduction will explore the ethical and legal implications of IoT in defence, highlighting key issues such as privacy, accountability, security, and compliance with international law, and provide a foundation for understanding how to navigate these challenges.

This chapter explores the ethical and legal implications of IoT-driven defence systems, including challenges such as the balance between autonomy and human control, the risk of privacy violations, the legal frameworks that govern their use, and the implications for national security. By addressing these challenges, the defence sector can move towards a more accountable and responsible integration of IoT technologies.

3.2. Ethical Challenges in IoT-Driven Defence

The integration of the IoT into defence operations has revolutionized military capabilities, enabling more efficient, responsive, and data-driven strategies. From smart surveillance systems and autonomous drones to real-time monitoring of soldiers' health and battlefield environments, IoT technologies have brought unprecedented innovation to the defence sector (Karale, 2021). However, with these advancements come significant ethical challenges that must be carefully examined and addressed.

The deployment of IoT devices in military contexts raises fundamental questions about privacy, accountability, and the potential for misuse. As IoT systems collect vast amounts of data – from civilian populations in conflict zones to the personal data of soldiers – concerns about surveillance, data protection, and the erosion of civil liberties become prominent. Additionally, the growing autonomy of military systems, including autonomous weapons and AI-driven decision-making processes, introduces complex ethical dilemmas surrounding human oversight, accountability for errors, and the potential for unintended harm.

Moreover, the use of IoT in defence poses risks of bias and discrimination, especially as IoT systems often rely on algorithms and machine learning that may perpetuate existing prejudices or produce skewed results. Fig. 3.1 shows the relationship of different challenges in IoT-driven defence. The question of who is responsible when IoT systems malfunction or cause harm is another crucial ethical issue, as decisions once made by humans may now be delegated to machines.

As IoT-driven defence systems become more integrated into military operations, it is critical to explore these ethical challenges in depth. This will ensure that technological advancements align with core ethical principles, such as respect for human rights, the protection of civilian lives, and the maintenance of accountability in warfare. In this context, understanding and addressing these ethical challenges is not only essential for ensuring the legitimacy of military actions but also for guiding the responsible use of emerging technologies in the future of defence operations (Weng, 2024).

The ethical challenges associated with IoT-driven defence operations are multifaceted, requiring careful reflection on the use of cutting-edge technologies in areas involving life, death, and national security. These concerns revolve around the autonomy of IoT systems, accountability for actions taken by autonomous devices, and the broader societal implications of surveillance and data collection.

3.2.1. Autonomy Versus Human Control in IoT Systems

One of the most significant ethical concerns in the use of IoT in defence is the autonomy of military systems, particularly autonomous weapons and unmanned vehicles. As IoT enables these systems to collect real-time data, process it locally, and take independent actions, there is an ongoing debate about the appropriate balance between autonomy and human oversight (Helkala et al., 2022; Karale, 2021; Taddeo et al., 2023; Weng, 2024).

Fig. 3.1. Ethical Challenges in IoT-Driven Defence Systems.

- **Autonomy in Combat Systems:** IoT-enabled autonomous systems, such as drones, robotic ground vehicles, and surveillance platforms, are increasingly able to operate without direct human intervention. These systems may identify targets, make tactical decisions, and execute missions. However, there is concern over whether these systems should be entrusted with lethal decision-making, especially in complex, unpredictable battlefield scenarios.
- **Human Control and Accountability:** The ethical challenge here is ensuring that humans retain control over critical decisions, particularly those involving the use of force. The central question is: who is responsible when an autonomous system causes harm? If a drone or automated ground vehicle mistakenly targets civilians, is the responsibility placed on the military personnel who deployed it, the developers who programmed it, or the machine itself?

The ethical principle of human dignity demands that decisions of life and death remain within human control, and thus it is imperative that IoT-driven systems in defence include mechanisms for human oversight and intervention, especially when autonomous systems are engaged in lethal operations.

3.2.2. Moral Accountability in Autonomous Military Devices

As IoT-enabled devices gain increasing autonomy, the question of moral accountability becomes more pressing. Autonomous weapons systems, such as AI-driven drones or robotic soldiers, raise the issue of who should be held accountable for their actions (Allhoff & Henschke, 2018; Koch, 2020).

- **Responsibility for Actions:** The question of whether machines can be held morally accountable is a matter of ongoing debate. Some argue that accountability should rest solely with the human operators, as the machines are only following predefined instructions or responding to programming. Others argue that the developers and manufacturers of the AI and machine learning models are responsible for ensuring that systems operate within ethical boundaries and international law.
- **Imposing Ethical Constraints:** One solution to this challenge is the "human-in-the-loop" (HITL) approach, which allows human operators to intervene and override automated systems when necessary. This ensures that ethical decision-making processes are upheld, especially in scenarios where the consequences of autonomous decisions are irreversible.

Ultimately, clear ethical guidelines must be established to ensure that AI/IoT systems operate in accordance with military ethics and respect the principle of proportionality – the idea that the use of force should not be excessive in relation to the threat posed.

3.2.3. Balancing National Security and Individual Privacy

The deployment of IoT devices in defence operations often requires the collection of vast amounts of data, including surveillance footage, biometric data, and geospatial information (Koch, 2021; Yaacoub et al., 2023). While this data is invaluable for enhancing national security, it raises concerns about individual privacy rights.

- **Mass Surveillance:** IoT-enabled surveillance systems, such as drones, facial recognition technologies, and biometric identification systems, can track individuals across wide areas. While these tools can enhance security and help detect terrorist activities or enemy movements, they also carry the risk of infringing on privacy rights, particularly when used in civilian areas or in ways that are not fully transparent.
- **Data Privacy:** The integration of IoT systems in defence also means collecting personal data, which raises concerns about how this information is stored, shared, and protected. Military organizations must ensure that data is not misused and that the rights of individuals are respected. The challenge lies in finding a balance between the security needs of the state and the privacy rights of individuals.

3.3. Legal Frameworks Governing IoT in Defence

The rapid integration of the IoT into defence operations has dramatically transformed the landscape of modern warfare, enabling military forces to enhance their operational efficiency, intelligence gathering, and decision-making capabilities. IoT devices, such as sensors, drones, autonomous weapons, and real-time data collection systems, play a pivotal role in both tactical and strategic military environments. However, as these technologies proliferate, they raise complex legal questions concerning the regulation, use, and oversight of IoT in defence (Fraga-Lamas et al., 2016).

The legal frameworks governing IoT in defence are rooted in a combination of international law, national legislation, and military regulations, which collectively seek to balance technological advancements with the protection of human rights, sovereignty, and the laws of armed conflict. These frameworks aim to ensure that the deployment of IoT systems in military operations adheres to well-established principles of IHL, human rights law, and cybersecurity regulations.

Key legal challenges arise in areas such as accountability for actions taken by autonomous IoT systems, data privacy for soldiers and civilians, the use of force in accordance with the laws of war, and cybersecurity risks posed by interconnected devices. For example, the use of autonomous weapons or lethal autonomous weapon systems (LAWS), which rely heavily on IoT sensors and AI, raises difficult questions about compliance with IHL and the attribution of responsibility in the event of unlawful harm.

Moreover, the increasing reliance on IoT technologies in military operations creates vulnerabilities that may be exploited by adversaries, necessitating robust legal frameworks around cyber defence and data protection to safeguard both military and civilian interests.

As IoT technologies continue to evolve, so too must the legal frameworks that govern their use in defence contexts. This ongoing challenge requires dynamic and flexible approaches to address the unique risks and opportunities posed by IoT, ensuring that military operations remain in compliance with international laws while maintaining the strategic advantages that these technologies provide.

This introduction explores the key legal frameworks that govern the use of IoT in defence, focusing on the intersection of international law, national security, and emerging technologies, while highlighting the need for continuous adaptation to address the evolving nature of warfare in the digital age.

The legal landscape surrounding the use of IoT in defence is complex and multi-layered, involving both international conventions and domestic laws. These frameworks are designed to ensure that IoT systems are used in compliance with established legal standards while also addressing emerging challenges posed by new technologies.

3.3.1. International Laws and Conventions

International law plays a crucial role in governing the use of IoT systems in defence, especially in matters related to warfare, surveillance, and human rights.

Several international conventions provide guidelines for the lawful use of military technologies (Heinl, 2014; Tzafestas, 2018):

- **Geneva Conventions:** The Geneva Conventions set out the rules for the protection of civilians and prisoners of war during armed conflict. They prohibit targeting civilians and mandate proportionality in the use of force. IoT-enabled autonomous weapons systems must comply with these rules, ensuring that such technologies do not violate the principles of distinction (between combatants and civilians) and proportionality.
- **The UN Charter:** The United Nations Charter emphasizes the principles of sovereignty and self-defence. The use of IoT systems in operations, especially those involving surveillance, must respect the sovereignty of states and avoid breaching international borders unlawfully.
- **Cybersecurity Laws:** The UN's Cybersecurity Framework and various international treaties on cyber warfare are critical when considering the security of IoT networks in defence applications. IoT systems are susceptible to cyberattacks, and international conventions are increasingly addressing the need for global cooperation in protecting military networks from malicious actors.

3.3.2. Domestic Regulations for IoT Deployment in Defence

Each country is responsible for establishing domestic regulations regarding the deployment and use of IoT technologies in defence. These laws must ensure compliance with international conventions while addressing national security concerns. Key areas include (Montasari, 2024; Swaniha & Sharanya, 2024; Tzafestas, 2018):

- **Defence Procurement Laws:** Governments must set clear policies for defence procurement, ensuring that IoT devices meet security, interoperability, and ethical standards. This includes regulations on the use of foreign technology and oversight of the development and deployment of IoT systems.
- **Cybersecurity Regulations:** Domestic laws must ensure that IoT devices used in defence are secure from cyber threats. Regulations must establish guidelines for testing, patching, and securing devices against potential breaches.
- **Data Protection Laws:** As IoT systems collect massive amounts of data, including sensitive information, countries need robust data protection regulations to ensure that the data collected is not misused, that it is stored securely, and that citizens' privacy rights are respected.

3.4. Privacy Concerns in IoT-Enabled Defence Systems

The use of IoT technologies in defence operations has brought remarkable advancements in military capabilities, from real-time surveillance and autonomous drones to the monitoring of soldiers' health and battlefield conditions.

However, as IoT systems become more embedded in defence, they also present significant privacy concerns that must be carefully managed to avoid unintended consequences. These concerns revolve around the collection, storage, and use of vast amounts of sensitive data, which can affect both individuals in conflict zones and military personnel themselves.

The use of IoT devices in military operations inevitably leads to the collection of vast amounts of data, which has significant implications for privacy (Alcántara Suárez & Monzon Baeza, 2023; Montasari, 2023; Payal et al., 2021). Given that IoT systems can monitor individuals, track movements, and gather biometric data, addressing privacy concerns is paramount to ensure that defence operations do not infringe on citizens' rights.

3.4.1. Data Collection and Surveillance Risks

IoT-enabled defence systems, particularly those used for surveillance, create risks to the privacy of civilians, especially in conflict zones. Devices such as drones, cameras, and sensors can be deployed to gather real-time intelligence, track movements, and monitor specific areas (Helkala et al., 2022; Karale, 2021; Weng, 2024). However, these systems can inadvertently infringe on the privacy of individuals, particularly when:

- **Invasive Surveillance**: IoT-based surveillance technologies can monitor large groups of people in public or private spaces without their knowledge or consent. In areas of military conflict, this often includes civilians who may not be directly involved in the hostilities but are still subject to continuous surveillance. The use of these systems may violate individuals' right to privacy, as guaranteed by international human rights law, including the Universal Declaration of Human Rights and the International Covenant on Civil and Political Rights (ICCPR).
- **Unintended Data Collection**: IoT devices can unintentionally collect sensitive data from individuals who are not the intended targets of surveillance. For example, facial recognition systems or location-tracking technologies could capture and store information about innocent civilians, raising concerns about data retention, consent, and how long such data is kept or shared.

The proliferation of IoT-enabled surveillance systems, such as drones, cameras, and biometric sensors, poses significant risks to privacy. Mass surveillance programs in defence can monitor individuals without their consent, raising concerns about the extent of data collection and its use.

3.4.2. Impact of Data Breaches on National Security

IoT systems are increasingly used to monitor the physical and psychological well-being of military personnel. Wearable sensors and connected devices track soldiers' health metrics, movement, and even psychological state to improve operational effectiveness and safety (Allhoff & Henschke, 2018; Koch, 2020; Yaacoub et al., 2023). While these technologies can enhance soldier welfare, they also raise several privacy issues:

- **Personal Data Collection**: Wearable IoT devices, such as health monitors or body cameras, collect a wide range of personal data, including physiological information (e.g. heart rate, stress levels), location data, and potentially even behavioural patterns. This data is often stored in centralized databases, making it vulnerable to misuse or unauthorized access.
- **Informed Consent**: The ethical collection and use of personal data rely on obtaining informed consent from individuals. Soldiers, like civilians, have the right to know how their data will be used and to provide explicit consent. However, in military environments, where hierarchical structures and operational urgency often prevail, ensuring informed consent and safeguarding privacy may be challenging.
- **Misuse of Personal Data**: The data collected from IoT devices can be misused, either intentionally or unintentionally, for purposes beyond the soldier's health and safety. For instance, personal data could be used to profile soldiers, monitor their behaviour outside of military operations, or even penalize them for actions unrelated to their duties.

Data breaches involving IoT devices can have severe consequences for national security. If sensitive information – such as intelligence data, locations of military assets, or personnel data – is accessed by malicious actors, it could compromise military operations or endanger the lives of soldiers and civilians.

3.4.3. Strategies to Ensure Privacy Compliance

To address these privacy risks, defence organizations must adopt clear privacy policies and compliance strategies (Fraga-Lamas et al., 2016; Koch, 2021; Yaacoub et al., 2023):

Data Minimization: Only collect data that is necessary for the operation of IoT systems. One of the fundamental principles of privacy law is data minimization, which requires that only the data necessary for a specific purpose is collected and retained. This is crucial for reducing privacy risks and ensuring compliance with data protection laws like the General Data Protection Regulation (GDPR) in Europe.

- **Selective Data Collection**: Defence systems should be designed to collect only the essential data needed for operational purposes. For example, IoT devices used in surveillance should focus on gathering intelligence directly relevant to military objectives, minimizing the capture of incidental personal information about civilians.
- **Anonymization and Pseudonymization**: Where possible, the data should be anonymized or pseudonymized to reduce the risk of identification. For example, location data from soldiers or surveillance systems can be anonymized to protect individuals' identities, especially in non-combat contexts.

- **Temporal Data Retention**: Limit the duration of data retention to only what is necessary for military purposes. Data should be securely deleted once it is no longer needed to fulfil the operational or strategic goal.

Data Encryption and Secure Storage: Ensure that all collected data is encrypted and stored securely to prevent unauthorized access. Transparency is key to ensuring privacy compliance. The more open defence agencies are about their data practices, the more they can build trust and ensure that privacy rights are respected.

- **Clear Privacy Policies**: Defence organizations must develop clear, comprehensive privacy policies that outline how data is collected, stored, processed, and shared. These policies should be communicated to both military personnel and civilians who may be affected by IoT systems.
- **Data Access and Auditing**: Establish systems of oversight that ensure data is accessed only by authorized personnel for legitimate purposes. Regular audits should be conducted to verify compliance with privacy policies and to ensure that the data is being handled appropriately. These audits should include assessments of IoT systems for potential privacy violations or unauthorized access.
- **Chain of Responsibility**: Clearly define the roles and responsibilities of those handling personal data, from the design phase through to deployment. This ensures accountability for any violations of privacy, both from a technical and operational standpoint.
- **Anonymization:** Where possible, anonymize personal data to protect individuals' privacy while still utilizing the information for operational purposes.

3.5. Cybersecurity and Legal Liabilities

The use of IoT technologies in defence operations has introduced significant advancements in the efficiency, effectiveness, and real-time capabilities of military systems. From autonomous drones to smart sensors, IoT devices play a crucial role in modern warfare, intelligence gathering, and logistics. However, the integration of these technologies into defence systems also introduces substantial cybersecurity risks and legal liabilities (Fraga-Lamas et al., 2016; Heinl, 2014; Swaniha & Sharanya, 2024; Tzafestas, 2018). These concerns need to be carefully addressed to protect both the military infrastructure and individuals from potential harm while ensuring compliance with relevant legal frameworks.

3.5.1. Cybersecurity Risks in IoT-Driven Defence Systems

IoT devices are inherently vulnerable to a range of cyber threats due to their connectivity, scale, and often limited security measures. When deployed in defence contexts, these vulnerabilities can have far-reaching consequences, especially when adversaries exploit weaknesses in IoT systems to gain unauthorized access, disrupt operations, or cause harm.

- **Data Breaches and Unauthorized Access**: IoT devices collect vast amounts of sensitive data, including classified military intelligence, personnel information, and operational details. If these devices are compromised, it can result in the theft or unauthorized disclosure of critical data, which could be used by adversaries or malicious actors to undermine national security.

- **Targeting of Critical Infrastructure**: Many defence systems, such as weaponry, communication networks, and surveillance platforms, are increasingly reliant on interconnected IoT devices. A successful cyberattack on these systems could lead to the disruption of military operations, malfunctioning of autonomous weapons, or interference with communication channels, all of which could jeopardize national security and endanger lives.
- **Vulnerabilities in Autonomous Systems**: Autonomous weapons and unmanned systems, which rely heavily on IoT sensors and artificial intelligence (AI), are particularly susceptible to cyberattacks. Hackers could manipulate these systems to alter their behaviour, leading to unintended consequences such as targeting civilians, misdirected attacks, or failure to carry out orders as intended.
- **Denial of Service (DoS) Attacks**: Distributed Denial of Service (DDoS) attacks on IoT infrastructure could incapacitate military IoT systems, potentially shutting down vital surveillance, communication, or navigation devices. The attack could render defence operations ineffective, delay critical military actions, or cause loss of operational control.
- **Supply Chain Attacks**: As IoT systems in defence increasingly rely on third-party vendors for hardware and software solutions, there is a growing risk of supply chain vulnerabilities. Malicious actors may compromise devices during manufacturing or through software updates, introducing hidden malware or backdoors that could be exploited during military operations.

3.5.2. Legal Liabilities Arising from Cybersecurity Failures

The increasing sophistication and complexity of IoT-driven defence systems require military agencies and contractors to be fully aware of their legal responsibilities and liabilities regarding cybersecurity breaches. Legal frameworks are evolving to hold parties accountable for failures to adequately secure IoT devices and systems, both domestically and internationally.

a. Liability for Data Breaches

Data breaches involving IoT systems in defence can result in the exposure of sensitive information, leading to national security threats, reputational damage, and legal consequences.

- **Civil Liability**: If an IoT-driven defence system is compromised and results in the theft of classified or personal data (e.g., military personnel details or mission-critical intelligence), the responsible parties – whether government agencies, contractors, or third-party service providers – could face lawsuits for negligence, breach of contract, or failure to secure sensitive information. In cases where civilian data is also affected (e.g. surveillance data from conflict zones), affected individuals or organizations might bring legal actions under national data protection laws or international human rights law.

- **Contractual Liability**: Military contractors providing IoT devices and services are contractually bound to ensure that their products meet certain security standards. If a cybersecurity failure results from a contractor's negligence or failure to implement adequate protections, they may be held liable under the terms of the contract, leading to financial penalties, lawsuits, and potential termination of the contract.

b. Non-Compliance with Data Protection Laws

As defence systems increasingly use IoT technologies to collect and process data – often involving personal or sensitive data – the legal risks of non-compliance with data protection regulations are significant.

- **General Data Protection Regulation**: If IoT systems collect data on civilians, especially in conflict zones, defence agencies must comply with GDPR (if operating within the European Union or dealing with EU citizens' data). GDPR imposes strict rules on data collection, processing, storage, and security, and breaches can result in substantial fines (up to 4% of annual turnover) as well as reputational damage. Non-compliance could lead to legal action by affected individuals or regulatory bodies.
- **International Human Rights Law**: The collection of data on civilians in conflict areas must adhere to international human rights law, including the International Covenant on Civil and Political Rights (ICCPR), which protects individuals from arbitrary interference with their privacy. Failure to safeguard civilian privacy through IoT surveillance systems may result in legal consequences for both military organizations and contractors.

c. Attribution of Cyberattacks

In the context of military operations, attribution of cyberattacks is a significant challenge. Cyberattacks targeting IoT systems can originate from various actors – state-sponsored hackers, non-state actors, or cybercriminals – and can be difficult to trace or attribute to a specific individual or group.

- **Attribution Issues in Warfare**: International law, particularly the Law of Armed Conflict (LOAC), requires clear rules regarding the use of force, including when it comes to cyberattacks. If an IoT system is compromised and the adversary uses it to cause harm (e.g. disabling a weapon system or directing a drone to attack civilians), determining whether this constitutes an act of war and how to respond legally can be complicated. International law does not yet provide clear standards for the legality of cyberattacks in warfare, especially as it pertains to IoT devices.

- **Responsibility for Cyberweapons**: If IoT systems are attacked and used in violation of international law, determining who is legally responsible can be difficult. The actors responsible could include the military forces deploying the systems, contractors who built the technology, or even third-party vendors who provided cybersecurity solutions. Additionally, the accountability of manufacturers (in the case of defective IoT devices or weak security protocols) could be legally questioned, especially if a cyberattack is caused by flaws in the system's design or deployment.

d. Failure to Implement Adequate Security Measures

Failure to implement adequate cybersecurity measures can expose parties to legal consequences under national laws or international agreements.

- **Negligence Claims**: If a breach of security occurs due to failure to implement reasonable cybersecurity measures (e.g. not encrypting sensitive data or failing to update software vulnerabilities), defence agencies or contractors could face negligence claims. This could result in financial compensation, penalties, or even reputational harm.
- **Compliance with National Cybersecurity Laws**: Countries like the United States have specific laws governing cybersecurity in defence operations, including the Cybersecurity Information Sharing Act (CISA) and FISMA (Federal Information Security Modernization Act). Non-compliance with these national laws can lead to penalties, sanctions, or loss of government contracts.

3.5.3. Mitigation Strategies for Cybersecurity Risks and Legal Liabilities

To reduce cybersecurity risks and mitigate legal liabilities associated with IoT-driven defence systems, the following strategies should be implemented:

- **Robust Cybersecurity Frameworks**: Develop and enforce comprehensive cybersecurity frameworks to ensure that IoT devices are protected throughout their lifecycle – from design and development to deployment and decommissioning. This includes regular security audits, penetration testing, and compliance with international cybersecurity standards (e.g. ISO/IEC 27001).
- **Cyber Hygiene Practices**: Ensure that all IoT devices in defence systems are updated with the latest security patches and that strong encryption and authentication protocols are implemented. Devices should be secured against both external and internal threats through multi-layered defences.
- **Clear Liability Clauses in Contracts**: When engaging contractors, ensure that clear cybersecurity and liability clauses are included in contracts, specifying the security standards that must be met and the consequences for failing to comply. This will help shift responsibility and reduce legal risk in the event of a breach.

- **Incident Response Plans**: Develop and regularly test comprehensive incident response plans for IoT-related cybersecurity breaches. These plans should address immediate steps to contain and mitigate damage, procedures for informing affected parties, and compliance with legal requirements regarding breach notification.
- **Cybersecurity Training and Awareness**: Regularly train military personnel and contractors on cybersecurity best practices and the legal implications of cyber-attacks. Training should emphasize how to prevent, detect, and respond to security threats and the potential legal consequences of mishandling IoT data or failing to secure military IoT systems.
- **Legal Preparedness and Coordination**: Maintain close coordination with legal experts who specialize in cybersecurity and international law to ensure that military actions involving IoT systems comply with both domestic and international legal requirements. This will also help manage the legal complexities associated with cyberattacks and the attribution of responsibility. The increasing reliance on IoT devices in military operations presents new cybersecurity risks. Cyberattacks targeting IoT networks can disrupt operations, steal sensitive data, and compromise national security.
- **Liability for Cyberattacks:** Legal frameworks must address who is responsible for cyberattacks on IoT systems. Should the government be held liable for inadequate security measures, or should the manufacturers of the IoT devices face liability for flaws in design?
- **Cyber Defence Regulations:** Governments must implement robust cybersecurity standards and regulations for IoT devices in defence to mitigate the risks posed by malicious actors, including state-sponsored cyberattacks and non-state actors.

3.6. Ethical Decision-Making in IoT Defence Applications

The integration of IoT technologies into defence applications offers significant advantages, including enhanced operational efficiency, improved situational awareness, and the development of advanced autonomous systems. However, the use of IoT in defence also presents a complex array of ethical challenges that require careful decision-making to ensure that these technologies are used responsibly, safely, and in compliance with ethical standards. Ethical decision-making in IoT defence applications is particularly important because these systems often operate in high-stakes environments, involving life-and-death situations, national security, and the protection of human rights (Alcántara Suárez & Monzon Baeza, 2023; Montasari, 2023, 2024; Payal et al., 2021). This section explores key considerations for ethical decision-making in IoT defence applications, focusing on autonomy, accountability, privacy, fairness, and the broader impact on society.

3.6.1. Autonomy and the Use of Autonomous Weapons Systems

One of the most contentious ethical issues in IoT-driven defence applications is the use of autonomous weapons systems (AWS), which rely on IoT sensors, AI, and machine learning algorithms to make targeting and firing decisions without human intervention. The potential for these systems to act autonomously raises significant ethical questions:

- **Moral Responsibility**: Who is ethically responsible when an autonomous system makes a decision that results in unintended harm? In traditional military operations, accountability for actions taken by personnel is relatively straightforward. However, with autonomous systems, it becomes more difficult to assign responsibility, especially if the system makes a decision that contradicts IHL or results in civilian casualties.
- **Human Oversight**: A key ethical debate is whether human operators should have the ability to override autonomous systems at any time. Many argue that human oversight is essential to ensure that ethical decisions are made in real-time and that humans remain in control of life-and-death decisions. The absence of this oversight may lead to unanticipated consequences, particularly in fast-evolving combat situations.
- **Discrimination and Bias**: AI systems used in autonomous weapons are only as ethical as the algorithms that govern them. If these algorithms are poorly designed or inadequately tested, they may make biased or discriminatory decisions. For example, if the system disproportionately targets certain groups of people based on race, ethnicity, or other factors, it could lead to violations of IHL or human rights.

3.6.2. Accountability and the Attribution of Responsibility

With IoT devices and systems playing an increasing role in military operations, determining accountability for actions taken by these systems becomes a major ethical challenge. In cases where IoT systems cause harm or violate legal or ethical standards, identifying who is responsible can be complicated.

- **Responsibility for IoT System Failures**: If an IoT system malfunctions or is hacked, causing damage, loss of life, or violations of international law, who is held responsible? Is it the manufacturer who designed the IoT system, the military entity deploying it, or the contractors responsible for maintenance and cybersecurity? Ethical decision-making must take into account the shared responsibility among all stakeholders involved in the system's development, deployment, and operation.
- **Chain of Command and Accountability**: In military operations, there is a well-established chain of command. When IoT systems are integrated into decision-making processes, it becomes vital to establish clear lines of accountability. Ethical decision-making should ensure that military leaders and operators are held accountable for their use of IoT technologies and that decisions are made in accordance with international laws and ethical principles.
- **Attribution in Cybersecurity Incidents**: IoT-driven defence systems are vulnerable to cyberattacks, which can result in the breach of sensitive information or the manipulation of military assets. Ethical decision-making in the event of a

cyberattack involves determining who is responsible for securing the system, how to respond to the attack, and how to protect both the military personnel and civilians affected.

3.6.3. Privacy and Civil Liberties

The use of IoT systems in defence operations – especially surveillance technologies – raises significant ethical concerns regarding privacy and civil liberties. These concerns are especially pronounced in conflict zones or areas where military IoT systems might be used to monitor civilian populations.

- **Surveillance and Privacy**: IoT systems can be used for surveillance, such as drones equipped with cameras or sensors to monitor enemy positions or civilian activity. However, this raises the question of whether civilians, especially in conflict zones, are being subjected to unwarranted surveillance. Ethical decision-making must balance the military's need for intelligence with the protection of civilian privacy.
- **Informed Consent**: For military personnel, IoT devices that collect personal data, such as health metrics, biometric data, or behavioural patterns, can infringe on privacy rights. Informed consent is a key ethical issue – military personnel should be aware of what data is being collected and how it will be used. Ensuring that soldiers have the ability to consent to data collection, or at least be informed about the extent of surveillance, is a critical ethical responsibility.
- **Data Security**: With large amounts of sensitive data being collected by IoT devices, ensuring the security of this data is essential. Ethical decision-making involves establishing data protection measures that prevent unauthorized access, data breaches, or misuse of information, particularly when that data relates to soldiers' health or civilians' personal information.

3.6.4. Fairness and Bias in AI and IoT Systems

IoT systems that rely on AI and machine learning are often used to make decisions in defence applications, such as targeting, surveillance, and strategic planning. However, these systems can inherit biases from the data they are trained on, leading to unfair or discriminatory outcomes.

- **Algorithmic Bias**: AI algorithms used in military IoT systems may be trained on biased data, which can result in discriminatory decisions. For instance, facial recognition technologies, used in both surveillance and targeting, have been shown to have higher error rates for certain demographics, particularly people of colour. Ethical decision-making must involve mitigating these biases by ensuring that AI systems are tested for fairness and transparency.
- **Access to Technology**: There is also an ethical issue around who controls and has access to military IoT technologies. Disparities in access to these technologies can lead to unequal power dynamics. Ethical decision-making should ensure that the use of IoT in defence is subject to international regulation, and

that powerful nations do not misuse or monopolize these technologies at the expense of others.

- **Human Versus Machine Decision-Making**: Ethical concerns also arise around the question of how much decision-making power should be delegated to machines. The delegation of life-and-death decisions to machines, such as in autonomous weapons systems, can raise ethical questions about whether humans should always be involved in these decisions, regardless of the efficiency of machines.

3.6.5. Impact on Society and International Law

The widespread use of IoT in military operations not only affects the immediate military context but can have broader implications for society, international relations, and global security.

- **Escalation of Conflict**: The deployment of advanced IoT systems in defence could lead to the escalation of conflicts, particularly if autonomous weapons systems are used without sufficient safeguards. Ethical decision-making involves considering the potential long-term consequences of these technologies, including the risks of triggering unintended conflicts, arms races, or violations of international law.
- **IHL**: All military actions, including those involving IoT-driven systems, must comply with IHL, which governs the conduct of armed conflict. This includes the principles of distinction (targeting only combatants and military targets), proportionality (avoiding excessive harm to civilians), and necessity (using force only when absolutely required). Ethical decision-making in the use of IoT in defence must ensure that systems are designed and used in a way that respects these principles.
- **Accountability in Global Governance**: As IoT technologies spread globally, there is an ethical obligation to establish international frameworks that regulate the use of IoT in defence. This could include agreements on the development and deployment of autonomous weapons, as well as norms for the protection of civilian infrastructure and the use of surveillance technologies.

Ethical decision-making in IoT-driven defence systems involves the development of AI algorithms that align with military ethics and international law. To ensure that AI systems make decisions that respect human rights and adhere to ethical standards, military organizations must focus on creating transparent, interpretable systems. These systems should be designed to enhance, not replace, human judgement, especially when it comes to decisions involving life and death.

3.7. IoT and the Rules of Engagement

The integration of the IoT into military operations is reshaping traditional concepts of warfare, particularly the Rules of Engagement (ROE) that dictate when, where, and how force can be used. IoT-enabled military systems, such as autonomous drones, sensor networks, and AI-driven decision-making tools, must operate within established ROE frameworks to ensure that engagements remain lawful, ethical, and aligned with the principles of just war theory – necessity, proportionality, and discrimination (Allhoff & Henschke, 2018; Helkala et al., 2022; Koch, 2020, 2021; Yaacoub et al., 2023).

- **Necessity:** IoT-driven military actions must be justified based on immediate threats or operational requirements, ensuring that force is used only when required to achieve a legitimate objective.
- **Proportionality:** Any response facilitated by IoT systems should be proportionate to the threat, minimizing collateral damage and unintended harm.
- **Discrimination:** IoT-enabled systems must be capable of distinguishing between combatants and non-combatants, reducing the risk of wrongful engagements.

While IoT enhances situational awareness and operational efficiency, there is a risk of automated escalation in conflict zones if IoT-driven systems lack proper controls. To mitigate this, human oversight is crucial – commanders and policymakers must ensure that IoT decisions in high-risk scenarios are subject to review by human operators, preventing unintended consequences or violations of international law. Moreover, fail-safe mechanisms should be embedded in IoT military systems to allow immediate intervention in case of errors or malfunctions.

As IoT continues to evolve, military forces must continuously update and adapt ROE to accommodate emerging technologies while upholding ethical and legal standards.

3.8. Policy Recommendations

To ensure the responsible and secure deployment of IoT in defence operations, the following policy recommendations should be considered:

- **Develop Clear Ethical Guidelines:** Establish a robust framework that defines ethical standards for IoT-driven military operations. This should emphasize accountability, transparency, and human oversight, ensuring that IoT technologies operate within ethical boundaries and do not engage in unlawful or indiscriminate warfare.
- **Ensure Legal Compliance:** Governments must create and enforce comprehensive legal frameworks that regulate IoT-driven defence operations, ensuring adherence to international law, human rights protections, and IHL. Special attention should be given to ensuring that IoT-enabled systems comply with the Geneva Conventions and United Nations protocols on armed conflict.
- **Enhance Cybersecurity Measures:** Strengthen cybersecurity protocols for IoT defence systems by implementing multi-layered security mechanisms, such as end-to-end encryption, intrusion detection, and real-time monitoring. This will prevent cyberattacks, hacking, and data breaches that could compromise military operations or national security.

- **Protect Privacy Rights:** IoT military applications often involve large-scale data collection, surveillance, and intelligence gathering. It is essential to implement policies that safeguard privacy rights, ensuring that surveillance operations do not lead to mass surveillance abuses or human rights violations. Clear guidelines must regulate the collection, storage, and use of IoT-generated data to prevent unlawful exploitation.
- **Establish Human-in-the-Loop (HITL) Systems:** Deploy IoT-based military solutions with built-in human oversight mechanisms that allow human operators to override autonomous decisions in complex combat scenarios. This ensures that critical engagement decisions are not left entirely to AI-driven IoT systems.
- **Strengthen International Cooperation:** Given the global nature of modern warfare, collaboration among allied nations is necessary to develop standardized IoT military policies, share best practices, and create global security protocols to prevent IoT misuse in conflicts.

By implementing these policy recommendations, defence organizations can harness the strategic advantages of IoT while ensuring compliance with ethical, legal, and security standards in modern warfare.

3.9. Discussion

The ethical and legal challenges associated with the IoT in defence operations are complex and multifaceted, requiring careful consideration at every stage of development and deployment. While IoT technologies offer significant advancements in surveillance, autonomous decision-making, and real-time situational awareness, they also raise critical concerns regarding accountability, privacy, cybersecurity, and compliance with international laws.

One of the foremost ethical dilemmas is accountability, particularly in the context of autonomous systems and decision-making processes. As IoT-enabled defence systems incorporate AI and machine learning, determining responsibility for actions taken by autonomous or semi-autonomous devices becomes increasingly difficult. This raises questions about liability in cases of unintended harm, operational failures, or breaches of IHLs. Clear mechanisms must be established to ensure that human oversight remains integral to the decision-making process and that military personnel remain accountable for the deployment and actions of IoT-driven systems.

Privacy concerns are another significant challenge, especially with the widespread use of interconnected sensors, surveillance systems, and biometric data collection. IoT technologies in defence often involve continuous data monitoring and tracking, which may infringe on the rights of both military personnel and civilians. The collection, storage, and processing of such data must be governed by strict data protection policies to prevent unauthorized access, misuse, or exploitation. Ensuring that personal and sensitive information is handled in accordance with privacy regulations is essential to maintaining ethical integrity in defence operations.

Cybersecurity is a critical legal and operational concern, as IoT networks in defence are highly susceptible to cyberattacks, hacking, and data breaches. The interconnected nature of IoT devices creates potential vulnerabilities that adversaries could exploit to gain access to classified information, disrupt communications, or manipulate military assets. Compliance with cybersecurity frameworks, implementation of robust encryption protocols, and continuous monitoring for cyber threats are necessary to protect the integrity of IoT-based defence systems. Additionally, defence organizations must work collaboratively with international partners to establish standardized security measures that address the unique risks posed by IoT technologies.

From a legal standpoint, the deployment of IoT in military operations must align with IHLs and conventions, including the Geneva Conventions and rules governing the use of autonomous weapon systems. The use of IoT in warfare raises concerns about proportionality, discrimination, and adherence to the principles of necessity and distinction. Any military application of IoT must ensure that it does not result in indiscriminate attacks, violate the rights of non-combatants, or contravene established legal norms. Furthermore, nations deploying IoT-enabled defence systems must engage in transparent discussions about regulatory compliance and ethical oversight to avoid potential violations of international treaties.

To address these ethical and legal challenges, it is imperative that IoT technologies in defence are developed and deployed within a framework that prioritizes human rights, legal compliance, and transparency. This requires multidisciplinary collaboration among policymakers, legal experts, technologists, and military leaders to establish guidelines that balance technological innovation with ethical responsibility. By integrating ethical considerations into the design and implementation of IoT in defence, we can mitigate risks while maximizing the strategic advantages of these technologies.

Ultimately, addressing these concerns is not just a matter of compliance but a fundamental necessity for maintaining global security, upholding international law, and fostering trust in the responsible use of IoT in military operations. By ensuring ethical governance, stringent cybersecurity measures, and adherence to legal frameworks, defence organizations can harness the full potential of IoT while safeguarding the principles of accountability, human rights, and operational integrity.

3.10. Conclusion

The integration of IoT in defence operations presents both transformative opportunities and formidable ethical and legal challenges that must be carefully navigated. The deployment of IoT-driven systems enhances surveillance, decision-making, and real-time situational awareness but also raises critical concerns regarding accountability, privacy, cybersecurity, and adherence to international laws. Ensuring that human oversight remains central to autonomous decision-making processes is essential to maintaining accountability and preventing unintended harm. Similarly, robust data protection measures are necessary to safeguard privacy, while stringent cybersecurity protocols must be implemented to counteract the risks of cyber threats and unauthorized access. From a legal perspective, compliance with IHLs, including the Geneva Conventions, is crucial to prevent violations related to proportionality, discrimination, and the rights of non-combatants. Addressing these multifaceted challenges requires a collaborative, multidisciplinary approach that balances technological innovation with ethical responsibility. By prioritizing transparency, legal compliance, and security, defence organizations can harness the potential of IoT while upholding global security, human rights, and operational integrity.

References

Alcántara Suárez, E. J., & Monzon Baeza, V. (2023). Evaluating the role of machine learning in defense applications and industry. *Machine Learning and Knowledge Extraction*, *5*(4), 1557–1569.

Allhoff, F., & Henschke, A. (2018). The Internet of Things: Foundational ethical issues. *Internet of Things*, *1*, 55–66.

Fraga-Lamas, P., Fernández-Caramés, T. M., Suárez-Albela, M., Castedo, L., & González-López, M. (2016). A review on internet of things for defense and public safety. *Sensors*, *16*(10), 1644.

Heinl, C. H. (2014, June). Artificial (intelligent) agents and active cyber defence: Policy implications. In *2014 6th International conference on cyber conflict (CyCon 2014)* (pp. 53–66). IEEE.

Helkala, K., Cook, J., Lucas, G., Pasquale, F., Reichberg, G., & Syse, H. (2022). AI in cyber operations: Ethical and legal considerations for end-users. In T. Sipola, T. Kokkonen, & M. Karjalainen (Eds.), *Artificial intelligence and cybersecurity: Theory and applications* (pp. 185–206). Springer International Publishing.

Karale, A. (2021). The challenges of IoT addressing security, ethics, privacy, and laws. *Internet of Things*, *15*, 100420.

Koch, W. (2020, July). On ethically aligned information fusion for defence and security systems. In *2020 IEEE 23rd International conference on information fusion (FUSION)* (pp. 1–8). IEEE.

Koch, W. (2021). On digital ethics for artificial intelligence and information fusion in the defense domain. *IEEE Aerospace and Electronic Systems Magazine*, *36*(7), 94–111.

Montasari, R. (2023). Internet of things and artificial intelligence in national security: Applications and issues. In Reza (Ed.), *Countering cyberterrorism: The confluence of artificial intelligence, cyber forensics and digital policing in US and UK National Cybersecurity* (pp. 27–56). Springer International Publishing.

Montasari, R. (2024). *National security in the Artificial Intelligence era: Challenges and implications of advanced technologies* [Doctoral dissertation, Cardiff Metropolitan University].

Payal, M., Dixit, P., Sairam, T. V. M., & Goyal, N. (2021). Robotics, AI, and the IoT in defense systems. In A. K. Dubey, A. Kumar, S. R. Kumar, N. Gayathri, & P. Das (Eds.), *AI and IoT-based intelligent automation in robotics* (pp. 109–128). John Wiley & Sons, Inc.

Santhi, K., Shri, M. L., Joshi, S., & Sharma, G. (2024, February). AI in defence and ethical concerns. In *2024 Second international conference on emerging trends in information technology and engineering (ICETITE)* (pp. 1–7). IEEE.

Swaniha, D., & Sharanya, E. (2024). Smart surveillance robot for military applications using IoT. *International Journal of Information Technology and Computer Engineering*, *12*(2), 38–45.

Taddeo, M., McNeish, D., Blanchard, A., & Edgar, E. (2023). 7 Ethical principles for artificial intelligence in the defence domain. In F. Cristiano, D. Broeders, F. Delerue, F. Douzet, & A. Géry (Eds.), *Artificial intelligence and international conflict in cyberspace* (p. 159). Routledge.

Tzafestas, S. G. (2018). Ethics and law in the internet of things world. *Smart Cities*, *1*(1), 98–120.

Weng, Y. (2024). Big data and machine learning in defence. *International Journal of Computer Science and Information Technology*, *16*(2), 25–35.

Yaacoub, J. P. A., Noura, H. N., Salman, O., & Chehab, A. (2023). Ethical hacking for IoT: Security issues, challenges, solutions and recommendations. *Internet of Things and Cyber-Physical Systems*, *3*, 280–308.

Chapter 4

Design of a Soft Computing Based Cryptosystem for Data Security in IoT in Defence Industry

Anirban Bhowmik[a] *and Sunil Karforma*[b]

[a]*Department of Computer Science, M.U.C. Women's College, WB, India*
[b]*Department of Computer Science, The University of Burdwan, WB, India*

Abstract

The military protects all citizens and should protect itself. The expanding use of information technology has boosted cyberattacks. The military industry must secure cyberspace with flexible and robust capabilities. The goal is to identify, protect, respond to, and prevent cyber attacks that could harm military systems, communication networks, operations, and Internet-based weapons and gadgets. Thus, information or data security is the main theme for robust communication system in military industry. In this chapter, the authors are trying to develop a cryptosystem that secures the communication of information in a wireless network. This system also helps in the defence industry for security in the Military Internet of Things. In any cryptosystem, the secret key is the backbone of any encryption and decryption process. The measurement of robustness in any cryptographic technique is based on the randomness of the secret key. Randomness implies the unbreakable cipher. Here, the authors have proposed a cryptosystem which includes a key generation process using a recurrent neural network, gravitational search algorithm, and genetic algorithm; a symmetric key-based key wrapping process for key transmission, and a format preserving encryption (FPE) technique for encryption and decryption algorithm. The proposed cryptosystem is suitable for fast, real-time applications. Military Internet of Things is such a real-time application that may use this system.

The Internet of Things in the Defence Industry:
Challenges and Solutions for Military Security, 81–106

doi:10.1108/978-1-83549-198-020261004

Different types of results and analyses suggest that the proposed scheme satisfies the demands of benchmarks such as maximum correlation, robustness, randomness, and complexity.

Keywords: Recurrent neural network; GSA; genetic operator; secret key stream; randomness; format preserving encryption

1. Introduction

Military institutions must contend with a constantly changing cyber security threats in military IoT. Cybercriminals are able to launch complex and prolonged cyber attacks against specific targets because they are usually well-resourced, extremely talented, and patient. Their goals are diverse and might be political or economical or espionage, since these individuals aim to obtain strategic intelligence that can help their own countries (Stallings, 2003).

Types of Cyber Attacks – Cyber attacks are of two types: *targeted and untargeted.*

Targeted cyber attack: This type of dedicated attack damages a specific user, organization, or company (Agarwal & Agarwal, 2013). It aims to gain access to important data from other users. The main aims of this type of attack are for financial gain, industrial espionage, stealing intellectual property, disrupting the system's process, political influence, etc. (Mahdi & Hassan, 2018).

Untargeted cyber attack: This is an attack that does not affect a specific designated target. It aims to generate huge losses by affecting multiple computers (Das & Veni Madhavan, 2004; Padhy, 2012).

Encryption Key (Secret Key): For wireless communication, the encryption algorithm (Kahate, 2008; Stallings, 2003) performs various substitutions and variations (Das & Veni Madhavan, 2004; Mahdi & Hassan, 2018) on the plaintext primarily based on the secret key. The encryption key must be unbiased of the plaintext and of the encryption algorithm (Bhowmik et al., 2020).

Recurrent Neural Network (RNN): A RNN (Haykin, 2004) distinguishes itself from a feed-forward neural network (Stinson, 2006) in which it has a minimum one feedback loop. A recurrent network can also include a hidden layer of neurons in which every neuron feeds its output signals back to the inputs of all of the other neurons. This is a shape of a layered network, we've got an input layer of source nodes that tasks into an output layer of neurons (computation nodes), but not vice versa. Here self-feedback loop is absent (Karakaya et al., 2017).

GSA: Here, we have used the gravitational search optimization algorithm (GSA) (Rashedi et al., 2009) for deciding good solutions. GSA is sort of a small synthetic world of masses obeying the Newtonian laws and guidelines of gravitation and movement. In this set of rules, agents are considered as items and their overall performance is measured by using their masses as well as their places. Using gravitational force, a lot of these items attract each different and as a result lower loads items action towards the heavier load items. Each mass (agent) has four specifications, which are position, inertial mass, active gravitational mass, and passive gravitational mass. Inertial and gravitational masses are determined by using a fitness function which is based on mass and velocity and the set of rules which are navigated by using properly adjusting the gravitational and inertial masses. Mathematical formulations are given below. Now, don't forget a set of *N* agents (loads). Here we define the position of the ith agent by:

$$X_i = (x_i^1, x_{i,}^2 x_i^3, \cdots x_i^d)\text{for } i{=}1{,}2{,}3\cdots N \tag{1}$$

where x_i^d represent the position of ith masses in the dth dimension. At a specific time *t*, the acting force on mass *i* from mass *j* is defined as follows:

$$F_{ij}^d(t) = G(t)\frac{M_{pi}(t)\times M_{aj}(t)}{R_{ij}(t)+\varepsilon}(x_j^d(t)-x_i^d(t)) \tag{2}$$

where $M_{pi}(t)$ is the latent gravitational mass of specialist *i*, $M_{aj}(t)$ is the vivacious gravitational mass of specialist *j*, *G*(*t*) is the gravitational predictable at time *t*, ε is a little customary and $R_{ij}(t)$ is the Euclidean distance among specialists *i* and *j*. The all-out power that follows up on the specialist (mass) *i* in a measurement. *d* is a haphazardly weighted amount of dth segments of the powers.

Discharged from different specialists (masses) is as per the following:

$$F_i^d(t) = \sum_{j\in K\,best,\, j\neq i} rand_j\, F_{ij}^d(t) \tag{3}$$

where *randj* is a random number in the interval [0, 1]. The set of first *K* agents is termed as *Kbest* with the best fitness values. Now the inertial masses of agents are calculated as follows.

$$m_i(t) = \frac{fit_i - worst(t)}{best(t) - worst(t)} \tag{4}$$

$$M_i(t) = \frac{m_i(t)}{\sum_{j=1}^{N} m_j(t)} \tag{5}$$

The fitness function is fit_i. Inertia mass is determined by the fitness function. Here, we treat a specialist whose mass is substantial as the best specialist. The best specialist has a higher fascination and walks all the more gradually. Presently, as indicated by laws of movement, let a^d(t) be the speeding up of the specialist *i* at time *t* in the dth course. So the formula is given underneath:

$$a_i(t) = \frac{F_i(t)}{M_{ii}(t)} \tag{6}$$

M_{ii} is the inertial mass of ith specialist. In this chapter, most noticeably *worst* (*t*) implies the least fitness function and *best* (*t*) implies the greatest fitness value.

During the pursuit, the specialists update their speed and area utilizing the accompanying conditions.

$$v_i^d(t+1) = rand_i X v_i^d(t) + a_i^d(t). \tag{7}$$

$$x_i^d(t+1) = x_i^d(t) + v_i^d(t+1). \tag{8}$$

Decreasing Function: The property of a decreasing function (Chakravorty & Ghosh, 2006) over an interval is, for every x_1 and x_2 in the interval, $x_1 < x_2, f(x_1) \geq f(x_2)$. The property of a strictly decreasing function over an interval is, for every x_1 and x_2 in the interval, $x_1 < x_2$, $f(x_1) > f(x_2)$. A modified GSA is used in this chapter. The GSA is modified according to the gravitational constant function. The complete structure of the chapter is provided in Table 4.1. Here we have used $f(y) = 2.7 * (0.7)^{(y/4.5)}$ which is a very slow decreasing function because in the GSA concept gravitational constant must decrease slowly with respect to time. The graphical representation of the function is given below through Fig. 4.1.

Table 4.1. Structure of the Chapter.

Serial No.	Item	Description
1	Introduction	General description about different concepts/ tools (like RNN, GA, Gray code, GSA, etc.) which are used in this chapter.
2	Literature Review	Discussion of previous work done in this field. Here we have discussed 11 papers for our work.
3	Objectives of the Proposed Scheme	Objective of our proposed cryptosystem with key features.
4	Proposed Methodology	Detailed algorithms and examples of the proposed scheme.
5	Result & Analysis	Detailed results, graph, charts, comparisons, etc.
6	Conclusion	Remarks on the proposed technique.

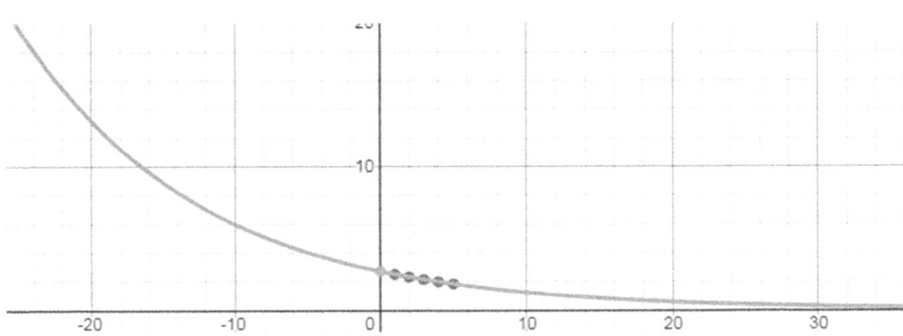

Fig. 4.1. Graphical Diagram of $(y) = 2.7 * (0.7)^{(y/4.5)}$ Function.

2. Literature Review

Conventional cryptography is based on mathematical computation and puzzles. A neural network-based cryptographic technique is based on neurocomputing, neurodynamic, and neurofuzzy concepts. In this chapter, we have used an ANN and a metaheuristics search technique for cryptographic key generation.

Pareek, Patidar and Sud, (2006) have used eight various kinds of operations utilized with 80-bit key to accomplish the encryption process based on two logistics maps.

Alsafasfeh and Arfoa (2011) introduced a new procedure depending on the use of multi-chaotic functions with Rossler attractor to generate the key for permutation all image pixels.

Alsafasfeh and Arfoa (2011) introduced two general tent chaotic maps to increase the degree of freedom and produced a versatile response that can fit a cipher application.

Behnia et al. (2008) proposed a novel photograph encryption scheme based on the chaotic tent map, to generate key flow by way of an ID chaotic tent map.

Amin et al. (2006) used DNA strands as a cozy key. They have not used real biological DNA strands, which is a virtual DNA cryptographic method, in their computing work.

Ghazi and Ali (2018) have provided a key stream generator procedure according to a dynamic composite LFSR stream cipher.

Sreelaja and Pai (2008) have suggested a key stream generation procedure for data encryption according to Ant Colony and the allocation of letters in the original message.

Sreelaja and Pai (2009) have introduced a key stream generator according to a 'Particle swarm optimization' for encrypting data or information. The disadvantage of these papers is that they enumerate the appearance of letters of the key stream in the original messages. This technique takes excessive time with respect to the overall time consumption for encryption, when the volume of the selected key stream is huge.

Ali (2018) has suggested a key stream generation method according to 3D chaotic maps and 'Particle swarm optimization' based random number generation, and tested it by some standard criteria.

Suresh et al. (2022) proposed a novel approach for generating the same public and private key pair based on two factors: fingerprint biometrics and password. A stable binary string is generated from the distances among pairs of minutiae points in a fingerprint using a gray code-based method. Here seed value is generated using the XOR operation between the Hash of the stable string generated from the fingerprint and the string generated from the hashed password. The proposed approach uses this seed value to generate two large prime numbers, which are used to generate the public and private key pair using the RSA method.

3. Objectives and Flow Diagram of the Proposed Scheme

From the literature review section, it is clear that the encryption key for different cryptosystems is generated using chaotic maps, neural networks, ACO, PSO (Pai, 2009; Ali, 2018), etc. But here we have proposed a soft computing-based cryptosystem where the session key is generated using RNN, GSA, and two-point crossover genetic operators (Agarwal & Agarwal, 2013. This session key and the symmetric key are the backbone of encryption and decryption of our proposed technique. This session key provides a restorative power over the symmetric key. So, this type of encapsulation among session key, symmetric key, and plain text reduces the vulnerabilities in wireless communication.

Key features of the proposed cryptosystem:

1. RNN is used to generate two sets of initial population vectors. From these two sets of initial population vectors, the gravitational search algorithm (GSA) provides the two best solutions. Now these two best solutions are given as input in the double-point genetic crossover operator to produce new offspring with strong features because of the exchange of genetic substances among the individuals of the chromosomal population (i.e. best solutions).
2. A gray code-based key wrapping algorithm (KWA) is proposed for exchanging a session key between the sender and receiver.
3. Modified format-preserving-encryption (FPE) technique is used for encryption-decryption purposes using a symmetric key and a session key.
4. A flow diagram of the proposed technique for clear understanding of each step is given below (Fig. 4.2).

The details algorithms are given in the next section.

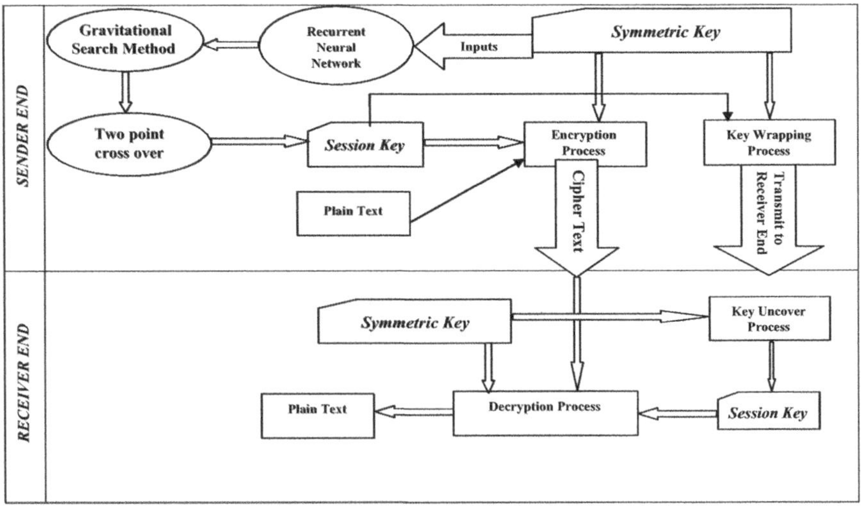

Fig. 4.2. Flow Chart of Proposed Technique.

4. Details About Proposed Technique

We divide our proposed technique into three sections. Each section is described by proper algorithms and examples for clear understanding. At first, we assumed that a symmetric key is negotiated between sender and receiver for wireless communications.

Section-1: Soft computing-based session key generation to produce cipher text.
Section-2: Key wrapping process for key exchange between sender and receiver through unguided media.
Section-3: Encryption & decryption process.

Detailed descriptions of each section are given below.

SECTION-1

Concepts:

(a) A recurrent neural network (RNN) is used for random number generation on the basis of two seed values. From these random numbers, we have generated two sets of m-dimensional n numbers of vectors which are random in nature. These n numbers of vectors are treated as the initial population for the gravitational search algorithm (GSA).
(b) Gravitational search algorithm is used for searching the two best solutions (m-dim vector) from two sets. Here we have modified the GSA by using a slowly decreasing function.
(c) Two points cross over operator in genetic algorithm (GA) is used on these two best solutions for best offspring generation. Now this offspring is used as session key.
(d) Three separate algorithms are given for three cases in Section-1. Thus Section-1 provides the session key for cipher text generation.

ALGORITHM-1 (Random vector generation through RNN)
Input: Two seed values.
Output: m-dimension n numbers of random vectors.
Method:
Step 1: $x[4], s_1, s_2, i, j, m_1, m_2, m_3, m_4, n, m, bs$.
Step 2: $s_1 \leftarrow$ first seed value and $s_2 \leftarrow$second seed value, bs$\leftarrow$bias value
Step 3: $m_1 \leftarrow$ activFunc $(s_1 * c_1 + s_2 * c_2 + bs)$, $m_2 \leftarrow$activFunc $(s_1 * c_3 + s_2 * c_4 + bs)$, $m_3 \leftarrow$ activFunc $(s_1 * c_5 + s_2 * c_6 + bs)$ and $m_4 \leftarrow$ activFunc $(s_1 * c_7 + s_2 * c_8 + bs)$. {/* initial values & c_i, i =1, 2... 8 are integer numbers.*/}
Step 4: for i = 1 *to n* //n numbers of vector.
Step 5: for j = 1 *to m* //m dimension vector.
{/* Step4 describes the unit delay in RNN*/}
Step 6: $x[1] \leftarrow ((m_2+m_3) \text{ xor } m_4)>>1$. $x[2] \leftarrow ((m_1+m_4) \text{ xor } m_3)>>1$.
$x[3] \leftarrow ((m_2+m_4) \text{ xor } m_1)>>1$. $x[4] \leftarrow ((m_1+m_3) \text{ xor } m_2)>>1$.
{/* Step 5 describes the linear combiner (summing junction) and output of activation function*/}

Step 7: m_1←Output1 ([2], [3], x[4]). Print(m_1%2). //output.
m_2← Output2 (x [1], x [3], x [4]). Print (m_2%2) //output.
m_3← Output3 (x [1], x [2], x [4]). m_4← Output 4 (x [1], x [2], x [3])
End for
End for
Step 8: End.
Output1:
Step 1: set w_1, w_2, w_3, w_4 as weight vector, bias and u_1 as integer.
Step 2: initialize weight vectors, bias.
Step 3: $u_1 \leftarrow w_1$*x[2] + w_2 * x[3] + w_3 * x[4]+bias.
Step 4: u_1←call *active_Func* (u_1).
Step 5: return (u_1).
Output2:
Step 1: set w_1,w_2, w_3, w_4 as weight vector, bias and u_2 as integer.
Step 2: initialize weight vectors and bias.
Step 3: $u_2 \leftarrow w_1$*x[1]+ w_2*x[3]+ w_3*x[4]+bias.
Step 4: u_2←call *active_Func* (u_2).
Step 5: return (u_2).
The pseudo code for Output3 and Output4 are same as Output1 and Output2.

Following is the pseudo code of the activation function.
active_Func (integer p): p is a parameter.
Step 1: Set r, n_1, n_2, n_3, n_4 as integer, op ← 0 and set n_1,n_2, n_3, n_4 as user defined number or any integer theory formula.
Step 2: if (p >= 0 && p <= n_1)
Step 3: $r = n_2 - p$.
Step 4: else if (p>= (n_1+1) && p<=n_3)
Step 5: $r \leftarrow n_4 - p$.
Step 6: else r←p% (n_1+1).
Step 7: Return (r)
Thus, the above algorithm provides the m-dimensional n numbers of random vectors. These vectors are used as the initial population for the next search algorithm.

ALGORITHM-2 (Modified Gravitational Search Algorithm)
If the encryption key is k bytes, then the number of population vectors should be (k + 1). Parameter Initialization
Step 1: Set initial values G_0 ←2.7, ∝ and ε.
Step 2: set the initial iteration$t$ ← 0.
Initial Population
Step 3: for i = 1 *to n* //n number of population.
Step 4: $x_i(t) \leftarrow (x_i^1(t), x_i^2(t), \cdots, x_i^n(t))$ //these population are from ALGORITHM-1.
End for.
Solution Update
Step 5: Evaluate the fitness function $f(x_i(t))$ for each agent in the population $x_i(t)$.
{/* here fitness function is based on mass & velocity. Heavier mass and low velocity provides fit agent.*/}

Step 6: Update gravitational constant G according to function $f(y) = 2.7 * (0.7)^{(y/4.5)}$ {/* the details of $f(y)$ are given at the result section.*/}
Step 7: for $i = 1$ *to* n
Step 8: for $j = i + 1$ *to* $n - 1$
Step 9: calculate $F_{ij}^{d}(t)$.
End for
Step 10: Calculate $F_i^{d}(t)$.
Step 11: Calculate inertial mass M_i from the equation (D).
Step 12: Calculate $a_i(t)$ for agent i by the equation (E).
Step 13: *Update velocity and position of agent i using the function (F) and (G).*
Step 14: *Set* $t \leftarrow t + 1$ *and repeat until termination criteria is satisfied.*
Step 15: *Return the best solution.*
Step 16: End program
This algorithm provides the best agent (solution) from the given population. The best agent is selected according to heavier mass and low velocity.

ALGORITHM-3 (Genetic Operator)
Here we have used double-point crossover genetic operator to generate the best characteristics offspring. This best offspring is the required session key (encryption key). Let the encryption key be k-byte.
Input: Two best agents (solution) by GSA (Algorithm-2).
Output: - Session key.
Method:
Step 1: bs1← best solution1 (best agent1) and bs2←best solution2 (best agent2).
Step 2: call twoPointCross (bs1, bs2).
{/*to generate best offspring 2-Point crossover from GA is used. Diagram of step 2 is given below.*/} Step 3: End.

The explanation of double-point crossover scheme in the genetic algorithm (GA) is given below with diagram (Fig. 4.3).(* shows the double point crossover start and ending point)

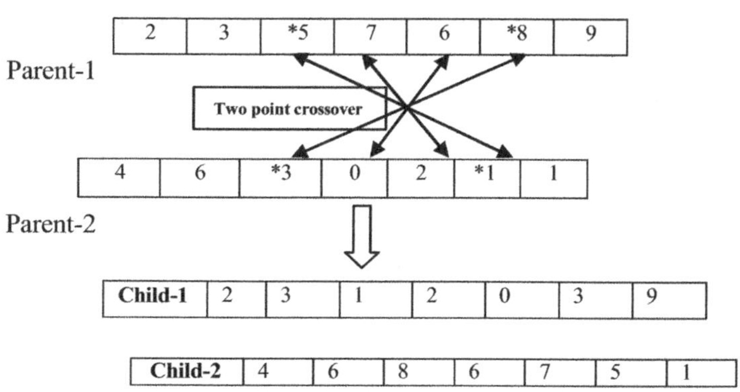

Fig. 4.3. Diagram of Step 2 of Algorithm-3.

Example:
Let the key size be 32 bits or 4 bytes. Let (26, 33) and (17, 20) be two seed values in RNN, and it generates two sets of 4-dimensional 5 vectors. Let set1 = {(4,6,11,7), (10,5,2,12), (32,20,3,26), (1,6,0,5), (15,8,17,2)} and set2 = {(4,16,3,6), (27,1,20,29),(9,40,36,6), (9,11,16,7), (2,2,7,18)}. Thus m = 4 & n = 5.
Now we apply the gravitational search algorithm (GSA) on set 1 and set 2 for searching the best solutions. Let bs1 = (32, 20, 26, 3) and bs2 = (9, 11, 16, 7).
bs1 = (00100000, 00010100, 00011010, 00000011) and bs2 = (00001001, 00000111, 00001011, 00010000).
Now we apply two-point cross-over operation from the genetic algorithm (GA) between each binary numbers from bs1 & bs2. Let the output of the cross-over operation is as follows:
Child-1 = (00010010, 00001010, 00011110, 00001001) & child-2 = (00001100, 00000110, 00010110, 00010010). Thus, we get two offspring in this generation. We select one of them according to the highest functional value of the given function, and this child is treated as the session key.
Function: $x=-1.0+ [3/(2^{22} - 1]vi$, where v_i *is vector component in binary form.*

SECTION-2

Concepts:

(a) Here we have emphasized on key wrapping process by which we can transfer the session key between sender and receiver.
(b) This wrapping process is treated as a secure channel for key transmission. In this process, the symmetric key is also used as authentication text (both user & message).
(c) In the key wrapping process, we have used symmetric key, session key, modular function, key wrapping function, and gray code. In this wrapping process, first we have generated key wrapping text (KWT) from symmetric key using a modular function. The size of KWT, the session key is the same as symmetric key. This KWT, symmetric key, and gray code conversion rule are used to wrap the session key for transferring.
(d) The modular function is $X_{n+1} = (a * X_n + C_n \oplus (X_n + 1)) \; mod \; M$, where $a = key\ size$, $M = 16$ for hexadecimal system and 127 for the ASCII system. $X_n = symmetric\ key\ element$, $n = 1,2,3, \ldots, n$ and

    $C_n = Any\ nonlinear\ function\ (each\ element\ of\ symmetric\ keyn,\ key\ length)$.

(e) The key wrapping function is $Wi = f(session\ keyi, grayCd(kwt_i + symmetric\ key_i))$, $i = 1,2,3, \ldots, n$,

    grayCd = gray code conversion, kwt_i= key wrapping text element & '+' means concatenation. The size of session key and symmetric key is the same. The wrapping process is described below via proper algorithm and example.

ALGORITHM-1 (Key wrapping process):

Input: session key, symmetric key.

Output: wrapped key (wkey) for secure session key transmission. Method:

Step 1: Set sesk [ ], symk [ ], kwtxt [ ], msbit [ ] [ ], lsbit [ ] [ ], wkeyH [ ], wkeyT [ ], ksize as arrays & variables.

Step 2: *ksize = get_length (symmetric key)*.

Step 3: for i=1 to ksize
$kwtxt[i] = (a * symk[i] + C_i \oplus symk[i]) mod\ M$.

Step 4: for i=1 to ksize
W[*i*] = *f*(*sesk*[*i*]*sesk*[*i*], *grayCd*(*kwtxt*[*i*] + *symk*[*i*]))
msbit [*i*][*N*]← *get_msb_Nbits* (*W*[*i*]) & *lsbit* [*i*][*N*] ← *get_lsb_Nbits* (*W*[*i*])/* N=4 for hex code & N=7 for ASCII code.*/

Step 5: *wkeyH* [*ksize*] = *msb*[1] + *msbit*[2] + *msbit*[3] + … + *msbit*[*ksize*].
wkeyT [*ksize*] = *lsb*[1] + *lsbit*[2] + *lsbit*[3] + … + *lsbit*[*ksize*].

Step 6: wkeyH [ ] and wkeyT [ ] are wrapped text for session key which are send to the receiver.

Step 7: End.

ALGORITHM-2 (Key uncover process)

Input: wkeyH [ ], wkeyT [ ] and symmetric key.

Output: Session key.

Method:

Step 1: Set sesk [ ], symk [ ], kwtxt [ ], auntxt [ ], wkeyH [ ], wkeyT [ ], tmptxt [ ], grytxt [ ], tmpsymk [ ],
ksize as arrays & variable.

Step 2: *ksize = get_length (symmetric key)*.

Step 3: for i=1 to ksize
$kwtxt[i] = (a * symk[i] + C_i \oplus symk[i]) mod\ M$.

Step 4: for i=1 to ksize
for j=1 to N /* N=4 for hex code & N=7 for ASCII code.*/
sesk[*i*][*j*] = *Xor_op* (*grayCd*(*kwtxt*[*i*]), *wkeyH*[*i*])
tmptxt[*i*][*j*] = *Xor_op* (*sesk*[*i*], *wkeyT* [*i*])
end for

Step 5: for i=1 to ksize
for j= 1 to N
grytxt[*i*][*j*] = *rev_grayCd* (*grayCd* (*kwtxt*[*i*]) + *tmptxt*[*i*])
auntxt[*i*][*j*] = *get_lsb_Nbits* (*grytxt*[*i*])
end for
tmpsymk[*ksize*] = *auntxt* [1] + *auntxt* [2] + *auntxt* [3] + … + *auntxt* [*ksize*]

Step 6: *if* (*psymk*[*ksize*] == *symk*[*ksize*]) *then Print "AUTHENTIC"*.
else Print "NOT AUTHENTIC".

{/*If the output of Step 6 provide the symmetric key i.e. print "AUTHENTIC", then sesk [ ] [ ] in step 4 provide the actual session key for encryption.*/}

Step 7: End.

Example:

Let symmetric key (symk [ ]) be $(A\ 5\ 4\ B)_{16}$ and session key (sesk [ ]) be $(8\ 6\ D\ 3)_{16}$. Now $X_{n+1} = (a * X_n + Cn \oplus (Xn + 1))\ mod\ M$, M=16 (Hexadecimal system). Let

$$C_n = [Celling(\frac{symk_n^2}{(a+1)}) + Floor(\frac{symk_n^3}{(a+n)}] + 1 \cdot$$

$A_1 = (4*10+1 \oplus 11) \bmod 16 = (2)_{16}$. $A_2 = (4*5+2 \oplus 6) \bmod 16 = (8)_{16}$.
$A_3 = (4*4+3 \oplus 5) \bmod 16 = (6)_{16}$. $A_4 = (4*11+4 \oplus 12) \bmod 16 = (4)_{16}$.
Thus kwtxt [4] is $(02\ 08\ 06\ 04)_{16}$.

Key Wrapping Process:-

Now from $Wi = (seskisesk_i, grayCd(kwtxti + symki), f(\ )$ produces XOR operation. We can generate wrapped text for the session key as follows.

$W[1] = f(sesk[1]sesk[1], grayCd(kwtxt[1] + symk[1]))$.
= f(10001000, grayCd (0010+1010)) = f (10001000, 00111111): H_1: 1011 & T_1: 0111. H denotes 4
MSBs & T denotes 4 LSBs.

$W[2] = f(sesk[2]sesk[2], grayCd(kwtxt[2] + symk[2]))$.
= f (01100110, grayCd (1000+0101)) = f (01100110, 11000111): H_2: 1010 & T_2: 0001.

$W[3] = f(sesk[3]sesk[3], grayCd(kwtxt[3] + symk[3]))$.
= f (11011101, grayCd (0110+0100))= f (11011101,01010110): H_3: 1000 & T_3: 1011.

$W[4] = f(sesk[4]sesk[4], grayCd(kwtxt[4] + symk[4]))$.
= f (00110011, grayCd (0100+1011)) = f (00110011, 01101110): H_4: 0101 & T_4: 1101.

WkeyH [ ] = $H_1 + H_2 + H_3 + H_4$ = 1011101010000101= $(B\ A\ 8\ 5)_{16}$.
WkeyT [ ] = $T_1 + T_2 + T_3 + T_4$ = 0111000110111101= $(7\ 1\ B\ D)_{16}$.

These wkeyH [ ] & wkeyT [ ] are transmitted to the receiver. Now receiver then uncovers the session key and also checks the authentication (both user & message) with the help of negotiated symmetric key.

Key Uncover Process:

Here symmetric key= $(A\ 5\ 4\ B)_{16}$ and key wrapping text (KWT)= $(02\ 08\ 06\ 04)_{16}$ are known. Now the process is as follows:

sesk[1]=(wkeyH[1] $\oplus$ grayCd (A_1)) and tmptxt[1]= (wkeyT[1] $\oplus$ sesk[1])
= 1000=$(8)_{16}$. = 1111

grytxt [1] = grayCd (grayCd (A_1) + tmptxt [1]) = 00101010 & auntxt [1] = *get_lsb_Nbits* (*grytxt*[1]) = 1010=$(A)_{16}$.

sesk[2]=(wkeyH[2] $\oplus$ grayCd (A_2)) and tmptxt[2]= (wkeyT[2] $\oplus$ sesk[2])
= 0110=$(6)_{16}$. = 0111

grytxt [2] = grayCd (grayCd (A_2) + tmptxt [2])= 10000101 & auntxt [2] = *get_lsb_Nbits* (*grytxt*[2])=0101=$(5)_{16}$.

sesk[3]=(wkeyH[3] $\oplus$ grayCd (A_3)) and tmptxt[3]= (wkeyT[3] $\oplus$ sesk[3])
= 1101= $(D)_{16}$. = 0110

grytxt [3] = grayCd (grayCd (A_3) + tmptxt [3]) = 01100100 &auntxt [3]= *get_lsb_Nbits* (*grytxt*[3])=0100=$(4)_{16}$.

sesk[4]=(wkeyH[4] ⊕ grayCd (A_4)) and tmptxt[4]= (wkeyT[4] ⊕ sesk[4])
= 0011= $(3)_{16}$. = 1110

grytxt [4]= grayCd (grayCd(A_4) + tmptxt[4])=01001011 &auntxt [4]= *get_lsb_Nbits* (*grytxt*[4])= 1011=$(B)_{16}$.

Thus session key= $(8\ 6\ D\ 3)_{16}$ and symmetric key= $(A\ 5\ 4\ B)_{16}$. This symmetric key provides both types of authentication user and message.

SECTION-3

Concepts:

(a) Robust encryption and decryption technique is the backbone of any cryptosystem. Here, we have tried to propose a strong encryption technique for cipher text generation.
(b) The plaintext is converted into 7-bit ASCII code (binary format). Plain text is divided into 'n' number of blocks, and each block size is equal to the key size.
(c) Extract three (3) LSB from each element of symmetric key and also extract two (2) LSB from each element of session key and create two arrays by incrementing 1 with each element.
(d) **C**ircular **L**eft **S**hift (CLS) operation is done on ASCII form plain text on the basis of the array based on three LSB of symmetric key.
(e) 'N' number of Gray conversion is done on the o/p of step (d) on basis of the array based on two LSB of session key.
(f) The output of step (e) is called the **P**artial **C**ipher **T**ext (pct).
(g) Session key passes through an algorithm (defined by the pseudo code below) which generates unique number in the array of session key. This modified array helps in the **F**ormat **P**reserving **E**ncryption (FPE). In FPE, each partial cipher text block is arranged as follows. Each block (partial cipher text) is collection of some characters. Tables 4.2–4.4 denote a block.
(h) *In sender end*, FPE is done on the output of step (e) i.e. pct as the following way.
    (i) If the session key contains multiple numbers of same elements, then we have to generate modified session key only for FPE, but this modified key is not the actual session key. The algorithm and example of this modification process is given.

Table 4.2. Representation of Partial Cipher Text and Corresponding Modified Session Key Elements.

Partial Cipher Text	**char-1**	**char-2**	**char-3**	**char-4**	...	**char-*n***
Modified Session key:	Session key element-1	Session key element-2	Session key element-3	Session key element-4	...	Session key element-*n*

(ii) Arrange the array of session key according to the ascending order and then also arrange the *char-i* accordingly. This arranged or modified *block-i (pct)* is the cipher text which will be transmitted to the receiver end. Thus as for example cipher text may be [char-4, char-2, char-1, char- 3,..., char-*n*], see Table 4.3.

Table 4.3. Cipher Text with Reordered Characters and Corresponding Modified Session Key Elements.

Cipher Text:	**char-4**	**char-2**	**char-1**	**char-3**	**...**	**char-*n***
Arranged modified session key (ascending order)	Session key element-4	Session key element-2	Session key element-1	Session key element-3	...	Session key element-n

(i) *In the receiver end*, the symmetric key & the session key are known. Now, reverse FPE (defined by Tables 4.2 and 4.3) is used to generate partial cipher text (pct) as follows.

Table 4.4. Cipher Text Character Reordering with Corresponding Modified Session Key Elements.

Cipher Text:	**char-4**	**char-2**	**char-1**	**char-3**	**...**	**char-*n***
Arranged modified session key (ascending order)	Session key element-4	Session key element-2	Session key element-1	Session key element-3	...	Session key element-n

Table 4.5. Partial Cipher Text and Corresponding Modified Session Key Elements.

Partial Cipher Text:	**char-1**	**char-2**	**char-3**	**char-4**	**...**	**char-*n***
Modified session Key	Session key element-1	Session key element-2	Session key element-3	Session key element-4	...	Session key element-n

(j) '*N*' numbers of gray to binary conversion on the output of reverse FPE on the basis of the array based on two LSB of session key. Table 4.5 shows the partial cipher text and its corresponding key elements.

(k) Circular **R**ight Shift (CRS) operation is done on the output of above step (l) on the basis of three LSB of symmetric key. The details algorithm is given below.

ALGORITHM-1(Data Encryption):

Input: Symmetric key, session key, plain text.

Output: Cipher text.

Method:

Step 1: Set thbit_symk [ ], twbit_sesk [ ], plntxt [ ], ciphtxt [ ], pct [ ], tmptxt [ ], md_sesk [ ], ksize as arrays & variables.

Step 2: thbit_symk [ ] = [extrt_3-bit_lsb (symk [ ])] + 01 & twbit_sesk= [extrt_2-bit_lsb (sesk [ ])] + 01.

{/* to avoid 00 case, one increment.*/}

Step 3: plntxt [ ] = plain text & plntxt [ ] = plntxt_blk***1*** [ ] +plntxt_blk*2* [ ] +...+plntxt_blk***n*** [ ]

{/*Plain text is divided into ***n*** number of blocks with equal size in binary form */}

Step 4: for n=1 to ksize {/* ksize denote the size of symmetric key*/}

tmptx_blk[**n**] [ ] = call *gray_Binary* (CLS (plntxt_blk[**n**][ ])) {/* circular left shift operation and then gray code end for conversion are done in each block*/}

Step 5: pct [ ] = tmptx_blk [**1**] + tmptx_blk [**2**] + tmptx_blk [**3**] +...+ tmptx_blk[**n**].

{/* Modified **F**ormat **P**reserving **E**ncryption***/}**

Step 6: md_sesk [ ] = call *unique_Numbs* (session key).

Step 7: ciphtxt [ ] = from steps (i) & (j) using Tables 4.2 and 4.3 in Section-2.

Step 8: End.

The output of step 7 is the cipher text which is to be sent to the receiver end. The definition of the function *unique_Numbs* (session key) is given below.

Def^{n}: *unique_Numbs* (*session key*)

{

Step 1: Check the multiplicity of each element in the array using linear search method.

Step 2: if multiplicity of any element≥2 then modifies the element as*element* = *element* +

array_position. After the first modification, the other elements after the modified element are put in the array as it is. Thus another array is created.

Go to step 1.

Step 3: if the multiplicity of each element in the array < 2 then step4.

Step 4: End.

}

Decryption is done on receiver end and it is the reverse process of encryption as defined in the steps (k), (l) and (m) above.

Example: Let the plain text be $(71\ 32\ 18\ 92)_{10}$ and symmetric key be (A 5 4 B) 16, session key $(8\ 6\ D\ 3)_{16}$. Now the array based on three-bit extraction from symmetric key is $(03\ 06\ 05\ 04)_{10}$, and the array based on two-bit extraction from session key is $(01\ 03\ 04\ 04)_{10}$. Shift operation is done on the basis of the array (03 06 05 04)$_{10}$ and gray code conversion is done on the basis of the array $(01\ 03\ 04\ 04)_{10}$.

Encryption Phase:
71: Binary form: $(1000111)_2$. After 3-bit shift operation, we get $(0111100)_2$. After gray code operation, we get (0100010).
32: Binary form: $(0100000)_2$. After 6-bit shift operation, we get $(0010000)_2$. After gray code operation, we get (0011110).
18: Binary form: $(0010010)_2$. After 5-bit shift operation, we get $(1000100)_2$. After gray code operation, we get (1000000).
92: Binary form: $(1011100)_2$. After 4-bit shift operation, we get $(1001011)_2$. After gray code operation, we get (1001111).
Thus partial cipher text = $(34\ 30\ 64\ 79)_{10}$. Now according to Format Preserving Encryption, we get

Partial cipher text	34	30	64	79
session key	8	6	D	3

Cipher Text	79	30	34	64
Session key (Ascending Order)	3	6	8	D

Thus cipher text= $(79\ 30\ 34\ 64)_{10}$ which is to be transmitted to the receiver side.
Decryption Phase:
Cipher Text = $(79\ 30\ 34\ 64)_{10}$. Symmetric key: $(A\ 5\ 4\ B)_{16}$. Session key: $(8\ 6\ D\ 3)_{16}$. $(03\ 06\ 05\ 04)_{10}$ for shift operation and $(01\ 03\ 04\ 04)_{10}$ for gray to binary conversion.
Reverse Format Preserving Encryption:
First, arrange the session key in ascending order, and we get $(3\ 6\ 8\ D)_{16}$. Now, from the following two tables, we get the partial cipher text.

Cipher Text	79	30	34	64
Session key (Ascending Order)	3	6	8	D

Then

Partial Cipher Text	34	30	64	79
Session key	8	6	D	3

Thus the partial cipher text = $(34\ 30\ 64\ 79)_{10}$.

34: Binary form: $(0100010)_2$. After gray to binary conversion, we get $(0111100)_2$. After 3-bit shift operation, we get (1000111).
30: Binary form: $(0011110)_2$. After gray to binary conversion, we get $(0010000)_2$. After 6-bit shift operation, we get (0100000).
64: Binary form: $(1000000)_2$. After gray to binary conversion, we get $(1000100)_2$. After 5-bit shift operation, we get (0010010).
79: Binary form: $(1001111)_2$. After gray to binary conversion, we get $(1001011)_2$. After 4-bit shift operation, we get (1011100).

Thus, plain text = (71 32 18 92).

If the session key contains multiple numbers of same elements, then for FPE, sender and receiver pass through an algorithm which generates unique numbers for session key which is defined in the ALGORITHM-1 in Section-2. An example is given below for proper understanding.

Let session key be (5 6 8 6 5 1). Here we should start the array position from 1.

Position	1	2	3	4	5	6
Session key	***5***	***6***	***8***	***6***	***5***	***1***
Step 1	5 Multiplicity=2	6	8	6	5	1
Step 2	6 (5+1)	6	8	6	5	1
Step 1	6 Multiplicity >2	6	8	6	5	1
Step 2	7 (6+1)	6	8	6	5	1
Step 1	7	6 Multiplicity=2	8	6	5	1
Step 2	7	8 (6+2)	8	6	5	1
Step 1	7	8 Multiplicity=2	8	6	5	1
Step 2	7	10 (8+2)	8	6	5	1
Step 1	7	10	8	6	5	1
Multiplicity of each element<2	7	10	8	6	5	1
Modified session key only for FPE	*7*	***10***	***8***	***6***	***5***	***1***

5. Results and Discussion

Results and analysis of the proposed technique are discussed here. The machine with the above configurations (Table 4.6) is used for all the programs and computational works in our scheme. NIST SP 800-22 Test Suit (Rutti, 2004) is used to show the statistical properties of the key stream. A good cryptosystem should be designed in such a way that it must robust against different types of cryptanalytic, statistical, and brute-force attacks (Al-Khateeb et al., 2017). Here, we have done the following experiments on our proposed scheme. The Cryptool interface is used for those tests.

Table 4.6. Machine Configuration for Our Experiment.

Type of computer	**Lenovo G80**
Type of processor	Intel® Pentium® CPU B951@210GHz
RAM	3GB
Compiler	Turbo C, Deb C++
Disc Drive	SA 9500326AS ATA
Operating System	Windows 7 Ultimate (32 Bits)

(a) Statistical Analysis
(b) Sensitivity Test
(c) Brute-Force Attack Analysis
(d) Randomness Test
(e) Encryption & Decryption time analysis.

5.1. Statistical Analysis

Intruders or hackers use the statistical analysis to decrypt and analyze the cipher text. So, any cipher text should be robust against any statistical attacks. To prove the robustness of our proposed scheme, we have derived the autocorrelation analysis and avalanche effect analysis.

Autocorrelation Analysis: Autocorrelation or serial correlation tests (Ghazi & Ali, 2018; Sreelaja & Pai, 2009; Suresh et al., 2022) describe the correlation amongst numbers and compare with the pattern correlation to the expected correlation of zero. It is also described because the correlation of a signal and with its not on time copy as a characteristic of delay. The evaluation of autocorrelation is used for locating repeating styles.

In statistics, the autocorrelation or serial correlation of a random manner is the Pearson correlation among values of the system at different instances. The mathematical formulation for Pearson correlation system is given beneath.

$$\mathrm{r} = \frac{\sum_{i=1}^{N}(x_i - \bar{x})(y_i - \bar{y})}{\sqrt{\sum_{i=1}^{N}(x_i - \bar{x})^2}\sqrt{\sum_{i=1}^{N}(y_i - \bar{y})^2}} \tag{6}$$

For autocorrelation, this coefficient is computed between the time collection and the identical time series lagged by means of a detailed range of periods. Here, only a graphical representation is given for our technique. Fig. 4.4 represents the autocorrelation analysis on the computed value of the proposed technique.

5.2. Key Sensitivity Analysis

Key sensitivity or avalanche effect means a single bit change in the secret key produces a completely different cipher text. The following result shows how our

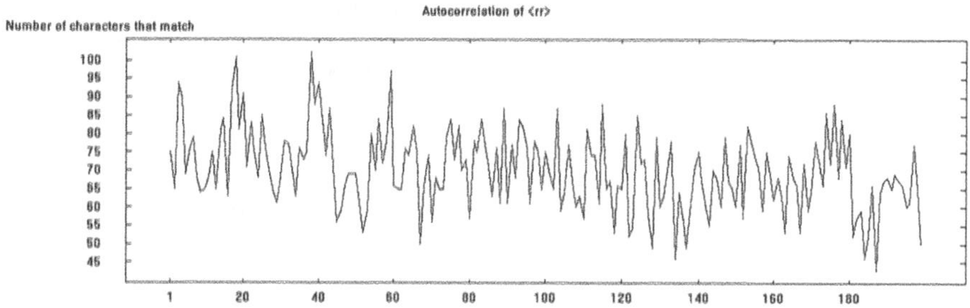

Fig. 4.4. Autocorrelation Analysis.

proposed encryption technique is sensitive with respect to the secret key. The avalanche effect is shown below only for the changed secret key and with a fixed secret key. Table 4.7 and Fig. 4.5 show the total scenario.

Table 4.7. Avalanche Effect: Change in Secret Key.

Key	ASCII Difference	Total Number of Added Characters	Total Number of Deleted Characters	Total Number of Changed Characters
cryptrnn@12345	0	3,525	3,541	2,542
cyyptann@12345	9	3,716	3,715	2,364
cryptBnn@12345	10	3,863	3,835	2,273
cryptann@1234**6**	98	3,927	3,876	2,218
cryptann**#**12345	32	3,615	3,613	2,453
cry**s**trnn@12345	71	4,264	4,248	1,892
cryptrnn@1234**z**	11	3,793	3,766	2,325
cryptrnn@12**4**45	122	3,866	3,844	2,245
cryptrnn@**0**2345	6	4,118	4,062	2,054
Aryptrnn@12345	69	4,084	4,079	2,041

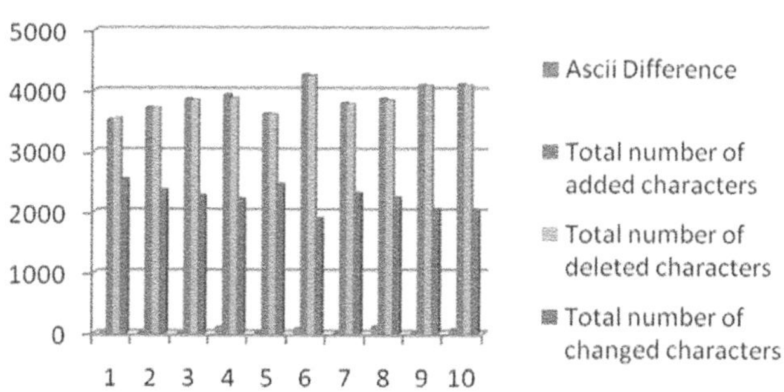

Fig. 4.5. Graphical Representation of Table 4.7.

Table 4.8. Relation Between Random Value and Bit Flip.

r-Value	Bit Flip in Cipher Text
2	131
4	146
3	131
5	123
3	202
7	149
9	218
11	175
9	134
16	107

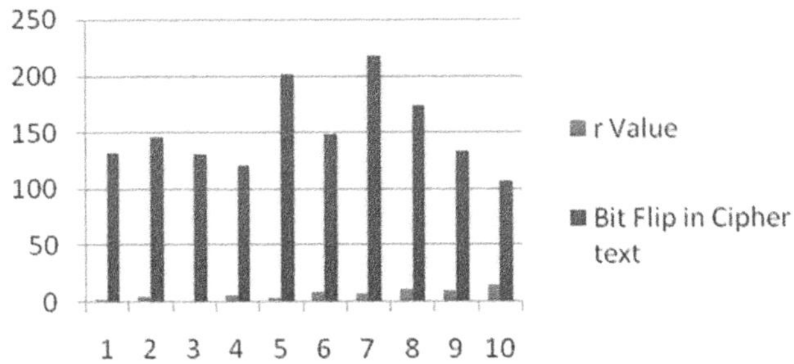

Fig. 4.6. Graphical Representation of Table 4.8.

Observation: We have shown the results of some attempts to decrypt an encrypted file with slightly different secret keys than the one used for the encryption of the original file. Table 4.4 shows the added characters, deleted characters, and changed characters with a slight change (one byte or two bytes) in secret key and Fig. 4.5 also shows the increasing and decreasing performance among added characters, deleted characters, and changed characters for one byte change in the key. It is clear that the decryption with a slightly different key fails completely, and hence the proposed encryption procedure is highly key sensitive.

Table 4.8 and Fig. 4.6 show the relation between the random value (a_1) in key generation and bit flip in plain text. This scenario shows that it is very hard to retrieve the key or predict key for intruders.

5.3. Security Analysis

Brute-Force Attack:

The large key space makes the brute-force attack (Bhowmik et al., 2020) impossible. Here, the attacker tries to translate the cipher text into plain text using every possible key with different combinations.

On average, half of all possible keys are enough for achieving success. Algorithms are known to all in most networking systems but a brute-force attack will be impossible if the algorithm uses a large key space.

If an eavesdropper properly assumes the inputs (public parameters) of the RNN structure, then it can act as a genuine participant. But it is very difficult for an eavesdropper to get access to the symmetric key and inputs.

5.4. Randomness Test of Keys

Randomness means all elements of the sequence are generated independently of each other, and the value of the next element in the sequence cannot be predicted. To prove the randomness of our secret key, we have done the following experiments.

(I) Frequency Test:

The frequency (or frequency inside a block) test (Karl, 2008; Rutti, 2004; Sheskin, 1997) is used to test the randomness of a sequence of zeros and ones. The test is based totally on the percentage of 0's and $1's$. Actually, it assesses the closeness of share of 1's to 0. The frequency within a block takes a look at is a refinement that examines the percentage of $1's$ within M-value block. The mathematical information is given below.

$$T_1 = \frac{(M0 - M1)^2}{M}$$

where $M0$: number of 0's in the key stream. $M1$: number of 1's in the key stream. M: total size of key stream. Table 4.9 and Fig. 4.7 show the results of the frequency test.

(II) Serial Test:

The serial test (Rutti, 2004; Wang et al., 2021) and chi-rectangular test (Sheskin, 1997; Wang et al., 2021) are comparable on frequency. The distinction is that the chi-square relative frequency takes a look at examines whether or not or no longer positive or negative values are consistent with a uniform distribution and the serial take a look at examines whether or not sequential and non-overlapping pairs of random numbers have a uniform distribution. This test focuses on frequency

Table 4.9. Results of the Frequency Test.

Key Size (Bits)	Test Results of Our Technique	Frequency Test on PRNG()
56	4596.257	4471.769
64	4525.146	4412.450
128	4661.585	4435.610
192	4619.969	4571.656
256	4633.421	4622.351
328	4722.320	4724.356

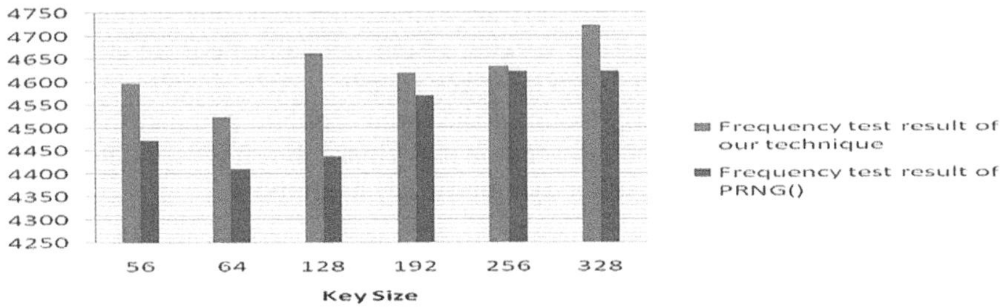

Fig. 4.7. Graphical Representation of Table 4.9.

distribution of pairs of samples. The random numbers are grouped right into a quite small quantity of businesses by using the usage of serial test.

The random numbers from the generator are mapped right into a quite small number of remarkable integer values from 10 to 181 by means of way of the modulo feature (Behnia et al., 2008). With those numbers of distinct values, the huge range of agencies additionally is affordable, from one hundred to 32,761. A chi-square test checks whether different pairs are similarly possible values. Table 4.10 and Fig. 4.8 show the serial test results and their graphical representation. The mathematical formulation is given below.

$$T_2 = \frac{4}{M-1}((M00)^2 + (M01)^2 + (M10)^2 + (M11)^2) - \frac{2}{M}((M0)^2 + (M1)^2) + 1$$

Table 4.10. Serial Test Results.

Key Size (Bits)	Serial Test of Our Scheme	Test on Key by prng()
56	4.0014	4.0636
64	4.1128	4.0973
128	4.1865	4.1843
192	4.2043	4.1992
256	5.0001	5.0173
328	5.1911	5.2201

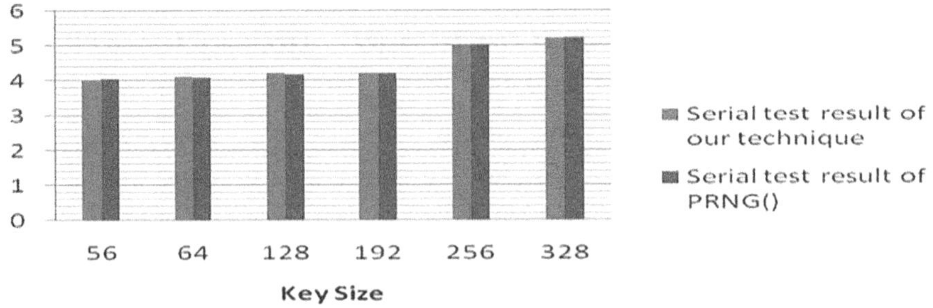

Fig. 4.8. Graphical Representation of Table 4.10.

where $M00$: number of $00's$ in the key stream. $M11$: Number of $11's$ in the key stream. $M01$: Number of $01's$ in the key stream. $M10$: Number of $10's$ in the key stream. M: Total size of key stream.

(III) Poker Test:

Poker test (Abd-El-Hafiz et. al., 2015; Ghazi & Ali, 2018; Karl, 2008) treats numbers grouped together as a poker's hand. Then the arms received are compared to what's anticipated the use of the chi-square take a look at. Given a series of n random numbers to be examined, it is proven that there may be a restriction based on n as to how large the value of ok can be. Table 4.11 and Fig. 4.9 show the results of the poker test and its graphical representation. In most cases, the poker test with extraordinary values of ok is applied to ensure that the underlying sequence is without a doubt random (Karakaya et al., 2017). The mathematical formula is given below.

$$T_4 = \frac{2^N}{\text{P}}\left(\sum_{j=1}^{2^N} M_j^2\right) - P \text{ where } M_j \text{ :number of appearance of the } j^{th} \text{ of length}$$

$$N.P = \frac{M}{N} \geq (5 * 2^N)$$

Table 4.11. Poker Test Result.

Key Size (Bits)	Results of Our Technique	Result of PRNG()
56	9.0233	9.0653
64	9.1245	10.0979
128	9.2443	10.1844
192	9.2565	10.1998
256	10.1077	11.7088
328	11.1176	11.7282

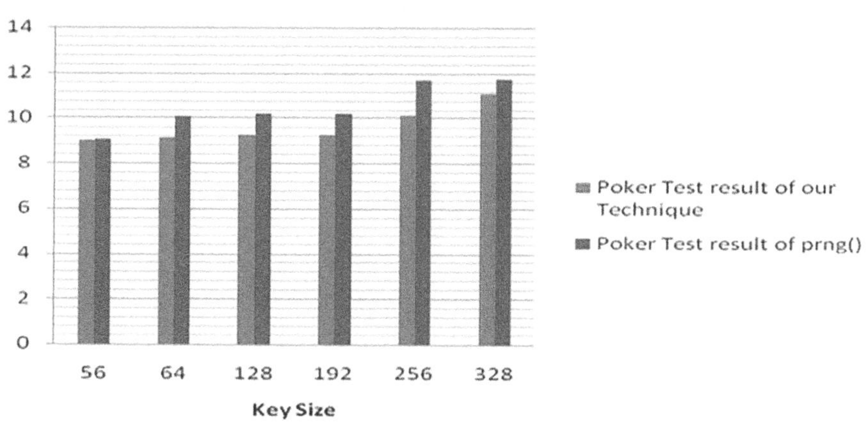

Fig. 4.9. Graphical Representation of Table 4.11.

Observations: Our technique generates an encryption key for a cryptographic application. So, according to the laws of cryptography, the key must be secure and robust. The randomness is a property by which we can impose both these properties. In our technique, we have proposed three modules, such as RNN, metaheuristics approach, and genetic operator for giving a high level of randomness and robustness in the generated key. We have proceeded with the important thing through five benchmark statistical tactics to check the randomness of the key. Each statistical test suggests whether or not the sequence is probably to a random collection or no longer. The end of every check is not exact, but as a substitute probabilistic. But our technique has passed most of the statistical tests. As a result, our proposed scheme generates a good key stream.

5.5. Comparative Study on Encryption and Decryption Time

Table 4.12 and Fig. 4.10 show the comparative analysis of encryption and decryption time among existing techniques and our proposed technique.

Table 4.12. Comparative Analysis on Encryption & Decryption Time.

	Tech.-1 (Behnia et al., 2008)	**Tech.-2 (Amin et al., 2006)**	**Tech.-3 (Ghazi & Ali, 2018)**	**Tech.-4 (Sreelaja & Pai, 2008)**	**Tech.-5 (Sreelaja & Pai, 2009)**	**Tech.-6 (Ali, 2018)**	**Proposed Tech.**
Key Generation Time (msec.)	1.102	1.023	0.975	1.14	1.401	0.998	1.011
Encryption Time (msec.)	2.202	2.158	2.235	2.126	2.106	2.203	2.134
Decryption Time (msec.)	2.203	2.157	2.236	2.125	2.107	2.204	2.136

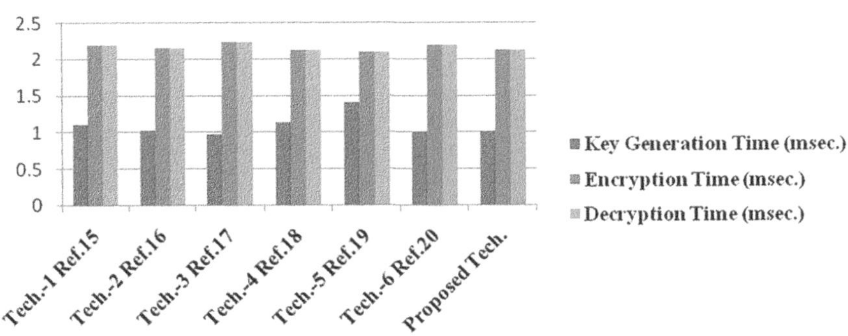

Fig. 4.10. Graphical Representation of Table 4.12.

6. Conclusion

The main goal of military communication is to improve and achieve a high-level cyber security. The study also made clear that there is no universally accepted definition of cyber security. Here, we have proposed a designed of a cryptosystem for data security in the defence sector. A robust cryptosystem is the backbone of cyber security. Although different types of cryptosystems exist, here we have emphasized on soft computing-based cryptosystem. Our proposed system encapsulated with a secured key generation process, secured key wrapping process, and encryption–decryption method. The use of RNN & GA for the key generation process is a novel approach and metaheuristics approach also provides extra flavour as well as robustness in our technique. All the statistical test results are presented in tabular form with a graphical diagram, and this proves that our scheme satisfies different benchmark statistical tests successfully.

Conflict of Interest

The authors declare that there is no conflict of interest.

References

Abd-El-Hafiz, S. K., Radwan, A. G., & AbdEl-Haleem, S. H. (2015). Encryption applications of a generalized chaotic map. *Applied Mathematics & Information Sciences*, *9*(6), 3215–3233.

Agarwal, N., & Agarwal, P. (2013). Use of artificial neural network in the field of security. *MIT International Journal of Computer Science & Information Technology*, *3*(1), 42–44.

Ali, R. A. (2018). Random number generator based on hybrid algorithm between particle swarm optimization (PSO) algorithms and 3D-chaotic system and its application. *Iraqi Journal of Information Technology.*, *8*(3), 1–20.

Alsafasfeh, Q. H., & Arfoa, A. A. (2011). Image encryption based on the general approach for multiple chaotic systems. *Journal of Signal and Information Processing*, *2*(3), 238–244.

Amin, S. T., Saeb, M., & El-Gindi, S. (2006). A DNA-based implementation of YAEA encryption algorithm. *Computational Intelligence*, *16*, 120–125.

Behnia, S., Akhshani, A., Mafmodi, H., & Akhavan, A. (2008). A novel algorithm for image encryption based on mixture of chaotic maps. *Chaos, Solitons & Fractals*, *35*(2), 408–419.

Bhowmik, A., Karforma, S., Dey, J., & Sarkar, A. (2020). Approximation algorithm and linear congruence: A state-of-art approach in information security issues towards internet of vehicles. In *Internet of vehicles and its applications in autonomous driving* (pp. 149–172). Springe.

Chakravorty, J. G., & Ghosh, P. R. (2006). *Advanced higher algebra*. U.N. Dhur and Sons Private Ltd. ISBN978-3-80673-67-7.

Das, A., & Veni Madhavan, C. E. (2004). *Public-key cryptography: Theory and practice*. Pearson Education.

Ghazi, A. A., & Ali, F. H. (2018). Robust and efficient dynamic stream cipher cryptosystem. *Iraqi Journal of Science*, *59*(2C), 1105–1114.

Haykin, S. (2004). *Neural network – A comprehensive foundation* (2nd ed.). Prentice-Hall.

Kahate, A. (2008). *Cryptography and network security*. Tata McGraw-Hill.

Karakaya, B., Celik, V., & Gulten, A. (2017). Chaotic cellular neural network-based true random number generator. *International Journal of Circuit Theory and Applications*, *45*(11), 1885–1897.

Keshav, & Yadav, A. K. (2026). A novel replace with: two-dimensional Logistic–Chebyshev–Sine hybrid chaotic map for secure color image encryption. *Multimedia Tools and Applications*, *85*(2), 92.

Raza, H., Singh, A., Erdenetsogt, T., Kabeer, M. M., Aslam, M. S., & Farooq, M. (2026). Machine Learning Driven Decision Making in the Modern Data Era. PERFECT: *Journal of Smart Algorithms*, *3*(1), 11–22.

Velásquez-Mejía, L., Vidal-Limon, A., Flores-Vargas, G., Ruiz-May, E., Scavone, P., de la Fuente-Nunez, C., & Zamora-Briseño, J. A. (2026). *Reviewing the Artificial Intelligence Boost for Accelerating the Development of Novel Antimicrobial Peptides.* Journal of Applied Microbiology, lxag036.

Weng, Y., Wu, J., Kelly, T., & Johnson, W. (2024). *Comprehensive overview of artificial intelligence applications in modern industries.* arXiv preprint arXiv:2409.13059.

Chapter 5

Quantum Computing and IoT: Transforming Cybersecurity in the Defence Sector

Mohd Nadeem[a], Suhel Ahmad Khan[b], Alka Agrawal[c] and Raees Ahamd Khan[c]

[a]*Department of Computer Science and Engineering, Shri Ramswaroop Memorial University, India*
[b]*Department of Computer Science, Indira Gandhi National Tribal University, India*
[c]*Department of Information Technology, Babasaheb Bhimrao Ambedkar University, India*

Abstract

The rapid advancement of digital technologies, particularly the Internet of Things (IoT) and quantum computing (QC), is reshaping modern military operations by enhancing real-time data collection, autonomous decision-making, and situational awareness. IoT-enabled systems, such as UAVs, battlefield sensors, and smart logistics, provide military forces with operational superiority but also introduce significant cybersecurity risks, including espionage, cyber sabotage, and unauthorized access. The emergence of QC further complicates this landscape, as quantum algorithms can break traditional encryption protocols, threatening the security of military communications and IoT infrastructure. However, quantum technologies also offer revolutionary cybersecurity solutions, such as Quantum Key Distribution (QKD) and Post-Quantum Cryptography (PQC), which leverage the principles of quantum mechanics to ensure secure communication. Despite these advancements, challenges such as the technological maturity of quantum solutions, high implementation costs, and global competition in quantum research pose obstacles to widespread military adoption. This chapter explores the interplay between QC and military

The Internet of Things in the Defence Industry:
Challenges and Solutions for Military Security, 107–134

Published under exclusive licence by Emerald Publishing Limited
doi:10.1108/978-1-83549-198-020261005

IoT security, addressing both the vulnerabilities of IoT systems and the potential of quantum-enhanced security frameworks. By integrating quantum-safe cryptographic techniques, defence organizations can fortify military IoT infrastructure, mitigate cyber threats, and maintain strategic superiority in an era of increasing digital warfare.

Keywords: Military IoT security; quantum computing; cybersecurity threats; quantum cryptography; post-quantum cryptography (PQC)

1. Introduction

The rapid advancement of digital technologies has ushered in a new era of connectivity and automation, with the IoT and QC at the forefront of this transformation. Among the many sectors experiencing this technological revolution, the defence industry stands out as one of the most critical areas of application. The integration of IoT into military operations has led to the development of smart battlefields, where real-time data collection, autonomous decision-making, and enhanced situational awareness significantly improve strategic and tactical operations. The deployment of IoT-enabled devices, including unmanned aerial vehicles (UAVs), remote surveillance networks, battlefield sensor grids, smart logistics, and weaponized IoT systems, has transformed modern warfare by providing military forces with greater efficiency, precision, and operational superiority (Ochoa & Vazquez, 2020). However, this growing reliance on interconnected networks has also introduced substantial cybersecurity challenges, making military IoT infrastructure vulnerable to sophisticated cyber threats.

One of the most pressing concerns in military IoT security is the exploitation of vulnerabilities by adversaries. Given the complexity and widespread connectivity of IoT devices, data breaches, unauthorized access, espionage, and cyber sabotage have emerged as major threats to national security (Khan & Khan, 2025). Adversarial entities, including state-sponsored hackers and terrorist groups, can exploit security loopholes to disrupt critical defence operations, manipulate military intelligence, or gain unauthorized control over IoT-enabled military assets. Moreover, traditional security measures, such as public-key cryptography, which have long been used to protect sensitive military communications and data transmissions, are increasingly proving to be inadequate against evolving cyber threats. This issue is further exacerbated by the emergence of QC, which has the potential to break conventional encryption protocols, rendering current cybersecurity defences obsolete (Luo & Xu, 2022).

QC, with its ability to perform complex calculations at an exponentially faster rate than classical computers, presents a double-edged sword for the defence sector. On one hand, quantum algorithms such as Shor's algorithm can easily crack widely used encryption standards, including RSA and Elliptic Curve Cryptography (ECC), posing a significant risk to military data security. On the other hand,

QC also offers a groundbreaking solution to cybersecurity challenges through the development of quantum cryptography. Unlike classical cryptographic methods, which rely on computational complexity, quantum cryptography is based on the fundamental principles of quantum mechanics, making it inherently secure against eavesdropping and cyberattacks. Technologies such as QKD ensure that encryption keys remain secure, as any attempt to intercept or tamper with quantum-encoded information leads to its immediate detection. This characteristic makes quantum cryptography a highly promising solution for securing classified military communications, IoT-based sensor networks, and autonomous defence systems (Turk et al., 2025).

Despite the promising advantages of quantum-enhanced cybersecurity, the integration of quantum technologies into military IoT infrastructure presents numerous challenges. One of the primary obstacles is the technological maturity and scalability of QC and quantum cryptography. While significant progress has been made in research and development, practical implementation remains limited due to hardware constraints, high costs, and the need for specialized quantum communication infrastructure (Sanborn, 2021). Furthermore, ensuring the compatibility of quantum-safe security solutions with existing military networks requires extensive modifications to defence communication systems, which could be both time-consuming and resource-intensive. Another major challenge is the global race towards quantum supremacy, where multiple nations are investing heavily in quantum research, raising concerns about the potential weaponization of quantum technology in cyber warfare. If adversarial nations achieve quantum superiority first, they could undermine the cybersecurity of defence infrastructures worldwide, leading to severe geopolitical consequences (Radanliev, 2024).

In this chapter, we will explore the intersection of QC and IoT security in the defence sector, examining how emerging quantum technologies can enhance the protection of military IoT infrastructure. We will begin by identifying the key threats and vulnerabilities associated with IoT deployment in military environments, followed by an overview of the fundamental principles of QC and its implications for cybersecurity. The chapter will then delve into the integration of quantum security measures, such as QKD and PQC, into IoT-based defence networks. Additionally, we will analyze the challenges and limitations of implementing quantum-enhanced security solutions in real-world military operations. Lastly, we will discuss future prospects and research directions, highlighting ongoing efforts to develop quantum-resistant cybersecurity frameworks that can safeguard military assets in the era of QC (Akhai & Kumar, 2024).

As global defence organizations prepare for the quantum age, it is imperative to adopt a proactive approach in developing robust, quantum-resistant security architectures. By integrating advanced quantum-safe cryptographic techniques into military IoT infrastructure, defence agencies can mitigate cybersecurity risks, enhance operational resilience, and maintain a strategic advantage in an increasingly digitized and interconnected battlefield. The future of military cybersecurity will depend on the ability to harness quantum innovations while simultaneously developing countermeasures against quantum-powered cyber threats.

2. Understanding the Cybersecurity Landscape in Defence

The digital transformation of military operations has significantly enhanced the effectiveness of defense strategies, but it has also introduced a complex cybersecurity landscape that demands attention. As defense systems increasingly rely on interconnected networks, cloud computing, artificial intelligence (AI), and the IoT, the risk of cyber threats has escalated. Cybersecurity in defense is no longer limited to protecting computer networks; it now encompasses safeguarding critical infrastructure, intelligence systems, and battlefield operations from cyberattacks, espionage, and data breaches. Adversaries, ranging from state-sponsored hackers to terrorist organizations, continuously exploit vulnerabilities to disrupt military operations and compromise national security (Paul et al., 2025).

To ensure military resilience, a comprehensive understanding of cybersecurity threats and vulnerabilities is essential. Among these, IoT systems present a unique set of security challenges due to their widespread use in modern defense applications. Addressing these vulnerabilities and implementing robust cybersecurity measures is crucial to safeguarding military assets, securing communications, and ensuring the integrity of operations (Khatoon & Riaz, 2025).

2.1. Key Threats and Vulnerabilities in IoT Systems

IoT technology has revolutionized military operations by providing real-time data analytics, enhanced surveillance, and improved decision-making capabilities. However, the interconnected nature of IoT devices in defense applications also introduces numerous security risks. These risks stem from unauthorized access, cyberattacks, and system vulnerabilities that adversaries can exploit to disrupt military operations or gain strategic advantages (Khan & Khan, 2025; Luo & Xu, 2022; Sanborn, 2021; Turk et al., 2025).

2.1.1. Unauthorized Access and Data Breaches

IoT systems used in military environments generate vast amounts of sensitive data, including troop movements, surveillance footage, and intelligence reports. If these systems are not adequately secured, they become prime targets for unauthorized access and data breaches. Weak authentication mechanisms and poorly configured security settings allow adversaries to infiltrate IoT networks, potentially leading to stolen military intelligence or manipulated information. The consequences of such breaches can be severe, including the compromise of national security and the exposure of classified information to hostile entities.

2.1.2. Distributed Denial-of-Service Attacks

One of the most significant threats to military IoT infrastructure is the potential for Distributed Denial-of-Service (DDoS) attacks. In these attacks, compromised IoT devices are exploited to flood military networks with excessive traffic, rendering communication systems and command centres inoperable. The ability to disrupt these critical systems during wartime or covert operations can severely impact military effectiveness. The 2016 Mirai botnet attack demonstrated how unsecured IoT devices could be weaponized, and similar attacks targeting military infrastructure could have catastrophic consequences (Zangana, 2025).

2.1.3. *Malware and Ransomware Infections*

Many IoT devices operate on outdated or unpatched firmware, making them susceptible to malware and ransomware infections. Adversaries can deploy malicious software to compromise military IoT networks, potentially locking out users, disabling critical operations, or demanding ransom payments (Santiago, 2023). Ransomware attacks on defense systems could result in the loss of control over surveillance equipment, weapons systems, or logistical databases, thereby jeopardizing military operations.

2.1.4. *Supply Chain Vulnerabilities*

The security of IoT systems extends beyond direct military networks to include the supply chains that produce and maintain these devices. Many military IoT components are manufactured by third-party vendors, which increases the risk of tampered hardware, embedded malware, or unauthorized access points (Santiago, 2023; Zangana, 2025). If adversaries compromise the supply chain, they can introduce vulnerabilities that remain undetected until activated during critical missions. Strengthening supply chain security through rigorous vetting, encryption, and continuous monitoring is essential to mitigating these risks.

2.1.5. *Man-in-the-Middle Attacks*

Wireless communications between IoT devices in defense applications are particularly susceptible to Man-in-the-Middle (MitM) attacks. In such attacks, adversaries intercept and manipulate data transmissions, allowing them to alter or eavesdrop on sensitive information. If an attacker gains control over communication links between drones, command centres, or battlefield units, they can misdirect military forces or compromise real-time decision-making. Implementing end-to-end encryption and secure authentication protocols is vital to countering this threat (Zangana, 2025).

2.1.6. *Insider Threats*

The human element remains one of the most significant vulnerabilities in any cybersecurity framework. Insider threats in military IoT environments can arise from personnel who intentionally or inadvertently compromise security. Whether due to negligence, coercion, or malicious intent, insiders can provide adversaries with access to IoT networks, disable security features, or leak classified data. Regular cybersecurity training, strict access controls, and behavioural monitoring can help mitigate the risks associated with insider threats (Gopireddy, 2024).

2.1.7. Lack of Standardized Security Protocols

Despite the growing reliance on IoT technology in defense applications, there is a lack of universal security standards governing these systems. Many IoT devices have limited processing power, making it difficult to implement robust encryption and intrusion detection mechanisms. Additionally, inconsistencies in security protocols across different military units and allied forces can create gaps that adversaries may exploit. Developing and enforcing standardized cybersecurity frameworks for IoT in military operations is critical to ensuring consistent and reliable protection (Rastogi et al., 2024).

2.2. The Role of Cybersecurity in Military Defence

As cyber threats continue to evolve, the role of cybersecurity in military defense has become increasingly vital. Cybersecurity ensures the protection of critical infrastructure, enhances operational resilience, and safeguards national security against adversarial attacks. Military organizations worldwide are integrating advanced cybersecurity measures to counter cyber warfare strategies, secure communication networks, and prevent unauthorized access to sensitive data (Gopireddy, 2024; Santiago, 2023).

2.2.1. Protecting Critical Infrastructure and Military Networks

Military operations depend on a vast network of interconnected systems, including command centres, surveillance platforms, radar installations, and weapons control systems. These infrastructures are prime targets for cyberattacks, which can disrupt operations or provide adversaries with valuable intelligence (Baseri et al., 2024). Implementing robust cybersecurity measures, such as firewalls, intrusion detection systems, and secure cloud storage, helps prevent unauthorized access and ensure operational continuity.

2.2.2. Enhancing Threat Intelligence and Cyber Warfare Capabilities

Threat intelligence plays a crucial role in modern military cybersecurity strategies. Cyber defense units continuously monitor emerging threats, analyze cyberattack patterns, and develop countermeasures to mitigate risks. AI and machine learning algorithms are increasingly used to detect anomalies in network behaviour, predict potential cyber threats, and automate threat response mechanisms. Proactive threat intelligence enables military forces to anticipate and neutralize cyber threats before they escalate into full-scale attacks (Rastogi et al., 2024).

2.2.3. Securing Military IoT and Cloud-Based Systems

As military operations rely more on cloud-based services and IoT ecosystems, securing these digital environments is paramount. Zero-trust security models, which enforce strict authentication and access control policies, are being adopted to protect sensitive military data. Strong encryption protocols, blockchain-based data verification, and multi-factor authentication (MFA) further enhance the security of cloud-based and IoT-integrated military systems (Gopireddy, 2024).

2.2.4. Cyber Resilience and Incident Response Strategies

Cyber resilience is a fundamental aspect of modern military cybersecurity planning. Defense organizations establish comprehensive incident response plans to ensure rapid recovery from cyberattacks. Simulated cyber drills and war games help assess military preparedness, allowing cybersecurity teams to refine their response strategies (Khan et al., 2024). By fostering resilience, military forces can maintain operational effectiveness even in the face of cyber disruptions.

2.2.5. Cybersecurity Training and Awareness

A well-trained workforce is essential for maintaining cybersecurity in defense environments. Regular training programs educate military personnel on best cybersecurity practices, ensuring that they recognize and mitigate potential threats. Ethical hacking exercises and penetration testing further identify vulnerabilities in military networks before adversaries can exploit them (Thirupathi et al., 2025).

3. QC Fundamentals

To understand how QC can revolutionize cybersecurity in defence IoT systems, it is essential to first grasp the fundamental principles behind this technology. QC offers a paradigm shift in computational power by leveraging the principles of quantum mechanics, which fundamentally differ from classical computing methodologies.

3.1. Basic Principles of QC

QC is based on the principles of quantum mechanics, which govern the behaviour of particles at the subatomic level (Bellante et al., 2025). The key principles that distinguish QC from classical computing are as follows.

3.1.1. Superposition

Superposition is the ability of quantum bits (qubits) to exist in multiple states simultaneously. Unlike classical bits, which can be either 0 or 1, a qubit can be in a state of 0, 1, or both at the same time. This property enables quantum computers to process vast amounts of data in parallel, exponentially increasing computational efficiency. For example, while a classical computer must evaluate each possible solution one by one, a quantum computer can evaluate multiple solutions at once, drastically reducing computation time for complex problems.

3.1.2. Entanglement

Entanglement is a quantum phenomenon where two or more qubits become correlated in such a way that the state of one qubit instantly influences the state of the other, regardless of the distance between them. This property enables quantum computers to perform highly coordinated calculations and enables secure communication methods, such as QKD, which is critical for defence cybersecurity (Baseri et al., 2024; Gopireddy, 2024; Rastogi et al., 2024). Entanglement allows quantum processors to transmit information instantaneously, making them highly efficient for parallel processing and secure data exchange across military networks.

3.1.3. Quantum Interference

Quantum interference refers to the way quantum states interact with each other when a measurement is performed. By carefully controlling quantum interference, quantum algorithms can enhance the probability of correct answers while reducing incorrect solutions. This property plays a crucial role in quantum error correction and quantum algorithms like Shor's algorithm (used for breaking cryptographic systems) and Grover's algorithm (used for searching large databases efficiently). These three principles together form the foundation of QC and differentiate it from classical computing, enabling it to solve certain problems exponentially faster (Rastogi et al., 2024).

3.2. Comparison Between Classical Computing and QC

Table 5.1 shows the comparison between classical computing and QC according to their features. While classical computers are highly efficient for general-purpose computing, they struggle with problems requiring massive parallel processing, such as:

Table 5.1. Comparative Analysis of Classical Computing and QC.

S. No.	Feature	Classical Computing	QC
1	Data Representation	Uses binary bits (0 or 1)	Uses qubits (superposition of 0 and 1)
2	Processing	Sequential (one calculation at a time)	Parallel (multiple calculations at once)
3	Computation Speed	Limited for complex problems	Exponential speedup for certain problems
4	Encryption Impact	Uses traditional cryptographic methods (e.g. RSA, ECC)	Capable of breaking classical encryption, but also enables quantum cryptography
5	Applications	General computing, databases, and traditional cybersecurity	Cryptanalysis, optimization, simulations, and secure communications

- Breaking cryptographic keys (RSA-2048 encryption can take thousands of years for a classical computer, but a quantum computer could break it in minutes).
- Complex simulations in defence applications, such as battlefield strategies or nuclear reaction modelling.
- Optimization of large-scale defence networks, enhancing response time and resource allocation.

QC, with its ability to process multiple solutions simultaneously, offers a revolutionary approach to solving these challenges.

3.3. Quantum Supremacy: Opportunities for Cybersecurity

Quantum supremacy is the stage where a quantum computer can outperform the most powerful classical supercomputers for specific computational tasks. Google's announcement of quantum supremacy in 2019, where its quantum processor completed a task in 200 seconds that would take the world's best supercomputer 10,000 years, marked a significant milestone in this domain. The implications of quantum supremacy for cybersecurity are profound, particularly in the defence IoT landscape, where data security is paramount (Khan et al., 2024; Thirupathi et al., 2025).

3.3.1. Challenges Posed by QC to Cybersecurity

a. Breaking Classical Encryption

- Most military and defence networks currently rely on public-key cryptographic algorithms like RSA (Rivest-Shamir-Adleman) and ECC for secure communication.
- Quantum computers can easily break these encryption methods using Shor's algorithm, which efficiently factors large prime numbers.
- This means that once large-scale quantum computers become accessible, existing defence encryption standards will be obsolete, exposing military IoT systems to data breaches and cyber espionage.

b. Threats to Secure Communication

- Secure communication methods such as VPNs (Virtual Private Networks), SSL/TLS encryption, and blockchain security will be compromised if adversaries develop quantum decryption capabilities.
- Quantum-enabled adversaries could intercept encrypted military messages and decode them instantaneously (Bellante et al., 2025).

3.3.2. Opportunities: Quantum-Resistant Cybersecurity

Despite these threats, QC also provides new opportunities for enhancing cybersecurity in defence IoT systems.

a. Quantum-Resistant Cryptography

- Researchers are developing PQC algorithms that are resistant to quantum attacks.
- Lattice-based cryptography, hash-based cryptography, and code-based cryptographic methods are being explored as potential solutions to secure military networks against quantum threats.

b. QKD

- QKD leverages quantum mechanics to create an unbreakable encryption protocol.
- Unlike traditional encryption, which depends on computational complexity, QKD ensures security by detecting any interception attempts (Rastogi et al., 2024).
- The BB84 protocol is one such QKD method that enables tamper-proof defence communications.

c. Quantum Random Number Generators (QRNGs)

- Traditional random number generators (RNGs) used for cryptographic keys rely on deterministic algorithms, making them potentially predictable.
- QRNGs leverage quantum mechanics to generate truly random numbers, ensuring highly secure encryption keys that cannot be easily deciphered.

d. Secure Military IoT Networks

- Quantum algorithms can be integrated into AI-driven cybersecurity models for real-time threat detection and mitigation in defence IoT ecosystems.
- Quantum-enhanced intrusion detection systems (IDS) can analyze vast datasets in real-time, identifying cyber threats before they materialize (Çakal & Özdemir, 2024).

4. Integration of QC with IoT

The integration of QC with the IoT represents one of the most promising frontiers in the evolution of digital technologies. Both QC and IoT are individually transformative, but their combination has the potential to redefine how we secure, analyze, and process data in real-time, especially within critical sectors such as defence, healthcare, smart cities, and manufacturing.

This chapter delves into the synergies between QC and IoT, highlighting how QC can enhance IoT systems in terms of security, data processing capabilities, and overall efficiency. It also explores the challenges and opportunities that arise from integrating these technologies, especially in complex environments like defence and military applications.

4.1. The Role of QC in Enhancing IoT Systems

4.1.1. Quantum-Enhanced Data Processing

At the core of IoT systems is the need to process and analyze massive amounts of data generated by billions of connected devices (Çakal & Özdemir, 2024; Qadri et al., 2024). While traditional computing struggles to handle this volume of data efficiently, QC can provide new computational paradigms that significantly enhance data processing capabilities.

- **Quantum Parallelism:** Quantum computers leverage the principles of superposition and entanglement, enabling them to process multiple possibilities simultaneously. This is in stark contrast to classical computing, which processes information sequentially. As a result, QC can dramatically improve the speed and efficiency of data analysis, especially for tasks like pattern recognition, optimization, and machine learning in IoT systems.
- **Optimization of IoT Networks:** Many IoT systems require real-time optimization, such as determining the best paths for data transmission in a network or optimizing energy usage in smart grids. Quantum algorithms, like Quantum Annealing, have the potential to solve complex optimization problems far more efficiently than classical algorithms, improving the performance and energy efficiency of IoT networks.
- **Real-Time Decision Making:** IoT systems, particularly those used in defence and military applications, often require real-time decision-making. QC can enhance real-time analytics and provide decision-makers with more accurate and faster insights, crucial for high-stakes environments such as autonomous vehicle navigation, military surveillance, or disaster response.

4.1.2. Quantum Cryptography for IoT Security

One of the most promising applications of QC for IoT is in the field of security. As IoT systems expand, the number of entry points for cyberattacks grows exponentially, making them increasingly vulnerable to traditional cyber threats (Qadri et al., 2024). QC, however, holds the potential to revolutionize encryption and data protection in IoT systems.

- **QKD:** One of the key components of quantum cryptography is QKD, which uses the principles of quantum mechanics to create a secret key that is secure from eavesdropping. QKD ensures that even if an adversary intercepts the key exchange, they will not be able to decrypt the communication because any attempt to measure the quantum states will disrupt them, making the interception detectable. In IoT applications, QKD can secure communications between sensors, actuators, and control systems.
- **Quantum-Resistant Cryptography (PQC):** Quantum computers have the potential to break existing encryption schemes like RSA and ECC, which are widely used in securing IoT communications. PQC algorithms are being developed to withstand quantum attacks. These algorithms will be essential for protecting IoT devices and networks once large-scale quantum computers become

operational. IoT devices, especially in sensitive applications like defence, healthcare, and finance, must be retrofitted or upgraded with PQC to ensure they remain secure against future quantum threats.

4.1.3. Quantum Random Number Generation

In traditional cryptographic systems, pseudo-random number generators (PRNGs) are used to create cryptographic keys. However, these PRNGs can be vulnerable to attacks if the algorithms behind them are discovered or if an attacker has access to significant computational resources. Quantum computers, on the other hand, can generate true random numbers based on quantum processes, which are inherently unpredictable.

- **QRNGs:** QRNGs leverage the inherent randomness of quantum mechanics to produce random numbers that are not subject to any algorithmic bias or predictability. This feature can be used in IoT systems to generate stronger cryptographic keys and ensure that sensitive data transmissions between IoT devices, such as in military communications or financial transactions, remain secure.
- **Applications in Secure IoT Devices:** Quantum random number generation can be embedded into IoT devices such as smart sensors, drones, and wearables, providing them with a robust foundation for cryptographic security (Bellante et al., 2025; Çakal & Özdemir, 2024). By using QRNGs, these devices can ensure that their communications and data storage remain resistant to future quantum-enabled decryption attempts.

4.2. Challenges and Opportunities in Quantum-IoT Integration

While the integration of QC with IoT offers substantial benefits, it also presents significant challenges that must be addressed to realize its full potential.

4.2.1. Technical Challenges

- **Quantum Hardware Limitations:** Current quantum computers are still in the early stages of development, with limitations such as qubit decoherence, error rates, and hardware stability. These issues must be resolved before large-scale quantum-IoT integration can be achieved (Pătraşcu, 2021).
- **Scalability and Deployment:** QC resources are currently expensive and limited in availability. Developing scalable quantum solutions for IoT networks remains a complex task.
- **Integration Complexity:** IoT networks are highly diverse, with various protocols, devices, and architectures. Ensuring seamless integration of QC with existing IoT infrastructure requires substantial research and development.

4.2.2. Opportunities and Future Directions

- **Advancements in Quantum Hardware:** As QC technology matures, advancements in quantum processors and qubit stability will make quantum-IoT integration more viable.

- **Hybrid Classical-Quantum Models:** In the near term, hybrid models that combine classical computing with quantum accelerators can be used to enhance IoT applications while overcoming current quantum hardware limitations.
- **Quantum AI for IoT:** The fusion of QC and AI can create powerful IoT analytics frameworks capable of detecting patterns and anomalies in real-time, benefiting fields like predictive maintenance, cybersecurity, and healthcare monitoring.
- **Quantum IoT for Defence and National Security:** Defence and military applications will benefit significantly from quantum-IoT integration, particularly in areas like secure battlefield communication, quantum radar systems, and cryptographic resilience against cyber warfare.

The integration of QC with IoT has the potential to revolutionize data security, processing efficiency, and decision-making capabilities across various industries. While challenges remain, ongoing advancements in quantum hardware, cryptographic techniques, and hybrid computing models will pave the way for a secure and efficient quantum-IoT ecosystem (Çakal & Özdemir, 2024). As organizations and governments invest in quantum research, the next decade will likely witness groundbreaking applications that redefine how IoT systems operate in our interconnected world.

4.3. Key Applications of QC in Defence IoT

The convergence of QC and the IoT in the defence sector is poised to revolutionize security, intelligence, and battlefield operations. QC's ability to process massive datasets exponentially faster than classical computers makes it a powerful tool for cybersecurity, autonomous systems, and real-time decision-making in defence applications (Bellante et al., 2025).

4.3.1. Quantum-Powered Defence Communications

Secure and reliable communication is a cornerstone of military operations. Given the increasing sophistication of cyber threats and the potential for quantum-powered adversaries to break classical encryption schemes, integrating quantum cryptographic techniques into defence IoT networks is crucial.

a. QKD for Military IoT Networks

QKD leverages quantum mechanics to enable secure encryption key exchange, making data transmission immune to interception. In military IoT, QKD can:

- Protect command-and-control (C2) systems from eavesdropping.
- Secure sensitive data from satellites, UAVs, and ground troops.
- Provide a future-proof encryption mechanism that remains secure against quantum-enabled cyberattacks.

b. Quantum-Enabled Satellite Communications

Military IoT networks span vast geographic regions, including remote battlefields, deep-sea environments, and space-based assets. Quantum satellites can facilitate ultra-secure communication by transmitting encryption keys via quantum states, ensuring that intercepted messages cannot be reconstructed (Bellante et al., 2025).

Key advantages include:

- Long-range secure communications for deployed forces.
- Enhanced network resilience against cyber warfare.
- Secure coordination between different military branches and allied nations.

4.3.2. Autonomous Military Systems and QC

Autonomous defence systems, including UAVs, robotic soldiers, and unmanned ground vehicles (UGVs), rely on IoT-enabled sensors and AI-driven algorithms to navigate and operate in complex environments. QC significantly enhances these systems by improving machine learning models, sensor data processing, and real-time optimization.

a. Quantum Machine Learning for Autonomous Defence Systems

QC can accelerate the training and inference of machine learning models, enabling autonomous military systems to:

- Recognize threats and respond in real time.
- Adapt to dynamic battlefield environments by processing vast amounts of sensor data.
- Perform predictive analytics for mission planning and risk assessment.

For example, a quantum-enhanced UAV fleet could process terrain data, identify enemy movements, and dynamically re-route to avoid threats while maintaining mission objectives.

b. Optimization of Logistics and Supply Chains

Military logistics is a highly complex domain requiring real-time optimization of supplies, personnel, and equipment. QC can solve logistical challenges by:

- Optimizing troop and resource deployment to maximize efficiency.
- Enhancing maintenance scheduling for defence IoT assets.
- Reducing operational costs and response time through better supply chain analytics.

Quantum-based algorithms, such as Quantum Annealing, can process multiple scenarios simultaneously, ensuring optimal decision-making in time-sensitive military operations.

4.3.3. Real-Time Threat Detection and Response

A robust threat detection and response mechanism is critical for modern military IoT networks. QC can enhance cyber threat analysis, physical security monitoring, and predictive intelligence, ensuring faster and more accurate response mechanisms (Rastogi et al., 2024).

a. Quantum-Enhanced Threat Detection

Military IoT networks collect massive amounts of data from drones, satellites, wearable sensors, and battlefield surveillance systems. QC can:

- Analyze encrypted threat intelligence much faster than classical computing.
- Detect cyber threats, enemy movements, and operational risks in real time.
- Predict future attack vectors using quantum-enhanced AI models.

By leveraging quantum machine learning, defence agencies can filter out false positives and focus on genuine threats, ensuring a more effective response strategy.

b. Dynamic Response and Decision Making

Decision-making in military operations is time-critical, requiring simultaneous analysis of multiple factors such as intelligence reports, logistics, and environmental conditions. Quantum-powered decision support systems can:

- Model multiple battlefield scenarios within seconds.
- Optimize mission strategies dynamically based on live updates.
- Enhance situational awareness for defence personnel.

For example, quantum algorithms could rapidly simulate counterattack strategies based on real-time battlefield intelligence, giving military commanders a tactical edge. QC is set to redefine defence IoT by providing unbreakable encryption, enhancing autonomous military systems, and improving real-time threat detection. As quantum technology matures, its integration with defence IoT will create next-generation military networks capable of resisting cyber threats, optimizing missions, and ensuring strategic superiority in modern warfare.

5. Quantum Cryptography in Defence Applications

Quantum cryptography is poised to revolutionize military cybersecurity by leveraging the principles of quantum mechanics to ensure unprecedented levels of data security. Traditional cryptographic methods, such as RSA and ECC, rely on mathematical problems that are computationally difficult to solve. However, with the advent of quantum computers, these encryption techniques will become increasingly vulnerable to attacks. Quantum cryptography offers a fundamental shift in securing military communication, intelligence operations, and defence networks by providing cryptographic methods that are theoretically unbreakable (Pătraşcu, 2021).

5.1. QKD for Secure Communication

One of the most well-known quantum cryptographic techniques is QKD, which allows two parties to securely exchange cryptographic keys. Unlike classical key distribution methods, which can be intercepted without detection, QKD is inherently secure due to the principles of quantum superposition and Heisenberg's Uncertainty Principle (Bellante et al., 2025; Thirupathi et al., 2025). In a QKD system, quantum states of photons (e.g. polarization states) are used to encode the cryptographic key. If an adversary attempts to eavesdrop on the key exchange, the quantum state collapses due to measurement, introducing detectable anomalies. This means that any intrusion can be identified, ensuring the security of military communications.

5.1.1. Advantages of QKD in Defence

- **Unbreakable Encryption:** QKD ensures that encryption keys cannot be intercepted or copied without detection.
- **Eavesdropping Detection:** Any attempt to listen in on the quantum transmission disturbs the system, alerting the communicating parties.
- **Long-Term Security:** Unlike classical cryptographic methods that may become obsolete with QC, QKD remains secure even against future computational advancements.

5.1.2. Challenges in Military QKD Deployment

- **Infrastructure Requirements:** QKD requires specialized optical fibre networks or satellite-based communication systems, which may be challenging to implement in remote or battlefield scenarios.
- **Limited Transmission Distance:** Ground-based QKD systems using fibre optics are currently limited to a few hundred kilometres due to signal loss, requiring quantum repeaters for long-distance communication.

Despite these challenges, ongoing research and advancements in satellite-based QKD networks are enabling practical implementations for global military communication.

5.2. PQC for IoT Devices

While QKD is ideal for high-security communications, its deployment in military IoT devices, such as UAVs, sensor networks, and battlefield communication systems, is still under development. These devices often have limited processing power and cannot yet support the complex infrastructure required for quantum communication (Çakal & Özdemir, 2024).

To address this, PQC is emerging as a crucial component of military cybersecurity. PQC algorithms are designed to be secure against quantum computer attacks while remaining compatible with classical computing hardware. Unlike QKD, PQC does not rely on quantum physics but instead uses advanced mathematical problems that even quantum computers cannot efficiently solve.

Key Features of PQC for Military IoT

- **Quantum-Resistant Algorithms:** Techniques such as lattice-based cryptography, hash-based cryptography, and multivariate polynomial cryptography ensure resilience against quantum attacks.
- **Computational Feasibility:** PQC can be deployed on standard military-grade processors, making it suitable for embedded IoT devices in battlefield operations.
- **Seamless Transition:** Military organizations can gradually transition from classical cryptographic methods to PQC without requiring quantum hardware.

The National Institute of Standards and Technology (NIST) has been working on standardizing PQC algorithms, which are expected to be widely adopted in military applications over the next decade.

5.3. Real-World Use Cases of Quantum Cryptography in Defence

Several nations and military organizations are actively exploring and deploying quantum cryptography for defence applications. Some of the most promising use cases include:

5.3.1. Satellite-Based QKD for Military Communication

- China has successfully demonstrated quantum-secured communication via its Micius satellite, which enables secure QKD transmissions between ground stations separated by thousands of kilometres (Qadri et al., 2024).
- The European Union is working on the Quantum Communication Infrastructure (QCI) initiative, which aims to establish a quantum-secured network for Europe's defence and intelligence services.
- The United States is investing in quantum-secured satellite communication to enhance cybersecurity for its global military operations.

5.3.2. Secure Battlefield Communications

- Military forces require secure communication between bases, naval fleets, and aircraft to prevent interception by adversaries. QKD can be integrated into radio-frequency (RF) and optical communication systems to enhance the security of military networks.
- Submarine Communication: Quantum cryptographic methods are being explored for secure undersea communication, where conventional encryption techniques are vulnerable to eavesdropping.

5.3.3. Defence Intelligence and Cryptographic Upgrades

- Intelligence agencies are incorporating quantum-secured encryption for highly sensitive data storage and transmission.
- Command and Control Networks are being upgraded with quantum-resistant cryptographic solutions to mitigate potential threats from QC advancements.

Quantum cryptography is set to play a transformative role in military cybersecurity, providing unparalleled security against both classical and quantum cyber threats (Pătraşcu, 2021). QKD enables secure communication channels that cannot be compromised, while PQC ensures that military IoT devices remain resilient against quantum attacks. As nations invest in quantum research and infrastructure, the deployment of satellite-based QKD, battlefield communication security, and quantum-resistant encryption will become integral to modern defence strategies.

6. Enhancing IoT Security Through Quantum Technologies

The integration of the IoT into military and defense applications has significantly increased the number of connected devices, creating new vulnerabilities to cyber threats. While traditional encryption methods are effective against current cyberattacks, the advent of QC poses a substantial risk to conventional cryptographic systems. However, quantum technologies do not merely represent a challenge – they offer a groundbreaking opportunity to enhance IoT security through advanced quantum-based mechanisms. From real-time threat detection to quantum cryptographic protocols, these technologies can fortify military IoT networks against evolving cyber threats (Santiago, 2023).

6.1. Real-Time Threat Detection and Prevention

QC has the potential to revolutionize real-time threat detection in IoT systems by leveraging quantum-enhanced algorithms that can analyze vast amounts of data at unprecedented speeds. Conventional machine learning-based cybersecurity solutions are constrained by computational limits, which hinder their ability to detect sophisticated cyber threats in real time.

By employing quantum machine learning (QML) techniques, IoT security systems can rapidly process high-dimensional data streams from military sensors, surveillance systems, and critical infrastructure. Quantum-enhanced anomaly detection models, such as quantum Boltzmann machines and quantum support vector machines (QSVMs), can identify minute deviations in network behaviour that may indicate a cyberattack (Bellante et al., 2025). These quantum models can detect zero-day vulnerabilities, unauthorized access attempts, and other cyber anomalies faster than classical approaches, reducing the risk of large-scale cyber incidents in military IoT networks.

Furthermore, quantum-based predictive analytics can forecast potential attack vectors by simulating various threat scenarios in a fraction of the time required by traditional computational methods. This predictive capability enhances proactive defense mechanisms, enabling military cybersecurity teams to counteract potential threats before they materialize.

6.2. Securing IoT Networks in Military Applications

In military IoT systems, securing data at every stage – collection, transmission, and storage – is critical to national security. Conventional encryption techniques, such as RSA and ECC, are vulnerable to quantum attacks, necessitating a shift towards quantum cryptographic protocols that ensure data confidentiality, integrity, and authenticity (Khan et al., 2024).

- **QKD:** One of the most promising quantum security techniques is QKD, which leverages quantum mechanics principles to generate and distribute encryption keys that are resistant to interception. Unlike classical key exchange methods, QKD ensures that any attempt to eavesdrop on the key exchange alters the quantum state of the transmitted particles, immediately alerting both parties to potential intrusions. In military IoT networks, QKD can safeguard mission-critical communications, secure battlefield sensor data, and protect classified intelligence transmissions.
- **Quantum Blockchain for Military IoT Security:** Blockchain technology is increasingly being explored for securing IoT ecosystems, but classical blockchain frameworks face scalability and computational efficiency challenges. Quantum blockchain, an emerging technology, enhances security by utilizing quantum entanglement and quantum-resistant cryptographic mechanisms. In military applications, quantum blockchain can provide tamper-proof security for supply chain management, weapon system integrity verification, and military logistics tracking, ensuring that critical data remains immutable and resistant to cyber threats (Pătraşcu, 2021).
- **PQC:** As quantum computers pose a threat to existing cryptographic standards, military organizations must transition towards quantum-resistant encryption algorithms. Post-quantum cryptographic methods, such as lattice-based, hash-based, and code-based encryption, provide long-term security solutions that can withstand attacks from quantum adversaries. Implementing these techniques in military IoT networks ensures the protection of sensitive information even in a post-quantum era.

6.3. Leveraging QRNGs

Randomness is the foundation of secure encryption, but traditional PRNGs rely on deterministic algorithms that can be exploited by sophisticated cyber attackers. QRNGs leverage the inherent randomness of quantum mechanics to generate truly unpredictable numbers, ensuring cryptographic keys are completely secure (Thirupathi et al., 2025).

- **Unbreakable Encryption for Military IoT Devices:** QRNGs generate high-entropy random numbers that are impossible to predict, making them ideal for military-grade encryption. By incorporating QRNG-generated cryptographic keys, IoT devices used in defense applications can achieve an unparalleled level of security, protecting critical data against brute-force attacks and decryption attempts.

- **Secure Authentication and Access Control:** QRNG-based cryptographic keys can be used for MFA and zero-trust security models in military IoT networks. This ensures that only authorized personnel and devices can access sensitive systems, mitigating the risk of insider threats and unauthorized intrusions.
- **Enhancing IoT Communications Integrity:** In military operations, secure communication channels are paramount. QRNGs enable the development of cryptographic protocols that safeguard drone communications, satellite transmissions, and battlefield command networks against eavesdropping and cyber interference.

Quantum technologies represent a paradigm shift in IoT security, offering unprecedented capabilities in encryption, threat detection, and network protection. By integrating quantum-enhanced machine learning, quantum cryptographic protocols, and QRNG-based security mechanisms, military IoT networks can achieve robust defense against cyber threats while ensuring the integrity and confidentiality of mission-critical data (Khatoon & Riaz, 2025; Paul et al., 2025; Zangana, 2025). As QC continues to evolve, adopting quantum-secure IoT architectures will be essential for safeguarding national security in the digital battlefield.

7. Challenges in Adopting QC for Defence IoT

The adoption of QC in defence IoT systems offers numerous opportunities for securing critical military networks and communication infrastructures. However, integrating quantum technologies into the existing military IoT ecosystem presents several challenges that must be addressed before large-scale implementation is feasible (Baseri et al., 2024; Gopireddy, 2024). These challenges span technological, logistical, regulatory, and security domains, necessitating substantial efforts from both the military sector and private industry. Below, we explore the key challenges in adopting QC for defence IoT and potential solutions to mitigate these barriers.

7.1. Technical Challenges

7.1.1. Scalability of Quantum Hardware

One of the most significant challenges in adopting QC for defence IoT systems is the scalability of quantum hardware. While quantum computers have demonstrated promise in applications such as cryptography and optimization problems, the technology is still in its early stages.

- **Current State of Quantum Hardware**: Today's quantum computers are noisy, error-prone, and limited in the number of quantum bits (qubits) they can handle. Quantum error correction techniques are still under development and require substantial computational resources, making it difficult to scale quantum systems for military IoT applications (Baseri et al., 2024; Khan et al., 2024; Rastogi et al., 2024).

- **Impact on Defence IoT**: Military IoT systems, such as autonomous drones, sensor networks, and communication channels, generate vast amounts of data requiring rapid and secure processing. Currently, classical computing solutions remain essential due to the limitations of QC.
- **Possible Solution**: Incremental advancements in QC hardware, such as quantum annealing and quantum simulators, may provide interim solutions. Military agencies can also invest in hybrid quantum-classical systems to address immediate needs while waiting for quantum technology to mature.

7.1.2. Quantum Communication Infrastructure

For QC to be effective in securing military IoT systems, it must be paired with quantum communication networks capable of securely transmitting quantum keys and information.

- **Current Limitations:** Existing quantum communication networks have a limited range, require line-of-sight communication, and depend on specialized infrastructure such as quantum repeaters and satellites. High development costs and technical complexity further hinder widespread deployment.
- **Military Application Challenges:** Defence IoT systems often operate in dynamic environments (land, air, sea, and space), requiring a stable quantum communication network. Deploying and maintaining such a system across various military assets is highly challenging.
- **Possible Solution:** Research collaborations and public–private partnerships could focus on advancing quantum repeaters and space-based quantum communication initiatives. Quantum satellites can play a crucial role in enabling secure long-range military communication.

7.2. Compatibility with Existing Defence Infrastructure

Most military IoT systems rely on classical computing and traditional cryptographic protocols such as RSA and ECC. Transitioning these systems to quantum-safe solutions presents significant compatibility challenges (Bellante et al., 2025; Çakal & Özdemir, 2024; Khan et al., 2024; Thirupathi et al., 2025).

- **Encryption Protocols**: Existing cryptographic methods must be replaced or supplemented with PQC algorithms resistant to quantum attacks. These algorithms are still under development, and their implementation within military infrastructure will require extensive testing.
- **Cost and Complexity of Integration**: Retrofitting existing defence IoT systems with quantum-safe encryption is costly and complex, requiring upgrades to hardware, software, and communication protocols.
- **Possible Solution**: A phased integration approach using hybrid cryptographic solutions that combine classical and quantum-safe protocols can provide security without immediate overhauls. Modular upgrades targeting high-value assets first can facilitate a smoother transition.

7.3. High Costs and Resource Constraints

Developing and implementing QC, quantum communication infrastructure, and post-quantum cryptographic systems involve high costs and resource demands.

- **Initial Investment:** The upfront expenses for quantum hardware, communication infrastructure, and personnel training are substantial, making short-term justification challenging.
- **Ongoing Maintenance and Operational Costs:** Quantum systems require specialized personnel and regular maintenance, adding to long-term operational costs.
- **Possible Solution:** Governments and defence agencies can adopt collaborative funding models with industry and research institutions. Strategic investments in quantum-resistant encryption for mission-critical systems can yield faster returns on investment (Çakal & Özdemir, 2024; Pătraşcu, 2021; Qadri et al., 2024).

7.4. Lack of Quantum Expertise

QC and quantum communication require highly specialized expertise in theoretical physics, computer science, and engineering, posing a significant challenge.

- **Training and Education**: The demand for QC professionals is growing, but military and industrial training programs have yet to keep pace.
- **Interdisciplinary Collaboration**: Effective integration of QC in defence IoT requires collaboration across multiple disciplines, adding complexity to team-building efforts.
- **Possible Solution**: Long-term investments in training military personnel and broader workforce development programs are necessary. Public–private partnerships with universities and research labs can accelerate workforce readiness.

7.5. Vulnerabilities of Early-Stage Quantum Technologies

While QC enhances security, early-stage quantum systems may introduce new vulnerabilities.

- **Quantum Side-Channel Attacks**: Weaknesses in quantum hardware implementation may expose systems to cyber threats.
- **Quantum Cryptanalysis**: Future advancements in quantum algorithms could compromise existing quantum-resistant encryption methods.
- **Possible Solution**: Continuous research in quantum cybersecurity, including rigorous testing and adaptive security frameworks, will be crucial to mitigating potential vulnerabilities (Santiago, 2023).

7.6. Lack of Standardization and Global Consensus

The lack of universal standards for quantum-safe encryption and quantum communication in defence IoT leads to uncertainty in implementation and interoperability.

- **International Cooperation**: The global race for quantum supremacy requires international agreements and standards to ensure secure communication and prevent misuse.
- **Possible Solution**: Collaboration with international standardization bodies (e.g. ISO, IEEE) and government-led initiatives can accelerate the development of global quantum security standards. Military alliances like NATO can work towards interoperability of quantum-enabled defence systems (Baseri et al., 2024).

Adopting QC for defence IoT presents transformative opportunities for enhancing cybersecurity and securing military infrastructure. However, significant challenges remain, including hardware scalability, infrastructure development, integration with legacy systems, economic constraints, workforce training, security risks, and regulatory issues.

Fig. 5.1 shows the challenges associated with the adoption of QC computing for IoT in a hierarchical format. Addressing these challenges requires a collaborative approach, incremental development, and strategic investments in quantum

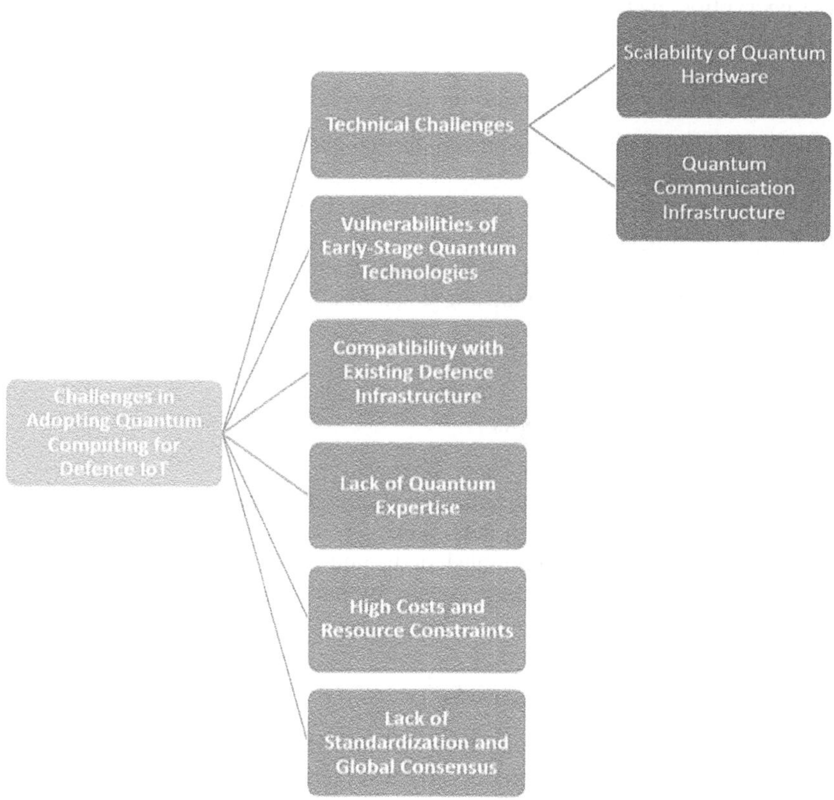

Fig. 5.1. Challenges Associated with the Adoption of QC for Defence IoT.

technologies. While QC holds immense potential for revolutionizing defence IoT security, careful planning and phased implementation will be essential to unlocking its full benefits (Khan et al., 2024).

8. Future Prospects of QC and IoT in Defence Cybersecurity

The convergence of QC and the IoT in the defence sector represents a paradigm shift in cybersecurity. These emerging technologies offer the potential to revolutionize military security by providing enhanced encryption, real-time threat detection, and unprecedented resilience against cyberattacks. However, their adoption also introduces challenges that need to be carefully addressed. Below, we explore key areas where QC and IoT will shape the future of defence cybersecurity (Khan & Khan, 2025; Luo & Xu, 2022; Sanborn, 2021; Turk et al., 2025).

8.1. Quantum-Resistant Cryptography: The New Standard for Defence

Current cryptographic systems, such as RSA and ECC, are vulnerable to QC threats, particularly from Shor's algorithm, which can efficiently break these encryption methods. This necessitates a shift towards quantum-resistant cryptography to ensure the security of military communications and IoT networks.

8.1.1. Transitioning to Post-Quantum Cryptographic Algorithms

- The NIST is actively working on standardizing PQC algorithms that are resistant to quantum attacks.
- Defence organizations must invest in research and development to integrate PQC into military IoT infrastructures.
- Hybrid cryptographic models will ensure a smooth transition by combining classical encryption with quantum-resistant algorithms until full adoption is feasible.

8.1.2. Deploying QKD Networks

- QKD leverages quantum mechanics to enable ultra-secure key exchanges that cannot be intercepted without detection.
- Military forces will need to establish dedicated QKD infrastructures, including satellite-based QKD networks, to secure global communications.

8.2. QKD in Military IoT Networks

QKD offers the most promising approach for securing communication channels within military IoT ecosystems. By leveraging quantum principles, QKD ensures that encryption keys remain secure, even against adversaries equipped with quantum computers (Bellante et al., 2025; Çakal & Özdemir, 2024; Khan et al., 2024; Thirupathi et al., 2025).

Advantages of QKD for Military Networks

- **Unbreakable Security:** Any eavesdropping attempt on a QKD channel disturbs the quantum state of the transmitted particles, making interception detectable.
- **Global Secure Communication:** With satellite-based QKD, military units can securely communicate across vast distances, even in hostile environments.
- **Scalability and Flexibility:** QKD can be integrated into existing IoT systems, ensuring robust security for battlefield communications, logistics, and intelligence operations.

Future advancements in quantum communication infrastructure, such as quantum repeaters and enhanced quantum satellite networks, will play a crucial role in making QKD a practical solution for military cybersecurity.

8.3. Quantum-Enhanced Machine Learning for Threat Detection

Military IoT systems generate vast amounts of data, requiring advanced threat detection mechanisms. QC can enhance machine learning models to provide real-time threat analysis and response.

Potential Benefits

- **Improved Anomaly Detection:** Quantum machine learning models, such as QSVMs and quantum neural networks, can detect sophisticated cyberattacks with higher accuracy.
- **Advanced Classification and Prediction:** Quantum computers can analyze complex data patterns, enabling predictive threat modelling and better classification of attack vectors.
- **Rapid Processing of Large Datasets:** Military IoT networks generate massive amounts of sensor data. Quantum-enhanced ML can process this information efficiently, leading to faster threat mitigation.

By integrating QC with IoT security frameworks, defence agencies can strengthen their cyber resilience and improve real-time decision-making capabilities.

8.4. Quantum Random Number Generation for Cryptographic Keys

Cryptographic security relies on the generation of truly random numbers to create secure encryption keys. Traditional RNGs use algorithmic methods that can be predicted by quantum-powered adversaries (Khan et al., 2024).

Advantages of QRNGs

- **Unpredictable Encryption Keys:** QRNGs use quantum properties to generate truly random numbers, ensuring robust cryptographic security.

- **Stronger Encryption Standards:** Quantum randomness enhances security for military IoT networks, making them resilient against both classical and quantum attacks.
- **Essential for Future-Proof Security:** As QC capabilities advance, QRNGs will become a standard for secure military communications.

8.5. QC for Post-Quantum Security in Military Supply Chains

Military supply chains involve interconnected IoT systems for logistics, inventory management, and transportation tracking. Securing these systems against cyber threats is critical for maintaining operational readiness.

Key Applications of QC in Military Supply Chains

- **Post-Quantum Cryptographic Protection:** Ensuring data integrity and confidentiality within supply chain networks by implementing quantum-resistant encryption.
- **Enhanced Security for IoT Logistics Systems:** Preventing cyberattacks targeting military logistics through quantum-secure authentication protocols.
- **Quantum Signatures for Component Verification:** Using quantum-based signatures to verify the authenticity of military equipment and components, preventing supply chain tampering.

As QC matures, its role in securing military logistics and supply chains will become increasingly significant, ensuring end-to-end cybersecurity for defence operations.

8.6. The Road Ahead: Overcoming Challenges in Quantum Adoption for Military IoT

Despite the promising advancements in QC and IoT security, several challenges must be addressed before widespread adoption in the defence sector (Pătraşcu, 2021).

Key Challenges

- **Scalability and Infrastructure Development:** The deployment of quantum technologies requires substantial investment in quantum communication networks, satellite systems, and secure IoT architectures.
- **Integration with Legacy Systems:** Transitioning from classical to quantum-secure systems is complex and requires gradual upgrades, testing, and workforce training.
- **Standardization and Regulatory Frameworks:** Establishing international standards for quantum encryption and secure communication is critical for interoperability between allied defence forces.
- **Operational Readiness and Practical Implementation:** While quantum technologies are advancing, their real-world deployment in military scenarios will require continued research, pilot programs, and collaboration among defence agencies, academia, and industry.

The future of QC and IoT in defence cybersecurity is poised for transformative growth. As military organizations navigate the transition to quantum-resistant cryptographic standards, invest in QKD networks, leverage quantum-enhanced machine learning, and integrate QRNGs, they will significantly enhance the security and resilience of their cyber infrastructures. While challenges remain, strategic investments and global collaboration will ensure that quantum technologies become an integral part of modern military cybersecurity, safeguarding defence systems against both classical and quantum threats.

9. Conclusion

QC stands at the intersection of both challenge and innovation for the defense sector, particularly in the domain of cybersecurity. The advent of quantum computers threatens conventional cryptographic algorithms, such as RSA and ECC, which currently safeguard military communications and classified data. The ability of quantum algorithms like Shor's algorithm to efficiently factor large numbers could render these encryption methods obsolete, exposing sensitive military systems to unprecedented cyber threats. However, this same quantum capability can be harnessed to develop more robust defense mechanisms. QKD, for instance, offers an unbreakable encryption paradigm by leveraging the fundamental principles of quantum mechanics, such as superposition and entanglement, to establish secure communication channels that are impervious to interception or decryption by adversaries, even those equipped with quantum computers.

Beyond cryptography, QC also presents transformative opportunities in optimizing logistics, strategic simulations, and AI applications in military operations. Quantum-enhanced machine learning can improve threat detection by rapidly analyzing vast datasets and identifying patterns indicative of cyber intrusions or enemy manoeuvers. Additionally, quantum algorithms can optimize complex defense supply chains, reducing operational costs and enhancing efficiency in battlefield logistics. By investing in post-quantum cryptographic solutions and integrating quantum-resistant security frameworks into IoT-enabled defense networks, military organizations can mitigate potential risks while leveraging quantum advantages. Ultimately, proactive adaptation to quantum advancements will be essential for maintaining technological superiority, ensuring national security, and safeguarding critical military assets in an era of rapidly evolving cyber warfare.

References

Akhai, S., & Kumar, V. (2024). Quantum resilience and distributed trust: The promise of blockchain and quantum computing in defense. *Sustainable security practices using blockchain, quantum and post-quantum technologies for real time applications* (pp. 125–153). Springer Nature Singapore.

Baseri, Y., Chouhan, V., & Ghorbani, A. (2024). Cybersecurity in the quantum era: Assessing the impact of quantum computing on infrastructure. *arXiv preprint arXiv:2404.10659*.

Bellante, A., Fioravanti, T., Carminati, M., Zanero, S., & Luongo, A. (2025). Evaluating the potential of quantum machine learning in cybersecurity: A case-study on PCA-based intrusion detection systems. *Computers & Security*, *154*, 104341. https://doi.org/10.1016/j.cose.2025.104341

Çakal, K., & Özdemir, S. (2024). Transforming military security: Quantum age blockchain architecture for IoBT – PARS. *2024 International Conference on Smart Applications, Communications and Networking* (SmartNets). (pp. 1–6). https://doi.org/10.1109/SmartNets61466.2024.10577697

Gopireddy, R. R. (2024). Securing the future: The convergence of cybersecurity, AI, and IoT in a world dominated by intelligent machines. *European Journal of Advances in Engineering and Technology*, *11*(8), 91–95.

Khan, M. A., & Khan, M. A. (2025). Securing IoT in the post-quantum era: Implementation, challenges, and future directions. *IEEE Communications Standards Magazine*. https://doi.org/10.1109/MCOMSTD.2025.3584658

Khan, H. U., Ali, N., Ali, F., & Nazir, S. (2024). Transforming future technology with quantum-based IoT. *The Journal of Supercomputing*, *80*(15), 22362–22396. https://doi.org/10.1007/s11227-024-06251-1

Khatoon, A., & Riaz, R. (2025). Quantum computing impacts on smart city cybersecurity through resilient defense framework: Quantum computing impacts on resilient cybersecurity frameworks for smart cities. *Ubiquitous Technology Journal*, *1*(1), 23–31.

Luo, Z., & Xu, L. (2022). Securing IoT in military networks using quantum cryptography. *Quantum Information Processing*.

Ochoa, O. F., & Vazquez, S. J. (2020). Quantum computing for cybersecurity: Current state and future directions. *Journal of Cybersecurity and Privacy*, *14*(3), 41–58.

Pătraşcu, P. (2021). Emerging technologies and national security: The impact of IoT in critical infrastructures protection and defence sector. *Land Forces Academy Review*, *26*(4), 423–429.

Paul, S., Choudhury, N. R., Pandit, B., & Dawn, A. (2025). Integration of AI and Quantum computing in cybersecurity: A comprehensive review. *Integration of AI, quantum computing, and semiconductor technology* (pp. 287–308). IGI Global. https://doi.org/10.4018/979-8-3693-7076-6.ch014

Qadri, S., Malik, J. A., Shah, H., Raza, M. A., Alsanoosy, T., & Saleem, M. (2024). Innovating with quantum computing approaches in block-chain for enhanced security and data privacy in agricultural IoT systems. In M. G. Sumithra, M. Sathyamoorthy, M. Manikandan, R. K. Dhanaraj, & M. Ouaissa (Eds.), *Computational intelligence in internet of agricultural things* (pp. 339–370). Springer Nature Switzerland.

Radanliev, P. (2024). Cyber diplomacy: Defining the opportunities for cybersecurity and risks from artificial intelligence, IoT, blockchains, and quantum computing. *Journal of Cyber Security Technology*, *9*(1), 28–78.

Rastogi, R., Arya, L., & Sharma, Y. K. (2024). Quantum-secured healthcare data and cybersecurity innovations in the era of Industry 5.0. In U. K. Lilhore, S. Dalal, V. Dutt, & M. Radulescu (Eds.), *Industrial quantum computing: Algorithms, blockchains, industry 4.0* (pp. 199–218). Walter de Gruyter GmbH & Co. KG.

Sanborn, A.D. (2021). *Quantum key distribution for secure military IoT communications: Challenges and opportunities*. Quantum Science and Technology.

Santiago, H. (2023). No Fight. No Flight. Just Innovation! How the most pressing need in cybersecurity today could propel the development of quantum computing. In G. Reza Djavanshir (Ed.), *Digital strategies and organizational transformation* (pp. 179–210). World Scientific Publishing Co. Pte. Ltd.

Thirupathi, L., Akshaya, B., Reddy, P. C., Harsha, S. S., & Reddy, E. S. (2025). Integration of AI and quantum computing in cyber security. In B. Mishra (Ed.), *Integration of AI, quantum computing, and semiconductor technology* (pp. 29–56). IGI Global.

Turk, Y., Zeydan, E., Blanco, L., & Liyanage, M. (2025). Quantum technologies for the Internet of Military Defense Things. In *2025 IEEE International Mediterranean Conference on Communications and Networking* (*MeditCom*) (pp. 1–6). IEEE. https://doi.org/10.1109/MeditCom64437.2025.11104321

Zangana, H. M. (2025). Introduction to modern cybersecurity. In H. M. Zangana (Ed.), *Defense in depth* (Chapter 1). https://doi.org/10.1002/9781394340750.ch1

Chapter 6

Securing the Battlefield: Overcoming Challenges and Implementing IoT Solutions in Military Defence

Kritika Khandelwal

Department of Business Administration, Manipal University Jaipur, India

Abstract

Integrating the Internet of Things (IoT) into the defence industry marks the beginning of a new era in military operations, offering unprecedented advancements in efficiency, real-time situational awareness, and strategic decision-making. IoT-enabled devices and systems facilitate seamless communication, automation, and data collection across diverse military environments. However, the rapid pace of technological advancement presents significant security challenges that must be addressed to ensure the integrity and functionality of military systems. This chapter provides a comprehensive examination of the challenges associated with IoT adoption in military contexts, including vulnerabilities to cyber-attacks, data privacy concerns, and the complexities of managing and securing vast networks of interconnected devices. It also explores innovative solutions and strategic frameworks designed to mitigate these risks, ensuring the development and deployment of robust and resilient military IoT systems. By analyzing current technologies, security practices, and future trends, this chapter offers valuable insights into safeguarding national defence infrastructures against emerging threats in the evolving IoT landscape.

Keywords: IoT in defence; military cybersecurity; cyber threats; defence technology; network resilience

The Internet of Things in the Defence Industry: Challenges and Solutions for Military Security, 135–148

doi:10.1108/978-1-83549-198-020261006

1. Introduction

1.1. The Role of IoT in Modern Defence Operations

The latest addition to the defence industry's technological arsenal is the IoT, which has revolutionized military operations by enhancing data connectivity and situational awareness. IoT has emerged as a game-changer for defence management, playing a crucial role in optimizing safety, efficiency, and decision-making processes. By integrating various smart devices and sensors, IoT facilitates seamless data collection and real-time information sharing, equipping military personnel with invaluable intelligence during missions (Lewis, 2016).

The deployment of IoT-enabled technologies in military environments has significantly improved battlefield awareness. Devices such as drones, surveillance systems, and wearable technologies embedded in soldiers' gear allow real-time monitoring of troop movements and battlefield conditions. Additionally, body-worn IoT systems provide biometric and environmental data that enhance both soldier performance and medical response during combat operations (Russell & Abdelzaher, 2018). These advancements not only enhance operational efficiency but also reduce risks by enabling rapid responses to emerging threats.

Beyond battlefield applications, the defence sector has leveraged IoT for a wide range of operational functions, spanning logistics, communication, intelligence gathering, and reconnaissance. In logistics, IoT solutions optimize supply chain management by tracking the movement of military equipment, ensuring that resources are delivered precisely when and where they are needed. This is particularly critical in Just-in-Time (JIT) production systems, where a single missed delivery can disrupt entire assembly lines and operational readiness (Greengard, 2015).

IoT also transforms military communication networks, fostering a more interconnected command structure. Secure and real-time communication between soldiers and command centres allows for better coordination and data-driven decision-making. However, as IoT integration in defence operations expands, new security challenges have surfaced. The increased reliance on networked systems exposes military infrastructures to cyber threats, espionage, and unauthorized data access (Gartzke, 2013).

1.2. Security Challenges and the Need for Resilience

As military forces incorporate thousands of IoT devices into their networks, ensuring the security and reliability of these systems becomes paramount. While IoT enhances operational efficiency, it simultaneously introduces vulnerabilities that adversaries can exploit. Cyberattacks on IoT-enabled military systems could lead to data breaches, system manipulation, and even disruptions in mission-critical operations (Taddeo, 2019). The potential for cyber espionage and infiltration necessitates robust security measures to safeguard sensitive military information.

Securing military IoT infrastructure requires a multi-layered approach that addresses both hardware and software vulnerabilities. As IoT devices proliferate across military environments, the challenge is not only to secure individual endpoints but also to develop a resilient and adaptable security framework that can withstand sophisticated cyber threats. Information privacy, data integrity, and system reliability must be preserved, even in highly dynamic and adversarial settings.

1.3. Strategic Solutions for Military IoT Security

To mitigate these risks, military organizations must adopt advanced cybersecurity strategies tailored to IoT systems. This includes the implementation of sophisticated encryption mechanisms, secure communication protocols, and robust authentication techniques to prevent unauthorized access. Additionally, artificial intelligence (AI) and machine learning (ML) play a crucial role in threat detection by providing early warnings on potential cyber intrusions and system vulnerabilities. AI-driven predictive analytics can help military operators preemptively address security breaches before they escalate into full-scale attacks (Stojmenovic & Wen, 2014).

This chapter delves into the security challenges associated with military IoT deployment and explores existing and emerging solutions. It examines state-of-the-art technologies designed to enhance the security of IoT-driven defence operations, including blockchain-based authentication, intrusion detection systems (IDSs), and decentralized network architectures. By understanding these solutions and their strategic implementations, military stakeholders can fortify their IoT infrastructures against cyber threats, ensuring operational continuity and national security.

2. IoT Integration in Military Operations

2.1. Key Applications of IoT in Defence

The IoT has revolutionized military operations, improving situational awareness, decision-making, and operational efficiency by connecting various sensors, devices, and systems across the battlefield. Fig. 6.1 shows the key applications of IoT in defence.

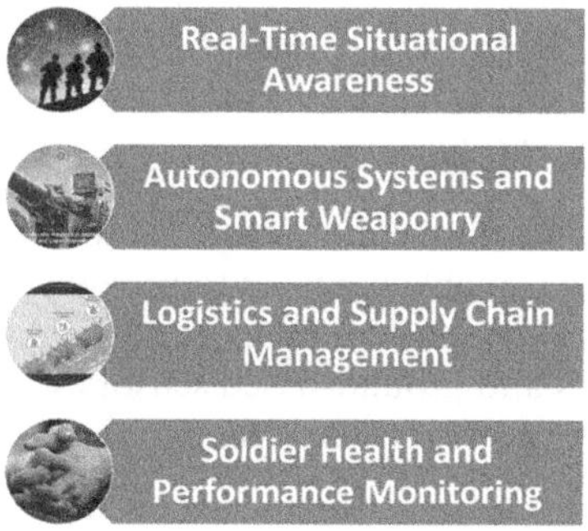

Fig. 6.1. Key Applications of IoT in Defence.

2.1.1. Real-Time Situational Awareness

IoT-enabled sensors gather real-time data on environmental conditions, enemy movements, and troop locations, providing commanders with actionable intelligence. This enables quicker and more effective decision-making on the battlefield (Borgia, 2014). For instance, unmanned aerial vehicles (UAVs) and ground-based sensors equipped with IoT technology can stream live data to command centres, enhancing operational awareness.

2.1.2. Autonomous Systems and Smart Weaponry

IoT is vital in autonomous military systems such as drones and robotic vehicles. Advanced use systems utilize a combination of sensors and AI to collect data in an environment with the minimum amount of human oversight possible. This is beneficial for increasing the accuracy and decreasing the risks of human forces in war zones (Gubbi et al., 2013).

2.1.3. Logistics and Supply Chain Management

It includes real-time tracking of equipment and supply parts that help military logistics. The military has onboarded sensors through vehicles, containers, and storage units to measure the status and locations of resources by tracking the waste or delay in reaching life-critical operations on time (Da Xu et al., 2014).

2.1.4. Soldier Health and Performance Monitoring

Wearable IoT devices can monitor soldiers' vital signs, including heart rate, body temperature, and fatigue levels, alerting commanders to any health issues in real-time. This enhances troop safety and ensures soldiers receive timely medical attention (Rayes & Salam, 2019).

2.2. Benefits of IoT-Enabled Military Systems

The integration of IoT technologies in military systems provides several advantages that enhance the effectiveness of defence operations:

2.2.1. Improved Decision-Making

Real-time data on environmental conditions, enemy movements, and troop positions is collected using IoT-enabled sensors to provide ground commanders with actionable insights. This allows faster and more efficient decision-making in combat (Borgia, 2014). UAVs and ground-based sensors with IoT technology would be able to provide live data streams back to command centres, providing operational transparency.

2.2.2. Enhanced Communication

Autonomous military systems – like drones and robotic vehicles – depend on IoT technologies to advance the accuracy with which they acquire facts from various telemetry assets. Such systems rely on aggregations of connected sensors and accessible AI, which gather vast amounts of data to process without much human involvement. This will help improve the canvas size; hence, miniaturizing these systems increases flexibility and reduces the dangers for human personnel during combat operations (Gubbi et al., 2013).

2.2.3. Cost Savings and Predictive Maintenance

Using IoT sensors to monitor the condition of military equipment, the defence sector can implement predictive maintenance practices, lowering the risk of unexpected equipment failure. This improves operational uptime and lowers maintenance costs (Da Xu et al., 2014).

2.2.4. Increased Soldier Safety

Wearable IoT devices can track a number of soldiers' vital signs, including heart rate, body temperature, and how tired they are – all without the need to do an ECG or blood test. In this case, it is simply done by asking the network for real-time updates on conditions as requests come in from commanders who want that information sent straight to their phones. It improves the safety of troops and allows soldiers to get medical help where needed (Rayes & Salam, 2019).

3. Security Challenges in Military IoT Implementation

Although military operations greatly appeal to IoT, they may also bring some security hurdles. IoT has undergone significant evolution in recent years due to the identified security risks and challenges and its highly interconnected nature, which increases vulnerability to cyber-attacks and data breaches.

3.1. Cybersecurity Threats and Vulnerabilities

Military IoT systems face significant challenges due to their vulnerability to cyber threats. IoT networks comprising hundreds of devices, sensors, and communication channels aggravate the case by their distributed nature. Cyber-attacks like Distributed Denial of Service (DDoS), data breaches, and malware are high-level risks. For example, in 2016, the Mirai botnet attack demonstrated how insecure IoT devices are by hacking them and using them to orchestrate massive DDoS attacks (Kolias et al., 2017).

From a military standpoint, an adversary might use these vulnerabilities to deny the operation of communication systems, intercept sensitive data, and influence autonomous agents. As such risks increase, more necessary security measures will be taken to protect military IoT networks (Stojmenovic & Wen, 2014).

3.2. Data Privacy and Integrity

Securing and maintaining data privacy is very important for military IoT systems. Vital information related to troop movements, logistics, and intelligence data is exchanged through IoT networks, making them a soft target for cyber espionage and data manipulation (Yan et al., 2014).

One of the biggest challenges is that data traverses between its source and destination if it has not been tampered with. Data fidelity is just one such factor, which, when compromised, may lead to severe consequences, for instance, misinformation that can disrupt an information process on a battlefield (Roman et al., 2013). This data is critically important, which is precisely why encryption and secure data transmission protocols must be upheld to protect it, ensuring its integrity and confidentiality.

3.3. Managing Large-Scale IoT Networks

Another significant challenge is managing large-scale military IoT networks. Thousands of interconnected devices, including drones, vehicles, ground sensors, and communication devices, are frequently included in military IoT systems (Alaba et al., 2017). Ensuring that all devices are secure and updated with the most recent security patches is daunting, as each device presents a potential entry point for attackers.

Different device types are heterogeneous (due to various manufacturers or communication protocols), which enables and complicates them all at once (Lin et al., 2017). Military IoT systems need to allow every device to collaborate securely.

3.4. Physical Security of IoT Devices

Military IoT implementation also involves physical security. Furthermore, IoT devices deployed in military applications can be placed in a physical location such as remote border areas or somewhere hostile where various enemies could tamper with and destroy them. These examples indicate that adversaries can easily capture or destroy surveillance drones, ground sensors, and communication devices, leading to defective network performance (Gubbi et al., 2013).

IoT devices must be hardened against physical attacks to minimize these risks, and device hardening or tamper detection measures must be incorporated.

3.5. Insider Threats

A particular concern is insider threats – cases in which people within the military or defence contractors misuse their access to IoT systems. Authorized insiders can leverage IoT networks to access critical systems, potentially leading to the theft of sensitive information or acts of sabotage (Maras, 2015). Considering the importance of military IoT systems, it is essential to control insider threats by implementing proper access controls and monitoring these constantly, along with a regular audit of all activities inside the IoT networks.

3.6. Securing Communication Protocols

IoT devices, especially in the military context, are vulnerable to eavesdropping, jamming, and spoofing because of their communication protocols. Most IoT devices use wireless communication, which can be easily intercepted to obtain information compared with wired systems (Stojmenovic & Wen, 2014). The communication channels should be protected by encryption, authentication protocols, and secure routing mechanisms to prevent adversaries from eavesdropping or altering the data.

4. Strategic Frameworks for Mitigating Security Risks

Given the numerous security threats introduced by IoT integration in military operations, reliable frameworks are necessary to deal with these risks. A pragmatic perspective is needed, which pays attention to developing robust cybersecurity, reinforcing data privacy measures, and ensuring IoT systems are resilient against malicious fields. These sections detail strategies to tackle these pain areas using advanced encryption, AI, blockchain technology, wireless secure communication protocols, CISSP certification, etc.

4.1. Advanced Encryption Techniques

One of the primary tactics in securing military IoT is advanced encryption. When data is captured between various commanding and control centres, it needs to remain private; this way, encryption allows for masking of transmitted information from when it is sent across multiple devices in the IoT, whereas now, if someone had detected or intercepted, they steal what has been taken. Military data requires secure encryption standards like Advanced Encryption Standard (AES) and Elliptic Curve Cryptography (ECC), which are used in military-grade security of military operations (Alaba et al., 2017). With these forms of encrypted data, it becomes impossible for malicious parties to make sense of the information even if they intercept it.

Moreover, encryption should be placed across all layers in the IoT structure at the data transmission, storage, and storage and processing stages. For example, data integrity in combat environments is crucial to the success of operations; hence, end-to-end encryption has been an essential component of military infrastructures (Stallings, 2018).

4.2. AI and ML for Threat Detection

ML and AI could be a big part of how the military protects its IoT systems. These technologies can analyze massive amounts of data to comprehend patterns around suspicious activities that could be misused to detect and act against cyber threats before they strike. Layer AI may process input packets and identify possible attacks before turning them into attacks with more damage (Zhou et al., 2018). An AI-based IDS can help with intrusion deactivation, too.

ML algorithms predict the emergence of vulnerabilities within the IoT and suggest measures for upcoming security precautions. AI systems and ML techniques may also help provide necessary resilience for military IoT networks (Khan & Salah, 2018). To achieve this, the security landscape is learned from new threats daily and adapts to attacks as new techniques are developed.

4.3. Blockchain for Secure Data Transmission

As a blockchain, it ensures that the IoT systems will be secured in military conditions. Blockchain can disseminate information through its distributed ledger, making it difficult for malicious actors to obtain the data. Additionally, because there is no central point where all of the data is stored, it is more difficult for hackers to break into the network. Data transitions are more secure as the transactions are verified and encrypted in a blockchain system (Dorri et al., 2017).

For example, blockchain can track resource transport, along with a trained and maintained support package for equipment and assurance that communications between different IoT devices are genuine (Kshetri, 2017). A key benefit of using blockchain is its ability to create inherently immutable audit trails that can be relied upon to assess the trustworthiness of data in an IoT system.

4.4. Secure Communication Protocols

Secure communication protocols are another crucial element of a strategic security framework. IoT devices rely on wireless communication, so they are suitable for eavesdropping, jamming, and spoofing. To prevent these risks, it is essential to use communication protocols with strong encryption and authentication between nodes and their integrity control (Stojmenovic & Wen, 2014).

This includes options like Transport Layer Security (TLS) and Datagram Transport Layer Security (DTLS), commonly used to encrypt data and prevent it from being changed while moving. The approach is to have PKI (public key infrastructure) as a preferred way for devices within the network to be authenticated and authorized, along with normalizing the use of digital certificates.

4.5. Continuous Monitoring and Security Audits

As cyber threats constantly evolve, IoT networks must be monitored around the clock so that potential vulnerabilities can be quickly identified or attacks detected in real-time. Security Information and Event Management (SIEM) systems can aggregate substantial data from diverse IoT devices and analyze anomalies within this data to identify potential security incidents (Kolias et al., 2017).

Regular security audits must ensure all IoT devices have the latest firmware and networking patches. By performing audits, military operators can detect outdated or vulnerable devices that attackers could exploit and solve those issues before they are exploited (Alaba et al., 2017).

4.6. Multi-Layered Defence Approach

Defence-in-depth: A layered defence strategy uses multiple security controls to safeguard IoT systems against various attacks. A wide range of safeguards have been proposed, from physical security measures (e.g. tamper-resistant hardware), network-level protections (e.g. firewalls and intrusion prevention systems) to application-level countermeasures based on secure coding practices, e.g., code signing, input validation or authentication data access control mechanisms; communication over encrypted channels; execution of privilege-epoch dependent functions only under the proper situation (Gubbi et al., 2013).

A single point of failure for military organizations will be eliminated by implementing security on every layer of the IoT architecture. Additionally, it guarantees that the entire system is safeguarded from breach if a layer is compromised (Yan et al., 2014).

5. Case Studies of IoT Solutions in Defence

IoT technologies have reshaped the functioning of the defence sector, improving its efficiency with security and quick decision-making techniques. These few successful case studies have proven IoT efficiency in military applications.

5.1. IoT-Enabled Battlefield Surveillance Systems

One of the most effective uses of IoT in the military is battlefield surveillance. IoT devices, such as UAVs and ground sensors, have been integrated into networks to monitor and assess real-time battlefield conditions. The US military, for example, uses drones and remote sensors as part of IoT-enabled surveillance systems to get real-time information on where enemies are and where troops are moving (Gubbi et al., 2013).

These devices benefit from high-resolution video feeds and real-time battlefield monitoring (via the same additional sensors) needed to supplement military commanders' decision-making process, which should result in an overall increase in operational effectiveness (Lin et al., 2017).

5.2. IoT in Military Logistics and Supply Chain Management

The emergence of IoT technologies for all ecosystem layers is imperative in enhancing how logistics and supply chain management practices work within military operations. For instance, the United States Department of Defence (DoD) is already leveraging Radio Frequency Identification (RFID) and IoT sensors for tracking military supplies and equipment. To keep track of shipments, vehicles, and supplies as they move in real-time, the DoD has utilized IoT devices throughout combat operations – for example, in Iraq or Afghanistan (Zhong et al., 2017).

In a world where every military unit relies on quick acquisition during critical operations, this model makes the supply chain visible in real time, leading to better resource distribution and reduced lag times. Logistics efficiency is speed using the IoT.

5.3. IoT and Smart Military Bases

The idea of smart military bases is built on a backbone of using IoT technologies to assist in controlling energy use, improving security measures, and optimizing infrastructure. US military bases use IoT-enabled devices on electrical grids to consume less energy and work under more sustainable operation conditions. Monitoring energy utilization, personnel movement, and security breaches at military bases through sensors deployed throughout are captured in real-time for faster threat detection (Gubbi et al., 2013).

The advent of these IoT-enabled surveillance and monitoring solutions at military bases provides security and energy efficiency in operations.

5.4. IoT in Autonomous Systems and Drones

Autonomous systems such as drones and unmanned ground vehicles (UGVs) rely on IoT to conduct surveillance and reconnaissance missions. A great example of an IoT-enabled platform that does intelligence, surveillance, and reconnaissance (ISR) work is the US Air Force's MQ-1 Predator drone. Equipped with sensors and cameras, the drone transmits real-time data back to the command centre, where military personnel can monitor battlefield conditions remotely (Austin, 2011).

The capability of IoT-powered drones to transmit and collect data in real-time makes them much needed on the battlefield. This minimizes human risk while delivering practical intelligence.

5.5. Challenges and Lessons Learned

The IoT technologies have worked wonders for us in varied ways, but simultaneously, they unbolt an array of gateway issues. The Mirai botnet attack was a critical incident that endangered potential IoT systems. This significant-scale distributed cyber-attack targeted hundreds of thousands of IoTs, including home network routers and IP cameras, by taking benefits from weak security protocols, turning these into bots for performing massive DDoS attacks (Kolias et al., 2017). Faced with this nature, the need to reinforce security for IoT systems on military applications is highlighted.

A big challenge is ensuring that many IoT systems from different platforms can talk together harmoniously. In military systems, devices from multiple vendors are typically implemented and thus need to interact securely (Lin et al., 2017).

6. Future Trends and Technologies in Military IoT Security

Unlike standard technology, the pace of change in military IoT system security is still very fast. As new challenges face the defence sector, several key trends and technologies are poised to significantly bolster security in this domain and fortify IoT systems within military applications. Among these advancements are quantum computing, blockchain, ML, and AI, which will significantly affect the future of security for military IoT.

6.1. AI and ML for Security

Adopting AI and ML is a trend that will play an even more significant role in defending military IoT networks. They outperform many existing solutions regarding real-time data analysis for predictive threat assessment, automating the detecting anomalies and (possibly harmful) trends that indicate a cybersecurity incident (Kshetri, 2017). AI-powered systems in military settings allow decision-makers to recognize and mitigate risks before they snowball and increase response time for the reliability of operations.

In this way, AI may be used to analyze patterns in network traffic and recognize odd activities that could indicate a security breach (e.g. an unauthorized device trying to gain access over the sensitive network). ML models can also learn to identify never-before-seen cyberattack tactics, providing an adaptive defence layer that grows better with time.

Furthermore, AI and ML are valid for regular security tasks like patch management with system updates to prevent established vulnerabilities from impacting IoT components (Al-Turjman, 2019). AI can assist military companies in becoming less dependent on human error, speeding up the security process, and generally upgrading the IoT network's security.

6.2. Blockchain Technology for IoT Security

Blockchain, a decentralized ledger technology, represents a promising solution for enhancing the security of IoT systems in military applications. A principal advantage of blockchain is its capacity for secure, tamper-resistant data sharing across various devices and networks, thereby ensuring data integrity and authenticity (Dorri, 2016). In military IoT settings, where devices frequently function in hostile or contested conditions, safeguarding data integrity is essential.

Blockchain can be helpful for military organizations as it provides a secure delivery path to IoT devices and ensures data integrity where malicious agents will not intercept or tamper with sensitive information during the transition. Likewise, a blockchain can also be helpful for secure identification measures of IoT Devices so that it becomes more difficult to inject unauthorized devices into the network (Samaniego et al., 2016). Smart contracts on the blockchain can automate specific security processes, such as identifying which devices are permitted access to your network based on their identity.

Blockchain has enormous potential for enhanced cybersecurity, and innovations similar to the ones mentioned earlier related to 5G – such as the IoT – but it also presents significant problems regarding scaling up or uncontrolled energy use, making it challenging to incorporate in military applications. However, research on this topic is still being developed, and they are trying to find a way for Blockchain-based military IoT systems to benefit from using Gross Domestic Products (GDPs) (Conoscenti et al., 2016).

6.3. Quantum Computing Impacts

Quantum computing represents both an opportunity and a threat to IoT security in military applications. Quantum computers can address intricate computational challenges at a significantly faster pace than classical computers, potentially resulting in advancements in the security of IoT networks (Gidney & Ekerå, 2021). Quantum encryption methods, including quantum key distribution (QKD), provide nearly unbreakable security by utilizing the principles of quantum mechanics (Pirandola et al., 2020). This could be particularly beneficial in securing military communications and protecting sensitive data from cyberattacks.

Conversely, quantum computers may present a considerable challenge to current cryptographic techniques. Present encryption standards, including RSA and ECC, face threats from advanced quantum computers, which have the potential to break encryption keys significantly quicker than traditional computers (Shor, 1999). Military IoT systems relying on traditional encryption methods may become vulnerable once quantum computers reach sufficient maturity.

One approach is for defence organizations to look at post-quantum cryptography – or newer encryption algorithms that are quantum-safe (Bernstein & Lange, 2017) and suitable against potential future implemented attacks. For example, quantum computing is a sunrise today. However, it could have been done with military IOT systems if one was future-compliant and could be post-quantum or hybrid cryptosystems decades out.

7. Conclusion

Integrating the IoT into military defence systems revolutionizes modern military operations. IoT's capabilities, such as enhanced situational awareness, automation, and improved decision-making processes, are invaluable in ensuring operational success. However, IoT technology adoption has several serious drawbacks, notably regarding data privacy, cybersecurity, and managing large, intricate networks.

The risks associated with IoT in military contexts are heightened due to the sensitivity of defence-related information and the potentially catastrophic consequences of security breaches. Vulnerabilities such as cyberattacks, unauthorized data access, and compromised networks necessitate developing advanced security measures to protect military IoT systems. To address these challenges, several technologies and strategies have been identified as crucial for strengthening IoT security, including encryption protocols, resilient network architectures, and IDSs.

In the future, new technologies like blockchain, quantum computing, and AI will be crucial in improving the security and robustness of military IoT systems. AI and ML will make predictive threat analysis and automated responses possible, while blockchain technology can offer safe, unhackable communication and data exchange across military networks. Quantum computing will simultaneously present new opportunities for sophisticated encryption and necessitate that defence systems adjust to possible quantum threats.

As the IoT landscape changes, military organizations must continue to be proactive in achieving system security. This will require ongoing investment in research, technology development, and collaboration across the defence sector and with private technology firms. By leveraging innovative security solutions and staying ahead of emerging threats, military IoT systems can be fortified to protect national defence infrastructures and ensure continued operational effectiveness in the face of an ever-changing security landscape.

References

Alaba, F. A., Othman, M., Hashem, I. A. T., & Alotaibi, F. (2017). Internet of Things security: A survey. *Journal of Network and Computer Applications*, *88*, 10–28.

Al-Turjman, F. (Ed.). (2019). *Artificial intelligence in IoT*. Springer.

Austin, R. (2011). *Unmanned aircraft systems: UAVS design, development and deployment*. John Wiley & Sons.

Bernstein, D. J., & Lange, T. (2017). Post-quantum cryptography. *Nature*, *549*(7671), 188–194.

Borgia, E. (2014). The Internet of Things vision: Key features, applications and open issues. *Computer Communications*, *54*, 1–31.

Conoscenti, M., Vetro, A., & De Martin, J. C. (2016, November). Blockchain for the Internet of Things: A systematic literature review. In *2016 IEEE/ACS 13th international conference of computer systems and applications (AICCSA)* (pp. 1–6). IEEE.

Da Xu, L., He, W., & Li, S. (2014). Internet of things in industries: A survey. *IEEE Transactions on Industrial Informatics*, *10*(4), 2233–2243.

Dorri, A. (2016). Blockchain in Internet of Things: Challenges and solutions. *arXiv preprint arXiv:1608.05187*.

Dorri, A., Kanhere, S. S., Jurdak, R., & Gauravaram, P. (2017, March). Blockchain for IoT security and privacy: The case study of a smart home. In *2017 IEEE international conference on pervasive computing and communications workshops (PerCom workshops)* (pp. 618–623). IEEE.

Gartzke, E. (2013). The myth of cyberwar: bringing war in cyberspace back down to earth. *International Security*, *38*(2), 41–73.

Gidney, C., & Ekerå, M. (2021). How to factor 2048 bit RSA integers in 8 hours using 20 million noisy qubits. *Quantum*, *5*, 433.

Greengard, S. (2015). *The Internet of Things*. The MIT Press.

Gubbi, J., Buyya, R., Marusic, S., & Palaniswami, M. (2013). Internet of Things (IoT): A vision, architectural elements, and future directions. *Future Generation Computer Systems*, *29*(7), 1645–1660.

Khan, M. A., & Salah, K. (2018). IoT security: Review, blockchain solutions, and open challenges. *Future Generation Computer Systems*, *82*, 395–411.

Kolias, C., Kambourakis, G., Stavrou, A., & Voas, J. (2017). DDoS in the IoT: Mirai and other botnets. *Computer*, *50*(7), 80–84.

Kshetri, N. (2017). Can blockchain strengthen the Internet of Things? *IT Professional*, *19*(4), 68–72.

Lewis, J. A. (2016). *Managing risk for the Internet of Things*. Center for Strategic & International Studies.

Lin, J., Yu, W., Zhang, N., Yang, X., Zhang, H., & Zhao, W. (2017). A survey on Internet of Things: Architecture, enabling technologies, security and privacy, and applications. *IEEE Internet of Things Journal*, *4*(5), 1125–1142.

Maras, M. H. (2015). Internet of Things: Security and privacy implications. *International Data Privacy Law*, *5*, 99.

Pirandola, S., Andersen, U. L., Banchi, L., Berta, M., Bunandar, D., Colbeck, R., & Wallden, P. (2020). Advances in quantum cryptography. *Advances in Optics and Photonics*, *12*(4), 1012–1236.

Rayes, A., & Salam, S. (2019). *Internet of Things from hype to reality* (pp. 1–35). Springer International Publishing.

Roman, R., Zhou, J., & Lopez, J. (2013). On the features and challenges of security and privacy in distributed internet of things. *Computer Networks*, *57*(10), 2266–2279.

Russell, S., & Abdelzaher, T. (2018, October). The internet of battlefield things: the next generation of command, control, communications and intelligence (C3I) decision-making. In *MILCOM 2018-2018 IEEE military communications conference (MILCOM)* (pp. 737–742). IEEE.

Samaniego, M., Jamsrandorj, U., & Deters, R. (2016, December). Blockchain as a service for IoT. In *2016 IEEE international conference on internet of things (iThings) and IEEE green computing and communications (GreenCom) and IEEE cyber, physical and social computing (CPSCom) and IEEE smart data (SmartData)* (pp. 433–436). IEEE.

Shor, P. W. (1999). Polynomial-time algorithms for prime factorization and discrete logarithms on a quantum computer. *SIAM Review*, *41*(2), 303–332.

Stallings, W. (2018). *Effective cybersecurity: A guide to using best practices and standards*. Addison-Wesley Professional.

Stojmenovic, I., & Wen, S. (2014, September). The fog computing paradigm: Scenarios and security issues. In *2014 federated conference on computer science and information systems* (pp. 1–8). IEEE.

Taddeo, M. (2019). Three ethical challenges of applications of artificial intelligence in cybersecurity. *Minds and Machines*, *29*, 187–191.

Yan, Z., Zhang, P., & Vasilakos, A. V. (2014). A survey on trust management for Internet of Things. *Journal of Network and Computer Applications*, *42*, 120–134.

Zhong, R. Y., Xu, X., Klotz, E., & Newman, S. T. (2017). Intelligent manufacturing in the context of industry 4.0: A review. *Engineering*, *3*(5), 616–630.

Zhou, W., Jia, Y., Peng, A., Zhang, Y., & Liu, P. (2018). The effect of IoT new features on security and privacy: New threats, existing solutions, and challenges yet to be solved. *IEEE Internet of Things Journal*, *6*(2), 1606–1616.

Chapter 7

Wars and Logistics: The Transformative Influence of the Internet of Things on Military Operations

Anurag A. S. and Johnpaul M.

Department of Management Studies, Central University of Kerala, India

Abstract

Logistics has always been the backbone of the military since the inception of the first army. This chapter explores the profound impact of the Internet of Things (IoT) on military logistics. Beginning with a discussion of the historical evolution of military logistics, it proceeds to define IoT and explore its various applications. The core of the chapter focuses on the military applications of IoT, including logistics, surveillance, virtual training, and connected soldiers. The chapter also addresses the challenges faced by the military in implementing IoT solutions. Understanding these challenges is crucial for developing strategies to mitigate them and ensure the successful integration of IoT into military operations. Furthermore, the chapter considers the future potential of IoT in military logistics. This comprehensive analysis highlights the impacts of IoT on military logistics, emphasizing the need for ongoing technological advancements and strategic solutions to overcome implementation obstacles.

Keywords: Connected soldiers; fleet management system; Internet of Battlefield Things; Internet of Things; military logistics; supply chain; unmanned aerial vehicle

The Internet of Things in the Defence Industry:
Challenges and Solutions for Military Security, 149–166

doi:10.1108/978-1-83549-198-020261007

Introduction

> 'Amateurs talk about tactics, but professionals study logistics' – Gen. Robert H. Barrow (Straight, 2022)
>
> 'An army marches on its stomach'. – Napoleon Bonaparte (Glenn, 2023)

These quotes are from two significant military figures: General Robert H. Barrow, a United States Marine Corps general who served during the late 20th century, and Napoleon Bonaparte, the French emperor and military commander of the early 19th century. Despite the different eras and contexts in which they lived, both statements underscore a timeless truth about warfare: logistics is crucial to success. General Barrow's insight highlights that, beyond battlefield strategies, victory often hinges on logistical planning and execution. Similarly, Napoleon's observation underscores the practical reality that soldiers' effectiveness relies heavily on their sustenance and supply lines. These perspectives from two military leaders from different times illustrate the crucial role logistics has played in warfare throughout history. In modern warfare, logistics is more important than ever. An army's power and capability can be measured by measuring its logistical capacity. Therefore, streamlining and improving logistics operations is vital for defense. One of the most significant and efficient modern technologies capable of transforming military logistics into a more streamlined and effective function is the IoT.

IoT is a comparatively new technology that is still under constant upgrades and development. A precise definition for IoT is still not available (Li et al., 2015). Several researchers have proposed their interpretations of what constitutes IoT, indicating the ongoing development and refinement of its definition. In an editorial published in the *International Journal of Communication Systems*, the authors view IoT as a networked interconnection of everyday objects equipped with ubiquitous intelligence, creating a highly distributed network of devices that communicate with humans and each other through embedded systems (Xia et al., 2012). Similarly, it is also defined as the extension of network connectivity and computing capabilities to everyday objects, devices, sensors, and items, enabling them to autonomously generate, exchange, and consume data without human interference (Rose et al., 2015). These are some of the ways researchers have already described the IoT. By considering these definitions and our understanding, in this paper, we define IoT as the interconnection of several embedded devices, such as Radio-Frequency Identification (RFID) tags, sensors, and actuators capable of communicating with each other through a network.

The term 'Internet of Things' was first used by Kevin Ashton in the title of one of his 1999 presentations (Ashton, 2009). The context of the presentation was to use RFID devices in Procter & Gamble's (P&G) supply chain. During the same time, RFID became the 'thing' along with the rising popularity of the internet. The Auto-ID Center at MIT, funded by major corporations, revolutionized RFID technology by creating low-cost tags that stored serial numbers, transforming RFID into a networking tool for automated supply chain tracking and communication over the Internet (Landt, 2005). This was the dawn of the groundbreaking concept that we know today as IoT. Since its inception, IoT has transformed in various ways. RFID is no longer the only thing in the IoT. It encompasses a wide variety of devices beyond RFID, such as different sensors, actuators, wearables like smartwatches and fitness trackers, home automation devices such as smart lights and smart appliances, smart city infrastructure, healthcare devices, and different devices and sensors used for agricultural purposes. Today, the applications of IoT have expanded across various sectors, including but not limited to environmental and disaster monitoring, home automation, consumer asset tracking, pilgrim monitoring, agriculture, transportation, healthcare, smart metres, waste management, surveillance, smart grids, and the military (Ramson et al., 2020).

Background and Literature Review

Warfare has been a critical part of human civilization since its inception. Over time, various military strategies were developed, including set-piece battles and raiding. However, the most notable strategy during this period was advanced siege warfare (Cohen, 2024). A siege involves surrounding enemy territory and cutting off their logistics and supplies. This strategy aims to force the enemy to abandon their position and surrender. Although it was often a much slower process, siege warfare was widely used because it could overcome castles and fortified cities with minimal bloodshed. By isolating the enemy and depriving them of resources, besiegers could achieve victory without the need for direct, large-scale combat. This method of warfare was effective in reducing casualties and ensuring a more controlled conquest of fortified locations.

The prevalence of strategies like siege warfare throughout history highlights the critical role of logistics in military success. The greatest conquerors in history, such as Alexander the Great and Genghis Khan, placed great importance on their military logistics. When the Mongols began their invasions, their most critical strength was not their arsenal or the size of their army but their logistics. A well-planned and strategized logistics system acted as the backbone of the Mongol army (Lee, 2022). Even in modern warfare, logistics and Supply Chain Management (SCM) remain critical. Effective strategic plans for military operations must prioritize logistics to ensure sustained operations and readiness. The ability to efficiently manage resources and supplies directly influences the outcome of any military campaign.

The Evolution of Military Logistics Across Different Eras

There are several definitions available to describe military logistics. One of the well-accepted definitions of military logistics was put forward by NATO. According to NATO's *Handbook of Logistics*, military logistics is the science of planning and executing the movement and maintenance of military forces. It encompasses the design, development, acquisition, storage, transport, distribution, maintenance, evacuation, and disposal of vehicles, weapons, ammunition, fuel, and other supplies (NATO, 1997).

- *Neolithic Military Logistics*

The necessity of logistics emerged with the formation of the first armies, which can be traced back to the Neolithic period. During this era, humans began to develop farming, establish permanent settlements, and create pottery. Concurrently, warfare evolved, as evidenced by the construction of defensive structures and the development of specialized weapons for combat, and this period marked the inception of deliberate innovation in military technology, transitioning from the use of simple hunting tools to the creation of purpose-built implements of war (Guilmartin, 2024). During this time, the logistics requirements primarily involved the supply of food and water for warriors.

- *Antiquity Military Logistics*

The emergence of early civilizations in Mesopotamia, Egypt, the Indus Valley, and China marked the onset of the use of iron tools and weapons. This epoch also witnessed the zenith of Greek and Roman civilizations. These developments also prompted the emergence of novel warfare strategies and logistical imperatives. Spanning from the Peloponnesian War to the collapse of the Roman Empire, ancient warfare strategies showcased a spectrum of tactics and logistical methodologies (Cohen, 2024). Rome's strategic doctrine was distinguished by institutional robustness and the adaptability of the Roman legion. At the same time, logistical operations primarily relied on human labour and meticulous resource allocation, notwithstanding limited advancements in transportation technology (Guilmartin, 2024).

- *Medieval Military Logistics*

During the medieval period, we witnessed the emergence of European kingdoms, the protracted conflicts of the Hundred Years' War, and the significant geopolitical event of the fall of Constantinople. This epoch was characterized by a multitude of military engagements, leading to the evolution of both strategies and logistical requirements. Military formations in medieval Europe varied widely, encompassing Swiss pikemen, Western European mounted chivalry, and Arabian light cavalry. Notably, the Byzantine Empire employed advanced weaponry, such as Greek fire, to repel adversaries. Warfare strategies of the period included both overthrow and exhaustion tactics, with sieges playing a pivotal role. However, logistical impediments such as limited food reserves and inadequate transportation infrastructure often impeded the pace of military campaigns. In contrast, regions like East and Central Asia, epitomized by the Mongols, witnessed swift and decisive conquests facilitated by favourable terrain and disciplined cavalry forces (Cohen, 2024).

- *Early Modern Military Logistics*

The early modern period set the stage for transformative developments in military strategy and logistics. The scientific revolution revolutionized military logistics, fostering a strategic evolution that would shape the course of warfare for centuries to come. As described in the book (Van Creveld, 1997), the European armies grew during the late 16th century, even surpassing 100,000 troops in some instances. This expansion brought logistical challenges as reliance on pillaging enemy territories for supplies became unsustainable. Consequently, strategic priorities shifted towards securing supply routes rather than solely military objectives, notably affecting sieges. Napoleon revolutionized warfare by dispersing his forces widely to optimize available resources, prioritize mobility, and establish regular supply lines. Unlike earlier methods of living off the land, his approach demanded meticulous logistical planning to sustain large armies and guarantee sufficient ammunition for campaigns.

- *Modern Military Logistics*

The modern period, shaped by industrialization, has witnessed profound changes in military logistics, evolving alongside technological advancements and socioeconomic upheavals. Advances in weapons technology, such as the rifled musket and breech-loading artillery, significantly increased firepower, requiring corresponding changes in logistical support to accommodate the heightened destructive potential of these weapons. The Industrial Revolution provided the capacity to produce munitions, food, transport, and other necessities on a large scale, enabling the support of mass armies and their logistical needs. There was a revolution in management and organization techniques, allowing for the more effective operation of military establishments through improvements in coordination, communication, and strategic planning. The emergence of transportation and communication innovations, including the railroad, steamship, telegraph, and later electronic communication methods, revolutionized logistical methods. Steam-powered ships and later developments in motor transport further enhanced logistical capabilities by enabling the rapid movement of troops and supplies over land and water (Leighton, 2023).

- *Contemporary Military Logistics*

The digital revolution, global interconnectedness, and environmental challenges characterize the 21st century. According to the article published by Brown (2023), military logistics have evolved to meet the demands of contemporary warfare, encompassing conventional conflicts, cyber threats, counterterrorism operations, and humanitarian missions. This evolution necessitates an adaptable and responsive logistics framework enhanced by the integration of GPS, real-time tracking, and data analytics to optimize SCM. The author also argues that the deployment of Unmanned Aerial Vehicles (UAVs) and autonomous vehicles has significantly expedited the delivery of critical supplies to frontline troops and the collaborative efforts between different branches of the armed forces and international partners, facilitated by interconnected logistics networks, ensure the rapid deployment of multinational forces. Agile supply chains, prepositioned stockpiles, and mobile logistics units enable quick resource shifting across various operational theatres, maintaining effectiveness in dynamically changing environments (Brown, 2023).

Internet of Things

The rise of digital technology has been a sudden and revolutionary game-changer across all fields. Digitalization has streamlined everyday tasks and transformed how we communicate, work, and access information. The military has also embraced the latest technologies. Recently, several disruptive technologies have emerged, transforming supply chain and logistics processes.

Innovations such as blockchain, predictive analytics, digital twins, cloud computing, and the IoT are reshaping the landscape, making operations more efficient and effective.

IoT has undergone significant evolution in its functionality, the integration of devices, and its operation since its inception. Currently, IoT has been extensively categorized into various types according to the areas of implementation and the functions they perform. When IoT is utilized solely for personal purposes involving consumer products like smart home appliances, smartphones, and smartwatches, it falls under Consumer IoT (Loi et al., 2017). On the other hand, when IoT applications extend to functions such as environmental monitoring or access controls for commercial or public places, they transition into Commercial IoT (Hernandez, 2019). Industrial IoT helps to create a factory environment where all the industrial functions are interconnected and automated to improve efficiency (Dhirani et al., 2021). Infrastructure IoT finds widespread application in projects related to smart buildings and smart cities. Among these categories, Military IoT is also of utmost importance in military operations and defense strategies. It ensures uninterrupted connectivity within the military domain and aids in information-gathering and decision-making processes (Cameron, 2018).

Components of IoT

- *IoT Devices*

There are several devices used in IoT, such as sensors, actuators, and RFID. Sensors automate applications by detecting and responding to changes in physical conditions (Sehrawat & Gill, 2019). Based on their features, sensors are classified into various types (see Table 7.1). On the other hand, an actuator is a device that receives an electrical signal from a PLC and converts it into a physical action. RFID is a technology that uses radio waves to identify objects by transmitting data from an RFID tag to a reader. Fig. 7.1 shows the graphical representation of components of IoT. An RFID tag contains a microchip for storing information and an antenna for transmitting this information to a reader. An RFID reader

Table 7.1. Types of Sensors Used in IoT. Source: Sehrawat and Gill (2019).

Types of Sensors		
Proximity Sensors	Humidity Sensors	Temperature Sensors
Position Sensors	Water Quality Sensors	Chemical Sensors
Occupancy Sensors	Infrared Sensors	Pressure Sensors
Motion Sensors	Gyroscope Sensors	Optical Sensors
Velocity Sensors		

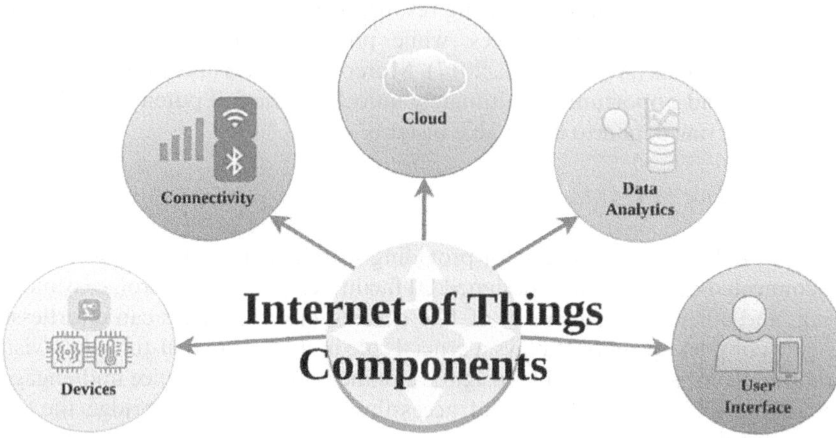

Fig. 7.1. Most Important Components of IoT (Author).

uses inductive coupling to communicate with RFID tags, converting the transmitted data into a digital format that computers can understand (Angeles, 2005).

- *Connectivity*

The next component of IoT is connectivity, which is the critical factor that links the devices to each other. There are various methods used for IoT connectivity depending on the system's application. For smaller systems operating over short distances, technologies such as Bluetooth, ZigBee, WiFi, and Optical Wireless Communication are employed. For broader applications, technologies like Long-Term Evolution and the 5th Generation (5G) technologies are primarily utilized, along with licenced and unlicenced versions of Low Power Wide Area Network technology (Ding et al., 2020).

- *Cloud*

The Cloud plays a pivotal role in IoT by serving as the central platform for storing, processing, and analyzing the vast amounts of data generated by IoT devices. Cloud functions streamline advanced analytics and IoT device monitoring, aiming to minimize execution time, costs, and energy usage (Bali et al., 2020).

The IoT cloud serves as a crucial backbone for efficiently handling the immense data volumes produced by IoT devices and applications. It is a tool for gathering, processing, and storing real-time data.

- *Data Analytics*

In IoT systems, data analytics plays a crucial role in extracting valuable insights from the massive amounts of data generated by interconnected devices and sensors. Data analytics plays a pivotal role in IoT systems. It enables real-time insights, enhancing decision-making agility and operational efficiency by predicting maintenance needs and optimizing resources. Understanding user behaviour facilitates personalized experiences, while predictive maintenance minimizes downtime and costs (Ahmed et al., 2017). Moreover, it fuels innovation by uncovering trends and opportunities, ultimately unlocking the full potential of IoT by transforming raw data into actionable insights.

- *User Interface (UI)*

The UI in IoT systems is crucial for providing seamless interaction between users and connected devices. A well-designed UI facilitates intuitive control, easy monitoring, and efficient management of IoT devices, ensuring users can effortlessly navigate complex systems. It plays a crucial role in delivering real-time data visualization, alerts, and actionable insights, enhancing user experience and engagement. By prioritizing usability and accessibility, the UI helps bridge the gap between sophisticated IoT technologies and everyday users, making advanced functionalities accessible and beneficial for all.

Applications of IoBT

By integrating advanced IoT technologies into various aspects of military infrastructure, forces around the world are enhancing their operational capabilities. The military applications of the IoT are rapidly transforming the landscape of defense operations. Fig. 7.2 shows the applications of Internet of Battle Things (IoBT) and their sub-areas. The IoT, which is designed specifically for military purposes, can be referred to as the Internet of Battlefield Things (IoBT).

Awareness of Battlefield in Advance: Unmanned aerial drones equipped with cameras and sensors to survey the battlefield allow for mapping the terrain and identifying enemy positions. These data can be transmitted to the command centre in real-time with the help of an IoBT system, aiding officers in making quick and strategic decisions (Prolim, n.d.).

Connect Soldiers System (CSS): The CSS is an IoBT-based network that links all soldiers in a troop into a unified communication system. The intelligent gadgets worn by the soldiers continuously transmit data from various parts of the battlefield to a central base in real-time. The CSS revolutionizes battlefield operations by offering comprehensive and uniform situational awareness, which significantly enhances command speed and initiative.

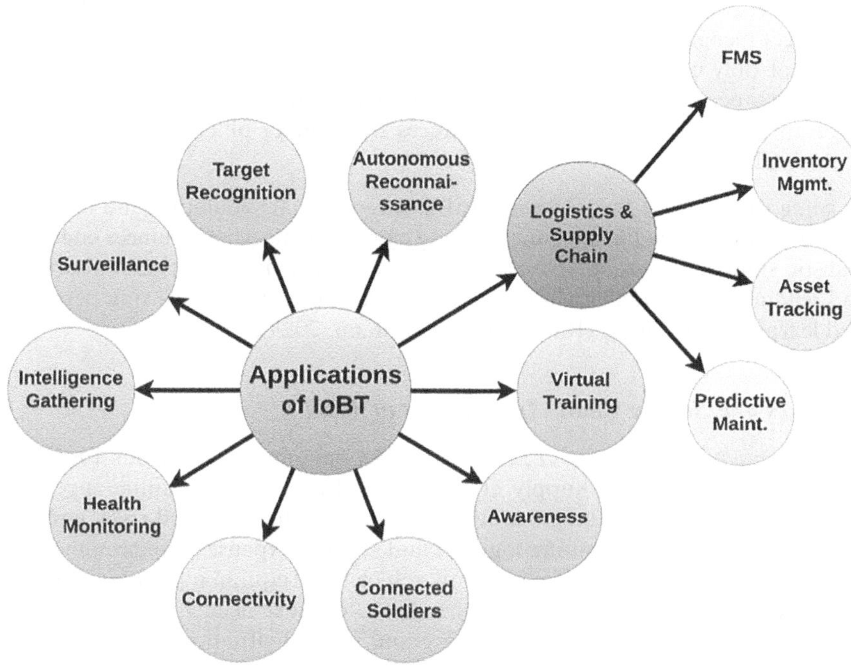

Fig. 7.2. Applications of IoBT (Author).

Communication and Connectivity: An effective IoBT system enables the efficient and real-time connectivity of a large number of active and passive devices, thus maintaining uninterrupted information sharing and ensuring complete situational awareness.

Soldier Health Monitoring: Advancements in IoBT offer promising capabilities for early detection, diagnosis, and treatment of soldier health issues in the field. This includes timely identification of casualties and prediction of injury outcomes. Wearable technology plays a significant role in remotely monitoring various physiological signs (Kang et al., 2020).

Intelligence Gathering: IoBT plays a crucial role in intelligence gathering by facilitating the coordination and flow of information among soldiers and sensors. By utilizing IoBT devices, soldiers can collect data from various sources and transmit it to the base. These devices enable real-time monitoring of the battlefield, allowing for rapid adjustments to mission strategies based on changing threats (Farooq & Zhu, 2017).

Surveillance & Remote Monitoring: Through interconnected devices, IoBT enables real-time data collection and analysis across diverse operational environments. Surveillance in IoBT extends beyond traditional borders, offering military forces unprecedented visibility into remote or hostile areas while minimizing human risk. The use of UAVs with IoBT has drastically improved the capabilities of military surveillance (Saraswat et al., 2022).

Target Recognition and Autonomous Reconnaissance: IoBT enables rapid and precise target recognition by analyzing vast amounts of data in real time. This capability not only enhances situational awareness but also empowers autonomous reconnaissance. The ability of a UAV to conduct missions without the direct involvement of humans drastically reduces the number of casualties (Saraswat et al., 2022).

Training with Virtual Environments: IoBT-based virtual simulation and real-time feedback systems enable dynamic learning environments where trainees engage in realistic simulations using virtual reality (VR), improving situational awareness and readiness. Instructors can tailor training activities easily, ensuring personalized learning experiences (Raman & Vyakaranam, 2024).

Logistics and Supply Chain Applications of IoBT

Fleet Management System (FMS): An FMS encompasses various functions like management of the supply chain, driver, fuel, vehicle maintenance, and transportation. It is a strategic tool for mitigating vehicle-related risks, enhancing productivity, and trimming logistics and staffing expenses (Nagarajan et al., 2020). The IoBT has revolutionized how vehicles and equipment are transported with FMS. Logistics operations in a military context need to be transparent and dynamic to adapt to ever-changing and critical situations. Implementing an IoBT system allows every fleet movement to be tracked. By continuously monitoring data from the vehicles and machinery, the IoBT system can detect deviations from standard patterns, aiding in informed decision-making for the entire transportation system.

Inventory Management: RFID scanners can scan and update the status of items in the cloud in real-time. By comparing historical data and real-time data, any IoT system is capable of automatically identifying items prone to shortage and can place orders accordingly. IoBT can increase transparency in inventory management, reduce loss, and increase efficiency. Using an efficient IoBT system for inventory management will effectively reduce inventory carrying costs by up to 10% (Zheng & Carter, 2015). An IoBT system can effectively track the status of containers during transit and while in storage around the world. This capability allows for the precise identification of a container's location and the detection of any tampering or unauthorized access attempts. This feature of IoT improves shipment monitoring, problem identification, and accountability (Zheng & Carter, 2015).

Asset Tracking: An effective asset tracking system typically includes a tagging system, such as RFID tags or barcodes, to mark assets with unique identifiers. These tags are read by a device that encrypts the details, which are then communicated via a UI that decrypts the information. The IoBT enhances asset tracking by monitoring the location and condition of military equipment. IoBT ensures the security of asset transfers by providing real-time tracking and alerts for any deviations from planned routes. Users receive immediate notifications on their monitoring devices, ensuring swift responses to potential issues. This system ensures the efficient and secure movement of assets, which is critical for maintaining operational continuity and security.

Predictive Maintenance: Predictive maintenance involves continuously monitoring machines and equipment to identify potential causes of failure and addressing them before they occur (Mobley, 2002). This method is very crucial for the defense sectors to maintain optimal performance. In a military base, several assets will require frequent maintenance, such as vehicles, aircraft, weapons, infrastructure, naval vessels, and UAVs. IoT will continuously collect vast amounts of data from these assets and check for anomalies in the working pattern. Predictive maintenance improves output quality and reduces unnecessary downtime. IoT enables remote monitoring of assets, making it possible to perform checks in scenarios where regular physical inspections are complex (zu Wickern, 2019).

Challenges in Implementing IoBT

Ethical Implications of Autonomous Systems

The advancements in 5G technology have enhanced IoT capabilities, providing faster and more reliable connectivity for IoT devices. Continued advancements in AI, ML, and quantum computing are expected to drive the next generation of IoT innovations. However, as IoT technology expands, the volume of data flowing into the system will be enormous, and it will be shared among various systems (Righetti et al., 2018). Due to this fact, the IoT system raises several concerns, such as informed consent, privacy, information security, physical safety, and trust (Allhoff & Henschke, 2018). Additionally, IoT devices may collect personal or sensitive data from users, potentially breaching their privacy. However, the key to a secure system lies in allowing only authorized access to collected data. Thus, the misuse of the data can be prevented. Unlike older military devices, web-connected devices are vulnerable to external cyberattacks. Breaches in operational plans could lead to strategic disadvantages and endanger lives. Therefore, ensuring robust cybersecurity measures is crucial to safeguard the integrity and confidentiality of military data. Confidence in IoT systems relies on the reliability of devices, the accuracy of data collected, and the effectiveness of security measures. Lack of trust among military personnel could impede operational efficiency, leading to hesitation or refusal to use critical IoT applications. Addressing these concerns with comprehensive strategies and robust security measures enables the military to harness the benefits of IoT while mitigating associated ethical issues.

Managing the Large Data Acquired by the Devices

IoT devices generate enormous amounts of data. Each of these data has its unique features, and combining all of them and managing them effectively is not a simple task. Abbasi et al. (2017) have proposed a framework for addressing the data management challenges expected in the future of IoT. The proposed data management framework consists of nine layers designed to handle the complexities of IoT data efficiently (Abbasi et al., 2017). Further studies are essential to enhance the capability of IoT systems to manage the extensive data gathered by devices effectively. Such systems should possess the capacity to handle structured, semi-structured, and unstructured data simultaneously, processing it promptly to derive actionable insights. Throughout these operations, data security and safeguarding against potential breaches and privacy infringements are to be ensured.

Interoperability of the IoBT System Employed

As the IoBT system evolves into a complex network of interconnected devices experiencing rapid expansion, the significance of interoperability becomes critical. According to Noura et al. (2019), interoperability can be comprehended through various perspectives. First is device interoperability, which pertains to the ability of devices to communicate with one another and integrate new devices into the existing system. Network interoperability signifies the system's capacity to communicate with analogous systems through diverse networks. Syntactical interoperability concerns compatibility with the data structure or encoding format employed by multiple systems. Semantic interoperability entails enabling diverse agents, services, and applications to exchange information and data meaningfully, notwithstanding disparities in data formats, models, schemas, and operational procedures, thereby facilitating seamless communication and collaboration across IoT systems. Lastly, platform interoperability refers to the capability of different software platforms or systems to interact seamlessly with one another (Noura et al., 2019). Without interoperability, IoBT systems will struggle to manage data from different devices and other systems. Adding new devices to the system will be challenging. Interoperability challenges undermine the seamless connectivity, scalability, security, and cost-effectiveness of IoBT systems, hindering their ability to realize their full potential in military applications.

Durability of the Hardware

Military operations often take place in harsh and unforgiving environments, including extreme temperatures, high humidity, sandstorms, and rugged terrain. Such conditions can compromise the structural integrity and functionality of delicate electronic components, leading to system failures and mission disruption. As with any other military equipment, IoBT devices should also be manufactured under military standards. It should be able to withstand severe battlefield conditions, rough usage, and harsh weather (Pant, 2019).

Difficulty in Recruiting and Retaining Skilled Personnel

Recruiting individuals possessing the requisite skill sets to operate this system presents a significant challenge. Several factors contribute to the complexity of the recruitment process and impede the military's capacity to attract and retain qualified personnel in this specialized domain. According to Schröder (2022), military organizations confront significant challenges in recruiting and retaining talent owing to rapid technological advancements and shifting workforce demographics. Moreover, the author suggests that the attraction of talent necessitates the provision of appealing career trajectories, customized compensation packages, and the establishment of a digitalized work environment. The incorporation of flexible career pathways and horizontal recruitments emerges as imperative measures to accommodate non-lifelong careers and address shortages in specialized skills. Furthermore, the optimized utilization of reserves and the professionalization of human resource functions are deemed essential for effective talent management within military contexts (Schröder, 2022).

Cases of Practical Application of IoT in Military Logistics

The Textron-Kodiak Collaboration

On 20 May 2024, a story was uploaded to Kodiak's website, in which they announced their collaboration with Textron Systems Corporation (Kodiak, 2024). Textron is a military vehicle developer, and Kodiak is the developer of self-driving technology, especially for the defense market. These two companies are collaborating to develop an autonomous military vehicle. Textron has extensive experience in designing and developing air, land, and sea vehicles for defense. In contrast,

Kodiak has prior experience with military technology applications, having revealed its first autonomous military test vehicle in December 2023. According to the article published by Hope (2024) on this collaboration, the author highlights the details of the project, such as the project will see Kodiak's autonomous technology, the Kodiak Driver, integrated into a purpose-built prototype from Textron. This new project is notable for being the first instance where Kodiak's technology is integrated into a vehicle designed without any space for a human driver. The vehicle will feature Kodiak's DefensePods, adapted from their modular SensorPods used in commercial trucks. These DefensePods are quick-swap sensor enclosures designed for rapid replacement in the field. Kodiak and Textron officially unveiled the vehicle (RIPSAW M3), equipped with the Kodiak Driver, and conducted driverless demonstrations in September 2024. They will also explore further opportunities with the US Department of Defense and allied militaries to advance automated ground vehicle technology (Hope, 2024). Kodiak and Textron's innovative vehicle has the potential to transform military logistics significantly. The autonomous operation of the vehicle reduces risks to personnel, particularly in hazardous environments such as combat zones or areas with explosive threats. Its deployment capability in remote or inaccessible areas without human intervention enhances logistical reach and operational flexibility. Additionally, the vehicle's autonomous system can collect and analyze data in real-time, providing valuable insights into logistics operations and facilitating more informed decision-making. Such advancements possess the capability to revolutionize military logistics by improving efficiency, safety, flexibility, and strategic capabilities while concurrently reducing costs and fostering innovation.

AI Incorporation Initiative in the Indian Army

As an emerging world economy that boasts one of the largest and most powerful military forces equipped with advanced weaponry and technology, India has already initiated several schemes to implement AI technologies and IoT into its defense sector. According to Lobo (2024), the Army Chief General of India spoke at the NDTV Defence Summit about the initiatives India plans to implement in the coming years. These include Natural Language Processing (NLP), facial recognition, vehicle tracking, and satellite imagery analysis. NLP, a system that understands and processes human language, aims to enhance communication and intelligence analysis. AI-driven facial recognition technology will bolster security and surveillance, while vehicle tracking can improve the operational and logistical capabilities of military vehicles. Satellite imagery analysis will facilitate border monitoring and reconnaissance operations. Furthermore, India has embarked on creating a high-powered computing AI cloud similar to those already adopted by countries such as the UK and the US. This AI cloud will enable quicker data processing and decision-making by leveraging vast amounts of data for strategic advantages. The integration of 5G-powered IoT will be utilized for smart surveillance, telemedicine, drone control, and training purposes. IoT devices will enhance surveillance capabilities by providing real-time monitoring and intelligence gathering. Additionally, IoT will enable telemedicine services for military personnel, allowing for remote diagnosis and treatment, particularly in remote or battlefield conditions. Advanced control systems for drones, facilitated by IoT, will improve their operational range, efficiency, and responsiveness. For military training purposes, virtual environments using AR and VR will be employed. To ensure the successful implementation of these projects, India is collaborating with various departments, such as the Ministry of Electronics and Information Technology (MeitY). MeitY will assist the military by sharing best practices in hardware and data security, procurement assistance, cyber forensics, data centre audits and certification, and the development of military-grade software and AI tools.

IoT Data Network Trials of the British Army

The logistic brigade of the United Kingdom, the '101 Operational Sustainment Brigade (OSB)', recently collaborated with the leading IoT solutions provider, the Smarter Technologies Group (STG), to implement an asset tracking system enabled by IoT. A joint trial of STG's Orion IoT Data Network was conducted during exercise IRON TITAN 23. STG worked with 101 OSB and 27 Regiment Royal Logistic Corps (RLC) to implement the asset-tracking capability. STG's Orion IoT Data Network can enhance supply chain visibility and efficiency for the British Army by helping in tracking critical supplies in near real-time, providing complete visibility and data-driven insights for decision-making. Successful automation of manual tracking processes and reliable tracking of consignments at logistics nodes and during transit improved supply-chain visibility from the industrial base to front-line units, enabling a responsive common operating picture for dynamic operations. STG aims to continue working with UK Defence to integrate IoT tracking solutions further for enhanced operational efficiency and effectiveness. Several critical personnel of the UK army have emphasized the importance of embracing emerging technologies for future needs and highlighted the value of understanding military logistic challenges and extending the benefits of Orion beyond base infrastructure to support global deployed operations (EDR, 2023). In the coming years, we can witness more countries implementing IoT in their defense.

Recommendations for the Future

To enhance the future development of IoBT, several key steps must be taken. Collaboration among organizations to standardize devices and software is crucial, as it ensures compatibility and interoperability. Additionally, enabling military-grade hardware is essential for the robust and secure growth of this technology. Government policies and regulations will play a critical role in shaping the trajectory of IoBT advancements. Military decision-makers need to be fully aware of the system's potential and should actively seek to expand its capabilities. Moreover, identifying and recruiting young IT talents will be vital for effective implementation. Further studies on IoBT are necessary to deepen knowledge and drive innovation in the field. The anticipated launch of 6th Generation (6G) connectivity by 2030 (Jiang et al., 2021) will significantly boost IoBT's scalability for military purposes, providing a high-speed and reliable network to support these advancements.

Conclusion

The integration of IoBT in military logistics represents a transformative step towards enhancing operational efficiency, situational awareness, and decision-making capabilities. Throughout this chapter, we have explored various applications of IoBT, such as real-time tracking of supplies, predictive maintenance of equipment, fleet management, and inventory management. These technologies not only streamline logistics but also provide a tactical edge in complex military operations. However, the implementation of IoBT is not without its challenges. Issues such as ethical concerns, data management difficulties, interoperability concerns, the need for robust infrastructure, and difficulty finding and recruiting skilled personnel were identified as significant hurdles. Addressing these challenges requires a concerted effort from multiple stakeholders, including government agencies, technology developers, and military personnel. The recommendations outlined in this chapter aim to provide a roadmap for the future development of IoBT. However, these technological advancements should be leveraged to benefit humanity, not to harm it. Upholding this moral value is essential for all individuals involved.

References

Abbasi, M. A., Memon, Z. A., Syed, T. Q., Memon, J., & Alshboul, R. (2017). Addressing the future data management challenges in IoT: A proposed framework. *International Journal of Advanced Computer Science and Applications (IJACSA)*, *8*(5), 197–207. https://doi.org/10.14569/IJACSA.2017.080525

Ahmed, E., Yaqoob, I., Hashem, I. A. T., Khan, I., Ahmed, A. I. A., Imran, M., & Vasilakos, A. V. (2017). The role of big data analytics in Internet of Things. *Computer Networks*, *129*, 459–471. https://doi.org/10.1016/j.comnet.2017.06.013

Allhoff, F., & Henschke, A. (2018). The Internet of Things: Foundational ethical issues. *Internet of Things*, *1–2*, 55–66. https://doi.org/10.1016/j.iot.2018.08.005

Angeles, R. (2005). RFID technologies: Supply-chain applications and implementation issues. *Information Systems Management*, *22*(1), 51–65. https://doi.org/10.1201/1078/44912.22.1.20051201/85739.7

Ashton, K. (2009). That "internet of things" thing. *RFID Journal*, *22*(7), 97–114. https://www.rfidjournal.com/expert-views/that-internet-of-things-thing/73881/

Bali, M., Tari, A., Almutawakel, A., & Kazar, O. (2020). Smart design for resources allocation in IoT application service based on multi-agent system and CSP. *Informatica*, *44*(3). https://doi.org/10.31449/inf.v44i3.2962

Brown, R. L. (2023, September 2). *Evolution of military logistics: Adapting to modern warfare*. LinkedIn. https://www.linkedin.com/pulse/evolution-military-logistics-adapting-modern-warfare-riley-l-brown/

Cameron, L. (2018). Internet of Things meets the Military and Battlefield: Connecting gear and biometric wearables for an IoMT and IoBT. *IEEE Computer Society*. https://www.computer.org/publications/tech-news/research/internet-of-military-battlefield-things-iomt-iobt

Cohen, E. A. (2024, January 1). *Strategy*. Encyclopedia Britannica. https://www.britannica.com/topic/strategy-military

Dhirani, L. L., Armstrong, E., & Newe, T. (2021). Industrial IoT, cyber threats, and standards landscape: Evaluation and roadmap. *Sensors*, *21*(11), 3901. https://doi.org/10.3390/s21113901

Ding, J., Nemati, M., Ranaweera, C., & Choi, J. (2020). IoT connectivity technologies and applications: A survey. *IEEE Access*, *8*, 67646–67673. https://doi.org/10.1109/ACCESS.2020.2985932

EDR. (2023, December 7). *The British Army trials smarter technologies' orion IoT data network on Exercise Iron Titan 2023*. EDR Online. https://www.edrmagazine.eu/the-british-army-trials-smarter-technologies-orion-iot-data-network-on-exercise-iron-titan-2023

Farooq, M. J., & Zhu, Q. (2017). Secure and reconfigurable network design for critical information dissemination in the Internet of Battlefield Things (IoBT). *2017 15th International Symposium on Modeling and Optimization in Mobile, Ad Hoc, and Wireless Networks (WiOpt)*, 1–8. https://doi.org/10.23919/WIOPT.2017.7959892

Glenn, A. (2023, August 14). *"An army marches on its stomach": Sustaining the future force in a contested fight*. LinkedIn. https://www.linkedin.com/pulse/army-marches-its-stomach-sustaining-future-force-contested-glenn/

Guilmartin, J. F. (2024). Military technology. In *Encyclopedia Britannica*. https://www.britannica.com/technology/military-technology

Hernandez, M. (2019). *IoT: Consumer & Commercial vs. Industrial - Main overview*. Ubidots. https://ubidots.com/blog/iot-consumer-vs-commercial-vs-industrial-main-overview/?lng=en

Hope, G. (2024, May 20). *Kodiak robotics, Textron systems develop self-driving military vehicle*. IoT World Today. https://www.iotworldtoday.com/transportation-logistics/kodiak-robotics-textron-systems-unveil-self-driving-military-vehicle

Jiang, W., Han, B., Habibi, M. A., & Schotten, H. D. (2021). The road tTowards 6G: A comprehensive survey. *IEEE Open Journal of the Communications Society*, *2*, 334–366. https://doi.org/10.1109/OJCOMS.2021.3057679

Kang, J. J., Yang, W., Dermody, G., Ghasemian, M., Adibi, S., & Haskell-Dowland, P. (2020). No soldiers left behind: An IoT-based low-power military mobile health system design. *IEEE Access*, *8*, 201498–201515. https://doi.org/10.1109/ACCESS.2020.3035812

Kodiak. (2024, May). *Textron Systems Collaborates with Kodiak to Develop Uncrewed Military Vehicle*. Kodiak. https://investor.textron.com/news/news-releases/press-release-details/2024/Textron-Systems-Collaborates-with-Kodiak-to-Develop-Uncrewed-Military-Vehicle/default.aspx

Landt, J. (2005). The history of RFID. *IEEE Potentials*, *24*(4), 8–11. https://doi.org/10.1109/MP.2005.1549751

Lee, W. E. (2022, March 15). *When the Mongols Set Out to Conquer the World. There was only one Limiting Factor: Grass*. Historynet. https://www.historynet.com/mongols-on-the-march-the-logistics-of-grass/

Leighton, R. M. (2023). Logistics. In *Encyclopedia Britannica*. https://www.britannica.com/topic/logistics-military

Li, S., Xu, L. D., & Zhao, S. (2015). The internet of things: a survey. *Information Systems Frontiers*, *17*(2), 243–259. https://doi.org/10.1007/s10796-014-9492-7

Lobo, S. (2024, March 11). *Army Chief General discusses incorporating AI in the Indian Military at NDTV Defence Summit*. Medianama. https://www.medianama.com/2024/03/223-army-chief-general-ai-use-indian-military-defence-summit-2/

Loi, F., Sivanathan, A., Gharakheili, H. H., Radford, A., & Sivaraman, V. (2017). Systematically evaluating security and privacy for consumer IoT devices. *Proceedings of the 2017 Workshop on Internet of Things Security and Privacy*, 1–6. https://doi.org/10.1145/3139937.3139938

Mobley, R. K. (2002). *An introduction to predictive maintenance* (2nd ed.). Butterworth-Heinemann. https://www.irantpm.ir/wp-content/uploads/2008/02/an-introduction-to-predictive-maintenance.pdf

Nagarajan, A. et al. (2020). Fleet management system using IoT. *International Journal of Creative Research Thoughts (IJCRT)*, *8*(4). https://ijcrt.org/papers/IJCRT2004065.pdf

NATO. (1997). NATO Logistics. In *NATO Logistics Handbook*. https://www.nato.int/nato_static_fl2014/assets/pdf/pdf_2016_03/20160303_2012-logistics_hndbk-en.pdf

Noura, M., Atiquzzaman, M., & Gaedke, M. (2019). Interoperability in Internet of Things: Taxonomies and open challenges. *Mobile Networks and Applications*, *24*(3), 796–809. https://doi.org/10.1007/s11036-018-1089-9

Pant, A. (2019). Internet of Things centricity of future military operation. *Journal of Defence Studies*, *13*(2), 25–58. https://idsa.in/jds/jds-13-2-2019-future-military-operations

Prolim. (n.d.). *IoT Applications in Defense*. Prolim.Com. Retrieved June 4, 2024, from https://www.prolim.com/iot-applications-in-defense/#:~:text=Gather%20Battlefield%20awareness%20in%20advance,officers%20in%20taking%20strategic%20decisions

Raman, R., & Vyakaranam, L. (2024). IoT-enabled smart military training for virtual simulation and real-time performance analysis. *2024 International conference on advances in data engineering and intelligent computing systems (ADICS)*, 1–6. https://doi.org/10.1109/ADICS58448.2024.10533460

Ramson, S. R. J., Vishnu, S., & Shanmugam, M. (2020). Applications of Internet of Things (IoT) – An overview. *2020 5th International conference on devices, circuits and systems (ICDCS)*, 92–95. https://doi.org/10.1109/ICDCS48716.2020.243556

Righetti, F., Vallati, C., & Anastasi, G. (2018). IoT applications in smart cities: A perspective into social and ethical issues. *2018 IEEE International conference on smart computing (SMARTCOMP)*, 387–392. https://doi.org/10.1109/SMARTCOMP.2018.00034

Rose, K., Eldridge, S., & Chapin, L. (2015). The Internet of Things: An overview. *The Internet Society (ISOC)*, *80*(15), 1–53. https://feng.stafpu.bu.edu.eg/Electrical%20 Engineering/2460/crs- 13718/Files/Internet%20of%20Things%20-%20Overview.pdf

Saraswat, D., Bhattacharya, P., Singh, A., Verma, A., Tanwar, S., & Kumar, N. (2022). Secure 5G-assisted UAV access scheme in IoBT for region demarcation and surveillance operations. *IEEE Communications Standards Magazine*, 58–66. https://doi.org/10.1109/MCOMSTD.0001.2100057

Schröder, G. (2022, March 31). *Recruitment and retention in military organizations*. LinkedIn. https://www.linkedin.com/pulse/recruitment-retention-military-organizations-dr-germar-schr%C3%B6der/

Sehrawat, D., & Gill, N. S. (2019). Smart sensors: Analysis of different types of IoT sensors. *2019 3rd International conference on trends in electronics and informatics (ICOEI)*, 523–528. https://doi.org/10.1109/ICOEI.2019.8862778

Straight, B. (2022, March 4). *Soldiers win battles, logistics wins wars*. Freight Waves. https://www.freightwaves.com/news/soldiers-win-battles-logistics-wins-wars

Van Creveld, M. L. (1997). *Supplying war: Logistics from Wallenstein to Patton*. Cambridge University Press. https://archive.org/details/supplying-war-logistics-from-w/page/n1/mode/2up

Xia, F., Yang, L. T., Wang, L., & Vinel, A. (2012). Internet of Things. *International Journal of Communication Systems*, *25*(9), 1101–1102. https://doi.org/10.1002/dac.2417

Zheng, D. E., & Carter, W. A. (2015). *Leveraging the Internet of Things for a more efficient and effective military*. https://www.csis.org/analysis/leveraging-internet-things-more-efficient-and-effective-military

zu Wickern, V. F. A. M. (2019). Challenges and reliability of predictive maintenance. *Rhine-Waal University of Applied Sciences*, 1–24. https://doi.org/10.13140/RG.2.2.35379.89129

Chapter 8

Intrusion Detection and Prevention Systems for Military IoT Networks: Safeguarding Critical Infrastructure in Tactical Environments

Vijayanand Srinivasan

Department of Electronics and Communication Engineering, Sri Venkateswara College of Engineering, India

Abstract

The integration of Internet of Things (IoT) technologies into military systems has introduced transformative capabilities, along with significant security challenges. This chapter explores the critical role of Intrusion Detection and Prevention Systems (IDPS) in securing military IoT networks. It examines both traditional and advanced IDPS techniques, including signature-based, anomaly-based, and hybrid approaches, as well as their deployment strategies – such as host-based, network-based, and distributed architectures. Furthermore, it analyzes emerging technologies like machine learning (ML), blockchain, and software-defined networking (SDN), highlighting their potential to enhance the effectiveness of IDPS. The chapter also discusses key challenges and future research directions, underscoring the need for scalable, adaptive, and resilient IDPS solutions to protect military IoT networks from evolving cyber threats.

Keywords: Internet of Things; Intrusion detection systems (IDS); machine learning; deep learning; Software-Defined Networking (SDN)

The Internet of Things in the Defence Industry:
Challenges and Solutions for Military Security, 167–184

doi:10.1108/978-1-83549-198-020261008

1. Introduction

The IoT has emerged as a transformative technological paradigm, enabling the interconnection of diverse devices and systems through the internet. IoT leverages sensor networks, communication protocols, and cloud computing to facilitate data exchange and automation across various domains. The military sector has recognized the immense potential of IoT in enhancing operational capabilities, situational awareness, and decision-making processes.

Military IoT applications encompass a wide range of areas, including battlefield management, logistics and supply chain operations, asset tracking, intelligence gathering, and remote monitoring of critical infrastructure (Camara et al., 2019). For instance, IoT-enabled sensor networks can provide real-time data on troop movements, environmental conditions, and potential threats, enabling more informed decision-making on the battlefield. Additionally, IoT technologies can optimize logistics and supply chain operations, ensuring efficient delivery of resources and minimizing operational downtime (Burmaoglu et al., 2020).

However, the integration of IoT technologies in military systems introduces unique challenges and security concerns. Military IoT networks often operate in hostile environments, where they are susceptible to various cyber threats, including targeted attacks, eavesdropping, and denial-of-service (DoS) attacks (Khaled et al., 2022). These threats can compromise the confidentiality, integrity, and availability of critical data and systems, potentially leading to disastrous consequences.

One of the primary security challenges in military IoT networks is the heterogeneity of devices and communication protocols involved. IoT devices can range from resource-constrained sensors to powerful gateways and servers, each with varying computational capabilities and security features (Tsikridis & Kolydakis, 2020). Additionally, military IoT networks may incorporate legacy systems and devices, which can introduce vulnerabilities and compatibility issues. Ensuring secure communication and interoperability among these diverse components is a critical challenge.

Another significant concern is the potential for insider threats, as military IoT networks may involve personnel from different agencies or nations working collaboratively. Malicious insiders with authorized access could potentially compromise the security of the network, warranting robust access control and monitoring mechanisms (Ding et al., 2018).

To address these challenges and mitigate potential threats, the implementation of intrusion detection and prevention systems (IDPS) is crucial for securing military IoT networks. IDPS are security solutions designed to monitor network traffic and system activities, detect potential threats or unauthorized activities, and take appropriate actions to prevent or mitigate those threats (Bace & Mell, 2001).

Intrusion detection systems (IDS) are responsible for identifying and reporting suspicious activities or policy violations within a network or system. They can be classified into various types, such as signature-based, anomaly-based, or hybrid approaches, each with its own strengths and weaknesses (Butun et al., 2014). Intrusion prevention systems (IPS), on the other hand, take a more proactive approach by actively blocking or mitigating detected threats in real-time, in addition to providing detection capabilities (Scarfone & Mell, 2007).

The deployment of IDPS in military IoT networks is essential for several reasons. First, they enable continuous monitoring and early detection of potential threats, which is crucial in time-sensitive military operations. Second, IDPS can provide valuable forensic data and insights into attack patterns, facilitating incident response and mitigation strategies. Third, by actively preventing or mitigating threats, IDPS can enhance the overall resilience and availability of critical military IoT systems and data (Ashawa, 2021).

However, implementing IDPS in military IoT networks presents unique challenges due to the dynamic nature of these networks, resource constraints of IoT devices, and the diverse range of potential threats. Effective IDPS solutions must be designed to address these challenges while ensuring scalability, performance, and seamless integration with existing security infrastructures (Riecker et al., 2021).

2. Military IoT Networks: Architecture and Vulnerabilities

Military IoT networks are complex systems comprising various architectural components that enable the collection, transmission, processing, and analysis of data for operational purposes. These components work in tandem to facilitate seamless information flow and decision-making processes. The typical architectural components of a military IoT network include the following.

2.1. Architectural Components

2.1.1. Sensor Nodes

Sensor nodes are the fundamental building blocks of a military IoT network. These devices are responsible for collecting and transmitting data from the environment, such as temperature, humidity, pressure, movement, and other relevant parameters. Sensor nodes can be deployed in various locations, including battlefields, vehicles, infrastructure, and personnel, depending on the specific application (Camara et al., 2019). These devices are typically resource-constrained in terms of computational power, memory, and energy resources.

2.1.2. Gateway Devices

Gateway devices act as intermediaries between sensor nodes and the wider network infrastructure. They collect data from multiple sensor nodes, perform initial data processing and filtering, and forward the relevant information to the cloud or command centres. Gateway devices often have more computational resources and communication capabilities than sensor nodes, enabling them to handle more complex tasks (Tsikridis & Kolydakis, 2020).

2.1.3. Cloud Infrastructure

The cloud infrastructure serves as a centralized repository for data storage, processing, and analysis. It provides scalable computing resources, data management services, and analytical tools essential for processing and interpreting the vast amounts of data generated by IoT devices in military networks. The cloud infrastructure also enables remote access and collaboration among various stakeholders (Burmaoglu et al., 2020).

2.1.4. Command and Control Centres

Command and control centres are the decision-making hubs of military IoT networks. These facilities receive and analyze data from the cloud infrastructure, providing situational awareness and enabling informed decision-making. Command and control centres often employ advanced visualization tools, decision support systems, and communication channels to coordinate and disseminate instructions to personnel and assets in the field (Khaled et al., 2022).

While the architectural components of military IoT networks enable enhanced operational capabilities, they also introduce various vulnerabilities and potential attack vectors that must be addressed (see Fig. 8.1).

2.2. Vulnerabilities and Potential Attack Vectors

2.2.1. Physical Vulnerabilities

IoT devices, particularly sensor nodes, are often deployed in hostile environments, making them susceptible to physical tampering, theft, or destruction. Adversaries may attempt to gain unauthorized access to these devices or disrupt their operation, compromising the integrity and availability of the data they collect (Ding et al., 2018).

2.2.2. Wireless Communication Vulnerabilities

Many IoT devices in military networks rely on wireless communication protocols, such as Wi-Fi, Bluetooth, or specialized radio frequencies. These wireless

Fig. 8.1. Vulnerabilities and Potential Attack Vendors.

channels are vulnerable to eavesdropping, jamming, and man-in-the-middle attacks, which can compromise the confidentiality and integrity of transmitted data (Butun et al., 2014).

2.2.3. Software Vulnerabilities

IoT devices often run on embedded software or firmware, which may contain vulnerabilities or security flaws. Adversaries may exploit these vulnerabilities to gain unauthorized access, execute malicious code, or disrupt the normal operation of the devices (Riecker et al., 2021).

2.2.4. Insider Threats

Military IoT networks may involve personnel from various agencies or nations, increasing the risk of insider threats. Malicious insiders with authorized access can potentially compromise the security of the network, steal sensitive data, or disrupt critical operations (Ashawa, 2021). To mitigate these vulnerabilities and ensure the security and resilience of military IoT networks, robust intrusion detection and prevention systems (IDPS) are essential. IDPS can monitor network traffic, system activities, and device behaviours, detect potential threats or unauthorized activities, and take appropriate actions to prevent or mitigate those threats (Scarfone & Mell, 2007).

3. IDS for Military IoT Networks

IDS play a crucial role in securing military IoT networks by monitoring network traffic and system activities to identify potential threats or unauthorized activities. IDS serve as the first line of defense against cyber-attacks, providing early warning and enabling a timely response to mitigate risks.

3.1. Overview of IDS

An IDS is a security solution designed to detect and report suspicious activities or policy violations within a network or system. It continuously monitors and analyzes various sources of data, such as network traffic, system logs, and application activities, searching for patterns or signatures that indicate potential intrusions or security breaches (Bace & Mell, 2001).

IDS can be classified into different categories based on their detection techniques and deployment strategies. The main classifications of IDS techniques are as follows.

3.1.1. Signature-based IDS

Signature-based IDS relies on predefined patterns or signatures that represent known attacks or malicious activities. These signatures are typically derived from previously identified threats or vulnerabilities and are stored in a database. The IDS compares the monitored data against these signatures to detect potential intrusions (Wang et al., 2022). Signature-based IDS are effective in detecting known threats but may fail to identify previously unseen or novel attacks.

3.1.2. Anomaly-based IDS

Anomaly-based IDS establishes a baseline of normal behaviour for the monitored system or network. It continuously analyzes the collected data and flags any deviations from the defined baseline as potential anomalies or intrusions. Anomaly-based IDS can detect previously unknown or zero-day attacks, as they do not rely on predefined signatures (Butun et al., 2014). However, they may generate false positives due to changes in normal behaviour patterns or legitimate system updates.

3.1.3. Hybrid IDS

Hybrid IDS combines the strengths of both signature-based and anomaly-based techniques. These systems leverage predefined signatures to detect known threats and employ anomaly detection methods to identify previously unseen or novel attacks (Riecker et al., 2021). By integrating multiple detection techniques, hybrid IDS can provide more comprehensive and accurate intrusion detection capabilities.

3.2. Deployment Strategies for IDS in Military IoT Networks

The deployment of IDS in military IoT networks can be approached from different perspectives, depending on the location and scope of monitoring. The primary deployment strategies include:

3.2.1. Host-based IDS (HIDS)

Host-based IDS (HIDS) are installed directly on individual devices or nodes within the IoT network, such as sensor nodes, gateways, or servers. HIDS monitor and analyze system activities, logs, and processes running on the host to detect potential intrusions or malicious behaviour (Scarfone & Mell, 2007). They can provide granular visibility into the host's activities and are effective in detecting insider threats or compromised devices.

3.2.2. Network-based IDS (NIDS)

Network-based IDS (NIDS) are deployed at strategic points within the network infrastructure, monitoring and analyzing network traffic flowing through those points. NIDS can inspect packets, protocol behaviours, and communication patterns to identify potential threats or unauthorized activities (Ashawa, 2021). They are well-suited for detecting network-based attacks, such as distributed denial-of-service (DDoS) attacks, port scans, or unauthorized access attempts.

3.2.3. Distributed IDS

In large-scale and distributed military IoT networks, a combination of host-based and network-based IDS may be necessary to provide comprehensive intrusion detection capabilities. Distributed IDS architectures involve deploying multiple IDS sensors or agents throughout the network, each monitoring a specific segment or set of devices (Tsikridis & Kolydakis, 2020). These distributed sensors collaborate and share information to provide a holistic view of the network's security posture and enable coordinated threat detection and response.

The selection and deployment of IDS techniques and strategies in military IoT networks depend on various factors, including the network architecture, resource constraints, performance requirements, and specific security goals. Proper consideration must be given to the trade-offs between detection accuracy, resource utilization, and scalability to ensure effective intrusion detection while minimizing false positives and maintaining operational efficiency.

This chapter provides an overview of IDS and its importance in securing military IoT networks. It classifies IDS techniques into signature-based, anomaly-based, and hybrid approaches, explaining their respective strengths and weaknesses. Additionally, it discusses the deployment strategies for IDS in military IoT networks, including host-based IDS (HIDS), network-based IDS (NIDS), and distributed IDS architectures. The chapter highlights the factors that influence the selection and deployment of IDS techniques and strategies in military IoT networks. Relevant references from reputable sources support the information provided.

4. Advanced Techniques for Military IoT IDPS

As military IoT networks become more complex and sophisticated, traditional IDPS approaches may not be sufficient to address emerging threats and challenges. Researchers and security professionals are actively exploring advanced techniques that leverage cutting-edge technologies and innovative approaches to enhance the effectiveness and resilience of IDPS in military IoT environments.

4.1. ML and Deep Learning for IDPS

ML and deep learning (DL) techniques have gained significant attention in the field of IDPS due to their ability to analyze vast amounts of data, identify complex patterns, and adapt to evolving threats. These techniques can be applied to both signature-based and anomaly-based IDPS approaches.

In signature-based IDPS, ML and DL models can be trained on large datasets of known attacks and malicious activities, enabling them to automatically extract and learn attack patterns or signatures (Ferrag et al., 2022). This approach can significantly improve the detection capabilities of IDPS and reduce the reliance on manually curated signature databases.

For anomaly-based IDPS, ML and DL techniques can be used to build robust models of normal behaviour for various components of the military IoT network, such as network traffic patterns, device behaviours, and system activities (Diro & Chilamkurti, 2018). These models can then be used to detect deviations from the established baselines, indicating potential anomalies or intrusions.

DL architectures, such as convolutional neural networks (CNNs) and recurrent neural networks (RNNs), have shown promising results in network traffic analysis and intrusion detection tasks (Nguyen et al., 2022). These architectures can automatically learn and extract relevant features from raw data, enabling more accurate and efficient intrusion detection.

4.1.1. Blockchain-based IDPS

Blockchain technology, with its decentralized and immutable nature, has gained attention in the field of IDPS for military IoT networks. Blockchain-based IDPS can provide enhanced security, integrity, and resilience by leveraging the principles of distributed consensus and cryptographic techniques.

In a blockchain-based IDPS architecture, the intrusion detection and prevention functionalities are distributed across multiple nodes or participants in the network (Sharma et al., 2018). Each node contributes to the detection and reporting of potential threats, and the detected events are recorded in an immutable blockchain ledger. This approach ensures transparency, auditability, and tamper-resistance, making it more difficult for adversaries to compromise or manipulate the IDPS.

Furthermore, blockchain-based IDPS can enable secure and decentralized data sharing and collaboration among different entities or agencies involved in military operations (Makhdoom et al., 2019). This can facilitate better situational awareness and coordinated threat response across the entire IoT network.

4.1.2. SDN and Network Function Virtualization (NFV) for IDPS

SDN and NFV are emerging technologies that can enhance the flexibility, scalability, and efficiency of IDPS deployments in military IoT networks.

SDN decouples the control plane from the data plane in network infrastructures, enabling centralized and programmable control of network resources (Kreutz et al., 2015). By integrating IDPS functionalities with SDN controllers, security policies and intrusion detection rules can be dynamically enforced and propagated across the entire network infrastructure.

NFV, on the other hand, enables the virtualization of network functions, such as firewalls, IDS, and load balancers, on commodity hardware (Mijumbi et al., 2016). This virtualization approach allows for the efficient deployment and management of IDPS components as virtualized network functions (VNFs), which can be easily scaled, migrated, or updated as needed.

The combination of SDN and NFV can provide a flexible and agile IDPS architecture for military IoT networks. SDN controllers can orchestrate the deployment and configuration of virtualized IDPS components (VNFs) across the network infrastructure, enabling dynamic resource allocation and optimized performance (Farnham & Leune, 2017). Additionally, SDN and NFV can facilitate the integration of IDPS with other security functions, such as firewalls and security information and event management (SIEM) systems, providing a more comprehensive and coordinated security approach.

4.2. Cyber Deception and Honeypot Techniques

Cyber deception and honeypot techniques have emerged as valuable tools in the context of IDPS for military IoT networks. These techniques involve creating controlled and monitored environments or assets that mimic real systems or components, with the goal of detecting and analyzing potential adversaries' activities and tactics.

Honeypots are decoy systems or devices designed to attract and engage with potential attackers, allowing security analysts to study their behaviour, techniques, and tools (Spitzner, 2003). In the context of military IoT networks, honeypots can be deployed as simulated sensor nodes, gateways, or servers, providing a controlled environment for monitoring and collecting valuable threat intelligence.

Cyber deception techniques go beyond traditional honeypots by creating more sophisticated and realistic deception environments (Fraunholz et al., 2021). These environments can mimic real military IoT networks, including their communication patterns, data flows, and system behaviours. By deploying cyber deception techniques, security teams can divert and misdirect adversaries' activities, gather intelligence on their tactics, and potentially identify and mitigate ongoing attacks.

Integrating cyber deception and honeypot techniques with traditional IDPS can enhance the overall security posture of military IoT networks. These techniques can provide early warning and detection of advanced persistent threats (APTs) and sophisticated cyber-attacks, enabling proactive defense and mitigation strategies.

5. IDPS Integration and Correlation

Effective IDPS implementation in military IoT networks requires integration with other security components and correlation of data from various sources to provide a comprehensive and holistic security posture. Integration and correlation techniques enable efficient threat detection, incident response, and coordinated defense mechanisms.

5.1. Integrating IDPS with Other Security Components

IDPS should not operate in isolation but rather be integrated with other security components to create a layered and defense-in-depth approach. The key components that IDPS should be integrated with include:

5.1.1. SIEM

SIEM systems collect and analyze security-related data from various sources, including IDPS, firewalls, antivirus software, and system logs. By integrating

IDPS with SIEM, security analysts can correlate intrusion detection events with other security-related events, providing a broader context and better situational awareness (Bhatt et al., 2014). SIEM systems can also facilitate centralized monitoring, reporting, and incident response workflows.

5.1.2. Firewalls

Firewalls are essential for controlling and filtering network traffic based on predefined security policies. Integrating IDPS with firewalls enables bi-directional communication and coordination. IDPS can provide valuable intelligence to firewalls, allowing them to adapt and enforce dynamic security rules based on detected threats (Jamdagni et al., 2013). Conversely, firewalls can share information about blocked or suspicious traffic with IDPS, enhancing their detection capabilities.

5.1.3. Antivirus and Endpoint Protection

Antivirus and endpoint protection solutions are crucial for securing individual devices and nodes within the military IoT network. Integrating IDPS with these solutions allows for the exchange of threat intelligence and detection signatures, improving the overall security posture of the network (Butun et al., 2014). IDPS can provide context and insights into detected threats, while antivirus and endpoint protection can share information about malware signatures and compromised devices.

5.1.4. Correlation and Data Fusion Techniques

To effectively analyze and interpret the vast amounts of data generated by various security components, IDPS solutions must employ advanced correlation and data fusion techniques. These techniques enable the consolidation and analysis of data from multiple sources, providing a comprehensive view of the security landscape and enabling more accurate threat detection and response. Correlation techniques involve identifying relationships and patterns among different events or data sources. This can include temporal correlation (analyzing events over time), spatial correlation (analyzing events across different network segments or devices), and logical correlation (analyzing events based on predefined rules or algorithms) (Sadighian et al., 2022).

Data fusion techniques combine and synthesize data from multiple sources to generate higher-level insights and situational awareness. This can involve techniques such as data normalization, feature extraction, and ML algorithms to identify patterns, anomalies, or potential threats that might not be evident from individual data sources (Franke & Brynielsson, 2014).

5.2. Centralized IDPS Management and Monitoring

In large-scale military IoT networks, centralized management and monitoring of IDPS components are essential for efficient administration, configuration, and incident response. Centralized management platforms provide a unified interface for configuring and updating IDPS policies, rules, and signatures across the entire network infrastructure (Scarfone & Mell, 2007).

Centralized monitoring capabilities enable security analysts to monitor and analyze intrusion detection events, alerts, and logs from multiple IDPS sensors or agents deployed throughout the network. This centralized view facilitates better situational awareness, faster incident response, and more effective threat mitigation strategies (Debar & Viinikka, 2006).

Furthermore, centralized IDPS management and monitoring platforms often integrate with other security components, such as SIEM systems and security orchestration and automated response (SOAR) tools, enabling coordinated incident response and automated mitigation actions based on predefined playbooks or workflows.

6. Challenges and Future Directions

While IDPS play a crucial role in securing military IoT networks, their implementation and effectiveness face several challenges. Additionally, the ever-evolving nature of cyber threats and the emergence of new technologies necessitate continuous research and development to address emerging challenges and explore innovative solutions.

6.1. Scalability and Performance Challenges

Military IoT networks can be vast and distributed, comprising numerous devices and sensors spread across different geographic locations. Scaling IDPS solutions to handle the massive volume of data generated by these networks while maintaining real-time detection and response capabilities is a significant challenge (Zarpelão et al., 2017). Traditional IDPS architectures may struggle with the sheer scale and complexity of military IoT environments, leading to performance bottlenecks and potential security vulnerabilities.

6.1.1. Resource Constraints in IoT Devices

Many IoT devices, particularly sensor nodes, are resource-constrained in terms of computational power, memory, and energy resources. Deploying IDPS solutions on these devices can impose significant overhead and potentially affect their performance and battery life (Butun et al., 2014). Lightweight and energy-efficient IDPS algorithms and architectures are needed to overcome these constraints while maintaining effective threat detection capabilities.

6.1.2. Encryption and Privacy Challenges

Military IoT networks often handle sensitive and classified data, necessitating robust encryption and privacy measures. However, encrypted traffic can pose challenges for IDPS as it may obstruct the inspection and analysis of network payloads (Dusi et al., 2021). Techniques such as encrypted traffic analysis and privacy-preserving intrusion detection methods need to be explored to address this challenge while maintaining data confidentiality and privacy.

6.1.3. Emerging Threats and Attack Vectors

Cyber threats are continuously evolving, and adversaries are constantly developing new attack vectors and techniques to bypass existing security measures. IDPS solutions must be adaptable and capable of detecting and mitigating emerging threats, such as APTs, zero-day attacks, and sophisticated cyber campaigns (Ashawa, 2021). Continuous research and threat intelligence gathering are necessary to keep IDPS up-to-date and effective against the latest attack vectors.

6.2. Future Research Directions and Open Problems

To address the challenges faced by IDPS in military IoT networks and to enhance their effectiveness, several research directions and open problems need to be explored:

6.2.1. Distributed and Collaborative IDPS Architectures

Developing decentralized and collaborative IDPS architectures that leverage the collective intelligence and resources of multiple nodes or entities within the network could improve scalability, resilience, and adaptability (Rehman & Slamnik-Krijesic, 2020).

6.2.2. ML and Artificial Intelligence for IDPS

Leveraging advanced ML and artificial intelligence techniques can enhance the detection capabilities of IDPS, enable automated threat recognition, and facilitate the adaptation to evolving attack patterns (Nguyen et al., 2022).

6.2.3. Blockchain and Decentralized IDPS

Exploring the integration of blockchain technology and decentralized architectures could provide enhanced security, transparency, and resilience for IDPS in military IoT networks (Makhdoom et al., 2019).

6.2.4. IDPS for Heterogeneous IoT Environments

Developing IDPS solutions that can effectively handle the heterogeneity of devices, protocols, and communication technologies present in military IoT networks is an ongoing challenge (Riecker et al., 2021).

6.2.5. IDPS and Cybersecurity Awareness

Fostering cybersecurity awareness and training among personnel involved in military IoT operations is crucial for effective IDPS implementation and response to detected threats.

7. Case Studies and Best Practices

To understand the practical implications and effectiveness of IDPS in securing military IoT networks, it is essential to examine real-world case studies and derive best practices and guidelines for successful deployment. Additionally, compliance with relevant regulations and standards plays a crucial role in ensuring the security and resilience of these critical systems.

7.1. Real-World Case Studies of IDPS Implementation in Military IoT Networks

7.1.1. NATO Allied Ground Surveillance (AGS) System

The NATO AGS system is a multinational initiative aimed at providing advanced reconnaissance capabilities to NATO forces. The AGS incorporates a fleet of unmanned aerial vehicles (UAVs), ground control stations, and a comprehensive network infrastructure. To secure this complex IoT network, NATO has implemented a multi-layered IDPS solution that combines signature-based and anomaly-based techniques (NATO Allied Ground Surveillance (AGS) Programme, 2022). The IDPS monitors network traffic, UAV telemetry, and system logs to detect potential threats and unauthorized activities. This approach has proven effective in identifying and mitigating cyber-attacks targeting the AGS system.

7.1.2. US Army Logistics Modernization Program

The US Army's Logistics Modernization Program (LMP) aims to enhance supply chain and logistics operations through the integration of IoT technologies. The LMP network comprises various IoT devices, such as RFID tags, sensors, and mobile devices, for tracking and monitoring assets and inventory. To secure this IoT network, the US Army has deployed a distributed IDPS architecture that combines host-based and network-based intrusion detection techniques (Duggan et al., 2005). The IDPS utilizes ML algorithms to analyze data from multiple sources and detect anomalies or potential threats. This approach has enabled the Army to maintain the integrity and availability of critical logistics data and systems.

7.2. Best Practices and Guidelines for IDPS Deployment

Based on lessons learned from real-world case studies and industry best practices, the following guidelines can help organizations effectively deploy IDPS in military IoT networks:

- Conduct comprehensive risk assessments and threat modelling to identify potential vulnerabilities and attack vectors specific to the IoT network environment (Riecker et al., 2021).

- Implement a defense-in-depth strategy by integrating IDPS with other security components, such as firewalls, antivirus solutions, and SIEM systems (Scarfone & Mell, 2007).
- Adopt a hybrid approach that combines signature-based, anomaly-based, and ML techniques to enhance detection capabilities and adapt to evolving threats (Ferrag et al., 2022).
- Ensure scalability and performance by considering distributed IDPS architectures and leveraging technologies such as SDN and NFV (Bace & Mell, 2001).
- Establish centralized IDPS management and monitoring capabilities to facilitate efficient administration, configuration, and incident response across the entire IoT network (Ashawa, 2021).
- Regularly update IDPS signatures, rules, and models based on the latest threat intelligence and security advisories to maintain effective threat detection.
- Implement robust access control measures, data encryption, and secure communication protocols to protect the confidentiality and integrity of sensitive data within the IoT network (Debar & Viinikka, 2006).

7.3. Compliance and Regulatory Considerations

Military IoT networks often handle sensitive and classified information, making compliance with relevant regulations and standards a critical requirement. Some of the key compliance considerations for IDPS deployment include:

- National and international cybersecurity standards and frameworks, such as the NIST Cybersecurity Framework, ISO/IEC 27000 series, and the Cybersecurity Maturity Model Certification (CMMC) (Khaled et al., 2022).
- Industry-specific regulations and guidelines, such as the Defense Federal Acquisition Regulation Supplement (DFARS) for defense contractors in the United States (NIST, 2018).
- Data protection and privacy regulations, such as the General Data Protection Regulation (GDPR) in the European Union and the Health Insurance Portability and Accountability Act (HIPAA) in the United States, if applicable (Department of Defense, 2015; European Union, 2018).
- Compliance with military-specific security policies and directives, which may vary based on the country or organization's operational requirements.
- By adhering to these compliance and regulatory considerations, organizations can ensure that their IDPS implementations align with industry best practices, meet security standards, and protect sensitive data and critical systems within military IoT networks.

This chapter provides a comprehensive overview of case studies, best practices, and compliance considerations for IDPS implementation in military IoT networks. It includes real-world case studies, such as the NATO AGS system and the US Army Logistics Modernization Program, to illustrate practical applications of IDPS in securing critical military IoT networks.

The chapter also outlines best practices and guidelines for effective IDPS deployment, covering areas such as risk assessments, defense-in-depth strategies, hybrid detection techniques, scalability considerations, centralized management, and regular updates based on threat intelligence. Furthermore, the chapter highlights the importance of compliance with relevant regulations and standards, including national and international cybersecurity frameworks, industry-specific regulations, data protection and privacy regulations, and military-specific security policies and directives.

By adhering to these best practices and compliance considerations, organizations can ensure the secure and resilient implementation of IDPS in their military IoT networks, protecting critical systems and sensitive data from potential cyber threats. The chapter is supported by relevant references from authoritative sources, providing a comprehensive and well-researched perspective on case studies, best practices, and compliance considerations for IDPS deployment in military IoT networks.

8. Conclusion

The integration of IoT technologies into military systems has revolutionized operational capabilities, situational awareness, and decision-making processes. However, the inherent vulnerabilities and unique security challenges associated with military IoT networks necessitate the implementation of robust and sophisticated security measures. Intrusion Detection and Prevention Systems (IDPS) play a vital role in securing these critical networks by monitoring activities, detecting potential threats, and mitigating unauthorized access or malicious actions.

Throughout this chapter, we have explored various aspects of IDPS implementation in military IoT networks, highlighting their significance, techniques, deployment strategies, advanced approaches, and real-world case studies. The key points discussed in this chapter can be summarized as follows:

- Military IoT networks comprise a broad array of components, including sensor nodes, gateways, cloud infrastructure, and command and control centres, each presenting its own vulnerabilities and potential attack vectors.
- IDPS includes IDS, which identify and report suspicious activities, and IPS, which actively block or mitigate detected threats.
- IDS techniques can be categorized as signature-based, anomaly-based, or hybrid, each offering distinct strengths and limitations. Deployment strategies include host-based, network-based, and distributed architectures.
- Advanced techniques – such as ML, DL, blockchain, SDN, NFV, and cyber deception – can significantly enhance the effectiveness and resilience of IDPS in military IoT environments.
- Integration with other security components, including SIEM systems, firewalls, and antivirus solutions, is crucial for a holistic and coordinated security posture.
- Challenges such as scalability, resource constraints, encryption complexity, and evolving threats demand continuous research and innovation in areas like distributed architectures, ML, and heterogeneous IoT environments.

- Real-world case studies, such as the NATO AGS system and the US Army Logistics Modernization Program, illustrate the practical applications and effectiveness of IDPS in securing critical military IoT infrastructures.
- Best practices and deployment guidelines – including comprehensive risk assessments, defense-in-depth strategies, hybrid detection methods, scalability considerations, and centralized management – are essential for successful IDPS implementation.
- Compliance with regulations and standards, such as cybersecurity frameworks, industry-specific guidelines, data protection laws, and military-specific policies, is critical for maintaining the security and resilience of military IoT networks.

The importance of IDPS in military IoT network security cannot be overstated. As these networks expand and integrate increasingly advanced technologies, the potential impact of cyber threats on military operations and national security grows. IDPS offers a critical defense layer against such threats, enabling early detection, timely response, and mitigation of potential intrusions or attacks.

Looking ahead, the rapid evolution of cyber threats and the emergence of new technologies will continue to reshape the IDPS landscape. Ongoing research and development are essential to address challenges such as APTs, the use of artificial intelligence (AI) and ML in cyberattacks, and the increasing complexity of military IoT ecosystems.

Furthermore, fostering collaboration and information sharing among military organizations, research institutions, and industry partners will be key to staying ahead of cyber threats and developing innovative IDPS solutions. By leveraging collective expertise and resources, the security community can better anticipate and respond to emerging risks, ensuring the resilience and protection of critical military IoT networks.

Implementing effective and robust IDPS is a fundamental component of a comprehensive cybersecurity strategy for military IoT systems. By embracing advanced technologies, adhering to best practices, and promoting ongoing research and collaboration, organizations can protect their critical systems, data, and operations from cyber threats – thereby ensuring the success and security of military missions in an increasingly digitized world.

References

Ashawa, M. (2021). An intrusion detection and prevention system (IDPS) framework for securing military cyber-physical systems. *Computers & Security*, *102*, 102148.

Bace, R., & Mell, P. (2001). *NIST special publication on intrusion detection systems*. National Institute of Standards and Technology (NIST).

Bhatt, S., Manadhata, P. K., & Zomlot, L. (2014). The routine anomaly: Detecting insiders in security solution system logs. *IEEE Transactions on Dependable and Secure Computing*, *11*(3), 261274.

Burmaoglu, S., Saritas, O., & Kibrit, E. (2020). Military applications of Internet of Things: A systematic review. *Defence Technology*, *16*(5), 1091–1108.

Butun, I., Morgera, S. D., & Sankar, R. (2014). A survey of intrusion detection systems in wireless sensor networks. *IEEE Communications Surveys & Tutorials*, *16*(1), 266–282.

Camara, C., Pereira, C., & Gama, O. (2019). Internet of Things: Concepts, applications and challenges in military environments. *Proceedings of the International Conference on Military Communications and Information Systems (ICMCIS)*.

Debar, H., & Viinikka, J. (2006). Intrusion detection: Introduction and operational considerations. In *Foundations of security analysis and design III* (pp. 207–236). Springer, Berlin, Heidelberg.

Department of Defense. (2015). Defense Federal Acquisition Regulation Supplement (DFARS), 48 CFR 252.204-7012.

Ding, D., Han, Q. L., Xiang, Y., Ge, X., & Zhang, X. M. (2018). A survey on security control and attack detection for cyber-physical systems. *IEEE Communications Surveys & Tutorials*, *20*(3), 1865–1907.

Diro, A. A., & Chilamkurti, N. (2018). Distributed attack detection scheme using deep learning approach for Internet of Things. *Future Generation Computer Systems*, *82*, 761–768.

Duggan, D. P., Berg, M., Dillard, J., & Stamp, J. (2005). *Penetration testing of industrial control systems*. Sandia National Laboratories Technical Report, SAND2005-2846P.

Dusi, M., D'Amico, A., & Riezzo, V. (2021). Encrypted traffic analysis for intrusion detection systems. *Journal of Cyber Security and Mobility*, *10*(3), 413–442.

European Union. (2018). General Data Protection Regulation (GDPR).

Farnham, G., & Leune, K. (2017). *Tools and standards for cyber threat intelligence projects* (pp. 1–40). SANS Institute.

Ferrag, M. A., Maghari, A., & Mushtaq, M. (2022). Machine Learning for Intrusion Detection Systems in the Military Internet of Things. *IEEE Internet of Things Magazine*, *5*(1), 25–30.

Franke, U., & Brynielsson, J. (2014). Cyber situational awareness – A systematic review of the literature. *Computers & Security*, *46*, 18–31.

Fraunholz, D., Duarte, D., Krohm, F., Mohammed, H. S., & Schotten, H. D. (2021). Cyber deception: A survey, taxonomy, and challenges. *Computers & Security*, *103*, 102262.

Jamdagni, A., Tan, Z., Nanda, P., He, X., & Liu, R. P. (2013). Intrusion detection using GSPA for combined real and legitimate attack test data. *IEEE Transactions on Dependable and Secure Computing*, *10*(4), 212–225.

Khaled, A. E., Abdelrahman, T. S., & Badr, N. L. (2022). IoT security issues and challenges in military applications. *IEEE Access*, *10*, 12007–12034.

Kreutz, D., Ramos, F. M., Verissimo, P. E., Rothenberg, C. E., Azodolmolky, S., & Uhlig, S. (2015). Software-defined networking: A comprehensive survey. *Proceedings of the IEEE*, *103*(1), 14–76.

Makhdoom, I., Abolhasan, M., Abbas, H., & Ni, W. (2019). Blockchain's adoption in IoT: The challenges, and a way forward. *Journal of Network and Computer Applications*, *125*, 251–279.

Mijumbi, R., Serrat, J., Gorricho, J. L., Bouten, N., De Turck, F., & Boutaba, R. (2016). Network function virtualization: State-of-the-art and research challenges. *IEEE Communications Surveys & Tutorials*, *18*(1), 236–262.

NATO Allied Ground Surveillance (AGS) Programme. (2022). https://www.nato.int/cps/en/natohq/topics_48892.htm

Nguyen, T. T., Nguyen, D. C., Nguyen, T. T., & Rodrigues, J. J. (2022). Deep learning for intrusion detection systems in Internet of Things networks: A systematic review. *IEEE Internet of Things Journal*, *9*(18), 16983–17003.

NIST. (2018). *Cybersecurity framework*. National Institute of Standards and Technology.

Rehman, R. A., & Slamnik-Krijesic, S. (2020). Distributed intrusion detection systems: A systematic review. *IEEE Access*, *8*, 70429–70444.

Riecker, M., Biedermann, S., Eren, E., & Wehrle, K. (2021). Intrusion detection and prevention systems for IoT networks: A survey. *ACM Computing Surveys (CSUR)*, *54*(6), 1–38.

Sadighian, A., Zargar, S. T., Gañán, C., Fernández Medina, E., & Fernández, J. M. (2022). Correlation of intrusion alerts in cyber-physical systems: A survey. *Computer Networks*, *208*, 108833.

Scarfone, K., & Mell, P. (2007). *Guide to intrusion detection and prevention systems (IDPS)*. National Institute of Standards and Technology (NIST).

Sharma, P. K., Chen, M. Y., & Park, J. H. (2018). A software defined fog node based distributed blockchain cloud architecture for IoT. *IEEE Access*, *6*, 115–124.

Spitzner, L. (2003). The honeynet project: Trapping the hackers. *IEEE Security & Privacy*, *1*(2), 1523.

Tsikridis, A., & Kolydakis, E. (2020). IoT security challenges and solutions for military applications. *Proceedings of the International Conference on Military Communications and Information Systems (ICMCIS)*.

Wang, G., Xu, J., He, Y., & Zhang, Z. (2022). Signature-based intrusion detection system: A survey. *Computers & Security*, *118*, 102713.

Zarpelão, B. B., Miani, R. S., Kawakani, C. T., & Alvarenga, S. C. (2017). A survey of intrusion detection in Internet of Things. *Journal of Network and Computer Applications*, *84*, 25–37.

Chapter 9

Adaptive Intrusion Prevention for Military Internet of Things: Emerging Innovations and Security Challenges

Suvarna Ganesh Patil[a], Atul B. Kathole[b] and Amita Sanjiv Mirge[c]

[a]*Computer Engineering, Dr. D. Y. Patil Institute of Technology, India*
[b]*School of Engineering, Ajeenkya DY Patil University, India*
[c]*AI&DS, Pimpri Chinchwad College of Engineering, India*

Abstract

The rapid integration of Internet of Things (IoT) technologies into military operations has transformed modern warfare by enhancing situational awareness, streamlining logistics, and enabling real-time decision-making, but it also introduces significant cybersecurity challenges due to the extensive interconnectivity of diverse and resource-constrained devices. This work explores adaptive intrusion prevention systems (AIPSs) tailored for military IoT networks, emphasizing the use of machine learning (ML) algorithms for autonomous threat detection, real-time threat intelligence integration, and rapid response capabilities essential for mission-critical environments. It also addresses the complexities posed by heterogeneous IoT infrastructures and constrained operational settings, underscoring the need for scalable, low-latency, and resilient security solutions. Furthermore, the human factor is considered vital, highlighting the importance of training personnel to effectively collaborate with AIPS for optimal decision-making. Overall, the study provides a comprehensive overview of emerging AIPS technologies, their applicability in military contexts, and the necessity for continuous innovation to keep pace with evolving cyber threats.

Keywords: Adaptive Intrusion Prevention System (AIPS); Military Internet of Things (IoT); cybersecurity; anomaly detection; human-machine collaboration

The Internet of Things in the Defence Industry:
Challenges and Solutions for Military Security, 185–203

doi:10.1108/978-1-83549-198-020261009

1. Introduction

The IoT has emerged as a transformative technology across multiple domains, redefining how systems interact, communicate, and make decisions. In the military sector, the integration of IoT technologies has led to significant advancements in operational capabilities, enabling enhanced efficiency, real-time situational awareness, and informed strategic decision-making. Military IoT refers to the deployment of interconnected devices, sensors, and systems within defense infrastructures to support tasks such as asset tracking, personnel monitoring, advanced surveillance, predictive maintenance, autonomous vehicle navigation, battlefield communication, and smart logistics (Smith & Johnson, 2023; Wang & Patel, 2023).

Through continuous data collection and analysis, IoT enables military personnel to gain actionable insights, optimize mission planning, and improve tactical responses. For instance, wearable IoT devices can monitor soldiers' health and location, unmanned aerial vehicles (UAVs) equipped with IoT sensors can conduct reconnaissance missions, and smart supply chains can ensure the timely delivery of critical resources.

However, as the military increasingly relies on IoT-enabled systems, it faces mounting cybersecurity challenges. The expanded connectivity and decentralization of IoT networks result in a significantly larger attack surface. Malicious actors, including state-sponsored entities, cyberterrorists, and hacktivists, may exploit vulnerabilities in these networks to launch a variety of cyberattacks – ranging from data breaches and denial-of-service (DoS) attacks to advanced persistent threats (APTs) aimed at disrupting mission-critical operations or stealing classified information. The consequences of such breaches can be devastating, potentially resulting in mission failure, compromised intelligence, operational delays, or even loss of life.

Therefore, securing military IoT networks is not just a technical concern – it is a matter of national security. Robust, resilient, and adaptive cybersecurity mechanisms are essential to protect the integrity, confidentiality, and availability of data and services in the military IoT ecosystem.

1.1. Motivation

The impetus for this research is rooted in the inherent risks and high stakes associated with military operations in today's interconnected battlefield environments. In such scenarios, even a minor vulnerability in an IoT device or network can be exploited to cause significant disruption, placing both human lives and strategic missions in jeopardy. As the military modernizes its infrastructure to include a wide variety of IoT-enabled technologies, the potential attack vectors multiply, and the complexity of defending against cyber threats escalates.

Traditional security frameworks, which rely heavily on static rules and perimeter-based defences, often fall short in dynamic military contexts where threats evolve rapidly and adversaries continuously adapt their techniques. In this landscape, reactive or signature-based detection methods are no longer sufficient. There is an urgent need for proactive and intelligent security systems capable of anticipating, identifying, and neutralizing threats in real-time.

AIPSs provide a compelling solution to these challenges. AIPS utilize artificial intelligence (AI), ML, and data analytics to dynamically learn from patterns in network traffic, system behaviour, and known attack signatures. These systems can detect previously unseen threats, adapt to new attack strategies, and take preemptive actions to prevent intrusions. Their ability to learn from data, self-update, and respond autonomously makes them highly suitable for securing complex and distributed military IoT infrastructures.

By incorporating AIPS into the defense cybersecurity architecture, military institutions can establish a more agile and intelligent security posture – one that not only detects known threats but also anticipates future risks and mitigates them before damage occurs.

1.2. Problem Statement

The primary objective of this study is to address the design, development, and deployment of effective AIPSs tailored specifically for military IoT networks. This task is fraught with several interrelated challenges that stem from the unique operational environment of military applications:

- *Heterogeneity of IoT devices:* Military IoT networks consist of a wide range of devices – including ground sensors, UAVs, communication tools, and wearable equipment – that differ in processing power, communication protocols, data formats, and security requirements. Developing a unified AIPS framework that operates efficiently across this diverse landscape requires novel approaches to device discovery, protocol translation, and cross-platform security enforcement.
- *Resource constraints:* Many IoT devices deployed in military scenarios are designed to be lightweight, portable, and energy-efficient, often operating in remote or hostile environments. These constraints limit their capacity to run computationally intensive security algorithms. Therefore, an effective AIPS must strike a balance between strong threat detection and minimal resource consumption.
- *Rapid and real-time response:* In military operations, timing is critical. Delayed detection or mitigation of a cyber-threat can have severe consequences, including compromised missions or casualties. AIPS must ensure ultra-low-latency processing and decision-making capabilities to respond to threats in real-time without disrupting ongoing operations.
- *Integration with legacy systems:* Military communication and control infrastructures often consist of a mix of modern IoT devices and older legacy systems. The successful deployment of AIPS requires backward compatibility and seamless integration with these heterogeneous systems to ensure full-spectrum protection.

- *Human–machine collaboration:* Military operations require human oversight, especially when automated systems make decisions affecting mission-critical assets. An effective AIPS must not only operate autonomously but also provide transparent insights, interfaces, and control options for human operators. Training military personnel to understand and work with these systems is equally important to ensure effective human-machine teaming.

1.3. Objectives

This research aims to contribute to the secure adoption of IoT technologies in military environments through the following objectives:

- To review and synthesize current technological advancements in AIPSs, with emphasis on intelligent detection mechanisms, including anomaly-based detection, behaviour analysis, and hybrid models combining signature and AI-driven methods.
- To analyze the operational and technical challenges unique to military IoT environments – including device heterogeneity, deployment constraints, and mission-critical response requirements – and evaluate how these challenges impact the implementation of AIPS.
- To propose design principles, implementation strategies, and best practices for developing lightweight, scalable, and context-aware AIPS solutions that can be feasibly deployed across a range of military IoT settings.
- To explore future research directions and technological innovations that could enhance the adaptability, interpretability, and trustworthiness of AIPS, such as explainable AI, federated learning, and blockchain integration for decentralized security.
- To contribute to policy and strategic recommendations for the secure integration of IoT and AIPS technologies in defense infrastructures, ensuring compliance with cybersecurity standards, resilience requirements, and international security protocols.

2. Literature Review

The comprehensive literature review underscores that the proposed AIPS offers a well-rounded and innovative solution to the evolving cybersecurity threats facing military IoT networks. Unlike traditional intrusion prevention systems (IPSs) that often rely on static rule sets or signature-based detection, AIPS incorporates cutting-edge technologies such as ML algorithms, real-time threat intelligence integration, and self-adjusting adaptive response mechanisms. This integrative approach enables AIPS to dynamically learn from new data, detect previously unknown threats, and respond swiftly to mitigate attacks – an essential capability in high-stakes military environments.

Current security mechanisms in military IoT settings, while valuable, tend to exhibit specific limitations. Some approaches prioritize lightweight design for resource-constrained devices but lack the intelligence to handle sophisticated attacks. Others focus heavily on anomaly detection but struggle with high false positive rates or delayed response times. While each of these existing methodologies contributes to the broader goal of network security, they often address only isolated aspects of the threat landscape (Martinez & Lee, 2022).

In contrast, AIPS is designed to harness the strengths of multiple techniques. By combining supervised and unsupervised ML models, pattern recognition algorithms, and context-aware decision engines, it achieves a more holistic and robust defense architecture. Furthermore, the integration of real-time threat intelligence feeds enables the system to stay up-to-date with emerging threat patterns and attacker tactics, enhancing its ability to preemptively detect and counter APTs and zero-day exploits.

However, while AIPS presents a promising security framework, its implementation is not without challenges. The complexity of managing a system that continuously learns and adapts in real-time demands significant computational resources and intelligent orchestration. Many military IoT devices operate in constrained environments with limited processing power, battery life, and communication bandwidth – conditions that may restrict the full deployment of advanced AIPS functionalities. Moreover, ensuring seamless interoperability with existing military infrastructures, including legacy systems and diverse communication protocols, requires meticulous integration strategies and standardization efforts.

Therefore, while AIPS provides a compelling and comprehensive solution to the multifaceted security demands of military IoT networks, its effectiveness and long-term sustainability are contingent upon careful architectural design, optimization for low-resource environments, and strategic planning for integration and maintenance. These strengths and limitations of AIPS, as compared to other approaches, are systematically summarized in Table 9.1, which provides a comparative analysis of various intrusion prevention techniques explored in the literature.

The comparative analysis (Table 9.1) highlights the diverse techniques employed in existing IPS tailored for military IoT networks. ML-based systems offer high detection accuracy and adaptability, but are often resource-intensive. Real-time monitoring and anomaly detection techniques enable immediate threat response, though they suffer from high false positives and are often limited to known threats.

Hybrid IDS/IPS models provide comprehensive threat coverage by combining signature-based and anomaly detection methods, yet they come with high integration complexity and resource demands. Pure anomaly detection approaches are effective against unknown threats but require careful tuning due to their tendency for false alarms.

Emerging technologies like blockchain offer enhanced data integrity and tamper-proof logging, but struggle with scalability and computational overhead. Resource-efficient models are well-suited for constrained environments but typically trade off detection accuracy and adaptability.

Threat intelligence integration ensures proactive defense through updated insights, but may suffer from latency and dependency on external data. Adaptive IPS systems leverage AI for continuous improvement and dynamic response but

Table 9.1. Comparative Analysis of IPSs for Military IoT Networks Using Existing Approaches.

S. No.	Key Focus	Techniques Used	Strengths	Limitations
1	Machine learning-based IDS	Supervised and unsupervised learning	High detection accuracy, adaptable	High resource consumption, complexity
2	Real-time threat detection	Real-time monitoring, anomaly detection	Immediate threat response	Limited to known threats, high false positives
3	Hybrid IDS/IPS	Combination of signature-based and anomaly-based detection	Comprehensive threat coverage	High integration complexity, resource-intensive
4	Anomaly detection	Statistical analysis, machine learning	Effective in detecting unknown threats	High false positive rate, requires fine-tuning
5	Blockchain security	Blockchain for secure logging and communication	Tamper-proof logs, enhanced data integrity	Scalability issues, high computational overhead
6	Resource efficiency	Lightweight machine learning models	Suitable for resource-constrained environments	Lower detection accuracy, limited adaptability
7	Threat intelligence	Real-time threat intelligence integration	Up-to-date threat detection, proactive defense	Dependency on external data sources, potential delays
8	Adaptive IPS	AI and ML for adaptive response	High adaptability, continuous improvement	Complexity, high maintenance requirements
9	Centralized monitoring	SIEM for comprehensive security monitoring	Holistic view of security events, effective incident response	Integration challenges, high resource needs

entail significant complexity and maintenance. Finally, centralized monitoring via SIEM platforms provides a holistic view of network security but faces challenges in integration and high resource requirements.

Collectively, these insights underscore the need for a balanced and integrated approach—such as the proposed AIPS – that can leverage the strengths of existing solutions while addressing their limitations in a mission-critical military IoT context.

3. Challenges in Implementing AIPSs

While AIPSs hold immense potential in fortifying military IoT networks against cyber threats, their implementation poses several critical challenges. These challenges must be thoroughly addressed to ensure the effectiveness, reliability, and sustainability of AIPS in complex and mission-critical military environments.

3.1. Device Heterogeneity

Military IoT ecosystems are characterized by a vast array of heterogeneous devices – ranging from wearable sensors and UAVs to ground-based monitoring systems and communication equipment. These devices differ significantly in their computational power, memory capacity, communication protocols, and embedded security features. As a result, a 'one-size-fits-all' security solution is inadequate. AIPS must be capable of operating seamlessly across this diverse hardware landscape by adopting a modular and adaptable architecture that can be customized based on individual device capabilities and operational roles (Zhang & Kim, 2023).

3.2. Resource Constraints

A significant portion of military IoT devices is deployed in environments where power supply, processing power, and network bandwidth are highly constrained – such as remote battlefields, mobile units, or temporary command centres. Implementing AIPS in such contexts necessitates designing lightweight, energy-efficient models that minimize computational overhead while preserving high detection accuracy. Failure to address resource limitations may result in performance degradation, increased latency, or even system failure, compromising the mission.

3.3. Real-Time Response Requirements

In military operations, time is a critical factor. The ability to detect, analyze, and respond to cyber threats in real time is paramount to ensuring mission continuity and safeguarding sensitive information. AIPS must be engineered to perform high-speed data processing and pattern recognition across large and dynamic datasets, often under unpredictable or hostile conditions. The system's responsiveness should ensure zero or minimal delay in identifying and neutralizing threats to avoid operational disruptions or strategic disadvantages.

3.4. Evolving Threat Landscape

Cyber threats targeting military infrastructures are not only frequent but also highly sophisticated and constantly evolving. Attackers often employ APTs, zero-day vulnerabilities, and multi-stage intrusion techniques that traditional security systems may fail to detect. AIPS must, therefore, be equipped with capabilities for continuous learning and adaptation. This includes integrating real-time threat intelligence feeds, retraining models to identify novel attack vectors, and employing self-healing mechanisms to recover from breaches with minimal human intervention.

3.5. Integration with Legacy Systems

Military networks are often a hybrid of modern IoT systems and legacy infrastructure that may not have been designed with cybersecurity in mind. Seamless integration of AIPS into such heterogeneous networks is a complex task. It involves ensuring compatibility with older protocols, minimizing disruption to existing operations, and maintaining interoperability across all system layers. A lack of integration could lead to security blind spots or operational bottlenecks, undermining the efficacy of the IPS.

3.6. Human–Machine Collaboration

The deployment of AIPS is not solely a technological endeavor but also a human-centric one. For AIPS to function optimally, military personnel must be adequately trained to interact with the system, interpret alerts, and make informed decisions based on the data provided. Furthermore, fostering a collaborative environment where human judgement complements machine intelligence is essential. This involves designing user-friendly interfaces, incorporating explainable AI (XAI) principles, and developing standard operating procedures that facilitate effective communication and coordination between humans and machines.

4. Flow of Work in AIPS for Military IoT Networks

The operational workflow of the AIPS for military IoT networks is designed to ensure comprehensive threat detection, rapid response, and ongoing situational awareness.

4.1. Data Collection from Distributed IoT Nodes

The process begins with IoT sensors, actuators, and communication modules deployed across the military environment. These components are responsible for continuously gathering a wide array of operational and environmental data. The sensors monitor parameters such as movement, temperature, positioning, and communication signals, while actuators respond to dynamic instructions based on real-time data. This raw data forms the foundation of security analytics and needs to be transmitted securely for further analysis.

4.2. Secure Data Transmission via Network Gateways

The collected data is then relayed through network infrastructure components such as gateways, routers, and switches. These components ensure secure, reliable, and low-latency transmission of information across different layers of the network. Given the sensitivity of military data, these gateways often incorporate encryption protocols and access control policies to safeguard the data in transit.

4.3. Threat Detection Through IDS and Anomaly Detection

Once the data reaches the network core, it is analyzed by an Intrusion Detection System (IDS) and anomaly detection modules. These systems use ML algorithms, historical threat data, and real-time threat intelligence (Brown & Davis, 2023) to inspect traffic patterns and system behaviour. Suspicious or abnormal activities – such as unauthorized access attempts, data exfiltration signals, or DoS indicators – are flagged for further evaluation. The IDS plays a crucial role in identifying both known and unknown (zero-day) threats.

4.4. Threat Mitigation through Adaptive IPS

Upon detection of a threat, the IPS takes immediate and autonomous action to block malicious traffic, isolate compromised nodes, or reroute communication to contain the threat. The AIPS integrates adaptive learning mechanisms to refine its responses based on evolving threat patterns and historical incidents. This allows the system to improve its accuracy and reduce false positives over time.

4.5. Centralized Monitoring and Event Correlation via Security Information and Event Management (SIEM)

To maintain holistic situational awareness, a SIEM system aggregates logs, alerts, and behavioural data from various endpoints and network segments. The SIEM performs correlation analysis to identify complex threat scenarios, prioritize incidents, and generate real-time alerts. By integrating with AIPS, the SIEM contributes to automated decision-making and strategic response planning.

4.6. Visualization and Human-in-the-Loop Response

A centralized dashboard presents security insights in a user-friendly, visual format – displaying metrics such as threat severity, affected devices, and real-time status updates. This enables military operators and analysts to quickly grasp the network's security posture. In the event of a major incident, the incident response team is activated to perform further investigation, containment, and remediation (Miller & Garcia, 2022). This human-in-the-loop model ensures accountability and supports adaptive tuning of automated defences.

5. Mathematical Modeling

To design an AIPS for Military IoT networks, we can use a combination of ML techniques and statistical methods. The goal is to detect anomalies and potential intrusions in real-time, adapting to new threats dynamically. Here's a mathematical model to represent the core components of AIPS:

Let D represent the dataset collected from various IoT devices in the military network, where $D = \{d1, d2, \ldots, dn\}$.

Feature extraction: Extract features F from the raw data D. Let F be the set of feature vectors, where $F = \{f1, f2, \ldots, fn\}$.

Anomaly detection model: Let X be the feature matrix, where each row $xi \varepsilon X$ represents a feature vector fi. Use a ML model M to detect anomalies. We can represent the anomaly score S as a function of $S = M(X)$

A high anomaly score indicates a potential intrusion.

$$\text{Alert} = \begin{cases} 1 & \text{if } S > T \\ 0 & \text{otherwise} \end{cases}$$

Threshold-based detection: Define a threshold T. If $S > T$, an intrusion alert is triggered:

The proposed AIPS is grounded in a systematic and dynamic framework that leverages ML to identify and respond to anomalies in real time. The following stages outline the functioning of the system, demonstrating how it evolves with changing threat patterns while maintaining high reliability and adaptability in military IoT environments.

5.1. Initialization

At the outset, the system initializes its core components:

- Dataset (D): A collection of historical and real-time data streams generated from military IoT devices.
- Feature matrix (X): Structured representations of the raw data, where each row corresponds to a device or event instance, and each column represents a specific feature (e.g. packet size, latency, signal strength).
- ML model (M): The core analytical engine trained to identify normal versus anomalous behaviour in network activities.
- Threshold (T): A predefined or dynamically learned value used to classify whether a given behaviour is benign or potentially malicious.

This initialization step lays the groundwork for systematic data ingestion and analysis, ensuring the system is primed for real-time operation.

5.2. Data Collection and Preprocessing

In this phase, the AIPS continuously collects streaming data from distributed IoT devices embedded in military infrastructure. Given the sensitive and diverse nature of this data, preprocessing is essential to ensure consistency, accuracy, and usability. Key activities include:

- Noise filtering and data cleaning: Removing irrelevant or corrupted entries that may hinder model performance.
- Feature extraction: Converting raw data into structured features that represent meaningful behavioural indicators.
- Feature matrix update: Integrating newly extracted features into the evolving matrix, ensuring the model has access to the most recent behavioural data.

This ongoing process allows the AIPS to maintain a comprehensive and up-to-date understanding of the system's operational context.

5.3. Anomaly Detection

Using the updated feature matrix, the AIPS employs the ML model MMM to assess each new feature vector. The anomaly detection mechanism works as follows:

- Anomaly score calculation: The model computes an anomaly score for each vector, indicating the degree of deviation from learned patterns of normal behaviour.
- Threshold comparison: If the computed score surpasses the predefined threshold TTT, the system classifies the instance as suspicious or malicious.
- Alert generation and logging: Upon detection of an anomaly, the system triggers an alert to security personnel and logs the event for forensic analysis and future learning (Taylor & Walker, 2023).

This stage ensures the AIPS actively monitors and flags abnormal activities with minimal delay, providing critical situational awareness in mission-critical environments.

5.4. Adaptive Learning

To remain effective against emerging threats and behavioural shifts in the network, the AIPS integrates adaptive learning mechanisms:

- Model update: At scheduled intervals or in response to significant changes in the data, the system retrains or fine-tunes the model MMM using the latest dataset DDD.
- Feedback loop: Information from detected incidents and analyst feedback may also be incorporated to refine the model's understanding of legitimate versus malicious behaviour.
- Dynamic threshold adjustment: The threshold TTT may be adaptively adjusted based on updated risk profiles, enhancing detection sensitivity while minimizing false positives.

This continuous learning capability ensures the AIPS does not become obsolete or vulnerable over time, allowing it to evolve alongside adversarial tactics.

The integration of initialization, dynamic data preprocessing, real-time anomaly detection, and adaptive learning in this mathematical model establishes a robust foundation for the development of a mission-ready AIPS. Tailored specifically for military IoT networks, this framework facilitates prompt threat identification and mitigation while adapting intelligently to an evolving security landscape. By aligning with the stringent requirements of defense infrastructures, the proposed approach ensures resilient and proactive cybersecurity measures for safeguarding sensitive military operations.

6. Proposed Work

The proposed AIPS framework is designed to address the unique security requirements of military IoT networks, which demand high levels of resilience, adaptability, and real-time response. The working diagram of the AIPS system architecture, outlines a multi-layered and integrated approach that combines edge computing, ML, and secure communication to deliver a robust intrusion prevention mechanism (Allen & Evans, 2023).

6.1. IoT Device Layer

This is the foundational layer of the AIPS architecture, comprising the frontline devices deployed in the field. These devices serve as both data sources and action points within the network.

- Sensors: Deployed in various tactical environments, these collect real-time environmental, operational, and situational data, which is critical for decision-making and security monitoring.
- Actuators: Act upon commands received from the control system, allowing physical responses such as initiating countermeasures, shutting down compromised nodes, or changing configurations.
- Communication modules: Facilitate secure data transmission between devices and other layers, supporting protocols like Zigbee, LoRa, or military-grade encrypted Wi-Fi.

6.2. Network Layer

The network layer acts as the bridge between distributed IoT devices and the centralized infrastructure, playing a vital role in initial security enforcement and data routing.

- Gateways: These serve as the first line of defense, aggregating data from multiple IoT nodes and performing preliminary security filtering. They enforce access control policies and validate data formats before passing information to the upper layers.

6.3. Data Aggregation and Edge Computing Layer

This layer is responsible for efficient data management and low-latency processing, crucial for real-time military applications.

- Data collectors: Accumulate and organize raw data from IoT nodes. Their design supports resilience and redundancy to prevent data loss or bottlenecks in hostile or bandwidth-constrained environments.
- Edge computing nodes: Positioned near the data source, these nodes conduct initial data analysis and threat detection using lightweight algorithms, thus reducing the load on the central system and minimizing communication delays.

6.4. AIPS Core Intelligence Layer

This is the heart of the IPS, where real-time analysis, learning, and threat mitigation are performed using advanced AI/ML capabilities.

- ML engine: Continuously ingests data to detect new intrusion patterns, self-tunes its algorithms based on operational feedback, and improves detection accuracy over time. It supports both supervised and unsupervised learning approaches.
- Anomaly detection module: Detects deviations from established behavioural baselines of devices and communication patterns. It flags suspicious activity and forwards alerts for further validation and action.

6.5. Centralized Command and Control Center

The centralized unit manages the overall security operations across the IoT network, integrating strategic decision-making and real-time response coordination.

- SIEM: Aggregates security logs, event data, and alerts from distributed components to provide a comprehensive and real-time view of the system's security posture. The SIEM supports incident correlation, forensic analysis, and automated threat prioritization.

6.6. Secure Communication Channels

Effective communication between components is fundamental to the success of AIPS, especially in sensitive military operations where data integrity and confidentiality are paramount.

- Secure communication protocols: All inter-layer and intra-layer communications are protected using military-grade encryption, secure key exchanges, and authentication protocols. These measures ensure end-to-end security during data transit and prevent interception or tampering by adversaries.

The proposed AIPS architecture ensures that all elements – from sensing and data collection to detection, decision-making, and response – are securely interconnected. Edge computing nodes enable fast, localized decision-making, while centralized systems provide strategic oversight and intelligence aggregation. The layered structure ensures redundancy, scalability, and adaptability in the face of dynamic threat environments, particularly in complex and geographically dispersed military deployments.

This comprehensive framework offers a holistic and adaptive solution to the growing challenges of cybersecurity in military IoT networks. It ensures rapid detection, precise classification, and effective response to both known and unknown threats, supporting mission continuity and national defense objectives (Thomas & White, 2023).

7. Result Analysis and Discussion

The Proposed AIPS was designed to address the evolving cybersecurity needs of military IoT networks. By integrating ML algorithms, real-time threat intelligence, anomaly detection, and adaptive learning, AIPS delivers dynamic and real-time protection against a broad spectrum of cyber threats. This section analyzes and discusses the performance of AIPS compared to traditional and modern IPSs (Harris & Robinson, 2022).

7.1. Comparative Evaluation Across Key Metrics

Table 9.2 presents a comparative analysis of AIPS with several existing approaches, including traditional IDS, heuristic-based IPS, static ML models, and hybrid IPS. The analysis is based on critical performance parameters such as detection rate, adaptability, false positive and false negative rates, response time, resource efficiency, integration ease, and maintenance requirements.

7.2. Visual Representation and Performance Insights

Figs. 9.1 and 9.2 provide a graphical representation of the comparative performance of various intrusion prevention approaches in military IoT networks.

In this bar chart shown in Fig. 9.1, we are comparing four algorithms (A–D) under eight major parameters in regards to security and efficiency. The highest detection rate and adaptability to new threats are always acquired by algorithm D (blue), but it has drawbacks with false negative rate and response time. Algorithms A (orange) is the most resource-efficient and responds the fastest, but loses its ability to adapt. Algorithms B (pink) and C (magenta) have moderate and balanced performance on most parameters with Algorithm C just a bit stronger on false positive rate control. All in all, algorithm D is more accurate and flexible whereas algorithm A is more efficient and the selection depends on the application.

Table 9.2. Comparative Analysis Using Different Parameters with Some Existing Approaches.

S. No.	Metric	Traditional IDS	Heuristic-Based IPS	Static ML Models	Hybrid IPS	Proposed AIPS
1	Detection rate	Moderate	Moderate	High	High	Very High
2	Adaptability to new threats	Low	Low	Moderate	High	Very High
3	False positive rate	High	Moderate	Moderate	Low	Low
4	False negative rate	Moderate	High	Moderate	Low	Very Low
5	Response time	Slow	Moderate	Moderate	Fast	Very Fast
6	Resource efficiency	High	Moderate	Moderate	Low	High
7	Ease of integration	High	Moderate	Moderate	Low	Moderate
8	Maintenance requirements	Low	Moderate	High	High	Moderate

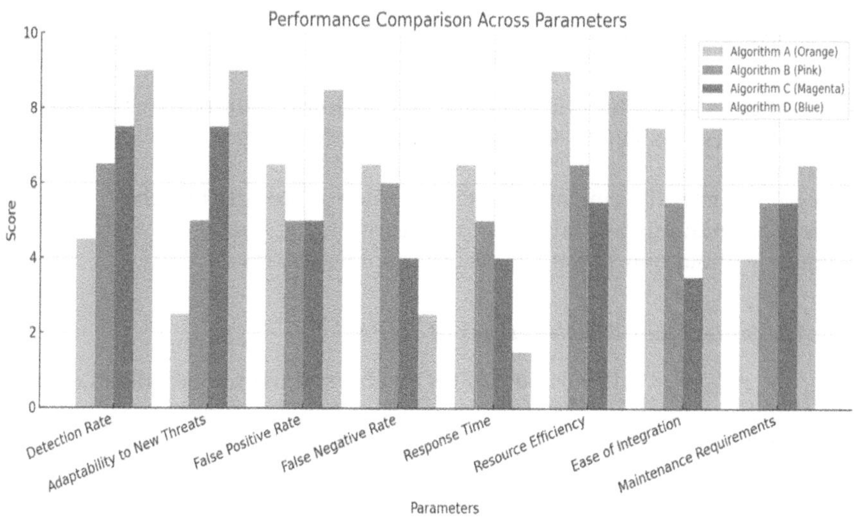

Fig. 9.1. Performance Comparison of IPS Approaches.

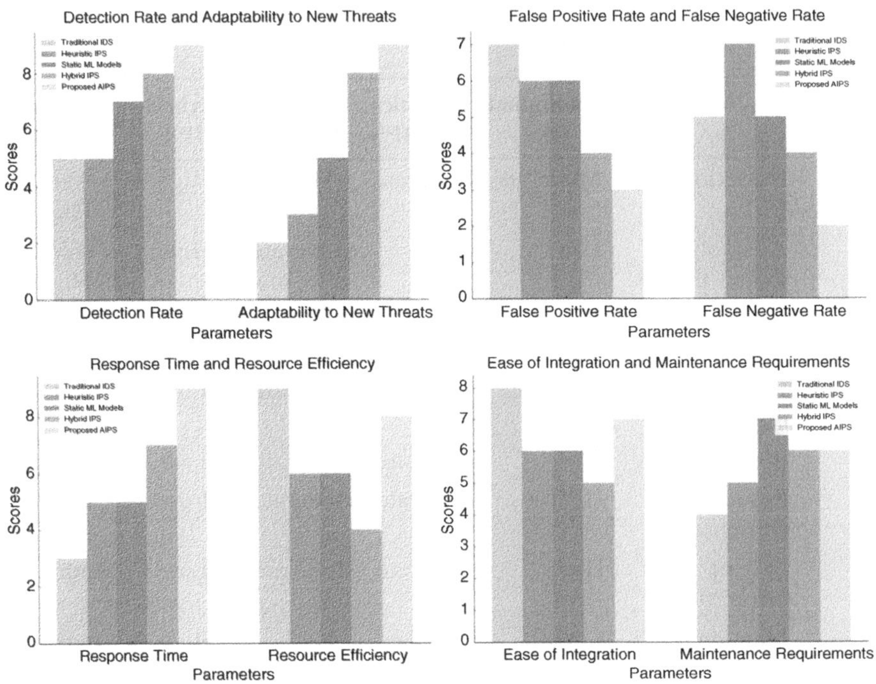

Fig. 9.2. Comparative Analysis Graphs Based on Key Performance Metrics.

These visual aids highlight the superiority of the proposed AIPS across most critical dimensions. AIPS shows marked improvement particularly in:

- Detection rate, which is crucial in high-risk, real-time operational environments;
- Adaptability, enabling it to remain effective even against novel and evolving threats;
- Response time, allowing immediate mitigation of security breaches;
- While maintaining low false positive/negative rates, ensuring operational continuity without unnecessary alerts or missed detections.

7.3. Advantages and Disadvantages of AIPS

While the proposed AIPS demonstrates notable strengths, especially in the context of military-grade cybersecurity, its deployment also introduces certain challenges. A balanced assessment is necessary for informed decision-making.

7.3.1. Advantages

- AIPS employs advanced ML algorithms and real-time threat intelligence, significantly increasing its ability to detect both known and zero-day attacks with high precision.

- Continuous learning from new threat data allows AIPS to stay ahead of adversaries, adapting in near real-time to shifting threat landscapes.
- Through intelligent anomaly detection, the system maintains a low false positive and false negative rate, improving trust and reducing alert fatigue among operators.
- The integration of fast-processing ML models and adaptive decision-making ensures that threats are identified and neutralized almost instantaneously, which is critical in military applications.
- By unifying multiple detection methodologies with threat intelligence feeds, AIPS offers a holistic view of network health and vulnerabilities.

7.3.2. Disadvantages

- The design and deployment of such an advanced system requires specialized technical skills, which may necessitate additional training for cybersecurity personnel.
- Integrating AIPS with existing and often outdated legacy military systems can be cumbersome and might lead to compatibility issues if not managed carefully.
- Continuous updates to ML models and integration of fresh threat intelligence are essential but can be resource- and time-intensive.
- Initial costs, including hardware, software licences, and personnel training, may be significant and require budgetary considerations.
- The success of AIPS hinges on the quality, variety, and representativeness of the training data. Poor or biased data can impair system performance.

The proposed AIPS represents a significant leap forward in securing military IoT infrastructures. Its performance across all major evaluation parameters suggests that it not only matches but surpasses many traditional and contemporary intrusion prevention mechanisms. However, successful real-world implementation depends on resolving integration challenges, managing complexity, and ensuring ongoing model maintenance.

8. Future Scope

The future of AIPSs for military IoT networks holds significant promise, driven by continuous advancements in technology and evolving security needs. Several key areas for future research and development include:

- As cyber threats become more sophisticated, there is a need for more advanced ML techniques that can better detect and respond to novel threats. Research into deep learning, reinforcement learning, and other advanced AI methodologies will be essential in developing more effective AIPS.
- Blockchain technology can provide enhanced security and transparency for military IoT networks. Future research could explore the integration of blockchain with AIPS to create tamper-proof logs of network activity, improving the system's ability to detect and respond to intrusions.

- The advent of quantum computing presents both opportunities and challenges for cybersecurity. Future AIPS could leverage quantum computing to enhance their processing power and threat detection capabilities, while also developing defences against potential quantum-based attacks.
- Enhancing the autonomy of AIPS to not only detect but also independently respond to threats can significantly reduce response times and improve overall network security. Future systems could employ autonomous drones or robots to physically address and neutralize threats in the field.
- As military IoT networks continue to grow and evolve, AIPS must be scalable and flexible enough to accommodate new devices and changing network configurations. Research into modular and adaptable AIPS architectures will be important for future deployments.

AIPSs are poised to play a critical role in securing military IoT networks against ever-evolving cyber threats. By leveraging cutting-edge technologies and addressing the unique challenges of military environments, AIPS can provide robust and adaptive security solutions that enhance the safety and effectiveness of military operations. Ongoing research and development, combined with a commitment to addressing ethical and legal considerations, will be essential in realizing the full potential of AIPS for military IoT networks. The future of military cybersecurity is dynamic and complex, but with continued innovation and collaboration, we can build resilient systems capable of defending against the threats of tomorrow.

9. Conclusion

The integration of IoT technology within military operations has brought about unprecedented capabilities, enhancing operational efficiency, situational awareness, and strategic decision-making. However, the proliferation of interconnected devices also introduces significant security vulnerabilities that can be exploited by sophisticated cyber threats. AIPSs have emerged as a crucial solution to address these vulnerabilities, offering dynamic, real-time protection tailored to the unique demands of military IoT environments.

Through this work, we have explored the latest innovations in AIPS, focusing on advancements in ML algorithms, anomaly detection techniques, and real-time threat intelligence integration. These technologies enable AIPS to learn from new data, identify emerging threats, and respond swiftly to mitigate potential attacks. The adaptive nature of these systems allows them to evolve alongside the threat landscape, providing robust and resilient security for military IoT networks.

We have also identified and analyzed several key challenges in implementing AIPS in military contexts. These include the heterogeneity of IoT devices, resource constraints, the need for rapid and real-time response, the evolving threat landscape, integration with existing systems, and the necessity for effective human-machine collaboration. Addressing these challenges is critical to the successful deployment and operation of AIPS in military IoT environments.

References

Allen, O., & Evans, P. (2023). AI-driven adaptive intrusion prevention. *Future Generation Computer Systems*, *152*(9), 450–465.

Brown, I., & Davis, J. (2023). Blockchain-enhanced security for IoT. *IEEE Internet of Things Journal*, *10*(8), 3200–3215.

Harris, S., & Robinson, T. (2022). Collaborative IDS for Military IoT. *International Journal of Distributed Sensor Networks*, *18*(7), 500–516.

Martinez, E., & Lee, F. (2022). Hybrid intrusion prevention for military IoT. *Computers & Security*, *120*(3), 45–59.

Miller, K., & Garcia, L. (2022). Resource-efficient IDS for IoT. *Journal of Systems and Software*, *195*(2), 75–89.

Smith, A., & Johnson, B. (2023). Advanced machine learning techniques for IDS in IoT. *Journal of Network and Computer Applications*, *205*(4), 101–115.

Taylor, M., & Walker, N. (2023). Threat intelligence integration in IDS. *Computers & Security*, *121*(6), 300–315.

Thomas, Q., & White, R. (2023). Security information and event management for IoT. *Journal of Information Security and Applications*, *75*(4), 200–214.

Wang, C., & Patel, D. (2023). Real-time threat detection in IoT networks. *IEEE Transactions on Information Forensics and Security*, *18*(2), 210–225.

Zhang, G., & Kim, H. (2023). Anomaly detection in military IoT networks. *Ad Hoc Networks*, *137*(5), 150–165.

Chapter 10

Exploring the Frontiers of 5G and 6G Networks: Virtualization Challenges and IoT Device Integration

Neha Katiyar[a], Hardeo Kumar Thakur[a], Kushal Pal Singh[b] and Anindya Ghatak[a]

[a] *Bennett University, India*
[b] *Malviya National Institute of Technology, India*

Abstract

Autonomous vehicles and virtual reality (VR) platforms rapidly increased due to the connectivity between the Internet of Things (IoT) technology; hence, the network connectivity demand also increased. Meeting the connectivity requirements of virtual platforms necessitates a high-speed, compatible, and wide-coverage network. Wide-area networks such as 5G and 6G support a variety of network and Internet of Things (IoT) devices. These networks have many communication features, such as Enhanced Mobile Broadband (eMBB), Ultra-Reliable, Low Latency Communications (URLLC), and massive machine type communications. These networks have advanced security features. The 5G technology cannot meet the technical requirements of IoT devices which consist of augmented reality (AR), VR, smart industry, intelligent traffic system, and other new application scenarios in the 2030s. Most of the technology research and standard studies about 6G have also been proposed. In this survey chapter, the authors performed a comparative study on 5G and 6G networks, virtualization-based multiple input multiple output (MIMO) technology, and Mobile Ad Hoc Network (MANET) techniques, challenges, and advantages in IoT devices. In this chapter, the authors discuss the network connectivity of various atmospheric layers, such as 5G and 6G network layers and the challenges

The Internet of Things in the Defence Industry:
Challenges and Solutions for Military Security, 205–225

doi:10.1108/978-1-83549-198-020261010

of 5G and 6G network connectivity. Finally, the authors discuss several lessons learned from the literature and also highlight the problems of open research directions of 5G and 6G networks for future research.

Keywords: 5G; 6G; IoT devices; network latency capacity; networks

1. Introduction

The 5G network has achieved significant breakthroughs in data rates, latency, mobility, and IoT devices' connectivity. It offers advanced features when compared to previous generations, such as 1G, 2G, 3G, and 4G. During the COVID-19 pandemic, 5G proved to be a game-changing, device-compatible network, enabling smooth access to technology for users. However, further enhancements and modifications are still needed to meet future demands.

These advancements are addressed by the 6G network, which was introduced through the 6Genesis flagship program in 2018. This program spanned eight years, with a budget of approximately ₹290 million, aiming to deliver a comprehensive 6G system. Globally, many countries are supporting and investing in the development of 6G. For instance, German companies are focusing on designing 6G networks integrated with quantum technologies, while China's Ministry of Industry and Information Technology has also prioritized 6G development. Both developed and developing nations are participating in the coordinated advancement of 6G technologies.

As for 5G, global investments are projected to reach USD 1.3 trillion by 2026. In the healthcare sector, the economic output enabled by 5G is expected to reach USD 1.1 trillion by 2035. According to the Immigration Health Surcharge (IHS) healthcare market report, 5G will support healthcare products worth approximately USD 1.0 trillion globally. Furthermore, both 5G and 6G base stations consume less power compared to their 4G counterparts.

The 6G network is expected to revolutionize various sectors, particularly healthcare. It guarantees key performance indicators (KPIs) while achieving a 5–10 times increase in spectral efficiency. It is also considered a key enabler of Industry 4.0. The 6G network is envisioned as the only technology capable of managing global data traffic up to 5 zettabytes by 2030. Its capabilities include terahertz frequency communication and spatial multiplexing, offering 1,000 times the capacity of 5G networks.

With seamless wireless connectivity and energy efficiency, the upcoming era of 6G is referred to as the 'Green 6G Network'. It aims to provide full-stack development with system-level requirements, addressing critical factors such as latency, throughput, and connectivity. The 6G network will be equipped with smart features to integrate with IoT environments, enabling intelligent automation.

In smart societal structures, 6G offers new degrees of freedom for enhancing wireless links and delivering unprecedented capacities. 6G devices and antennas are expected to be built with metamaterials, allowing wideband antenna implementations. It will also utilize radio-fibre technology to enable global and regional network coverage.

6G communication technology supports both short- and long-range user connectivity. It integrates with various wireless technologies, such as Wi-Fi, WiMAX, and Bluetooth, and provides secure data transmission across networks. The technology also presents a transformative synergy capable of replacing traditional copper cables and optical fibre with more advanced solutions.

6G also introduces promising research areas spanning terrestrial, ground, and space-level networks. It is currently being explored for satellite communication applications. In India, the Department of Telecommunications (DoT) is supporting various stakeholders in driving digital transformation and deploying emerging technologies. The 6G network will also support low-earth orbit (LEO) constellations for broadband coverage.

India's Department of Communication has projected a revenue opportunity of over $1 billion annually from 6G networks. Tata and Telesat have collaborated to enter India's emerging fast broadband space segment. With LEO satellite communication, India is poised to ensure inclusive 6G coverage, particularly in remote and underserved regions.

This survey paper presents a comprehensive literature review of 5G and 6G network technologies. It compares the two generations across various parameters, highlights their applications and challenges, and evaluates their performance through network simulations. Additionally, the chapter examines 5G and 6G in the context of stealth communication and atmospheric layer interactions.

2. Literature Survey

Ten years ago, concepts like machine learning (ML), artificial intelligence (AI), the IoT, and Industrial IoT (IIoT) were still in their infancy and saw limited application across most technical fields. The last decade marked a transitional phase across multiple generations of wireless communication – from 1G to 4G – and later ushered in the beginnings of 5G and research into 6G.

The first-generation (1G) network, introduced in the 1980s, was based on analog communication and only supported basic voice transmission with very limited capacity and security. This was followed by second-generation (2G) networks, which introduced digital communication, enabling both voice and text messaging through technologies like GSM (Global System for Mobile Communications). With the advent of third-generation (3G) networks, data transmission capabilities became feasible. Technologies like CDMA (Code Division Multiple Access) and packet-switched data enabled faster web browsing, mobile internet, and basic video calling, with speeds around 2 Mbps.

Fourth-generation (4G) networks further revolutionized mobile communication by incorporating high-speed data transfer and multimedia support. Technologies such as OFDM (Orthogonal Frequency Division Multiplexing) and wireless LAN integration allowed for streaming, gaming, and high-definition mobile content, reaching speeds of up to 100 Mbps to 1 Gbps under ideal conditions.

With the arrival of fifth-generation (5G) networks, wireless communication entered a new era characterized by ultra-high speed, low latency, massive device connectivity, and energy efficiency. The evolution continues with the sixth-generation (6G) networks, which promise even broader bandwidth, terahertz (THz) communication, AI-native operations, intelligent edge computing, and support for emerging paradigms such as tactile internet, holographic communication, and intelligent autonomous systems.

Giordani et al. (2020) critically evaluated the transition from 5G to 6G, comparing the key parameters across generations. The study noted significant differences in data transmission speeds: 2G supported up to 64 kbps, 3G up to 2 Mbps, 4G up to 100–1,000 Mbps, and 5G between 1 and 10 Gbps. In contrast, 6G is expected to operate at terahertz frequencies, delivering data rates up to 1 Tbps (terabits per second). The chapter emphasized the novel features of 6G, including new spectrum exploration (e.g. THz bands), classless network virtualization, Green Information and Communication Technology (ICT) (energy-efficient network design), and seamless integration of AI. Furthermore, it explored the potential of ML strategies to enhance dynamic network management, resource allocation, and security in 6G environments.

Huo et al. (2019) focused on the deployment of 5G applications and highlighted techniques that reduce deployment costs and improve energy efficiency. Their review encompassed operations using unlicensed spectrum, with emphasis on multiplexing techniques and dependencies on Wi-Fi, WiGig (Wireless Gigabit), and sub-6 GHz bands. Their proposed multiplexing architecture was based on three key broadband types: cellular broadband, WiGig basebands, and 2.45 GHz Wi-Fi basebands. The study also explored communication technologies such as 5G mmWave, Wi-Fi at 24 GHz and 60 GHz, 5G sub-GHz bands, and emerging 6 GHz mmWave technologies.

Huang et al. (2019) introduced the concept of Green 6G network architecture, proposing sustainable, energy-efficient technologies as a foundation for future networks. Both 5G and 6G are seen as enablers of energy-conscious infrastructure. The Green 6G framework aimed to reduce carbon footprints by integrating communication paradigms like symbiotic radio, blockchain-based security, and THz network optimization. LTE (Long-Term Evolution) networks were also discussed as a transitional technology within the green network context, providing a stepping stone between traditional cellular architecture and the envisioned 6G model.

A 2020 report by the International Telecommunication Union (ITU) (Lu & Zheng, 2020) emphasized the role of 6G as a convergence platform for next-generation technologies. The 6G vision is aligned with the needs of emerging ICTs, encompassing AI, VR, AR, IoT, and Industrial IoT. The ITU's strategic goals for 6G include supporting immersive experiences, intelligent sensing, and global hyper-connectivity.

Wang et al. (2020) highlighted the exploratory and disruptive potential of 6G. It pointed to key architectural elements such as real-time edge computing distribution, autonomous AI-based network management, and the evolution of inter-device communication protocols. The study also discussed the security and privacy concerns associated with AI integration in 6G, including challenges related to authentication, access control, malicious behaviours, and encryption methodologies.

An emerging area of interest is molecular and nanoscale communication over 6G networks. The research community has begun to explore how nanotechnology, coupled with advanced encryption and AI mechanisms, can enable secure and efficient nanoscale communications in biomedical, defence, and industrial applications. These applications include nano-sensors, bio-networking, and molecular-level diagnostics, driven by the ultra-low latency and high bandwidth of future 6G infrastructures.

2.1. Key Concepts of 5G and 6G Networks

The study by Tang et al. (2020) focused on the key concepts and challenges the 6G network faces in rural areas. They surveyed the rural area from the perspective of an advanced network. Most of the population resides in rural areas. The key challenges of the network are: (a) Low-income people cannot afford this network, and (b) the relevance of the network, (c) user capabilities of the network, and (d) infrastructure of the network. The major issues depended upon the population and per capita income per year. This chapter also highlights the use of electricity in the network, the energy efficiency, and cost efficiency of the advanced network.

Tariq et al. (2020) focused on the visionary technologies that enable the 6G network. They also differentiate between the 5G and 6G networks. The characteristics of 5G and 6G networks' differential are based on individual data rate, Data Latency (DL) data rate, unplanned latency, C-plane latency, mobility, and operating frequency. The 6G network provides an additional Degree of Freedom (DoF). The 6G network provides a block interface to enhance the security and privacy process. 5G and 6G also reduce the complications of cyber-attacks. Valero et al. (2022) focused on developing the 6G ecosystem procedure. The 6G network concentrates on the 6 Genes Flagship program. This program has all the fundamental techniques of enabling technology. The 6G Flagship program supports digitalization. Digitalization consists of 6G ultra-low latency communication of RAN protocols used as transceivers. The security technologies of the 6G network using RAN technology enable 6G network propagation modelling and communication theory. The 6G network technologies develop the fundamentals of network optimization in mm-Wave TH2bands.

Nawaz et al. (2019) focused on the 5G and 6G connecting wireless networks in real-time processing; they also performed research on quantum computing and highlighted the problem of uncertainty in quantum computing. They also focused on ML techniques to complete the procedure of quantum computing. The ML algorithm reviewed the stringing performance requirement for future communication networks in the 6G network infrastructure of the network edge. The user site increases thoroughly with strong processing and learning capabilities.

Sergiou et al. (2020) reviewed the various technologies of the 6G mobile communication network. This chapter encourages people to research complex systems on mobile communication networks. A complex system has its desired behaviours adaptively through network evolution, network robustness, and decentralization. These complex systems used the distributed system. The 6G advanced features make the network more complex and dynamic topology, TH2 frequencies. It also maintains the backhaul traffic, AI and ML techniques, and software-defined networking.

2.2. *Autonomous-Driven Network*

Zhang et al. (2020) worked on the 6G network and its communication techniques. This chapter focused on AI-assisted intelligent communication and elaborated on the driving forces. In the 6G network, topology and time frames are used. This chapter highlights the concept of a 6G network and its cost efficiency. The cost-efficient network reduces the cost 1,000 times compared to other networks. Viswanathan and Mogensen (2020) focused on the communication technique of the 6G era. They highlight the main interfaces, distributed computing between local devices and clouds, multisensory data, and multi-mapping strategies. They focused on the 6G network connectivity, such as smartphones and smart devices, flexible devices, skin-patchable devices, and cyborgs. The connectivity of the 6G network throughput is 100 Gbps. The latency and reliability of the network are 0.1 ms. The adaptability time of 6G connectivity is 1 sec. The response time of 6G connectivity is 1 sec.

Nawaz et al. (2021) focused on 5G wireless network research and the challenges of the 5G era. The research consists of man machine-type communication (m MTC) services; they used uncrewed aerial vehicles (UAVs) assisted communications and visible light communications (VLC) quantum communications, ML, and intelligent networks. Emu and Choudhury (2021) focused on the deep learning techniques used in the 6G network. Several research works have been proposed regarding the IoT ecosystem and IoT applications. In this chapter, they provided an algorithm for cost optimization and communication trade-off factors. They used the Virtual Network Function (VNF) relocation and communication cost deviation procedure. The deviation decreases by 8.95%, up to each epoch 5 with a batch size of 450, Kernel size 3. The activation function used in the algorithm is ReLU for optimization.

Jang et al. (2021) proposed a new enabling technology in the 6G network to accommodate a massive number of IoT devices. This technology is GFMA (Grant Free Multiple Access). The GFMA framework is used for random, resource, and Latin group hopping. These hopping devices are rapidly managing their connectivity to IoT devices. The GFMA procedure consists of transmission, reception, device activity detection, & channel estimation. The data decoding in GFMA is done with devices. Barakat et al. (2021) reviewed the 6G network connectivity with IoT devices. They reviewed the wide variety of implemented work in networking technologies like 6G and 5G. They reviewed various technologies like multimedia automation of factories, high-resolution techniques, and automotive vehicles. The main features they reviewed for the 6G network are IoT connectivity, time sensitivity applications, engineered applications, high fidelity connectivity, or advanced features of holographic connectivity. They also reviewed smart energy monitoring systems.

Ssengonzi et al. (2022) worked on the wave technology of the 6G network. The wave technology used in the 1G network is FDMA (frequency division multiple access). The second generation uses TDMA (time division multiple access). The 3G technology uses CDMA. The 4G used web technology (MIMO). The 5G used web technology for massive machine-type communication (MMTC). The 6G network used MIMO technology. Kukliński et al. (2021) researched the network slicing architecture. They proposed a modular architecture having a network slicing paradigm. They enable the domain slices, which are relatively easy to implement because of their global connectivity, low latency, and spectral efficiency.

The slicing approach of the 6G network has concerns about centralized issues, single domain orchestration only, reactive resource allocation, slice management variants, and slice orchestration variants. In this research paper, they also researched the network slicing procedure of the 6G network. They provided the concept of the RAN slicing protocol. The Radio Access Network (RAN) slicing protocols at three levels are network level slicing, next generation node B (g node B) level slicing, and packet level slicing. The protocol is automatic, and the RAN slicing protocol provides the Internet of Everything (IoE) concept. The networking technologies used AI and ML techniques.

Sim et al. (2020) worked on the deep neural network structure, which explains the power delay profiles with data inputs. They proposed deep learning-based methods for time-frequency domain synchronization on 5G networks. They set the new 5G standard for network establishment and worked on the LTE of the 5G network. They used a cellular network of 5G and performed channel modelling. The channel models categorized are – mm Wave CHANEL Model and SUB-6GHz Chanel Model. They used various performance methods for deep learning-based selection.

3. 5G Network

Mei et al. (2020) researched the network slicing procedure of the 6G network. They provided a concept of the RAN slicing protocol. The RAN slicing protocol is used at three levels: network-level slicing, next-generation Node B (g node B), and packet-level slicing. They designed a seven-automatic and RAN slicing protocol. The RAN slicing protocol provides the concept of IoE. The networking technologies used AI and ML techniques.

Liyanaarachchi et al. (2021) worked on the optimized waveform of 5G and 6G networks. They used the OFDM waveform optimization to complete the optimization process. The optimization process jointly minimizes low bounds for Doppler optimization. In this optimization technique, sample optimization is done analytically and computationally, and a feasible algorithm is used to present the task.

(Rahman et al., 2022) emphasize the 5G technology used to handle the issues of COVID-19 in different areas. The 5G technology improved health services, medical research, and various experiences for medical professionals. The design of the 5G Network is used for handling emergencies. The 5G network is also used in the healthcare sector, which has (a) limited resources and healthcare facilities, (b) challenges in health information systems, and (c) lacks in developing healthcare solutions. Cheng et al. (2022) and Zhang et al. (2020) researched the 5G network deployment on the network. They mainly focused on the 5G network deployment in the short- and long-term demand areas.

The methodology they used for the network deployment is system representations, boundaries, and base stations. The network architecture site types are Macrocell, Microcell, Picocell, and Femtocell. These types of cells are deployed in the various base stations. The power consumption by Macrocell base stations is 3 kW–10 kW and the power consumption of microcells is 150W to 300 kW and for picocells is 15W. The power consumption of fentocell is 10 W to 30 W.

Muteba et al. (2022) and Zhang et al. (2020) focused on designing the 5G network. They focused on lower-power wide-area technology for the LTE of the network. The narrow-band technology of the 5G network provides a solution for Low Power Wide Area Network (LPWAN) establishment. The narrowband techniques decreased the process of critical communications and increased their broadband area for communication. The narrowband techniques in IoT remove the congestion. Valero et al. (2022) focused on mobile telecommunication techniques in the network. The 5G group was established through the group of entities' demands and trustworthiness. The overview of reputation models' modules has started monitoring new iterations, direct and indirect start, trust data features and actions, etc. There are various modules: (1) an information gathering module, (2) a trust computation module, and (3) a trust storage module.

Stavroulaki et al. (2021) focused on the dedicated network. The dedicated 6G network is used for the dynamic distribution. That is used for smart warehousing, public safety, and highways. The main challenge Dedicate 6G is the mechanism for dynamic coverage and connectivity extension. The dedicated 6G concepts have the dynamic distribution of intelligence. It also supports features like CRATE-IOT, SECUREIOT, and IOT. Tang et al. (2020) researched the MIMO technologies using 5G and 6G networks. The MIMO technology can compensate for large path holes for high-frequency bands. The designing scenarios have smart warehousing. We can upgrade the design procedures for this. In this procedure, they enhanced the experience of public safety and connectivity. In this, they provide linking-level simulation specifications. The MIMO technology manages with the 5G network system level simulations 90%. That can be achieved by exceeding the throughput of 160 Gbps. Tariq et al. (2020) focused on studying this 6G network's cost-effectiveness, technological advancements, and speculative network analysis.

4. Comparative Study of 5G and 6G Networks

4.1. 5G and 6G Comparative Study on Different Measurements

5G has now been launched in various cities in India. 5G devices take over the market. 5G devices are sold out worldwide, and users are using these devices. 5G collaborates with various industries, such as academia networks, and investigates new modules. 5G technology works with all smart devices. 6G technologies and 5G technologies are different in various aspects, and the comparison is based on configuration, as shown in Table 10.1. The 6G network is highly intelligent. It consists of all smart technologies. The 6G network provides a smart grid, smart living, and human specializations. Various technologies like Wi-Fi, MANET, and WiMax support the 6G network. In 5G technology, things depend upon the touch screen. Regarding 6G technology, it depends upon gesturing and talking to devices, and 5G network-provided sensors with wearable devices. 6G network provides brain sensors that detect the information without wearable devices. 5G network supports the digital world efficiently, but the 6G network not only supports 5G network functionality but also consists of edge computing. These two networks have advanced techniques and a massive deployment of sensors. Still, it differs in various aspects like network deployment, network architecture, simulation environment, simulators, Quality of Service (QOS) parameters, mobile Wifimax configuration, 3D network architecture, and network virtualization. The comparative approach incorporates 5G and 6G network simulation, communication technologies, and stealth communication. Besides, many more future perspectives of 5G and 6G networks exist.

4.2. Comparison of 5G and 6G Networks on the Basis of Simulation

Simulation of 6G Network – The 6G simulation network depends upon the 3D representation environment, combining advanced 6G networking technology with MIMO channels and multimodal data and MANET technology. This cutting-edge 6G network simulator operates across various network activities, including processing Ray Tracing data, data point clouds, simulated camera images, and spatial positions. 6G technology is designed to encompass both terrestrial and extraterrestrial realms, providing integrated support for airspace networks spanning from the Earth's surface to outer space. 6G networks are mainly used for front and passive components and emitted electromagnetic waves with circular metres.

Table 10.1. Configuration of 5G and 6G Networks.

S. No.	Parameters of 5G Network	Parameters of 6G Network
1	Frequency bands 6 GHz	Frequency bands up to 6 GHz and used for non-RF bands
2	1 Gbps to 20 Gbps data rates	1 Tbps data rates
3	Network latency 5 ms	Network latency 5 ms
4	Dense architecture	Non-dense architecture
5	AR and VR devices do not connect easily	AR and VR devices connectivity
6	Gigahertz speed network	Terahertz speed network
7	Wi-Fi supported	Only support Wifimax
8	GFMA not supported	GFMA supported

Each beam is printed in predefined parameters. The 6G network simulation covered many aspects of performing the networking services in high aspects. It consists of a digital representation of gestures and objects. Suppose some sensor captures a person's gesture; then, four steps are applied to the gesture. The first one is ray tracing, which checks the data points on the cloud and the gesture's position through GPS. When the 6G network tracks everything, it will be sent to the communication system. Simulation Model of 5G Network – The network model and simulator encompass several components: application layer, 5G network services, 5G SIM systems, and 5G link systems.

The 5G simulations employ a diverse range of testing techniques. It encompasses service platforms, frequency carrier channels, and interface tools. The 5G simulator has a 5G connectivity network platform. The 5G simulator boasts a robust 5G network connectivity platform. This simulator shows two advanced features in Fig. 10.1: 5G web-based Graphical User Interface (GUI) and the cloud computing environment. The 5G simulation operation involves initiating a 5G device and transmitting data through 5G networking test techniques. These techniques access the interface tools and service platforms. The service platform, in turn, conveys the values to the 5G simulator for evaluation, scrutinizing the sim system, link system, and application layer. Furthermore, the 5G platform responds to the request, whether it's cloud-based or service-based request.

4.3. Comparison Between the 5G and 6G Networks Based on Stealth Communication

Incorporating In-Band Full-Duplex Connectivity (IBFD) into the network has revolutionized communication. With the deployment of 5G network connectivity, over 50 communication systems were integrated, seamlessly connecting to a

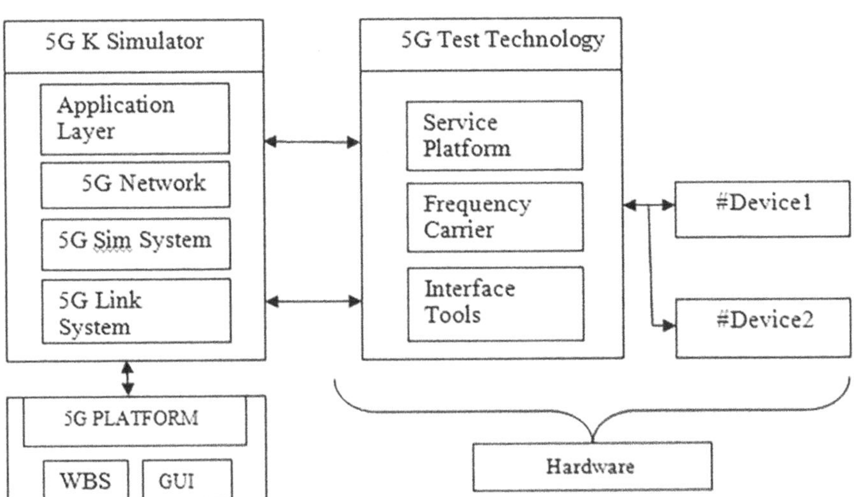

Fig. 10.1. 5G Network Simulation Model.

diverse range of 80 unique scenarios. With the advent of 6G network technology, we witness a significant leap in capabilities. The inclusion of IBFD, a key component, now supports the integration of over 70 communication systems, IoT enabling connectivity across a staggering 100 different measurement scenarios.

4.4. 5G and 6G Network Comparisons Concerning the Atmospheric Layer

The 5G network ranges and covers the area of the atmosphere. It covers various layers of the atmosphere. The layers are the troposphere, stratosphere, and mesosphere. The 6G network covers the range and area of the 6G network. It covers the troposphere, stratosphere, mesosphere, thermosphere, and exosphere. The 5G network covers LTE air interface, 5G air interface and RAN interface, front haul interface, and RAN-CN. The network connectivity procedure is shown in Figs. 10.2 and 10.3.

The rapid advancement in 5G and 6G technologies has introduced a wide array of novel applications, while simultaneously presenting significant technical challenges. According to Marco Giordani et al., 5G/6G enable transformative applications such as AR/VR, holographic teleportation, E-health, Industry 4.0, and robotics (Barakat et al., 2021). However, these innovations demand complex solutions in areas like real-time processing, scheduling, network topology optimization, scalability, and energy efficiency. Similarly, T. Huang et al. explored futuristic applications including THz and VLC, quantum communication, aerial networking, and energy harvesting. These require innovative licencing policies, cost-effective semiconductor materials, and decentralized network control mechanisms (Cheng et al., 2022).

Tongyi Huang and colleagues expanded the spectrum of applications by introducing ubiquitous 3D coverage, pervasive AI, advanced protocol stacks, and symbiotic radio (Emu & Choudhury, 2021). The implementation of these applications depends on energy conservation strategies, cost-effective antenna designs,

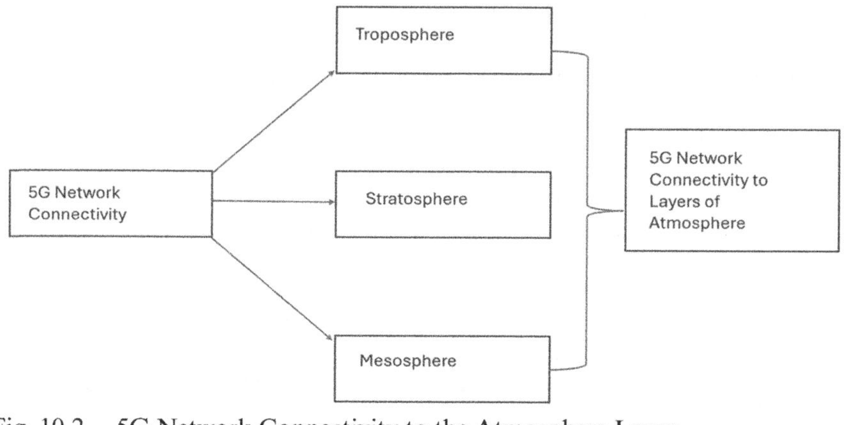

Fig. 10.2. 5G Network Connectivity to the Atmosphere Layer.

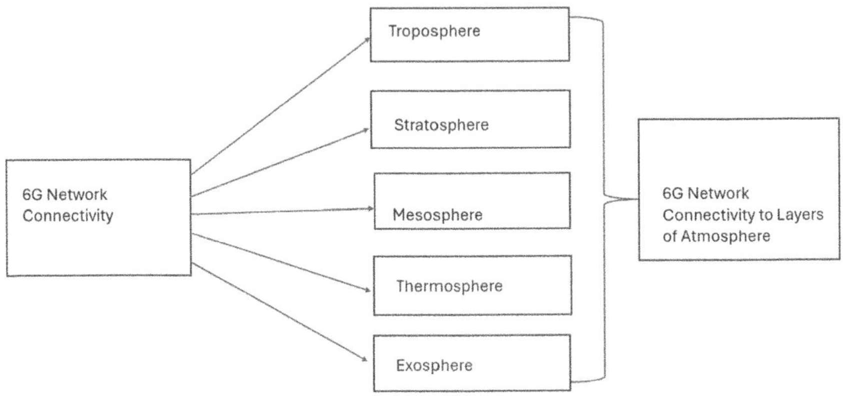

Fig. 10.3. 6G Network Connectivity to the Atmosphere Layer.

and backscatter communication. Yiming Huo et al. discussed the integration of WiFi/WiGig multiplexing, reconfigurable circuits, and beamforming architectures, but acknowledged the challenge in product design, field testing, and Terahertz equipment configuration (Giordani et al., 2020).

Minghao Wang emphasized the role of edge computing in real-time autonomous driving and introduced distributed AI, intelligent radio, and quantum communication. Challenges include maintaining privacy (location and system), device deployment, and supporting wireless brain-computer interactions (Huang et al., 2019). Eliyas Yaacoub proposed fibre space optics for satellite and UAV communications, aiming for increased capacity and lower costs. However, they faced challenges related to spectrum economics, rural IoT connectivity, and mesh backhaul setups (Huo et al., 2019).

Faisal Tariq et al. envisioned haptic and holographic communication, smart home and healthcare systems, and manufacturing automation (Jang et al., 2021). These require robust THz band management, fog networking, edge computing, and dynamic topology handling. Marcos Katz identified URLLC, embedded positioning, and distributed wireless computing, where challenges lie in quantum communication security, material innovation, and infrastructure management (Valero et al., 2022).

Syed Junaid Nawaz highlighted quantum communications, ultra-network access, non-orthogonal multiple access, and ML integration, with core issues such as throughput optimization, network capacity, and congestion management (Kukliński et al., 2021). Sergiou et al. addressed ultra-massive MIMO, reconfigurable intelligent surfaces, and scale-free architectures, but noted challenges in structural complexity, network adaptability, and resilience modelling (Liyanaarachchi et al., 2021).

F. Tang et al. brought vehicular communication to the forefront, including environmental modelling and rapid vehicular network response, while contending with multi-radio access, virtualization, and large-scale network management (Lu & Zheng, 2020). Zhang et al. introduced massive machine-type communications, digital twins, space-air-ground integration, and AI-assisted communications. These required precise channel estimation, portable algorithms, and traffic control mechanisms (Mei et al., 2020).

Viswanathan et al. delved into novel man–machine interfaces, ubiquitous computing, multi-sensory data fusion, and 6G air interfaces (Muteba et al., 2022). Spectrum sharing, hyper-specialized slicing, and open platform security remain significant hurdles. Nawaz et al. (2021) expanded on broadband speed, network slicing, virtualization, and tactile internet for IoT, facing challenges in bandwidth throughput, encryption, and 3D connectivity.

Mahzabeen Emu discussed the significance of virtual network functions, edge cloud networks, and ubiquitous digital connectivity, hindered by issues in network addressing and deep learning-based management (Nawaz et al., 2019). H. Janget focused on improving system performance via random hopping and reduced packet delays, with challenges in group hopping and latency control (Rahman et al., 2022).

Finally, Basel Barakat explored healthcare support through real-time object detection and RF sensing, while Charles Ssengonzi addressed intrusion detection, autonomous driving, and mobile communications. Both studies acknowledged the need for robust performance, time-sensitive data management, efficient planning, and cost-effective infrastructure deployment (Sergiou et al., 2020; Sim et al., 2020).

5. Future Work

While this chapter provides a comprehensive overview of 5G and 6G networks, including their technical attributes, applications, and challenges, several avenues remain open for future research and exploration.

First, deeper investigations into energy-efficient architectures for both 5G and 6G networks are necessary, particularly in the context of large-scale deployments and sustainable communication infrastructures. With the rising adoption of IoT and smart environments, optimizing power consumption across network layers will be crucial.

Second, terahertz communication – a cornerstone of 6G – requires further exploration in terms of device-level integration, signal propagation modelling, and cost-effective semiconductor material development. Future work should focus on overcoming the barriers related to high-frequency signal attenuation and hardware design limitations (Katiyar et al., 2022).

Third, while this study reviewed network connectivity across atmospheric layers, comprehensive simulation frameworks for SAGINs still need to be standardized. Future research should explore seamless handover, latency reduction, and security mechanisms within these hybrid communication architectures.

Fourth, the evolution of AI-driven self-organizing networks in 6G opens the door to predictive maintenance, dynamic resource allocation, and real-time optimization. Research into federated learning, edge AI, and reinforcement learning algorithms tailored for 6G performance goals remains a promising direction.

Moreover, quantum communication and quantum-resistant security protocols are expected to play a critical role in future networks. Developing scalable quantum key distribution frameworks and integrating them into existing network infrastructure is an emerging area that warrants thorough exploration.

Additionally, regulatory and spectrum management issues will need to evolve in parallel with technological advancements. Policies for THz spectrum allocation, interoperability among multi-vendor networks, and security governance in decentralized architectures should be examined in upcoming studies.

Finally, further work should be directed towards creating real-world testbeds and pilot projects that validate theoretical frameworks and simulate practical deployment scenarios. These experimental setups will enable researchers to assess performance metrics such as latency, reliability, and resilience under diverse environmental and user conditions.

Overall, future research in 5G and 6G technologies must continue to address scalability, adaptability, interoperability, and security while embracing innovation in AI, quantum technologies, and network virtualization to meet the dynamic demands of next-generation digital ecosystems.

6. Conclusion

This chapter presents an extensive review of the advanced techniques and evolving frameworks within 5G and 6G networks, emphasizing key technological elements such as MIMO, MANETs, and the emerging potential of terahertz (THz) connectivity. By conducting a comprehensive comparative analysis, we have highlighted the distinctive features, performance capabilities, and infrastructure advancements that differentiate 5G from its successor, 6G.

One of the focal areas of this study is the examination of atmospheric layer-based network connectivity, analyzing how 5G and 6G technologies function across terrestrial, aerial, and space-based environments. The configuration parameters and architectural considerations associated with these layers were thoroughly explored to understand the scope of scalable and seamless communication.

Moreover, the chapter delves into the enabling technologies that support the vision of ultra-fast, ultra-reliable, and intelligent networks. These include stealth communication mechanisms, advanced beamforming techniques, network slicing, quantum communication, and AI-driven network orchestration. Simulations and use-case scenarios were discussed to showcase the performance benefits and deployment challenges of 5G and 6G in real-world environments.

Table 10.2 provides a synthesized summary of diverse applications and corresponding challenges associated with 5G and 6G networks, compiled from recent scholarly contributions. This tabular analysis offers a holistic view of the ongoing advancements and the technical barriers that still need to be addressed for effective global implementation.

In essence, this chapter serves as a valuable resource for researchers, engineers, and practitioners by outlining both the foundational concepts and cutting-edge developments in next-generation networks. It aims to foster a better understanding of the comparative procedures and convergence pathways between the current and future network generations, paving the way for innovative solutions in digital communication systems.

Table 10.2. Applications and Challenges of 5G and 6G Networks.

5G and 6G Networks	Applications	Challenges
Giordani et al. (2020)	1) AR & VR	1) Scheduling, need for new network design
	2) Holographic (teleportation)	2) Modelling, topology optimization, and energy efficiency
	3) E-Health	3) Scalability, scheduling, and interference
	4) Industry 4.0	4) Real-time processing
	5) Robotics	5) Energy-efficient techniques
Huang et al. (2019)	1) THz communication	1) Spectrum horizons license with minimal cost
	2) VLC	2) Funded projects of THz technologies
	3) Quantum communication	3) Semiconductor materials are available at low cost
	4) Energy harvesting and management	4) Hard to satisfy different requests from servers
	5) Aerial network communication	5) Decentralized network control mechanism setup
Huang et al. (2019)	1) Ubiquitous 3D coverage	1) Efficient energy conservation
	2) Pervasive AI	2) Backscatter communication set up
	3) Advanced protocol stack	3) Semiconductor availability low cost
	4) Symbiotic radio	4) Designing of frequency reconfigurable antennas

(Continued)

Table 10.2. (*Continued*)

5G and 6G Networks	Applications	Challenges
Huo et al. (2019)	1) WiFi/WiGig multiplexing	1) Antenna and product design
	2) Highly flexible and re-configurable circuits designing	2) Field test of the beam forming techniques network architecture
	3) Beam forming techniques architecture used for network design	3) Enabling Terahertz technologies in equipment
	4) Low-noise amplifier network transmission	4) Configure system for WiFimax operation
Wang et al. (2020)	1) Real-time intelligent edge could facilitate autonomous driving response to unfamiliar environments in real-time	1) Deployment of AR and VR devices through cloud services using 5G and 6G networks
	2) Intelligent radio framework	2) Robotics connections and automated systems
	3) Distributed AI	3) System privacy
	4) Quantum communication for better security	4) Location privacy
		5) Wireless brain-computer interactions
Eliyas Yaacoub et al. (2020)	1) Fibre space optics is used for communications between High Altitude Platfrom (HAPs), UAVs, balloons, satellites, and/or between these entities and Grounded Signaling (GSs)	1) Spectrum and economic aspects
	2) Satellite backhaul connectivity	2) IoT connectivity in rural areas with the network o 5G and 6G technologies
	3) Increase in capacity and decrease in cost per Mb/s	3) Securing electronic transactions
	4) Hyper-connected people may be connected with different regions and different areas	4) Multihop/Mesh networks setup with backhaul connectivity

Faisal Tariq et al. (2020)	1) Haptic communication	1) Backhaul traffic access and network management
	2) Holographic communication	2) THz band frequency maintenance from blockage
	3) Smart home connectivity	3) Fog networking and edge computing
	4) Smart healthcare	4) Dynamic topology densification
	5) Automation & manufacturing	
Marcos Katz et al.	1) URLLC	1) Security for 6G
	2) Embedded positioning connection	2) Quantum communications monitoring
	3) Distributed intelligent wireless computing	3) Development of new low-loss materials and packaging solutions for adequate system performance
	4) Dynamic infra structure connectivity	4) Superfast connectivity infrastructure maintenance
Syed Junaid Nawaz et al. (2021)	1) Quantum communications	1) Network throughput
	2) Ultra network communications	2) Maintenance of network capacity
	3) Non-orthogonal multiple access of networks	3) Network congestion reduction
	4) ML-based communication systems	4) Backhaul network traffic management
Sergiou et al. (2020)	1) Ultra-massive MIMOs use a large number of antennas for frequency distribution	1) Network structural complexity
	2) Reconfigurable intelligent surfaces for network connectivity	2) Adaptability of the network
	3) Decentralized operation due to the network architecture	3) Modelling of a complex network
	4) Scale-free network architecture	4) Resilience of the 5G and 6G network

(Continued)

Table 10.2. (*Continued*)

5G and 6G Networks	Applications	Challenges
Tang et al. (2020)	1) Vehicular networking	1) Multiradio access challenge
	2) Vehicular communication	2) Future state prediction
	3) Vehicular security	3) Correlation recovering
	4) Accurate environment modelling	4) Network virtualization initialization
	5) Rapid response to the vehicular network	5) Large-scale network management on the vehicular network
Zhang et al. (2020)	1) Massive machine type communications	1) Channel estimation
	2) Digital twins for technology for smart manufacturing	2) THz transmission
	3) Space-Air-Ground integrated network (SAGIN) connections	3) Designing of portable and low-latency algorithm
	4) AI-assisted communications	4) Network traffic control
Viswanathan and Mogensen (2020)	1) New man–machine interfaces of 6G network	1) Spectrum sharing techniques
	2) Ubiquitous computing	2) Extreme performance of the network in terms of latency and reliability
	3) Multi-sensory data fusion to create multi-verse maps for network transmission	3) Hyper-specialized slicing of network maintenance
	4) 6G Air interface	4) Open platform security maintenance prevents various security attacks

Nawaz et al. (2014)	1) Enhancement of mobile broadband speed 2) Network function virtualization 3) Network slicing 4) Tactile internet for IoT devices connectivity	1) Throughput management of network bandwidth 2) 3-dimensional connectivity with 5G and 6G networks 3) Ultra-dense heterogeneous networks formation for energy conservation 4) Data encryption and security
Emu and Choudhury (2021)	1) Virtual network function 2) IoT devices network connectivity 3) Ubiquitous digital network environment 4) Edge cloud data network	1) Perpetual telecommunication 2) Network addressing 3) Deep learning aided approach in network management
H. Janget et al. (2019)	1) Random hopping 2) Improved system performance 3) Increased portability 4) Reduces network packet delay	1) Group hopping 2) IoT devices accommodation 3) Improving resource efficiency using hopping 4) Network latency management
Basel Barakat et al. (2021)	1) Healthcare professionals through a preventive and in-home care approach 2) Radio frequency sensing 3) Activity monitoring 4) Real-time object detection framework	1) Integrate the enabling technologies 2) Guarantee of robust performance 3) Time-sensitive applications 4) Time-sensitive datasets management
Charles Ssengonzi et al. (2022)	1) Intrusion detection techniques 2) Mobile communication 3) Mobile advertising 4) Autonomous driving	1) Reduced time for network planning 2) Service quality management 3) Infrastructure expenditure in a smaller amount 4) Network alarm management

References

Barakat, B., Taha, A., Samson, R., Steponenaite, A., Ansari, S., Langdon, P. M., Wassell, I. J., Abbasi, Q. H., Imran, M. A., & Keates, S. (2021). 6G opportunities arising from Internet of Things use cases: A review paper. *Future Internet*, *13*(6), 159. https://doi.org/10.3390/fi13060159

Cheng, X., Hu, Y., & Varga, L. (2022). 5G network deployment and the associated energy consumption in the UK: A complex systems' exploration. *Technological Forecasting and Social Change*, *180*, 121672. https://doi.org/10.1016/j.techfore.2022.121672

Emu, M., & Choudhury, S. (2021). Towards 6G networks: Ensemble deep learning empowered VNF deployment for IoT services. In *2021 IEEE 18th annual consumer communications & networking conference (CCNC)* (pp. 1–4). IEEE. https://doi.org/10.1109/CCNC49032.2021.9369515

Giordani, M., Polese, M., Mezzavilla, M., Rangan, S., & Zorzi, M. (2020). Toward 6G networks: Use cases and technologies. *IEEE Communications Magazine*, *58*(3), 55–61. https://doi.org/10.1109/MCOM.001.1900411

Huang, T., Yang, W., Wu, J., Ma, J., Zhang, X., & Zhang, D. (2019). A survey on green 6G network: Architecture and technologies. *IEEE Access*, *7*, 175758–175768.

Huo, Y., Dong, X., Xu, W., & Yuen, M. (2019). Enabling multi-functional 5G and beyond user equipment: A survey and tutorial. *IEEE Access*, *7*, 116975–117008.

Jang, H. S., Jung, B. C., Quek, T. Q., & Sung, D. K. (2021). Resource-hopping-based grant-free multiple access for 6G-enabled massive IoT networks. *IEEE Internet of Things Journal*, *8*(20), 15349–15360.

Katiyar, N., Srivastava, J., & Singh, K. P. (2022). A perspective toward 6G connecting technology. In D. K. Sharma, S. L. Peng, R. Sharma, & D. A. Zaitsev (Eds.), *Microelectronics and telecommunication engineering: ICMETE 2021* (Lecture Notes in Networks and Systems, Vol. 373, pp. 755–763). Springer. https://doi.org/10.1007/978-981-16-8721-1_70

Kukliński, S., Tomaszewski, L., Kołakowski, R., & Chemouil, P. (2021). 6G-LEGO: A framework for 6G network slices. *Journal of Communications and Networks*, *23*(6), 442–453.

Liyanaarachchi, S. D., Riihonen, T., Barneto, C. B., & Valkama, M. (2021). Optimized waveforms for 5G–6G communication with sensing: Theory, simulations and experiments. *IEEE Transactions on Wireless Communications*, *20*(12), 8301–8315.

Lu, Y., & Zheng, X. (2020). 6G: A survey on technologies, scenarios, challenges, and the related issues. *Journal of Industrial Information Integration*, *19*, 100158.

Mei, J., Wang, X., & Zheng, K. (2020). An intelligent self-sustained RAN slicing framework for diverse service provisioning in 5G-beyond and 6G networks. *Intelligent and Converged Networks*, *1*(3), 281–294.

Muteba, K. F., Djouani, K., & Olwal, T. (2022). 5G NB-IoT: Design, considerations, solutions and challenges. *Procedia Computer Science*, *198*, 86–93.

Nawaz, S. J., Sharma, S. K., Mansoor, B., Patwary, M. N., & Khan, N. M. (2021). Non-coherent and backscatter communications: Enabling ultra-massive connectivity in 6G wireless networks. *IEEE Access*, *9*, 38144–38186. https://doi.org/10.1109/ACCESS.2021.3062854

Nawaz, S. J., Sharma, S. K., Wyne, S., Patwary, M. N., & Asaduzzaman, M. (2019). Quantum machine learning for 6G communication networks: State-of-the-art and vision for the future. *IEEE Access*, *7*, 46317–46350. https://doi.org/10.1109/ACCESS.2019.2909490

Rahman, M. M., Khatun, F., Sami, S. I., & Uzzaman, A. (2022). The evolving roles and impacts of 5G enabled technologies in healthcare: The world epidemic COVID-19 issues. *Array*, *14*, 100178. https://doi.org/10.1016/j.array.2022.100178

Sergiou, C., Lestas, M., Antoniou, P., Liaskos, C., & Pitsillides, A. (2020). Complex systems: A communication networks perspective towards 6G. *IEEE Access, 8*, 89007–89030. https://doi.org/10.1109/ACCESS.2020.2993170

Sim, M. S., Lim, Y.-G., Park, S. H., Dai, L., & Chae, C.-B. (2020). Deep learning-based mmWave beam selection for 5G NR/6G with sub-6 GHz channel information: Algorithms and prototype validation. *IEEE Access*, *8*, 51634–51646. https://doi.org/10.1109/ACCESS.2020.2979173

Ssengonzi, C., Kogeda, O. P., & Olwal, T. O. (2022). A survey of deep reinforcement learning application in 5G and beyond network slicing and virtualization. *Array*, *14*, 100142. https://doi.org/10.1016/j.array.2022.100142

Stavroulaki, V., Calvanese Strinati, E., Carrez, F., Carlinet, Y., Maman, M., Draskovic, D., Ribar, D., Lallet, A., Mößner, K., Tosic, M., Uitto, M., Hadiwardoyo, S. A., Marquez-Barja, J., Garrido, E., Stamatelatos, M., Sarayeddine, K., Sánchez Vivas, P., Mämmelä, A., & Demestichas, P. (2021). DEDICAT 6G – Dynamic coverage extension and distributed intelligence for human-centric applications with assured security, privacy, and trust: From 5G to 6G. In *2021 Joint European Conference on Networks and Communications & 6G Summit (EuCNC/6G Summit)* (pp. 556–561). IEEE. https://doi.org/10.1109/EuCNC/6GSummit51104.2021.9482611

Tang, F., Kawamoto, Y., Kato, N., & Liu, J. (2020). Future intelligent and secure vehicular network toward 6G: Machine-learning approaches. *Proceedings of the IEEE*, *108*(2), 292–307. https://doi.org/10.1109/JPROC.2019.2956536

Tariq, F., Khandaker, M. R. A., Wong, K.-K., Imran, M. A., Bennis, M., & Debbah, M. (2020). A speculative study on 6G. *IEEE Wireless Communications*, *27*(4), 118–125. https://doi.org/10.1109/MWC.001.1900431

Valero, J. M. J., Sánchez, P. M. S., Pérez, M. G., Celdrán, A. H., & Pérez, G. M. (2022). Toward pre-standardization of reputation-based trust models beyond 5G. *Computer Standards & Interfaces*, *81*, 103596.

Viswanathan, H., & Mogensen, P. E. (2020). Communications in the 6G era. *IEEE Access*, *8*, 57063–57074. https://doi.org/10.1109/ACCESS.2020.2981745

Wang, M., Zhu, T., Zhang, T., Zhang, J., Yu, S., & Zhou, W. (2020). Security and privacy in 6G networks: New areas and new challenges. *Digital Communications and Networks*, *6*(3), 281–291. https://doi.org/10.1016/j.dcan.2019.11.006

Yaacoub, E., & Alouini, M.-S. (2020). A key 6G challenge and opportunity—Connecting the base of the pyramid: A survey on rural connectivity. *Proceedings of the IEEE*, *108*(4), 533–582. https://doi.org/10.1109/JPROC.2020.2976703

Zhang, S., Xiang, C., & Xu, S. (2020). 6G: Connecting everything by 1000 times price reduction. *IEEE Open Journal of Vehicular Technology*, *1*, 107–115. https://doi.org/10.1109/OJVT.2020.2990437

Chapter 11

Advancing Static Weapon Target Allocation: Research Insights and Future Directions

Dukuru Chiranjevi and Tarun Biswas

Department of Computer Science and Engineering, Indian Institute of Information Technology Ranchi, India

Abstract

With the proliferation of technology, the field of defense science and engineering is continuously advancing, and the accurate resolution of the Weapon Target Allocation Problem (WTAP) remains one of the primary concerns for any nation's safety and security. WTAP involves the precise allocation of a set of weapon resources to potential targets in such a way that the damage inflicted on the opponent is maximized. WTAP is well known for its non-deterministic polynomial-time hard (NP-hard) nature.

This work presents an in-depth study of the static WTAP, covering its characteristics, nature, formulation, performance issues, and potential research insights. The study contributes to a better understanding of key issues associated with WTAP, such as challenges in resource allocation, accurate assignment of resources, and precise mission planning and execution in dynamic defense environments.

Keywords: Weapon target assignment problem; resource allocation; defense services; non-deterministic polynomial-time hard; dynamic defense environments

The Internet of Things in the Defence Industry:
Challenges and Solutions for Military Security, 227–243

doi:10.1108/978-1-83549-198-020261011

1. Introduction

The precise allocation of war resources is a crucial aspect in determining the outcome of any war. Static Weapon Target Allocation (SWTA) addresses the challenge of allocating limited resources to targets in a way that ensures maximum damage to the opponent. Alternatively, it focuses on achieving successful deployment with minimal expenditure.

SWTA (Geng et al., 2022; Zhang & Wang, 2023) aims to assign available weapon resources to targets based on various factors such as weapon effectiveness, target priority, and other operational constraints. Numerous studies have been conducted to address the various aspects of SWTA using heuristic, metaheuristic, and hybrid techniques (Kline et al., 2019; Ruining & Yan, 2021; Shi et al., 2023), despite the diverse challenges it presents – such as high computational cost, resource constraints, target selection, handling uncertainties in available data, real-time decision-making, and operational limitations.

The core motivation behind the SWTA problem lies in its practical importance within real-time military operations, where optimizing the assignment of a limited number of resources is critical to mission success. Therefore, an accurate and efficient SWTA process significantly enhances the probability of mission success. In modern military warfare, the demand for precise and efficient target allocation has grown due to the increasing complexity and scale of threats brought about by technological advancements.

The primary motivation for this research stems from the fact that real-time decision-making environments demand high computational effectiveness. Consequently, expanding methodologies for SWTA can lead to more effective resource utilization and better support mission objectives while reducing operational costs. Moreover, analyzing the challenges of SWTA contributes to solving similar optimization problems in fields such as disaster management and earthquake response.

Additionally, the SWTA problem is inherently NP-hard and computationally intensive. Addressing this problem contributes to improving military performance, enhancing the efficient use of resources, and promoting interdisciplinary collaboration between the fields of operations research, computer science, and artificial intelligence.

Furthermore, the methodologies developed for SWTA can also be applied to disaster and earthquake management scenarios. These methods can be integrated with current systems and are well-suited for modern training environments and real-time military decision-making. As such, the WTA problem offers opportunities for innovative solutions, contributes to national security, and has significant real-world applications – making this an important and attractive field of study.

The overall contributions of this work are as follows:

- A comprehensive review of research on SWTA since 2018, including an analysis of the fundamental nature of the problem, its characteristics, applicable models, and solution approaches.
- A discussion of several potential future research directions.

The remainder of this chapter is organized as follows. Section 2 presents a systematic literature review of related algorithms. Section 3 outlines the models used and the problem formulation. Section 4 offers a comparative analysis of prominent existing works and highlights further research possibilities. Finally, Section 5 concludes the study with a discussion.

2. Related Works

A large number of SWTA have been proposed to solve the problem. Some of the relevant existing approaches are presented as follows.

Zhang and Wang (2023) explained the problem with the help of mathematical probabilities for intercepting targets. Markov decision process based on deep reinforcement learning (DRL) solution is highlighted. Two groups of computational simulations for the given problem are performed, and shown reinforcement learning (RL) method performs well. Geng et al. (2022) focus on air defense in the contemporary battles and the assignment of weapons. Proposed a Three-stage WTA Model using a new objective function. Iterated Sparrow Search Algorithm (SSA) for multi-stage weapon target assignment for improving effeciency. Solution for three-stage WTA problem using the modified sparrow search algorithm (MSSA) suggested multi-stage WTA model with better than sparrow search algorithm (SSA). Amalgamating the observation of MSSA effectiveness in solving WTA problems with SSA. Cross-section comparative results showed that MSSA has better stability when used in three-stage WTA models than SSA.

From the analysis of results obtained, MSSA converges faster and yields better solutions compared to SSA. Thus, modified SSA is observed to effectively solve multi-stage WTA problem with better performance compared with the original SSA. The future directions are associated with the interception cost and the radar feedback in real time. Kline et al. (2019) discussed WTA with different stages of WTA development. It shows improvement on its ability to make precise decision for assigning the resources. Ruining and Yan (2021) discussed about the enhancement of performance of genetic algorithm and WTA problem. Proposed improvements to the fitness function for solving WTA problem.

Fu et al. (2018) proposed a genetic algorithm (GA) based solution aiming for maximum extrapolation of local search ability. It integrates the hill climbing algorithm with strong local search ability to build up the hybrid GA for the weapon target assignment problem (WTAP). Experimentally, it has been shown that the hybrid GA has the ability to foster convergence. Zhai et al. (2021) proposed an improved particle swarm optimization (PSO)-based algorithm to address the WTA problem. It has been shown to NP complete and can be solved by the use of the improved PSO algorithm. Second improved PSO algorithm with decimal coding strategy. Nonlinear inverse tangent inertia weight was adaptively updated in the PSO.

Kline et al. (2020) proposed a metaheuristic-based WTA. It introduces linear function approximation and NP-complete SWTA Problem. Heuristic approach introduced for WTA problem to improve the solution. Metaheuristic performed better than the global optimization solver in 25 of the problems. An improved heuristic provided a better solution than the global optimization solver by at most 64%. Benchmarked heuristics and metaheuristics on 15-size problem proposed a new metaheuristic derived from the modified quiz problem. Guangsheng et al. (2020) highlight several heuristic and metaheuristic algorithms for the optimization of the SWTA problem.

Proposed a new metaheuristic algorithm to improve the existing technique for assignment of resources. Introduced a metaheuristic approach for the WTAP to support its optimization. Reviewed quiz problem heuristic and Metaheuristic techniques for weapon target assignment. Explained linear function approximation and NP-complete SWTA problem. Li et al. (2023) focus on the weapon target assignment (WTA) issue, which is a significant concern within the military operation research to determine the most effective arrangement of weapon systems to targets with multiple hostile objectives. Other conventional approaches like Mixed Integer Linear Programming (MILP) for instance, prove to be quite inefficient in terms of scalability and computational time especially in real time combat scenarios. Wang et al. (2021) mainly deal with the optimization of targeting of weapon systems in warfare. It handles the multi objective conflict of resource (weapons) distribution to multiple targets with the objectives of least destruction and greatest operational efficiency.

From the study, we can infer that by employing a GA for target assignment of a weapon, the result proves to encourage efficient utilization of weapons and resources in defense, As the outcomes show, the use of the GA helps to enhance the total performance of weapon allocation considering target priority and weapon characteristics. Zhang et al. (2022) analyzed on the multi-task assignment problem for heterogeneous unmanned aerial vehicles (UAVs) applying an improved simulated annealing (SA) particle swarm optimization (SAPSO) algorithm. The research tackles the issues brought up by the variability capacities of UAVs in terms of the ability to perform a certain task, speed, range, etc. The research makes a good contribution to advancing the best model of task allocation for UAVs in complex environments, hence forming a basic subsequent advancement of swarm intelligence techniques for UAVs.

Yang et al. (2022) proposed an opposition-based memetic algorithm (OMA) for the SWTA problem. The OMA demonstrates the enhancement of the solution quality emphasizing the innovative method and its applications for the optimization in the context of military use. Niu et al. (2021) discussed about advancement in the technology development of command and control facilities for small UAVs in defense, putting pressure on the use of several detecting equipment's for higher detection efficiency.

He et al. (2023) proposed a GA-based model for the allocation of multiple UAVs against multiple targets. It provides a mathematical model that takes into account all special features of UAVs that targets involved, including speed, operative range, and the force needed to attack the target. From the results of the study, the authors concluded that the use of the proposed approach could enhance the working performance of UAVs in different conditions of the battlefield. He et al. (2023) focused on the mission planning system for UAV where cooperation is mandatory due to the multiple target environment of the warfare. It sets up a multiple objective, where the goal is to reduce the path length and airborne time for UAVs while on missions.

This study also presents a new, improved adaptive GA to improve the outcome of traditional GAs by increasing crossover operators. Finally, by comparison of simulation experiments, the proposed method provides a correct solution to the WTA problem, the applicability is higher and the search capability is also stronger. The outcomes revealed that UAV swarms may learn the surrounding environment, and then enhance the efficiency of the undertaken tasks that contributed to enhance the mission success rate in military actions at war zones.

Fang et al. (2021) discussed the PSO algorithm for the WTAP where different task allocation criteria are used. This section covers PSO basics, namely it employs a population of feasible solutions that adapt their positions as individuals and collectively. What they learn in the process is to find the best assignments. The focus of the study is to ensure the use of multiple criteria for task allocation in order to tackle the issues of resource distribution in military operations with weapon system performance will enhance decision-making in tactical environments therefore to improve the utilization of resources in the missions is necessary.

3. Models and Problem Formulation

Table 11.1. Definitions of Notations.

Notation	Definition
C	$C = \{c_1, c_2, c_3, \ldots c_n\}$ a set of n number of command bases.
T	$T = \{t_1, t_2, \ldots, t_m\}$ a set of m number of target points.
R	$R = \{r_1, r_2, \ldots, r_x\}$ a set of x number of resources.
P_{ij}	Killing probability values of the resources at c_i.
T_j	Defending probability values of the resources at t_j.
$V_{i,j}$	Attacking score value of c_i to t_j i.e., $c_i \rightarrow t_j$.
$\theta_{i,j}$	the Boolean variable.
d_j	damage value of t_j.

Now, the WTAP is formulated as the follows, assume that a task C consists of n number of command basses where a set of x types of weapon resources are available. The resources at $C = \{c_1, c_2, c_3, \ldots c_n\}$ need to be deployed to the set of m number of target points as $T = \{t_1, t_2, t_3, \ldots t_m\}$ provided that the overall damage function (D_j) must be as maximum as possible. Table 11.1 shows the definitions of notations used here.

The D_j is computed as follows.

Static WTAP formulation: The actual problem formulations were created by Manne (1958), the scenario where the defender has $wi = 1. . . m$. weapon types need to defend against the target base $j = 1 \ldots n$. Each weapon type i has a probability of p_{ij} of killing target j, and each target has a destructive value vj. Decision variable Xij shows total no of weapons of type i allocated to target j.

$$\text{Minimize } (Dj) = \sum_{i=1}^{n} Vj \prod_{j=1}^{n} (1 - p_{ij}) Xij \tag{1}$$

where $\sum_{i=1}^{n} Xij \ <= wi$, for $i = 1, \ldots, m$.

A detailed discussion on several SWTA algorithms with possible research insights based on heuristic, metaheuristic, and hybridization techniques are discussed in Table 11.2–11.4, respectively.

4. Comparative Analysis with Possible Research Insights

The SWTA problem has garnered significant attention in recent years due to its strategic importance in modern military operations. The goal is to assign a limited set of weapon resources to various targets in a manner that maximizes operational effectiveness while minimizing cost and collateral damage. Given its NP-hard nature, the SWTA problem presents complex computational challenges that require advanced algorithmic strategies to address. Over time, researchers have proposed a wide range of heuristic, meta-heuristic, and hybrid approaches to solve the SWTA problem more efficiently and effectively.

Table 11.2 presents a comparative analysis of heuristic-based approaches for SWTA, focusing on the objectives, implementation methods, and potential improvements for each algorithm. These methods often rely on domain-specific knowledge and simpler optimization strategies, offering relatively fast solutions that can be suitable for time-constrained military applications. However, their performance may degrade in more dynamic or uncertain operational scenarios. Recent developments suggest the potential to enhance these heuristic approaches by integrating real-time data, machine learning techniques, and contextual decision-making frameworks.

Heuristic approaches have long served as effective tools for addressing the SWTA problem due to their computational simplicity and relatively fast execution times. Table 11.2 provides a comparative overview of several heuristic algorithms that have been implemented to solve SWTA, along with potential avenues for enhancement to improve their operational utility.

The Quiz Problem-based heuristic (2019) utilizes a branch and bound algorithm with a greedy approach to minimize damage at target zones. While this method has shown promise in structured scenarios, its limited exploration of the solution space could hinder adaptability in complex, real-world environments.

Table 11.2. Comparative Analysis of Heuristic Approach-Based SWTA with Possible Improvement.

Algorithms	Objectives	Implementation Methods	Further Possibilities
Quizprob-lem, 2019 (Kline et al., 2019)	Minimizing the damage at target zones	Branch and bound algorithm, greedy branch and bound heuristic algorithm is used	WTA problem may be considered with filtered beam search through Naive which is not considered yet
P-ALNS, 2023 (Shi et al., 2023)	Minimize the overall costs while fulfilling mission requirements.	Population-based adaptive large neighborhood search (P-ALNS) algorithm was used	Addition of real-time data and dynamic factors such as weather conditions, enemy movements, and changing mission priorities into the planning process to improve adaptability and responsiveness
MRBCH, 2019 (Xin et al., 2018)	Maximize the effectiveness of destroying incoming targets	Marginal return based constructive heuristic (MRBHC) is designed and implemented to solve static WTA in an effective manner	MRBCH algorithm in network-centric complex warfare scenarios involving additional constraints need to be applied for dynamic environments, or diverse types of sensors and weapons. Adapting the algorithm to handle evolving threats and changing operational conditions could improve its practical utility
QS-RRT, 2022 (Li et al., 2022)	Improve path planning to reach targets in an average time difference by coordinating attack efficiency	The QS-RRT (Quality Sampling Rapidly exploring Random Tree) Algorithm and the Improved Auction algorithm were used to implement	Can incorporate reinforcement learning, deep learning and machine learning to improve the decision-making process
New GA, 2018 (Fu et al., 2018)	Minimizing the damage at target bases	Hill climbing algorithm with strong local search ability was used	The usage of new GA Algorithm may greatly improves the search efficiency and optimization quality of the problem solving

A possible improvement would be the integration of a filtered beam search using naive approaches, which has not yet been explored. This could expand the search capability and provide better alternatives in high-complexity cases.

The P-ALNS (Population-based Adaptive Large Neighborhood Search), introduced in 2023, shifts focus to minimizing overall mission costs while still achieving mission objectives. The use of an adaptive population-based search allows for diverse solutions, enhancing flexibility. However, to increase its applicability in dynamic battlefield environments, this model can benefit from the integration of real-time operational data – including weather changes, enemy movements, and shifting mission priorities. This would enhance the model's responsiveness and robustness under evolving conditions.

The Marginal Return-Based Constructive Heuristic (MRBCH), 2019, emphasizes maximizing effectiveness in destroying incoming targets. Its strength lies in its capacity to prioritize targets based on marginal returns, making it efficient for static WTA problems. However, its applicability in network-centric warfare scenarios is limited due to its static nature. To extend its utility, MRBCH needs to evolve to support dynamic environments, accommodate multiple sensor types, and adapt to shifting operational constraints – essentially enabling it to handle evolving threats and multi-layered defense systems.

In 2022, the QS-RRT (Quality Sampling Rapidly-exploring Random Tree) algorithm, in combination with an improved auction mechanism, was introduced to optimize path planning and coordinate attack timings. While this approach improves average-time-to-target metrics, it could be significantly enhanced by incorporating machine learning techniques, including reinforcement learning and deep learning. These enhancements could enable more nuanced decision-making and adaptability in uncertain or adversarial contexts.

Finally, the New Genetic Algorithm (2018) applied a hill-climbing algorithm with a strong local search capability to minimize damage at target bases. This method improves convergence speed and ensures locally optimal solutions. However, its global optimization capabilities remain limited. By refining the GA implementation – such as by incorporating crossover and mutation strategies tailored to the SWTA domain – the efficiency and solution quality could be further improved.

In summary, while heuristic approaches provide practical solutions to the SWTA problem, especially in static or moderately complex scenarios, there remains significant scope for enhancing these models. Incorporating adaptive, data-driven techniques and real-time environmental feedback can bridge the gap between theoretical models and battlefield-ready decision-support systems.

Table 11.3 details various meta-heuristic approaches, which employ population-based or nature-inspired optimization techniques such as GAs, sparrow search, PSO, and co-evolutionary strategies. These methods aim to explore the solution space more thoroughly and are better suited for handling the non-linear, multi-objective nature of the SWTA problem. The analysis includes suggestions for further enhancement through hybridization, incorporation of real-time decision-making mechanisms, and integration with emerging technologies such as artificial intelligence and reinforcement learning.

Table 11.3. Comparative Analysis of Metaheuristic Approach Based SWTA with Possible Improvement.

Algorithms	Objectives	Implementation Methods	Further Possibilities
Co-Evolutionary Algorithm, 2021 (Huang et al., 2021)	Aircraft in a way that maximizes their respective rewards while minimizing losses	Coevolutionary algorithm and GA used to AWGTA scenarios	There is a possibility of multi-stage incorporation and real-time decision making by integration with machine learning enhances the AWGTA problem
GA, 2021 (Ruining & Yan, 2021)	Minimize threat by best allocation of resources	Fitness function considers computation cost. Make span is minimized by considering transfer time	Integration with other algorithms, like PSO and ant colony can improve performance
SSA, 2022 (Geng et al., 2022)	Maximize the total reward by intercepting missiles	Modified sparrow search algorithm that produced better results	Cost considerations can be done and real-time quick feedback can be taken with integration of machine learning possible
PSO, 2023 (Li et al., 2023)	Failure probability needs to be minimized	SAPSO, IAPSO, and SPSO was used in implementation	Can be focus on real-time battles data to work with dynamic situations of target movements Integration of GA and Ant colony can improve performance
CGA, 2020 (Altinoz, 2020)	Maximum kill probability with minimum number of resources	Constraint genetic algorithm, GA, PSO and firefly algorithm were used	Hybrid algorithms can be used. We can work on more complex battlefield scenarios. It can be applied on multi agent to yield better performance

(*Continued*)

Table 11.3. (*Continued*)

Algorithms	Objectives	Implementation Methods	Further Possibilities
Evolutionary algorithm, 2020 (Zhang et al., 2020)	Maximizing total damage by successfully intercepting resources at targets	Evolutionary algorithm, GA, improved artificial bee colony (ABC) algorithm, and binary tournament selection are used	Dependency constraints can be incorporated. Co- ordination among various multiple defense systems in real-time decision making is possible by adding uncertainty in target
GA, 2022 (Elfeky et al., 2022)	Enhancement of decision making with the representation of new chromosomes by assignment of drones to military vehicles	GA and composite heuristic algorithm is used	Incorporation of other technologies and test with applications can be done for opponent strategy. It can be used to more robustness of danger zone
TSA, 2022 (Yadav et al., 2022)	Aims to contribute to the military operations by providing a robust algorithm that can easily tackle the complexities of the WTA problem at war times	Improved tunicate swarm algorithm is used to provide an optimized solution	It can be applied to real-life applications like logistics, telecommunication, and military operations. It can also be used to multiple target tackle in complex scenarios

The comparative analysis presented in Table 11.3 provides an insightful overview of metaheuristic approaches applied to the Static WTAP, highlighting their respective objectives, implementation techniques, and possible areas for improvement. Metaheuristic methods are particularly valuable in solving NP-hard problems like SWTA due to their adaptability and efficiency in finding near-optimal solutions in complex and uncertain environments.

One of the key contributions in this space is the Co-Evolutionary Algorithm (2021), which focuses on optimizing aircraft deployment to maximize rewards while minimizing losses. This approach leverages the combined strength of co-evolutionary and GAs tailored to the Airborne Weapon-Target Assignment (AWGTA) scenario. Future enhancements could involve multi-stage incorporation and real-time decision-making, especially by integrating machine learning techniques to better adapt to evolving battlefield dynamics.

The Genetic Algorithm (GA, 2021) has also been explored for minimizing threats through optimal resource allocation. By incorporating a fitness function that considers computational cost and makespan, the algorithm effectively balances performance and efficiency. However, integrating additional metaheuristics such as PSO and Ant Colony Optimization (ACO) could further improve the solution space exploration and convergence rates.

In another significant approach, the SSA (2022) has been modified to intercept incoming missiles and maximize rewards. This variant has demonstrated promising results. Still, it could benefit from cost optimization considerations and real-time feedback mechanisms, possibly through machine learning integration, to respond to rapidly changing target dynamics.

The PSO-based approaches (SAPSO, IAPSO, and SPSO, 2023) aim to minimize failure probabilities during interception. These methods have potential in managing real-time battle data and dynamically adapting to target movement. Moreover, hybridizing PSO with GA or ACO can enhance performance in high-uncertainty environments.

Another notable contribution is the Constraint Genetic Algorithm (CGA, 2020), which combines CGA with PSO and the Firefly Algorithm to maximize kill probability using minimal resources. This hybrid approach is especially suited to multi-agent and complex battlefield scenarios. Future work could involve refining the algorithm for better coordination in high-density combat environments.

The Evolutionary Algorithm (2020) emphasizes maximizing total damage by successful interception and employs a diverse set of techniques, including GA, ABC, and binary tournament selection. The method shows promise in incorporating dependency constraints and facilitating multi-system coordination under uncertain conditions.

In 2022, another GA-based model explored enhanced decision-making by introducing new chromosome representations to assign drones to military vehicles. By combining GA with a composite heuristic, this model could be extended through integration with additional technologies for predicting opponent strategies and ensuring robustness in danger zones.

Lastly, the Improved Tunicate Swarm Algorithm (TSA, 2022) seeks to tackle the complexity of WTA problems in warfare scenarios. Its robust optimization capabilities make it applicable not just to military operations but also to domains like logistics and telecommunications. The algorithm could be further improved by adapting it to multi-target engagement scenarios and real-time mission updates.

In summary, the metaheuristic approaches covered in Table 11.3 exhibit significant progress in addressing SWTA challenges. Their continuous improvement through hybridization, real-time data integration, and AI-driven adaptability holds great potential for modern and future combat systems.

Table 11.4 highlights hybrid approaches that combine heuristic and metaheuristic methods to exploit the strengths of both strategies. These algorithms seek to improve the solution quality and robustness under varied and complex battlefield conditions. The integration of deep learning techniques, graph neural networks, and dynamic programming approaches has opened new frontiers for solving SWTA in real-time and uncertain environments. The table also explores opportunities for improving robustness, incorporating uncertainty modelling, and expanding applicability to real-world defense and logistics scenarios.

Hybrid approaches in solving the SWTA problem represent a fusion of heuristic, meta-heuristic, and machine learning-based methodologies, aiming to optimize performance by leveraging the strengths of different computational paradigms. Table 11.4 offers a comparative view of several hybrid algorithms developed in recent years, showcasing their objectives, implementation techniques, and the scope for future enhancements.

The GA proposed in 2022 (HuangFu et al., 2022) focuses on maximizing the kill probability by effectively assigning multiple weapons to designated targets. Although the use of GA demonstrates satisfactory optimization capabilities, the model still lacks the ability to adapt under uncertain operational conditions. To address this, future enhancements could incorporate uncertainty modelling regarding weapon effectiveness and environmental variations, which are critical in real-time warfare scenarios.

Similarly, the 2021 GA model (Ghanbari & Alaei, 2021) attempts to minimize threats by optimizing resource allocation. The implementation relies on a fitness function that factors in computational cost and make-span, thereby balancing efficiency and effectiveness. However, the performance of this model could further be improved through integration with other optimization techniques like PSO and ACO, allowing for deeper exploration and exploitation of the solution space.

The Greedy Heuristic and Modified Quiz Problem (GH and MQP) model from 2020 (Kline et al., 2020) aims to enhance the damage probability from incoming threats. Its implementation, although relatively straightforward, has potential for extension to multi-stage problems and dynamic assignment scenarios. Such enhancements would make it more applicable to real-time and evolving battlefield environments.

The SA based approach from 2023 (Elliott & Vatsan, 2023) takes an abstraction-driven approach to tackle large-scale SWTA problems. By incorporating linear programming techniques, the model can effectively address computational complexity. Nonetheless, future developments should consider integrating

Table 11.4. Comparative Analysis of Hybrid Approach Based SWTA with Possible Improvement.

Algorithms	Objectives	Implementation Methods	Further Possibilities
GA, 2022 (HuangFu et al., 2022)	The main goal is to improve the maximum killing probability of multiple weapons assigned to targets	Genetic algorithm was used to implement	Models can incorporate uncertainity, weapon performance and environmental conditions there is a possibility
GA, 2021 (Ghanbari & Alaei, 2021)	Minimize threat by best allocation of resources	Fitness function considers computation cost Make span is minimized by considering the transfer time	Integration with other algorithms like PSO and ant colony may improve performance
GH and MQP, 2020 (Kline et al., 2020)	Maximize the probability of destroying the missiles by assigning interceptors (weapons) to incoming missiles (targets)	Greedy heuristic and modified quiz problem is used	Can be applied to multi-stage problems and dynamic assignment problem
SA, 2023 (Elliott & Vatsan, 2023)	Solving the large weapon target assignment problem using abstraction approach	Use of linear programming and abstraction approach were used	Incorporation of new technologies like machine learning and artificial Intelligence is possibly enhance the outcome of assignment problem
DRL, 2023 (Zhang & Wang, 2023)	Minimize the damage caused by incoming threats and aims to minimize the cost of intercepting enemy targets	The RL agents were trained using the D3QN algorithm on experimental parameters called 'S1- L2'. Each parameter set contained two types of problems: known and unknown hit rates across various scales	Three-stage WTA model was proposed. A novel objective function can construct to emphasize the different benefits of shooting down missiles at different stages
DQN-GNN, 2024 (Zhang et al., 2024)	Minimize the destruction at all target zones	Implemented using deep Q learning and graph neural network	HTA need to be more robust framework Inclusion of obstacles and non-cooperative traffic can also be added to DQN-GNN algorithm simulations

artificial intelligence and machine learning techniques to further enhance the model's predictive accuracy and adaptive capabilities, especially under uncertain and high-stakes conditions.

A more recent and sophisticated approach involves DRL, as presented in 2023 (Zhang & Wang, 2023). This model, utilizing the Dueling Double Deep Q-Network (D3QN), was trained on experimental scenarios (termed 'S1-L2') covering both known and unknown hit rate problems. The introduction of a three-stage WTA framework highlights the algorithm's flexibility in addressing varying engagement priorities. Future improvements may lie in developing novel objective functions that prioritize strategic value, timing, and threat level of different targets during interception.

Lastly, the 2024 DQN-GNN hybrid model (Zhang et al., 2024) integrates Deep Q-Learning with graphical neural networks to reduce destruction at target zones. The use of GNNs enables the system to understand and process complex relationships among multiple entities in a battlefield. However, this model could be made more robust by simulating environments with non-cooperative traffic and physical obstacles. Enhancing the model's resilience to such real-world complexities will be critical for its deployment in actual defense operations.

Collectively, these hybrid models reflect an ongoing shift towards intelligent, adaptive, and context-aware weapon-target assignment systems. By combining classical optimization techniques with modern AI/ML frameworks, these approaches offer a promising path forward in enhancing the tactical efficiency and operational resilience of military decision-making systems.

5. Discussion

This study presents an in-depth investigation of the SWTA problem, examining it from its fundamental nature and characteristics to the operational mechanisms and challenges involved in real-time decision-making environments. The SWTA problem, being a classic combinatorial optimization issue in defense operations, requires precise and intelligent allocation of limited weapon systems to multiple targets to maximize mission effectiveness. Through this analysis, the study not only outlines the theoretical and practical aspects of the problem but also highlights several promising research directions that can guide future advancements in this domain.

A core focus of the investigation lies in the comparative evaluation of various algorithmic approaches – specifically, heuristic, meta-heuristic, and hybridization-based strategies. These methodologies have been analyzed in terms of their defined objectives, implementation mechanisms, and performance enhancement opportunities. The heuristic methods, although simple and fast, are often problem-specific and may not guarantee global optimality. On the other hand, meta-heuristic approaches such as GAs, SA, and RL provide a more flexible and powerful framework to address the complex and multi-objective nature of the SWTA problem. Furthermore, hybrid models – blending classical optimization with advanced learning mechanisms – are emerging as a promising frontier, offering a balance between computational efficiency and solution quality.

The key motivation behind this comparative analysis is to offer structured guidance for designing a unified and coherent algorithm that not only adapts to the static environment but also ensures improved efficiency, scalability, and robustness. Such an algorithm, when appropriately tailored, can significantly contribute to defense systems by enabling rapid and intelligent decision-making under constrained and uncertain battlefield conditions.

Additionally, this study emphasizes the need to extend research beyond the static paradigm to address the Dynamic Weapon Target Allocation (DWTA) problem. DWTA presents a more intricate and realistic scenario where targets and threats evolve over time, requiring continuous assessment and reallocation of resources. Solving DWTA demands adaptive algorithms capable of real-time learning and responsiveness to environmental changes.

Looking ahead, a significant leap in this field could be realized by incorporating principles from Quantum Computing and Quantum Artificial Intelligence. Approaches such as Quantum Machine Learning (QML) and Quantum Deep Learning (QDL) could provide exponential speed-ups and enable exploration of complex solution spaces that are otherwise computationally prohibitive using classical methods. These quantum-enhanced techniques can offer novel perspectives in handling large-scale, high-dimensional defense optimization problems like DWTA, opening up transformative possibilities in military strategic planning and autonomous systems.

The sustained interest in the WTAP – both static and dynamic – underscores its critical relevance to modern defense science and technology. By integrating classical optimization, AI, and emerging quantum technologies, future research can significantly enhance the resilience, precision, and adaptability of next-generation weapon-target assignment systems.

6. Conclusion

The study of the SWTA problem reveals its critical importance in enhancing the decision-making capabilities of modern defense systems. By systematically analyzing various algorithmic strategies – ranging from heuristic and meta-heuristic to hybrid approaches – this work highlights the strengths and limitations of existing solutions while identifying key areas for performance improvement. The comparative analysis underscores the necessity of designing a comprehensive and adaptive framework that can intelligently allocate limited weapon resources to optimize mission outcomes, even under constraints such as uncertainty, time sensitivity, and operational complexity.

Looking forward, the transition from static to dynamic DWTA environments presents both a challenge and an opportunity. Future research can benefit significantly from integrating advanced technologies such as quantum machine learning (QML), QDL, and reinforcement learning to address the dynamic nature of threats and evolving battle conditions. These innovations have the potential to revolutionize WTA systems by enabling real-time responsiveness, increased adaptability, and higher computational efficiency. The continued exploration and refinement of these approaches can serve as a foundation for the development of intelligent defense solutions, contributing meaningfully to the broader domain of national security and military technology.

References

Altinoz, O. T. (2020, July). Modeling of synchronous weapon target assignment problem for howitzer based defense line. In *2020 IEEE Congress on Evolutionary Computation (CEC)* (pp. 1–8). IEEE.

Elfeky, E., Cochrane, M., Crase, S., Elsayed, S., Sims, B., Essam, D., & Sarker, R. (2022, December). Coevolution with danger zone levels strategy for the weapon target assignment problem. In *2022 IEEE symposium series on computational intelligence (SSCI)* (pp. 596–603). IEEE.

Elliott, D. S., & Vatsan, M. (2023). *Efficient computation of weapon-target assignments using abstraction*. IEEE Control Systems Letters.

Fang, F., He, J., Li, Q., Ding, F., Liang, W., & Fei, A. (2021, October). Weapon-target assignment based on improved particle swarm optimization for different allocation criteria. In *2021 China Automation Congress (CAC)* (pp. 6628–6633). IEEE.

Fu, M., Li, M., & Sun, N. (2018, October). Study on the weapon target assignment problem using hybrid genetic algorithm. In *2018 IEEE 3rd advanced information technology, electronic and automation control conference (IAEAC)* (pp. 1583–1587). IEEE.

Geng, Z., Huang, Y., Zhang, H., & Chen, T. (2022, November). Improved sparrow search algorithm applied to multi-stage weapon target assignment. In *2022 International conference on cyber-physical social intelligence (ICCSI)* (pp. 98–103). IEEE.

Ghanbari, A. A., & Alaei, H. (2021). Meta-heuristic algorithms for resource management in crisis based on OWA approach. *Applied Intelligence*, *51*(2), 646–657.

Guangsheng, J., Xianming, S., Jing, C., Liqing, R., Minmin, Z., & Kang, L. (2020, December). A survey of intelligent optimization algorithms for weapon target assignment (WTA) problem. In *2020 Management science informatization and economic innovation development conference (MSIEID)* (pp. 50–54). IEEE.

He, Y., Su, Q., & Long, H. (2023, August). Task allocation of multi UAV based on genetic algorithm. In *2023 10th International conference on dependable systems and their applications (DSA)* (pp. 466–467). IEEE.

Huang, J., Li, X., Yang, Z., Kong, W., Zhao, Y., & Zhou, D. (2021). A novel elitism co-evolutionary algorithm for antagonistic weapon-target assignment. *IEEE Access*, *9*, 139668–139684.

HuangFu, Y., Fan, Y., Li, G., & Li, C. (2022). Adaptive grouping weapon-target assignment with field-of-view angle constraint. *IFAC-PapersOnLine*, *55*(3), 190–195.

Kline, A. G., Ahner, D. K., & Lunday, B. J. (2019). Real-time heuristic algorithms for the static weapon target assignment problem. *Journal of Heuristics*, *25*, 377–397.

Kline, A. G., Ahner, D. K., & Lunday, B. J. (2020). A heuristic and metaheuristic approach to the static weapon target assignment problem. *Journal of Global Optimization*, *78*, 791–812.

Kline, A., Ahner, D., & Hill, R. (2019). The weapon-target assignment problem. *Computers & Operations Research*, *105*, 226–236.

Li, Q., Hua, Y., Zhai, H., Li, Q., & Dong, X. (2022, July). Multi-agent weapon target assignment and cooperative path planning based on QS-RRT algorithm. In *2022 41st Chinese Control Conference (CCC)* (pp. 4909–4914). IEEE.

Li, S., He, X., Xu, X., Zhao, T., Song, C., & Li, J. (2023). Weapon-target assignment strategy in joint combat decision-making based on multi-head deep reinforcement learning (Vol. 11, 113740–113751). *IEEE Access*.

Li, X., Wu, G., Wang, Q., & Cen, J. (2023, November). Study on intelligent allocation of shipborne weapons air defense targets considering weapon capability constraints. In *2023 China Automation Congress (CAC)* (pp. 1858–1863). IEEE.

Niu, Y., Jin, X., & Wen, Z. (2021, September). Research on command and control technology in small-UAV defense system. In *2021 International conference on computer information science and artificial intelligence (CISAI)* (pp. 673–677). IEEE.

Ruining, L., & Yan, Z. (2021, June). Improved genetic algorithm for weapon target assignment problem. In *2021 International symposium on computer technology and information science (ISCTIS)* (pp. 19–23). IEEE.

Shi, J., Zhang, J., Lei, H., Liu, Z., & Wang, R. (2023). Joint mission and route planning of unmanned air vehicles via a learning-based heuristic. *Journal of Systems Engineering and Electronics*, *34*(1), 81–98.

Wang, C., Gao, J., Lv, N., Cao, Y., Zhao, S., & Wu, J. (2021, November). Multi-objective optimization of weapon target assignment based on genetic algorithm. In *2021 International conference on computer, Internet of Things and control engineering (CITCE)* (pp. 29–34). IEEE.

Xin, B., Wang, Y., & Chen, J. (2018). An efficient marginal-return-based constructive heuristic to solve the sensor–weapon–target assignment problem. *IEEE Transactions on Systems, Man, and Cybernetics: Systems*, *49*(12), 2536–2547.

Yadav, K., Alshudukhi, J. S., Dhiman, G., & Viriyasitavat, W. (2022). iTSA: An improved Tunicate Swarm Algorithm for defensive resource assignment problem. *Soft Computing*, *26*(10), 4929–4937.

Yang, Y., Yan, M., Liu, Z., & Wei, Z. (2022, November). Opposition-based memetic algorithm for the shared weapon target assignment problem. In *2022 China Automation Congress (CAC)* (pp. 1951–1956). IEEE.

Zhai, H., Wang, W., Li, Q., & Zhang, W. (2021, May). Weapon-target assignment based on improved PSO algorithm. In *2021 33rd Chinese control and decision conference (CCDC)* (pp. 6320–6325). IEEE.

Zhang, Y., Koch, S., Calvin, W. J. G., Srigrarom, S., & Stütz, P. (2024, March). Interception of multiple drone targets by heterogeneous chasers using heuristic task allocations with DQN-GNN guidance model. In *2024 SICE international symposium on control systems (SICE ISCS)* (pp. 7–13). IEEE.

Zhang, S., & Wang, Q. (2023, November). A reinforcement learning method for the weapon target assignment problem with unknown hit rate. In *2023 China Automation Congress (CAC)* (pp. 900–905). IEEE.

Zhang, J., Wen, P., & Xiong, A. (2022, October). Multi-task assignment research for heterogeneous UAVs based on improved simulated annealing particle swarm optimization algorithm. In *2022 International conference on cyber-enabled distributed computing and knowledge discovery (CyberC)* (pp. 284–288). IEEE.

Zhang, K., Zhou, D., Yang, Z., Kong, W., & Zeng, L. (2020). A novel heterogeneous sensor-weapon-target cooperative assignment for ground-to-air defense by efficient evolutionary approaches. *IEEE Access*, *8*, 227373–227398.

Chapter 12

Android Malware Detection Based on Intrinsic Feature Selection and False Omission Rate Metric

Naimisha Awasthi[a] *and Prateek Raj Gautam*[b]

[a]*Department of Computer Science and Engineering, Centre for Advanced Studies, AKTU, India*
[b]*School of Computer Science, UPES, India*

Abstract

With the rise of technology, data, and information, reliance on cyberspace has surged, creating a global virtual reality where users are virtually omnipresent. While this virtual realm fosters connectivity, it also disconnects users from physical reality, exposing them to various threats and attacks. To address these challenges, extensive exploration of cyberspace has led to the adoption of machine learning techniques. By employing a tree-based Decision Tree Feature Selection (FS) methodology, the authors meticulously selected and evaluated 135 critical features, significantly enhancing both model performance and interpretability. Among the various algorithms tested, the ensemble method Random Forest outperformed others, achieving an impressive accuracy rate of 98.74%. In addition to evaluating accuracy, the authors assessed the performance of each classification algorithm using the False Omission Rate (FOR) metric. This metric is valuable for evaluating a model's ability to prevent false negatives and generate accurate negative predictions. The Random Forest ensemble technique excelled across all evaluation metrics, achieving a FOR score of 0.024 – indicating superior performance in minimizing false negatives compared to other algorithms. Conversely, Naive Bayes underperformed in terms of accuracy, precision, and recall, while logistic regression proved to be the weakest performer in terms of the FOR metric. These outcomes

The Internet of Things in the Defence Industry:
Challenges and Solutions for Military Security, 245–258

Published under exclusive licence by Emerald Publishing Limited
doi:10.1108/978-1-83549-198-020261013

underscore the effectiveness of our FS process and highlight the FOR metric's strength in guiding feature-based predictive accuracy.

Keywords: Machine learning; threat detection; feature analysis; feature selection; feature importance

1. Introduction

Threats and attacks define this virtual world. With so many devices being monitored for threat detection and prevention, the existence of inexperienced users utilizing vulnerable technology raises the likelihood of an attack. Data, information, devices, and networks are all susceptible to various dangers and attacks. Threats are potential risks or threats caused by system or network faults. Viruses, attempted hacking, unauthorized access, data breaches, social engineering attacks, and device theft are all possible dangers. Attacks occur when these threats are identified and used against a specific system or network. An attack happens when a threat actor effectively exploits existing security measures, obtaining unauthorized access, interrupting services, stealing data, or inflicting harm. Attacks are frequently planned, targeted, and use specialized tactics or methodologies to attack vulnerabilities. There are different types of attacks that users are prone to, as shown in Fig. 12.1. Malware attacks are a regular and major concern in today's digital landscape.

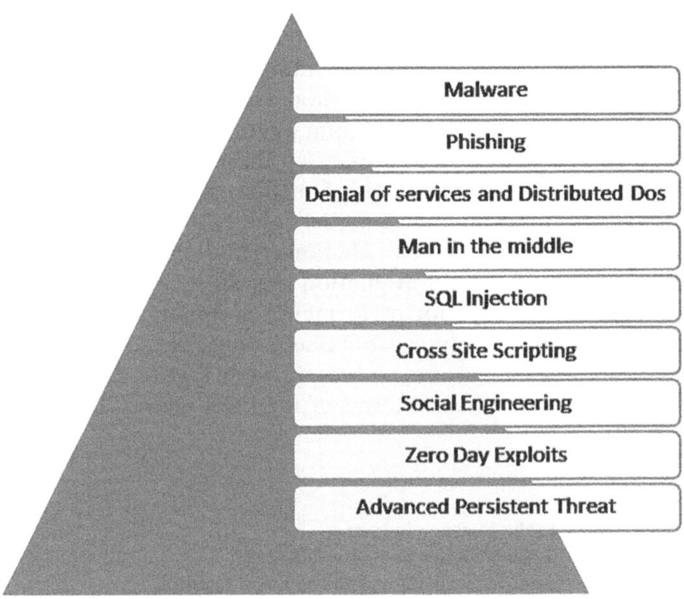

Fig. 12.1. Different Types of Attacks.

Malware is an acronym for malicious software, which refers to software or code that is expressly designed to exploit, harm, or compromise systems, devices, and networks without the user's knowledge. Malware assaults have become commonplace, affecting both corporations and people. Malware threats take many forms, including viruses, worms, Trojans, ransomware, adware, spyware, and keyloggers. To address the ever-changing nature of malware attacks, new detection and protection approaches are continually being developed. These strategies require taking into account numerous features and properties of malware. Evaluating these aspects helps security professionals detect and prevent malware infestations (Urooj et al., 2021). As hackers employ new and developing tactics to exploit vulnerabilities in systems and devices, there is an increasing requirement for unique ways and procedures for detecting and preventing attacks. This includes improving security on devices, systems, and networks that are prone to attacks. New technologies, particularly supervised and unsupervised machine learning algorithms, have significantly improved malware detection and prevention. These machine learning approaches have been effective in improving cyber security measures. Many of the advantages of machine learning entail having a dual nature on both ends, one as defender and one as aggressor. These methods may investigate complicated features and interactions in malware samples, yielding more precise and robust detection capabilities.

1.1. Feature Selection

In real-world concept learning environments, data may have multiple qualities, with just a subset relevant to the goal notion. Choosing the right qualities is crucial for faster learning and higher concept quality. To function properly, an accurate model must satisfy all requirements. This includes training the model using a large volume of data, as the law of large numbers indicates that performance and prediction accuracy grow with dataset size. As more data enters the model, its prediction ability improves, yielding more accurate results. One key quality that is sometimes missed is the model's interpretability, also known as the ability to discern underlying patterns that influence decisions or outcomes. This lack of interpretability makes it difficult to create a generalized model capable of greater prediction. As a result, the model must choose between performance and interpretability. This is where FS comes in. FS is more than just randomly selecting features to reduce training size or computing complexity; it is a technique for identifying significant features that are critical for decision-making and performance. Understanding features reveals how the model makes decisions, why particular decisions are made, and enables continuing monitoring and development to find underlying trends and improve overall model performance.

1.2. Android Malware

Unlike malware developed for computers and laptops, Android malware attacks the Android operating system, architecture, apps, and services. They are frequently spread and infected through unlicensed app stores, third-party applications, and malicious emails, files, and links that exploit Android's open environment, in contrast to tightly controlled apps available on sites such as the Apple Store. Malware built for Android smartphones, such as adware, false system upgrades, exploits weaknesses to deceive users by demanding permission, changing manifests, and modifying components such as SMS, call records, cameras, microphones, and contacts. Malicious code in Android malware attacks frequently hides between system calls and APIs to avoid detection. It then obtains unlawful data access and talks with command and control servers via trojans over HTTP, HTTPS, and custom protocols.

2. Literature Review

Chandrashekar and Sahin (2014) provide an overview of numerous FS strategies, with a particular focus on the Filter, Wrapper, and Embedded approaches. Their study emphasizes the importance of variable elimination in addressing various machine learning challenges. They also demonstrate the applicability of FS algorithms to commonly used datasets. Given the abundance of high-dimensional data, the literature offers a range of FS methods aimed at reducing processing time, enhancing prediction accuracy, and deepening the understanding of data, particularly in machine learning and pattern recognition applications.

Jovic et al. (2015) present a review of widely used FS techniques, emphasizing their practical applications. Beyond traditional methods such as Filter, Wrapper, and Embedded approaches, the study explores recent hybrid techniques and advanced topics. Recognizing the impracticality of exhaustive searches for optimal feature subsets, various search strategies are introduced. These FS techniques are applied across diverse tasks, including classification, clustering, and regression.

Guyon and Elisseeff (2003) examine the threefold objectives of FS: improving prediction performance, reducing computational costs, and promoting a better understanding of the data generation process. Their contributions span multiple dimensions – refining objective functions, constructing and ranking features, selecting features in multivariate scenarios, implementing efficient search techniques, and evaluating the validity of selected features.

Dash and Liu (1997) offer a comprehensive survey of FS methodologies from the 1970s to the present. The study outlines four essential steps in the FS process, categorizes methods based on generation procedures and evaluation functions, and explores innovative combinations of these components. Through examples and benchmark datasets, they compare different methods, assess their strengths and weaknesses, and provide practical guidelines tailored to various data types and domain requirements. The survey also discusses future directions and serves as a resource for both newcomers and practitioners.

Miao and Niu (2016) provide a detailed review of state-of-the-art FS techniques, supported by experimental validation. Their findings highlight the effectiveness of unsupervised FS algorithms, especially in enhancing clustering performance in machine learning tasks.

Venkatesh and Anuradha (2019) explore various FS techniques and observe that most are designed for static data. However, the rise of IoT and web-based applications has led to dynamic data generation, presenting new challenges such as noise, which may impact the accuracy of FS algorithms.

Liu et al. (2005) present an overview of FS considerations, including managing overfitting in small-sample classifiers, handling unlabeled data, using ensemble methods, and applying the minimum redundancy-maximum relevance criterion. The study also considers biological relevance, particularly in microarray data analysis.

Seyfari and Meimandi (2024) conduct experiments using the DREBIN dataset, which includes 410 samples of both benign and malicious Android applications. Their proposed method, utilizing a KNN classifier and 1908 permission features, achieves an impressive accuracy of 99.02%. These results outperform several recent studies, demonstrating the effectiveness of their approach.

Nikam and Deshmukh (2024) propose a hybrid FS technique that combines information gain, chi-square, and feature importance metrics for malware classification. They initially identify the top 20 features using each technique and evaluate the performance of various classifiers, including linear regression, SVM, KNN, decision trees, and XGBoost. The top 60 features are merged, and 11 hybrid features – common to at least two methods – are selected. Using these features, the classifiers show improved performance, with XGBoost achieving the highest accuracy (0.9866), precision (0.9900), recall (0.9833), and F1-score (0.9866). The results highlight the strength of the hybrid method in distinguishing between malicious and benign apps.

Muzaffar et al. (2022) review prior research on Android malware detection using machine learning. They categorize techniques into supervised, unsupervised, deep learning, and online learning approaches, further organizing them based on whether they employ static, dynamic, or hybrid features. The review provides valuable insights into the effectiveness of various detection strategies.

Kouliaridis and Kambourakis (2021) conduct a concise analysis of ML-based Android malware detection studies, summarizing trends and identifying key challenges. A major observation is the inconsistent use of parameters, datasets, analysis methods, and evaluation metrics across studies. To address this, the researchers propose a four-step converging scheme that could serve as a standard baseline for future research.

Faruk et al. (2021) advocate for the use of advanced technologies, especially artificial intelligence, in malware detection. They argue that AI techniques – including machine learning and deep learning – offer the potential to enhance the accuracy, speed, and adaptability of detection systems.

Hamed et al. (2018) present a Network Intrusion Detection System (NIDS) based on Recursive Feature Addition (RFA) and a bigram technique for FS. Tested on the ISCX 2012 dataset, the system benefits from improved feature representation and introduces a novel metric that combines accuracy, detection rate, and false alarm rate for performance evaluation. The results show notable improvements across multiple performance indicators.

Kok et al. (2019) address the growing threat of ransomware, which has become increasingly effective due to factors such as encryption technology, cyber currency, and the accessibility of attack tools. The study notes that machine learning – particularly regression algorithms – is commonly used for ransomware detection. However, the lack of protective models highlights the need for new ML-based detection systems.

Yang et al. (2024) propose AMDASE, a novel Android malware detection method that utilizes API semantics extraction to adapt to the evolving nature of Android threats.

Suciu and Lung (2023) introduce a genetic algorithm-based FS approach. By evaluating features through decision trees, the method selects the most effective individuals in the genetic algorithm population. The study demonstrates the practical benefits of this approach through improved classification performance, supported by experimental results.

Zhou et al. (2021) propose a FS method for decision trees by assigning weights to features and selecting the highest-weighted one at each tree level. Additionally, an algorithm is introduced to pre-screen and remove irrelevant features, leading to better classification outcomes.

Adhao and Pachghare (2019) emphasize the importance of training function-based FS. Using the CICIDS2017 dataset, they reduce the original 82 features to 15, achieving improved accuracy and reduced training time despite initial limitations in performance. Their machine learning approach successfully balances accuracy with efficiency.

Eslavath and Mummadi (2024) investigate how features such as call signals, intents, and commands influence app access for malware classification. With 215 sub-attributes in the dataset, traditional FS methods proved computationally expensive and yielded subpar accuracy. Their proposed embedded method integrates a non-linear customized SVM and cross-validation to reduce features to 74, significantly enhancing classification accuracy to 95.58%.

3. Methodology

3.1. Dataset

The dataset employed for analysis is taken from the Kaggle platform that comprises a total of 215 subdivided feature vectors or variables. Additionally, it includes a target variable referred to as class, which distinguishes between benign and malware instances. The dataset has been categorized into four overarching divisions: manifest permission, API call signature, intent, and command signature. These divisions were derived from a diverse set of 15,036 applications, encompassing 5,560 malware samples and 9,476 benign samples. The flowchart of methodology is shown in Fig. 12.2.

3.2. Decision Tree-based Intrinsic FS

Large databases and the necessity for effective machine learning algorithms have inspired substantial study on FS (Dash & Liu, 1997). This strategy combines

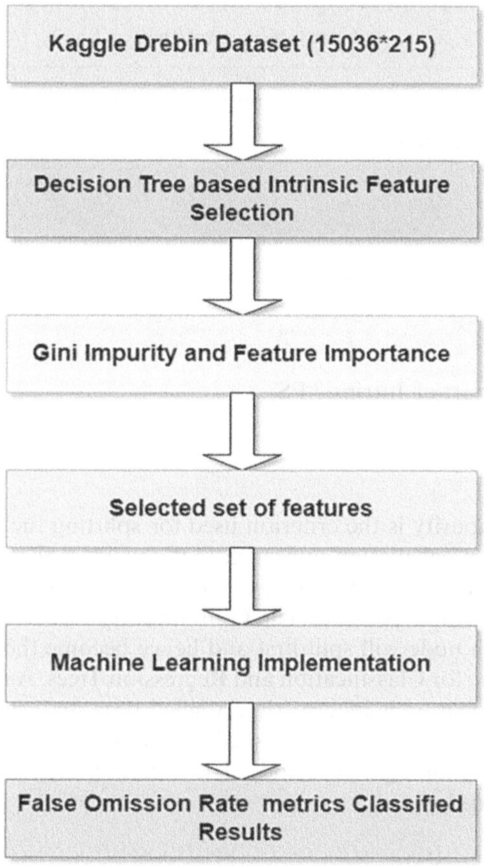

Fig. 12.2. Flowchart of Methodology.

the filter and wrapper methods, yielding a comprehensive FS model that makes it easier to choose acceptable features for machine learning models. This strategy lowers the requirement for manual feature engineering, saving both time and effort, also reducing the risk of overfitting by focusing on the most relevant features.

Decision tree-based algorithms and models, such as decision trees, are renowned for their strong predictive performance and the ability to provide feature importance metrics. These models iteratively search for optimal predictors and split points to create partitions that maximize homogeneity in predicted outcomes. If a predictor is not utilized in any split, it is considered functionally independent and is excluded from the model, ensuring that only relevant features contribute to predictions. This FS process enhances the model's interpretability and performance. A flowchart of the FS process is shown in Fig. 12.3.

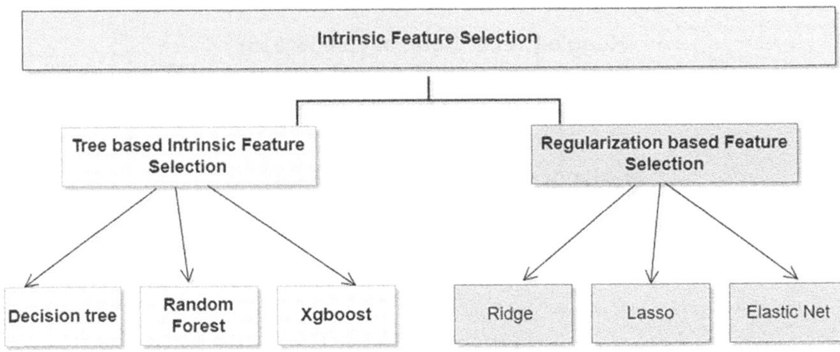

Fig. 12.3. Flowchart of Intrinsic FS.

3.2.1. Splitting

Generally, Gini impurity is the criterion used for splitting the node, as well as a feature contribution calculation approach that considers the possibility of randomly picking features. The process seeks to eliminate pollutants and produce the least polluted sample possible. The Gini impurity of each node is evaluated to determine which node will split first and hence become the root node. It is a well-known statistic for Classification and Regression Trees. A new sample is split recursively until a feature is incorrectly classified because it was labelled at random, and a halting condition is not satisfied, such as maximal depth, few observations each leaf, or attaining a pure node. The Gini impurity for a node N can be calculated using Eq. 1.

$$\text{Gini}(N) = 1 - \sum_{m=1}^{k} q_m^2 \tag{1}$$

where:

Gini(N) signifies the Gini impurity of node N, q_m represents the probability of a sample belonging to class m at the node, and k indicates the total number of classes.

3.2.2. Feature Importance

Feature importance quantifies how much each input variable contributes to the model's predictive performance. It identifies which features have the most impact on the model's ability to make accurate predictions. By analyzing feature importance scores, models can pinpoint the most influential features in the dataset. Understanding feature importance enables us to optimize the models effectively. By focusing on the most important features of the model's architecture we can get refined, fine-tune hyperparameters that improves overall performance. Feature importance helps prioritize variables for further analysis or feature engineering.

Feature importance provides valuable insights into the relationship between input variables and the target variable. It enhances the interpretability of machine learning models by highlighting the driving factors behind predictions. Mean decrease impurity is used by the Decision Trees to calculate the feature importance which is more specific to the models that are tree-based.

3.3. Machine Learning Implementation

3.3.1. Naive Bayes

Naive Bayes is an effective algorithm for text classification tasks, small training sets, categorical and discrete features, and real-time prediction applications. Its simplicity, efficiency, and ability to handle multi-class classification make it a popular choice for certain types of problems. However, its performance may degrade when the independence assumption is strongly violated or when dealing with continuous features. It is essential to consider the characteristics of the data and the assumptions of Naive Bayes when choosing it as the algorithm for a specific task.

3.3.2. K-Nearest Neighbour (KNN)

KNN is an effective algorithm for non-linear data, multi-class classification, small-dimensional feature spaces, and tasks where local patterns are essential. It is relatively easy to implement. It is a sparse algorithm. The choice of k and its computational cost should be considered when applying KNN to large datasets.

3.3.3. Support Vector Machine (SVM)

SVM is an effective algorithm when dealing with linearly separable data, nonlinear data with the help of the kernel trick, small- to medium-sized datasets, binary classification problems, and tasks where a clear decision boundary is present. It is less sparse as compared to KNN. Understanding the characteristics of the data and appropriately tuning hyperparameters can make SVM a powerful algorithm for classification and regression tasks.

3.3.4. Decision Tree

Decision trees are effective algorithms when dealing with non-linear data, multi-class classification, interpretability, handling missing values, and feature importance analysis. They are particularly useful when the focus is on understanding the decision-making process and generating interpretable models. They provide an efficient rule collection that is easy to understand and analyze, making them a valuable tool in data analysis and machine learning.

3.3.5. Random Forest

Random Forest classifier is a popular machine learning algorithm known for its effectiveness in both classification and regression tasks. It operates by constructing multiple decision trees based on various subsets of the dataset and features.

Each decision tree within the Random Forest acts independently, and the final prediction is made by averaging the outputs of these trees, resulting in improved accuracy and robustness. Random Forest is favoured for its ability to handle large datasets with high dimensionality and for providing insights into feature importance. Random Forest algorithm has the capability to reduce overfitting, handle missing values, and perform well with minimal hyperparameter tuning.

3.3.6. Logistic Regression

Logistic regression is a statistical approach used in machine learning to categorize binary data. Unlike linear regression, which predicts continuous values, logistic regression determines if a sample belongs to a particular class. It determines the relationship between one or more independent variables and the likelihood of an outcome. Logistic regression, often known as the sigmoid function, predicts the probability distribution of events.

4. FOR Metrics

The FOR is an indicator of model performance. FOR assists a decision tree in selecting features, reducing false negatives from projected negative data. The FOR handles the decision tree's recursive refining. Investigating the sources of false negatives allows you to improve the model's sensitivity to these errors, either by reselecting features or altering the tree's attributes to better detect class distinctions. The FOR is calculated as the ratio of false negatives (FN) to the total number of negative predictions, expressed as Eq. 2.

$$\mathrm{FOR} = \frac{FN}{TN + FN} \tag{2}$$

Eq. 2 represents the FOR. FOR quantifies the risk of false negatives among the negative predictions. The lower the False Negative (FN) and the higher the True Negative (TN) value, the better the output and results.

5. Result and Discussion

On implementing FS and feature importance through a tree-based decision tree, we have identified the 135 most important and relevant features. These features not only improve the performance but also the interpretability of the model. In addition to implementing machine learning algorithms for better classification in Fig. 12.4, we found that among all the algorithms, the ensemble algorithm that is Random Forest outperforms the others, non-ensemble, with an accuracy of 98.74% and FOR of 0.024. The outcome in the form of a bar graph in Fig. 12.5 indicates that, following the computation of FS selection and importance by a decision tree, features with greater importance tend to serve as root nodes more frequently, just like in Fig. 12.5 transact has the highest importance tends to be the root node in the decision tree. This suggests that these features are better at describing, classifying, and effectively splitting samples, thereby leading to accurate predictions.

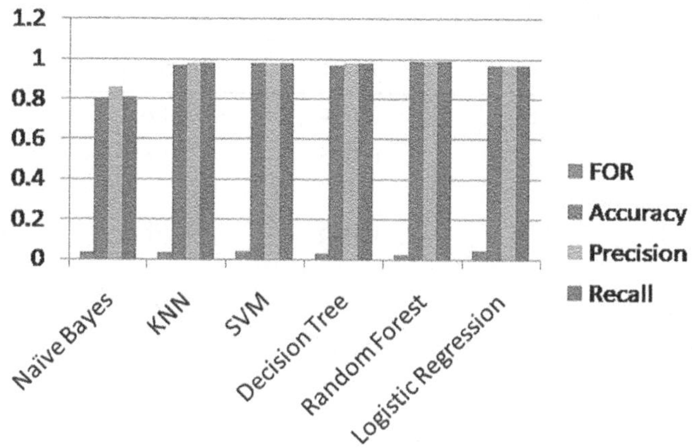

Fig. 12.4. Performance Metric of all the Algorithms in Percentage.

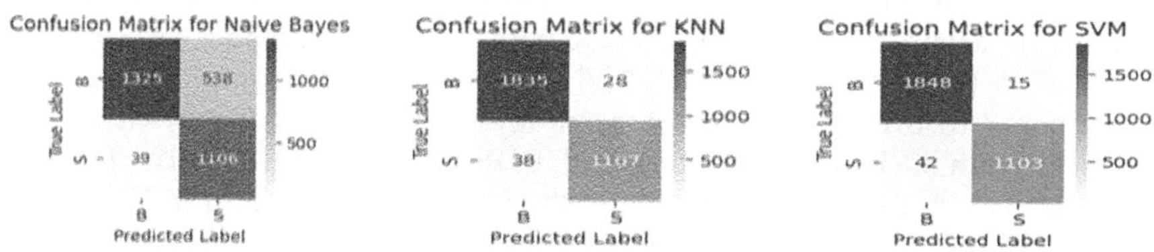

(a)Confusion Matrix of Naïve Bayes

(b)Confusion Matrix of KNN

(c)Confusion Matrix of SVM

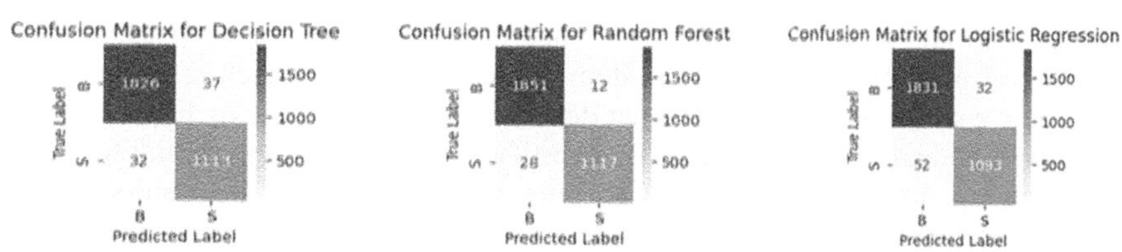

(d)Confusion Matrix of Decision Tree

(e)Confusion Matrix of Random Forest

(f)Confusion Matrix of Logistic Regression

Fig. 12.5. Confusion Matrix of Different Classifiers.

Table 12.1 shows the performance of different algorithms on different metrics considered, where each metric has its own significance. Using intrinsic decision trees to decrease the Android Dataset from 215 feature vectors to 135 features was the first step in the intriguing findings of using FS and FOR metric score in conjunction with other metrics. FS is the process of determining the relative importance of each feature before choosing it for further classification using a variety of algorithms, including Naive Bayes, k-Nearest Neighbour, Support Vector Machine, Decision Tree, Random Forest, and

Table 12.1. Metric Table.

Algorithm	Accuracy	FOR	Precision	Recall
Naive Bayes	0.80	0.034	0.86	0.81
k-Nearest Neighbour	0.97	0.033	0.98	0.98
Support Vector Machine	0.98	0.036	0.98	0.98
Decision Tree	0.97	0.027	0.98	0.98
Random Forest	0.99	0.024	0.99	0.99
Logistic Regression	0.97	0.045	0.97	0.97

Logistic Regression. Random Forest surpassed all other ensemble algorithms in terms of accuracy with 0.99%, FOR with 0.024%, precision with 0.99%, and recall with 0.99%. In contrast, Naive Bayes performs completely poorly as compared to others in terms of accuracy with 0.80, precision with 0.86, and recall with 0.81, but not in terms of FOR. For the FOR metric, logistic regression is a disaster with 0.045%, as shown in Table 12.1 and in Fig. 12.4, that can be clearly drawn from the Confusion Matrix of the algorithms shown in Fig. 12.6.

6. Conclusion and Future Scope

Malware threats remain a significant concern in today's digital landscape, with attackers continuously exploiting system vulnerabilities to breach sensitive data. An effective strategy to enhance threat detection involves the use of FS combined with machine learning techniques. By identifying and selecting essential features and applying machine learning algorithms, while evaluating the results across multiple performance metrics, accurate threat prediction and detection can be achieved.

The application of FS methods based on importance scores improves both the efficiency and effectiveness of machine learning models in classifying malware and benign files. This is achieved by reducing the size of feature vectors while ensuring that critical features for classification are preserved.

When considering dataset characteristics and specific problem requirements, FS proves to be a valuable approach for achieving accurate classification outcomes. For instance, Naïve Bayes yielded the lowest accuracy at 81%, a FOR of 0.033 (which still indicates relatively good performance), a precision of 86%, and a recall of 81%. In contrast, the ensemble algorithm Random Forest outperformed other models with an accuracy of 99%, a FOR of 0.024, a precision of 99%, and a recall of 99%. The low FOR value highlights the model's ability to minimize false negatives and correctly identify true negatives, thus reducing the risk of classifying malware as benign.

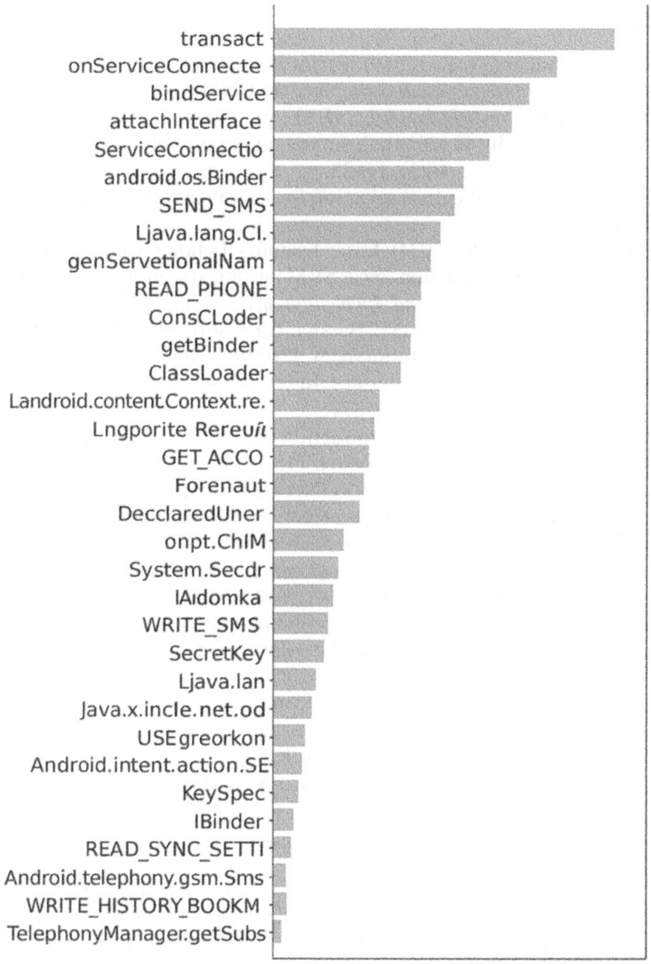

Fig. 12.6. Selected Features on the Basis of Their Importance Score.

On the other hand, Logistic Regression demonstrated comparatively poorer performance, with a FOR of 0.045, indicating a higher likelihood of misclassifying malware samples as benign. This underscores the importance of including FOR alongside traditional metrics like accuracy, precision, and recall when evaluating model performance.

These techniques and evaluation metrics play a crucial role in minimizing misclassification errors and enhancing the overall efficiency of machine learning models in cybersecurity applications.

Future research should explore diverse FS algorithms, such as Random Forest and XGBoost, to further improve performance, particularly with respect to FOR. Additionally, other methods like filter-based and wrapper-based approaches can be assessed in combination with FOR metrics to better identify false negatives and guide models towards improved detection capabilities.

References

Adhao, R. B., & Pachghare, V. K. (2019). Performance-based feature selection using decision tree. In *2019 international conference on innovative trends and advances in engineering and technology (ICITAET)*, IEEE, pp. 135–138.

Chandrashekar, G., & Sahin, F. (2014). A survey on feature selection methods. *Computers & Electrical Engineering*, *40*(1), 16–28.

Dash, M., & Liu, H. (1997). Feature selection for classification. *Intelligent Data Analysis*, *1*(1–4), 131–156.

Eslavath, R., & Mummadi, U. K. (2024). Ensic: Feature selection on android malware detection attributes using an enhanced non-linear SVM integrated with cross validator. *International Journal of Intelligent Systems and Applications in engineering*, *12*(2), 495–504.

Faruk, M. J. H., Shahriar, H., Valero, M., Barsha, F. L., Sobhan, S., Khan, M. A., Whitman, M., Cuzzocrea, A., Lo, D., Rahman, A. (2021). Malware detection and prevention using artificial intelligence techniques. In *2021 IEEE International conference on big data (big data)*, IEEE, pp. 5369–5377.

Guyon, I., & Elisseeff, A. (2003). An introduction to variable and feature selection. *Journal of Machine Learning Research*, *3*(Mar), 1157–1182.

Hamed, T., Dara, R., & Kremer, S. C. (2018). Network intrusion detection system based on recursive feature addition and bigram technique. *Computers & Security*, *73*, 137–155.

Jovic, A., Brki' c, K., & Bogunovi' c, N. (2015). A review of feature selection' methods with applications. In *2015 38th international convention on information and communication technology, electronics and microelectronics (MIPRO)*, IEEE, pp. 1200–1205.

Kok, S., Abdullah, A., Jhanjhi, N., & Supramaniam, M. (2019). Ransomware, threat and detection techniques: A review. *International Journal of Computer Science and Network Security*, *19*(2), 136.

Kouliaridis, V., & Kambourakis, G. (2021). A comprehensive survey on machine learning techniques for android malware detection. *Information*, *12*(5), 185.

Liu, H., Dougherty, E. R., Dy, J. G., Torkkola, K., Tuv, E., Peng, H., Ding, C., Long, F., Berens, M., Parsons, L., Yu, L., Zhao, Z., & Forman, G. (2005). Evolving feature selection. *IEEE Intelligent Systems*, *20*(6), 64–76.

Miao, J., & Niu, L. (2016). A survey on feature selection. *Procedia Computer Science*, *91*, 919–926.

Muzaffar, A., Hassen, H. R., Lones, M. A., & Zantout, H. (2022). An indepth review of machine learning based android malware detection. *Computers & Security*, 102833.

Nikam, U., & Deshmukh, V. M. (2024). Hybrid feature selection technique to classify malicious applications using machine learning approach. *Journal of Integrated Science and Technology*, *12*(1), 702–702.

Seyfari, Y., & Meimandi, A. (2024). A new approach to android malware detection using fuzzy logic-based simulated annealing and feature selection. *Multimedia Tools and Applications*, *83*(4), 10525–10549.

Suciu, M.-A., & Lung, R. I. (2023). Feature selection based on a decision tree genetic algorithm. In *International conference on hybrid artificial intelligence systems* (pp. 433–444). Springer.

Urooj, U., Al-rimy, B. A. S., Zainal, A., Ghaleb, F. A., & Rassam, M. A. (2021). Ransomware detection using dynamic analysis and machine learning: A survey and research directions. *Applied Sciences*, *12*(1), 172.

Venkatesh, B., & Anuradha, J. (2019). A review of feature selection and its methods. *Cybernetics and Information Technologies*, *19*(1), 3–26.

Yang, H., Wang, Y., Zhang, L., Cheng, X., & Hu, Z. (2024). A novel android malware detection method with API semantics extraction. *Computers & Security*, *137*, 103651.

Zhou, H., Zhang, J., Zhou, Y., Guo, X., & Ma, Y. (2021). A feature selection algorithm of decision tree based on feature weight. *Expert Systems with Applications*, *164*, 113842.

Chapter 13

Artificial Intelligence and Machine Learning Integration with IoT for Enhanced Defence Applications

Sarang Kumar[a], *Abhishek Kumar Pandey*[b], *A. K. Singh*[c] *and Omprakash Kaiwartya*[d]

[a]*Department of Computer Science, University of Agder, Kristiansand, Norway*
[b]*Center for Security, Theory and Algorithmic Research, IIIT Hyderabad, India*
[c]*Shri Ramswaroop Memorial University, India*
[d]*Department of Computer Science, Nottingham Trent University, UK*

Abstract

The integration of artificial intelligence (AI), machine learning (ML), and the Internet of Things (IoT) is revolutionizing the defence sector by enhancing operational efficiency, situational awareness (SA), and decision-making capabilities. IoT interconnects a vast network of smart devices, enabling continuous data collection from sources such as surveillance drones, autonomous vehicles, and intelligent weapon systems. AI and ML process this data in real time, identifying patterns, predicting threats, and optimizing battlefield strategies. These technologies play a crucial role in cybersecurity, autonomous defence systems, and predictive logistics, ensuring enhanced threat detection, automated responses, and resource optimization. AI-driven automation reduces human risk in high-stakes military operations while strengthening national security through intelligent cyber-defence mechanisms. Despite its transformative potential, the integration of AI, ML, and IoT presents challenges related to data security, ethical considerations, and interoperability. This chapter explores the impact of this technological convergence on defence, emphasizing its advantages, challenges, and future implications for modern warfare and strategic security.

The Internet of Things in the Defence Industry:
Challenges and Solutions for Military Security, 259–279

Published under exclusive licence by Emerald Publishing Limited
doi:10.1108/978-1-83549-198-020261014

Keywords: Artificial intelligence (AI); machine learning (ML); Internet of Things (IoT); defence technology; cybersecurity

1. Introduction

In recent years, the amalgamation of AI, ML, and the IoT has emerged as a transformative force across multiple industries. In the defence sector, this integration presents groundbreaking opportunities to enhance operational efficiency, strengthen national security, and improve decision-making processes. As modern warfare and security threats become increasingly complex and data-driven, the ability to collect, process, and analyze vast amounts of information in real time is paramount. AI and ML serve as critical enablers in this advancement, providing the intelligence necessary for automation, predictive analytics, and strategic decision support in defence operations.

The IoT plays a crucial role by interconnecting a vast network of smart devices, sensors, and autonomous systems, ensuring seamless data collection and communication across different platforms. IoT-powered technologies facilitate real-time surveillance, threat detection, battlefield monitoring, and logistics management, among other critical functions (bin Zainuddin et al., 2024). These interconnected devices gather continuous streams of data from various sources, such as unmanned aerial vehicles (UAVs), surveillance drones, smart combat gear, automated missile defence systems, and intelligent transportation units. However, raw data alone holds limited strategic value unless it is efficiently processed and analyzed – this is where AI and ML come into play (Ahmed, 2022; bin Zainuddin et al., 2024; Weng, 2024).

AI and ML are the driving forces behind the intelligent processing of defence-related data. AI-powered algorithms can sift through massive datasets, detect patterns, and identify anomalies that may indicate potential threats. ML models enhance SA by predicting enemy movements, optimizing battlefield strategies, and automating threat response mechanisms. With advancements in deep learning, neural networks, and natural language processing, AI and ML are becoming increasingly adept at deciphering complex battlefield environments, recognizing targets, and making split-second decisions with high accuracy (Ahmed, 2022; bin Zainuddin et al., 2024; Sarker et al., 2023; Weng, 2024).

One of the most significant advantages of AI and ML in defence is their ability to improve autonomous systems. Autonomous drones, robotic soldiers, unmanned naval vessels, and AI-powered missile systems are becoming essential components of modern defence strategies (Mahmood et al., 2022). These systems reduce human intervention in high-risk combat scenarios, minimizing casualties while maximizing operational efficiency. Furthermore, AI-driven automation plays a pivotal role in cyber warfare, where sophisticated algorithms can detect, counteract, and mitigate cyber threats in real time, thereby strengthening cybersecurity measures in defence infrastructure (Mohanta et al., 2020).

The fusion of AI, ML, and IoT is also revolutionizing logistics and supply chain management within the military. AI-powered predictive maintenance ensures that defence equipment remains in optimal condition, reducing downtime and preventing unexpected failures during critical operations. Smart logistics systems optimize resource allocation, streamline troop deployment, and enhance mission planning through real-time data analytics (Pasdar et al., 2024). Such advancements contribute to better strategic planning, cost-effectiveness, and improved readiness for military operations.

This article delves into the far-reaching implications of AI, ML, and IoT integration within the defence sector, focusing on key areas such as surveillance, cybersecurity, autonomous systems, and logistics. It highlights the transformative benefits these technologies offer, while also addressing the challenges, ethical considerations, and future prospects of their adoption. As defence agencies worldwide strive to enhance their capabilities, the convergence of AI, ML, and IoT is set to redefine modern warfare, bolstering national security and operational effectiveness in unprecedented ways.

2. Role of AI and ML in Enhancing IoT for Defence

The integration of AI and ML with the IoT is dramatically transforming the landscape of defence operations. IoT systems are inherently designed to gather vast amounts of data from an array of interconnected devices – sensors, satellites, drones, vehicles, and weapons – enabling a more connected and data-rich environment. However, the sheer volume and complexity of this data present significant challenges for human analysts and traditional systems (Sharma et al., 2021). AI and ML are the catalysts that allow defence forces to effectively process, analyze, and act on this data, turning it into actionable insights that can enhance SA, improve decision-making, and increase operational efficiency. Here's a deeper look at the specific roles AI and ML play in enhancing IoT for defence applications:

- **Real-time Data Processing and Analysis:** IoT devices generate massive amounts of data that require real-time processing to be useful in defence operations. AI and ML techniques, particularly edge computing and distributed AI, enable the immediate analysis of data at the point of collection, allowing for faster decision-making in critical situations (Alcántara Suárez & Monzon Baeza, 2023). For example, AI can analyze data from battlefield sensors to detect unusual patterns that may indicate enemy movement, changes in environmental conditions, or even potential threats. ML models are used to improve the accuracy of threat detection by learning from historical data and identifying complex patterns that would be difficult for humans to discern.
- **Enhanced Threat Detection and Predictive Analysis:** One of the most significant applications of AI and ML in IoT-enabled defence systems is in predictive analytics. Through the use of historical data, ML algorithms can be trained to identify early warning signs of potential threats, such as enemy activity, cyberattacks, or equipment failures. For instance, AI can continuously monitor

communications and sensor data to predict patterns of adversary behaviour or anticipate operational risks, allowing defence forces to take preemptive action (Chandra & Suresh, 2024). This predictive capability enhances SA, allowing military units to make informed decisions before threats escalate.

- **Autonomous Systems and Decision-Making:** AI and ML algorithms are essential for the operation of autonomous systems that are increasingly deployed in defence applications. IoT devices such as drones, UAVs, autonomous vehicles, and robotic systems are capable of gathering data from the battlefield in real time (Rani et al., 2025). AI and ML help these systems make intelligent decisions without human intervention. For example, AI-powered drones can autonomously identify and track targets, while ML algorithms allow them to adapt to changing conditions and unexpected events. This integration of AI and IoT also enables systems to improve over time, as the ML models learn from each interaction and enhance their capabilities.
- **Optimizing Resource Allocation and Logistics:** In defence, efficient management of resources and logistics is crucial for mission success. IoT systems collect data on various assets, such as fuel levels, ammunition, vehicle performance, and supply chain status (Karthikeyan et al., 2024). AI and ML can analyze this data to optimize resource allocation and logistical support, ensuring that military units have the right supplies at the right time and place. ML models can predict maintenance needs, preventing equipment failure before it occurs, and help optimize the distribution of resources across different units, reducing waste and ensuring mission readiness.
- **Cybersecurity and Threat Mitigation:** The integration of AI and ML with IoT also plays a critical role in cybersecurity within defence applications. IoT devices, while essential for SA and operational effectiveness, can also create vulnerabilities due to their interconnected nature. AI and ML algorithms are used to monitor and analyze network traffic, identify anomalies, and detect potential cyber threats in real time (Rani et al., 2025). ML models can adapt to new attack vectors, improving the ability to detect previously unseen or emerging cyber threats. AI-driven systems can also automatically respond to cyber incidents, isolating compromised devices, applying countermeasures, or alerting security teams to take action.
- **Improved Surveillance and Intelligence Gathering:** AI and ML significantly enhance the capabilities of surveillance systems powered by IoT. Using image recognition, speech recognition, and sensor fusion, AI algorithms can analyze video feeds, audio signals, and sensor data to identify potential threats or points of interest (Karthikeyan et al., 2024). For instance, AI-powered surveillance drones can process video feeds from cameras, detecting enemy soldiers, vehicles, or infrastructure in real-time, while ML models can track movement patterns to predict future enemy actions. This capability allows for more effective intelligence gathering and supports decision-making by providing accurate and timely information.
- **Operational Efficiency and System Health Monitoring:** AI and ML contribute to improving the health monitoring of IoT-enabled defence systems. Continuous monitoring of the performance of critical systems – such as communication

networks, weapons, and surveillance equipment – enables early detection of malfunctions or degradation (Esenogho et al., 2022). Through predictive maintenance models, AI can analyze data from various sensors to predict when an asset is likely to fail, allowing for preemptive repairs and minimizing downtime. This contributes to the overall operational efficiency, ensuring that defence systems are always ready for action.

- **Enhanced SA and Command and Control:** The fusion of IoT with AI and ML enables enhanced SA on the battlefield. By aggregating and processing data from a variety of IoT sources – such as surveillance cameras, satellites, GPS devices, and battlefield sensors – AI systems can create a comprehensive, real-time picture of the operational environment. ML algorithms can then analyze this data to detect anomalies, predict future movements, and optimize tactics (De Spiegeleire et al., 2017). For commanders, this provides an invaluable tool for making informed, data-driven decisions that can significantly improve mission outcomes.

The integration of AI and ML with IoT in defence applications marks a transformative shift in how military forces gather, process, and act upon critical information. These technologies not only enhance the operational capabilities of defence systems but also improve efficiency, reduce human error, and enable faster decision-making (Alharbi et al., 2022). From autonomous systems to predictive analytics and real-time data processing, the role of AI and ML is central to unlocking the full potential of IoT in defence, paving the way for smarter, more resilient, and more adaptive military operations. As these technologies continue to evolve, their impact on the defence sector will only grow, further enhancing national security and operational readiness.

2.1. Automated Decision-Making and Predictive Analytics

The integration of the IoT with automated decision-making and predictive analytics is transforming defence operations by enhancing efficiency, agility, and precision. Powered by advanced AI and ML algorithms, these technologies empower defence systems to make faster, data-driven decisions in dynamic and high-stakes environments. Automated decision-making systems, operating without direct human intervention, utilize predefined rules and adaptive learning models to respond to critical situations in real-time. IoT-enabled devices, including sensors, drones, and autonomous vehicles, generate vast amounts of data that require rapid processing and analysis (De Spiegeleire et al., 2017). AI and ML play a pivotal role in extracting actionable insights from this data, enabling threat prediction, resource optimization, and autonomous decision-making – all of which are essential components of modern defence strategies.

2.1.1. Key Components of Automated Decision-Making in Defence

- **Data Collection:** IoT devices are deployed on the battlefield, collecting data in real-time, such as environmental conditions, troop movements, and the status of assets like vehicles and weapons systems.

- **Data Analysis:** The collected data is processed using AI/ML models to identify patterns, assess threats, and determine optimal responses. For example, ML algorithms might analyze sensor data to detect patterns of enemy movement or recognize anomalies indicating a potential attack.
- **Actionable Insights:** Once the data is processed, the system can automatically initiate actions. For instance, if an IoT-enabled surveillance system detects enemy activity, it may autonomously alert command centres, trigger defensive systems, or even launch an automated countermeasure (such as deploying drones or activating automated defence systems).

2.1.2. Applications in Defence

- **Autonomous Vehicles and Drones:** Autonomous platforms, such as UAVs or autonomous ground vehicles, rely on automated decision-making to navigate and perform missions without direct human control (Alharbi et al., 2022). These systems can analyze real-time sensor data to avoid obstacles, identify threats, and adapt to changing battlefield conditions.
- **Target Identification and Engagement:** AI-powered automated systems can rapidly analyze data from sensors (e.g. thermal or infrared imagery) and make real-time decisions about targeting and engagement. For example, an IoT-connected weapons system may automatically lock onto a target identified by surveillance drones, reducing human decision-making delays and increasing operational efficiency.
- **Cybersecurity Defence:** IoT systems in defence are often exposed to cyber threats, but AI-based decision-making can help autonomously detect and mitigate attacks. For instance, when an IoT device is compromised, an AI-powered security system can take automated steps to isolate the threat, reconfigure network settings, or alert cybersecurity teams.

2.2. Real-Time Data Processing and Insights

The growing integration of IoT technologies in defence applications is revolutionizing how military operations are conducted, particularly in the realm of real-time data processing and insights. IoT devices, such as sensors, cameras, drones, and connected equipment, continuously gather vast amounts of data in real-time from the battlefield and operational environments. This data is essential for maintaining SA, making timely decisions, and ensuring mission success in the face of rapidly evolving threats (De Spiegeleire et al., 2017).

To harness the full potential of IoT in defence, it is crucial to process this data in real time and derive actionable insights that inform decision-making. Real-time data processing involves the immediate collection, analysis, and dissemination of information without delays, while the insights extracted from these data enable military personnel to respond quickly and effectively to changing conditions.

2.2.1. Real-Time Data Collection via IoT

IoT systems in defence environments consist of a diverse array of interconnected devices and sensors that continuously monitor various parameters across the battlefield (Alharbi et al., 2022; De Spiegeleire et al., 2017; Esenogho et al., 2022). These devices can include:

- **Surveillance Cameras**: Used for monitoring areas of interest, detecting movement, and identifying potential threats.
- **Drones and UAVs**: Collecting aerial imagery, video, and environmental data to support reconnaissance, target identification, and surveillance.
- **Environmental Sensors**: Measuring environmental factors such as weather, temperature, humidity, and atmospheric pressure to support mission planning and operational safety.
- **Smart Weapons and Vehicles**: Equipped with sensors to monitor performance, location, and status in real-time, enabling autonomous operations or support for human operators.
- **Wearables and Biometric Sensors**: Used to monitor the health and vitals of soldiers, providing data on stress levels, fatigue, and physical condition.

2.2.2. Real-Time Data Processing in Defence

Processing real-time data from IoT devices is critical for translating raw information into actionable insights. However, given the volume, velocity, and variety of data generated, traditional methods of data analysis are insufficient. This is where advanced edge computing, cloud computing, and AI-driven analytics come into play (Alharbi et al., 2022; Radanliev et al., 2020; Rani et al., 2024).

- **Edge Computing**: In defence, edge computing refers to processing data closer to the source, such as at the IoT device level or near the battlefield, rather than relying on distant data centres. This reduces latency and ensures that critical data is processed immediately. For example, if a drone detects an approaching enemy vehicle using its sensors, edge computing allows the drone to analyze the data and trigger an immediate response (e.g. evasive maneuvers or alerting command centres) without waiting for data to be transmitted back to a central server.
- **Real-Time Analytics**: AI and ML algorithms are deployed to process and analyze large volumes of incoming data streams. These algorithms can detect anomalies, recognize patterns, and make predictions based on historical data. For instance, data from IoT-enabled surveillance systems can be analyzed in real-time to detect unusual patterns of movement, such as the buildup of enemy forces in a specific location, which could indicate an imminent attack. By applying ML models to this data, systems can not only recognize threats but also predict future behaviours or developments, such as the likely route of an advancing enemy.
- **Data Fusion**: IoT devices in defence are often used in conjunction with multiple sensor modalities, such as cameras, thermal sensors, radar, and GPS. Sensor fusion integrates these disparate data sources into a unified, real-time picture of the battlefield. For example, combining thermal imagery from drones with radar data and ground sensor inputs can provide a more comprehensive

understanding of enemy movements, improving detection accuracy and reducing false positives. This fusion of real-time data ensures that decision-makers receive the most accurate and actionable insights.

2.2.3. Real-Time Insights for Defence Decision-Making

Once real-time data is processed, it needs to be transformed into actionable insights that inform military strategy and operations. These insights provide commanders and military units with the critical information they need to make informed decisions, adapt to changing battlefield conditions, and maintain operational superiority (Alharbi et al., 2022; Chipatiso, 2024; Radanliev et al., 2020; Rani et al., 2024).

2.3. Enhancing SA with IoT in Defence

SA in defence refers to the ability to perceive, understand, and predict the operational environment, including the status of friendly and enemy forces, terrain, weather conditions, and other dynamic factors. In modern warfare, enhanced SA is critical for making timely, informed decisions that ensure mission success, reduce risks, and improve the safety of personnel. The IoT plays a transformative role in enhancing SA in defence by providing real-time data from a wide array of interconnected devices, sensors, and platforms, enabling military forces to gain a comprehensive understanding of the operational environment.

IoT in defence connects various devices such as drones, sensors, cameras, vehicles, wearables, and satellites, creating an ecosystem of smart systems that continuously collect, transmit, and analyze data. This data is then used to generate actionable insights that support decision-making and improve overall SA.

2.3.1. Real-Time Data Integration for Comprehensive Understanding

One of the primary contributions of IoT to SA is its ability to integrate vast amounts of real-time data from multiple sources into a cohesive, actionable picture of the battlefield (Alharbi et al., 2022; Chipatiso, 2024). IoT devices, including surveillance drones, environmental sensors, and tactical communication networks, collect and transmit data such as:

- **Enemy Movements**: IoT-powered sensors, radar, and drones can track the movements of enemy forces in real time, providing military personnel with up-to-date intelligence about enemy positions, routes, and potential threats.
- **Environmental Conditions**: Sensors deployed in the field can monitor environmental factors like weather, temperature, and humidity, which are critical for mission planning, navigation, and safety. For example, understanding terrain conditions through IoT sensors can help determine optimal routes for troop movements or vehicle deployments.
- **Asset Health and Location**: IoT-enabled devices track the location, status, and health of critical assets, such as vehicles, aircraft, weapons systems, and

soldiers. This data helps military planners monitor the readiness of their assets and respond quickly to mechanical issues or combat-related damage.
- **Real-Time Communication**: IoT technologies enable seamless communication between all units, from infantry soldiers on the ground to command centres and higher-level decision-makers. Real-time communication between various sensors and units ensures that everyone involved in an operation has access to the same up-to-date information, improving coordination and reducing errors.

2.3.2. Enhanced Decision-Making Through AI and ML

While IoT devices collect and transmit data, the true value of this data is realized when it is analyzed and interpreted using advanced technologies like AI/ML (Rani et al., 2024). These technologies enable military forces to:

- **Analyze Large Data Streams**: IoT systems generate massive volumes of data, which can be overwhelming for human analysts to process manually. AI and ML algorithms can automatically process and filter this data, identifying key trends, patterns, and anomalies. For instance, ML models can learn to recognize patterns in troop movements or identify emerging threats based on historical and real-time data.
- **Predict Future Scenarios**: AI-powered predictive analytics can forecast potential enemy actions, such as likely attack locations or strategic movements. For example, IoT sensors can track the position of enemy vehicles, and ML models can predict their next likely positions, giving commanders a critical advantage in anticipating and countering enemy moves.
- **Automate Responses**: In some cases, IoT systems combined with AI can even automate responses. For instance, if a drone detects an approaching enemy vehicle using real-time sensor data, an AI system might automatically adjust the drone's flight path or activate defensive measures without waiting for human approval. This enables faster reactions in fast-paced, high-risk situations.

2.3.3. Improved Intelligence, Surveillance, and Reconnaissance

IoT plays a significant role in modern ISR operations. Through interconnected networks of drones, satellites, ground sensors, and other surveillance equipment, military forces can gather real-time intelligence that provides a clear and up-to-date view of the operational environment (Chipatiso, 2024; Rani et al., 2024). For example:

- **UAVs**: UAVs equipped with IoT sensors, cameras, and radar can fly over hostile or remote areas, providing surveillance data without putting human personnel at risk. These UAVs can transmit live video feeds, thermal imaging, and environmental data back to command centres, which can be analyzed for signs of enemy activity or movement.
- **Ground Sensors**: IoT-enabled ground sensors (such as motion detectors, acoustic sensors, or seismic sensors) are strategically placed to monitor and detect

enemy forces. These sensors can alert military units in real time when they detect movement, gunfire, or explosions, providing immediate intelligence that can guide tactical decisions.
- **Satellite Imagery and Geospatial Data**: Satellites integrated with IoT systems collect geospatial and environmental data that are crucial for mapping terrain, monitoring weather, and observing enemy activities from space. This data is used to enhance real-time SA by providing a broader view of battlefield dynamics.

2.3.4. Autonomous Systems for Enhanced SA

Autonomous systems, such as drones, ground robots, and autonomous vehicles, are increasingly deployed in defence to enhance SA (Alharbi et al., 2022; Chipatiso, 2024; De Spiegeleire et al., 2017; Radanliev et al., 2020; Rani et al., 2024). These systems, powered by IoT, can autonomously gather data, analyze the battlefield, and make decisions without human input. The key benefits of autonomous systems in enhancing SA include:

- **Independent Data Collection**: Autonomous systems can operate in environments that are too dangerous or difficult for humans, such as heavily contaminated areas or hostile territories. These systems continuously collect and send back real-time data to command centres, ensuring that commanders receive an uninterrupted flow of intelligence.
- **Adaptability**: Autonomous systems can adapt to changes in the operational environment. For instance, autonomous drones can adjust their flight paths based on real-time data from IoT sensors, such as avoiding obstacles or changing their course to capture new intelligence.
- **Faster Decision-Making**: These systems can make decisions in real time, reducing response times and increasing the agility of defence forces. For example, an autonomous ground vehicle (AGV) might identify a potential threat (such as a vehicle approaching a military base) and automatically deploy a countermeasure or alert nearby personnel without requiring human involvement.

2.3.5. SA for Soldiers on the Ground

IoT also plays a crucial role in improving the SA of individual soldiers in the field. Wearable IoT devices and smart helmets can provide soldiers with real-time information about their environment and the status of their mission (Alharbi et al., 2022; De Spiegeleire et al., 2017; Esenogho et al., 2022; Karthikeyan et al., 2024). These wearable technologies can include:

- **Location Tracking**: GPS-enabled IoT devices can track the location of soldiers, ensuring they stay within the designated area and enabling commanders to monitor troop movements. This is particularly useful in complex, urban, or hostile environments where visibility is limited.
- **Health Monitoring**: IoT-enabled sensors can monitor the health and vitals of soldiers, providing real-time data on stress levels, heart rate, body temperature,

and fatigue. This information can help commanders ensure that soldiers are fit for duty and provide early warnings if a soldier is in distress.

- **Augmented Reality (AR)**: Some wearable IoT devices use AR to provide soldiers with real-time overlays of battlefield information, such as enemy locations, friendly forces, and environmental hazards. This allows soldiers to navigate and respond to threats more effectively.

3. Applications of AI/ML-Driven IoT in Defence

The integration of AI and ML with the IoT is revolutionizing modern defence applications, enabling faster, more intelligent, and autonomous operations (De Spiegeleire et al., 2017; Esenogho et al., 2022; Karthikeyan et al., 2024; Rani et al., 2025). The real-time processing and analytics of data generated by IoT devices allow military forces to make faster, more informed decisions in dynamic and high-risk environments. AI and ML algorithms enhance IoT systems by enabling smarter automation, predictive capabilities, and adaptive responses. Below are key applications of AI/ML-driven IoT in defence.

3.1. Autonomous Systems and Unmanned Vehicles

Autonomous systems, particularly unmanned vehicles (land, air, and sea), are one of the most significant applications of AI/ML-driven IoT in defence. These systems leverage IoT sensors to gather real-time data, AI/ML to process and analyze that data, and automated decision-making systems to take action autonomously. Autonomous systems enhance operational efficiency, reduce human risk, and enable highly flexible and scalable operations in complex environments.

3.1.1. Unmanned Aerial Vehicles

- **Real-time Data Collection:** UAVs equipped with IoT sensors gather live data from the battlefield, including visual, infrared, and radar data, which is transmitted in real-time to control centres. AI/ML algorithms analyze this data to identify and track targets, monitor enemy movements, and assess potential threats without human input.
- **Autonomous Flight Paths:** AI enables UAVs to autonomously navigate and adapt to changing conditions, such as weather or enemy interference. ML algorithms can adjust flight paths based on real-time environmental data, ensuring efficient and safe operation in hostile environments.
- **Surveillance and Reconnaissance:** UAVs are increasingly used for surveillance and reconnaissance in areas where manned flights or human presence would be too risky. AI-driven UAVs can autonomously patrol large areas, identify points of interest, and make immediate decisions on whether to report or engage targets.

3.1.2. Autonomous Ground Vehicles

- **Navigational Autonomy:** AGVs are equipped with IoT sensors (such as LiDAR, GPS, and cameras) to navigate terrain without human control (Alharbi et al.,

2022; Chipatiso, 2024; De Spiegeleire et al., 2017; Radanliev et al., 2020; Rani et al., 2024). AI/ML algorithms process sensor data in real-time, enabling vehicles to avoid obstacles, follow predefined routes, and operate in hostile environments.

- **Logistics and Supply Chain Support:** AGVs in military applications can autonomously transport goods, supplies, and equipment across challenging terrains, reducing reliance on human convoys and improving efficiency. These vehicles are capable of navigating through forests, deserts, or even urban combat zones.
- **Mine Detection and Disposal:** AGVs, such as robotic deminers, use IoT sensors to detect landmines and unexploded ordnance. ML algorithms can distinguish between different types of debris and explosives, enabling timely and safe disposal operations without putting human lives at risk.

3.1.3. Unmanned Underwater Vehicles (UUVs)

- **Oceanic Surveillance:** UUVs are used to monitor submarine movements, gather data on marine conditions, and detect underwater mines or debris. IoT sensors provide real-time feedback, while AI-driven analytics help predict potential threats or identify changes in maritime activity.
- **Autonomous Navigation:** These vehicles can operate autonomously using IoT-based navigation systems and adapt to underwater conditions (e.g. water currents, temperature changes) in real-time. AI/ML algorithms optimize the vehicle's path, ensuring the mission is completed with minimal human intervention.

3.2. Smart Surveillance and Reconnaissance Systems

The combination of IoT, AI, and ML has transformed the way surveillance and reconnaissance operations are conducted. Smart surveillance systems use interconnected IoT devices, such as cameras, drones, satellites, and ground sensors, to monitor the environment continuously (Chipatiso, 2024; Johnson, 2019; Rani et al., 2024). AI and ML algorithms process the vast amounts of data generated to enhance the effectiveness of surveillance, provide actionable insights, and automate the identification and tracking of potential threats.

3.2.1. AI-Powered Surveillance Cameras and Sensors

- **Object Detection and Classification:** Surveillance systems using AI algorithms can process data from cameras and sensors to detect and classify objects of interest, such as vehicles, individuals, or suspicious movements. ML models trained on large datasets can recognize a wide range of objects in diverse environments, improving the accuracy and speed of detection.
- **Real-Time Alerts and Reporting:** IoT sensors integrated with surveillance cameras can send real-time alerts to command centres when a potential threat is detected. AI/ML algorithms can assess the severity of the threat and determine whether immediate action (e.g. deploying a drone, activating defensive systems) is required.

- **Facial Recognition and Behaviour Analysis:** In security-sensitive areas, AI-enabled cameras can perform facial recognition to identify individuals of interest. Furthermore, ML can analyze human behaviour and movement patterns to predict hostile intent, such as an approaching ambush or a covert infiltration.

3.2.2. Autonomous Drone Surveillance

- **Continuous Reconnaissance:** Drones equipped with IoT sensors and AI-driven systems can autonomously conduct reconnaissance over large areas for extended periods (Chipatiso, 2024). These drones can avoid obstacles, change their flight paths based on real-time data, and adapt to shifting environments.
- **Predictive Intelligence Gathering:** By processing data from IoT sensors (such as radar, thermal imaging, and motion detectors), AI/ML models can predict the movement and behaviour of enemy forces. For example, drones might autonomously track the location of a high-value target and adjust their flight paths based on predictions of enemy countermeasures or attempts to escape.
- **Swarm Intelligence:** IoT-enabled drone swarms, powered by AI and ML, can conduct coordinated surveillance operations. These drones can share data with one another in real-time, optimizing coverage and adapting to unforeseen changes on the battlefield. Swarm intelligence allows for flexible, large-scale surveillance missions that are harder for adversaries to detect or counter.

3.2.3. Satellite Imaging and Geospatial Data

- **High-Resolution Imagery Analysis:** AI/ML algorithms can process satellite images and geospatial data from IoT-connected platforms to analyze terrain, monitor troop movements, and detect anomalies in real-time. For instance, AI models can identify hidden infrastructure or clandestine enemy activity based on subtle changes in the environment, such as shifts in land use or unusual patterns of vehicle movement (Johnson, 2019).
- **Data Fusion for Enhanced SA:** By combining data from multiple IoT-enabled sources, such as UAVs, ground sensors, and satellites, AI algorithms can create a more comprehensive view of the operational environment. This integrated approach ensures better-informed decisions and reduces the risk of missing critical threats (Chipatiso, 2024).

3.3. Threat Detection and Countermeasure Strategies

The primary advantage of integrating AI, ML, and IoT in defence is the ability to automatically detect and respond to threats in real-time (Rani et al., 2024). By leveraging the combined capabilities of IoT sensors, AI models, and ML algorithms, military systems can improve their ability to predict, identify, and counter threats quickly and effectively. Graphical representation of threat detection strategies is shown in Fig. 13.1.

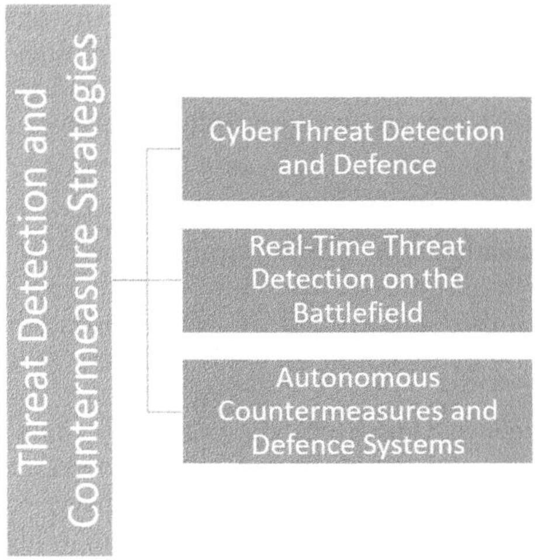

Fig. 13.1. Threat Detection and Countermeasure Strategies.

3.3.1. Cyber Threat Detection and Defence

- **Anomaly Detection:** In the context of IoT networks, cybersecurity is a critical concern. AI/ML systems can analyze patterns in network traffic from IoT devices and identify anomalies that may indicate a cyber attack or malicious activity. By using ML to continuously adapt to evolving cyber threats, defence systems can better protect IoT devices from hacking or malware attacks.
- **Automated Response Systems:** When a cyber-threat is detected, IoT-based AI systems can autonomously initiate countermeasures, such as isolating affected devices, reconfiguring network protocols, or triggering alerts to cybersecurity personnel. This reduces the time needed to mitigate threats, enabling faster recovery and minimizing damage.

3.3.2. Real-Time Threat Detection on the Battlefield

- **Missile and Projectile Detection:** IoT sensors deployed across the battlefield (such as radar, acoustic sensors, and thermal cameras) provide real-time data on incoming threats like missiles or artillery shells. AI-driven systems can instantly assess the trajectory of incoming projectiles and alert defensive systems, enabling automatic activation of countermeasures, such as active protection systems (APS) or intercepting drones (Esenogho et al., 2022; Karthikeyan et al., 2024).
- **Intrusion Detection:** ML algorithms can analyze data from ground-based IoT sensors to detect unauthorized personnel or vehicles in restricted zones. For example, an ML model trained on movement patterns might identify suspicious activity – such as the approach of an enemy combatant or a civilian vehicle straying into a military installation – and trigger an automatic security response.
- **Biometric Identification and Authentication:** AI-powered biometric systems, integrated with IoT sensors, can detect and authenticate individuals attempting

to access sensitive areas. These systems can identify hostile actors or verify the identity of personnel, reducing the chances of unauthorized infiltration.

3.3.3. Autonomous Countermeasures and Defence Systems

- **Smart Defence Systems:** AI-driven systems can control a variety of defence mechanisms, such as anti-drone technologies, anti-missile defence systems, and automated turrets (De Spiegeleire et al., 2017). These systems use IoT sensors to detect incoming threats, analyze them, and deploy appropriate countermeasures autonomously. For example, IoT sensors may detect a drone, AI algorithms analyze its size and trajectory, and the system autonomously launches a counter-drone missile or jamming signal.
- **Electronic Warfare and Jamming:** AI and IoT technologies enable military forces to deploy advanced electronic warfare strategies, such as disrupting enemy communications or GPS signals. By monitoring the electromagnetic spectrum in real-time, IoT sensors can detect signals from enemy assets, while AI-driven systems automatically decide the best method to counteract these threats, whether through jamming or spoofing.

4. Technological Challenges in AI/ML-IoT Integration in Defence

The integration of AI, ML, and the IoT in defence is transforming military operations, enhancing SA, decision-making, and operational efficiency. However, this convergence of cutting-edge technologies also presents a range of technological challenges that need to be addressed for successful deployment in defence applications (Esenogho et al., 2022). These challenges span various areas, from hardware limitations to cybersecurity concerns, and require continued innovation and collaboration to overcome. Fig. 13.2 shows the technological challenges in AI/AL-IoT integration in defence.

Fig. 13.2. Technological Challenges in AI/ML-IoT Integration in Defence.

4.1. Data Overload and Management

- **High Volume of Data:** IoT devices in defence generate vast amounts of real-time data from sensors, cameras, drones, vehicles, and other connected systems. Managing and processing this data efficiently is one of the most significant technological challenges. Large-scale data management systems need to handle this information, ensuring that only relevant data is retained and processed.
- **Data Integration:** IoT devices in defence typically use different communication protocols and generate data in various formats. Integrating data from diverse IoT devices into a coherent, unified system for analysis requires robust **data fusion** and **interoperability** solutions, which are often complex and require significant computational resources.

4.2. Latency and Real-Time Processing

- **Low Latency Requirements:** In defence operations, real-time decision-making s critical, and any delay in data processing can lead to missed opportunities or failure to respond to imminent threats. AI/ML models need to process and analyze data from IoT sensors instantly, and **edge computing** is often used to reduce latency. However, this increases the complexity of the network architecture and demands advanced algorithms that can work in real-time across distributed devices.
- **Bandwidth and Network Constraints:** In remote or hostile environments, maintaining reliable communication and sufficient bandwidth between IoT devices, sensors, and command centres can be challenging. Network disruptions or limited bandwidth can slow down data transmission, causing delays in SA and decision-making.

4.3. Security and Cybersecurity

- **IoT Security Vulnerabilities:** The more interconnected the IoT devices, the larger the attack surface. IoT devices in defence are often targets for cyberattacks, and securing these devices is crucial. They may be vulnerable to hacking, data breaches, or denial-of-service (DoS) attacks, compromising the integrity of military operations.
- **AI/ML Security Threats:** AI and ML models themselves can be vulnerable to adversarial attacks, where slight manipulations of input data can cause the models to make incorrect predictions or decisions. This poses a risk when AI/ML systems are used in mission-critical applications such as autonomous weapon systems or surveillance.
- **Encryption and Authentication:** Strong encryption protocols are necessary for securing the communication channels between IoT devices. Additionally, ensuring proper authentication of devices and users is essential to prevent unauthorized access and tampering with IoT networks and systems.

4.4. Hardware and Power Constraints

- **Battery Life and Power Consumption:** Many IoT devices in defence, especially those used in autonomous systems (drones, ground vehicles), rely on battery power. The energy consumption of these devices, especially those utilizing advanced AI/ML algorithms for processing data, can quickly drain battery life (Chandra & Suresh, 2024). Ensuring that IoT devices operate for extended periods in the field without frequent recharging is a significant challenge.
- **Durability and Ruggedization:** IoT devices deployed in military environments must be durable enough to withstand extreme conditions such as high temperatures, humidity, dust, shock, and vibrations. The hardware must be ruggedized to ensure reliable performance even in the most hostile environments.

4.5. Scalability and Integration Complexity

- **Integration with Legacy Systems:** Defence organizations often have complex, legacy systems in place, and integrating new AI/ML-IoT solutions with these existing systems can be difficult (Alcántara Suárez & Monzon Baeza, 2023). Ensuring compatibility between modern IoT sensors and older platforms requires time, expertise, and custom development.
- **Scalability Issues:** As military operations scale up, so do the requirements for data processing, network bandwidth, and computational power. Ensuring that AI/ML-IoT systems can scale to meet these demands while maintaining performance is a critical challenge.

5. Ethical and Operational Considerations in AI/ML-IoT in Defence

The use of AI/ML-driven IoT systems in defence raises important ethical and operational considerations (Sharma et al., 2021). These issues must be addressed to ensure that technology is used responsibly, safely, and in accordance with international law and human rights standards.

5.1. Autonomous Weapon Systems and Ethical Implications

- **Autonomy in Lethal Decision-Making:** AI-driven autonomous weapons, such as drones and unmanned ground vehicles, can make decisions about the use of force with minimal human intervention. This raises ethical concerns about accountability and responsibility. If an autonomous system makes an incorrect or harmful decision (e.g. targeting civilians), it may be difficult to assign responsibility.
- **Compliance with International Laws:** Autonomous systems must comply with international humanitarian laws, including the Geneva Conventions, which govern the conduct of war. Ensuring that AI systems are designed to comply with these laws and adhere to principles such as proportionality and distinction (i.e. distinguishing between combatants and civilians) is a complex ethical challenge.

5.2. Privacy and Surveillance

- **Mass Surveillance Risks:** IoT devices, such as surveillance cameras, drones, and biometric systems, can be used to monitor individuals in real time, raising concerns about privacy. In defence applications, especially in civilian areas, the potential for overreach and abuse of surveillance capabilities is a significant ethical issue.
- **Data Privacy:** The data collected by IoT devices often includes sensitive information, such as biometric data, health metrics, and location data. How this data is stored, shared, and used needs to be carefully managed to ensure that privacy rights are not violated.

5.3. Bias and Fairness in AI/ML Models

- **Algorithmic Bias:** AI and ML models used in defence applications, such as target identification or threat detection, are trained on large datasets (Alharbi et al., 2022). If these datasets are biased, the AI models may produce inaccurate or discriminatory results. For example, facial recognition systems may be less accurate for certain ethnic groups, leading to unfair treatment or wrongful targeting.
- **Transparency and Accountability:** As AI/ML systems are increasingly used to make critical decisions in military operations, ensuring that these systems are transparent and accountable is essential. Defence organizations need to develop mechanisms for auditing AI systems, understanding how decisions are made, and ensuring that they align with ethical and legal standards.

5.4. Human Oversight and Control

- **Human-in-the-Loop (HITL) Systems:** While autonomy is a key feature of many AI/ML-IoT systems, human oversight remains critical, especially in high-stakes military operations. Ensuring that humans maintain control over AI-driven systems – particularly those that involve the use of force – helps mitigate the risks of unintended escalation, errors, and ethical breaches (Chipatiso, 2024).
- **Decision-Making Transparency:** Ensuring that AI systems used in defence are interpretable and explainable is important for decision-making transparency. When critical decisions are being made, operators must be able to understand the reasoning behind the system's recommendations or actions.

6. Future Trends and Directions

As technology continues to evolve, the integration of AI, ML, and IoT in defence is expected to advance in several key areas. These advancements will enable more efficient, autonomous, and intelligent defence systems, but they will also introduce new challenges and considerations.

6.1. Advanced Autonomous Systems and Swarm Robotics

- **Swarm Intelligence:** One of the most promising directions for AI/ML-IoT in defence is the development of swarm robotics – groups of autonomous systems (drones, ground vehicles, robots) that can work together to perform complex tasks. These systems communicate with one another in real time, sharing data and making collective decisions to enhance SA and execute missions more efficiently.

- **Collaborative Autonomous Systems:** The future of autonomous defence systems will likely involve more collaboration between human operators and autonomous machines. AI-powered systems will assist soldiers on the ground by providing real-time analysis, suggesting optimal strategies, and performing support functions, such as resupply or reconnaissance, without direct human control.

6.2. AI-Powered Predictive Analytics and Decision-Making

- **Predictive Warfare:** AI and ML will continue to play a pivotal role in enabling predictive warfare, where military forces anticipate enemy actions, adapt to changing conditions, and take proactive measures (Alcántara Suárez & Monzon Baeza, 2023; Mohanta et al., 2020; Pasdar et al., 2024; Sharma et al., 2021). By processing vast amounts of real-time data from IoT sensors, AI systems will identify trends and make predictions about the future battlefield environment, improving decision-making and operational readiness.
- **Smart Command and Control Systems:** Command centres will evolve into AI-driven hubs that synthesize data from IoT devices, process this data with ML algorithms, and provide commanders with actionable insights in real-time. These systems will integrate various sensor data (ground, aerial, satellite) and create predictive models that help decision-makers plan missions and allocate resources more effectively.

6.3. Quantum Computing and AI-Enhanced Defence Systems

- **Quantum Computing:** The rise of quantum computing promises to revolutionize defence capabilities, particularly in areas like cryptography, materials science, and AI/ML applications. Quantum algorithms could enhance data processing speeds and enable more advanced ML models for real-time decision-making (Esenogho et al., 2022; Karthikeyan et al., 2024).
- **AI-Driven Cyber Defence:** As quantum computing evolves, so will the need for more advanced AI-based cyber defence systems. These systems will be capable of automatically detecting and countering cyber threats, ensuring the security of IoT networks and preventing adversaries from exploiting vulnerabilities in defence systems.

6.4. Integration of 5G and Edge Computing for IoT in Defence

- **5G Networks:** The integration of 5G networks with IoT systems will enhance the speed and reliability. By merging decentralized edge computing with ultra-fast 5G networks, 5G edge computing makes it possible to process data and make decisions in real-time right at the edge of the network. By incorporating 5G, this system takes advantage of the new generation of networks' superior data transfer speeds, reduced latency, and expanded capacity.

7. Conclusion

The integration of AI, ML, and the IoT is revolutionizing modern defence systems, enabling enhanced SA, predictive analytics, autonomous operations, and optimized logistics. By harnessing real-time data from interconnected IoT devices, AI-driven algorithms can detect threats, automate decision-making, and improve overall operational efficiency. Autonomous drones, robotic combat units, and AI-powered cybersecurity frameworks are reshaping defence strategies, reducing human risks, and ensuring rapid response to emerging threats. However, alongside these advancements, challenges such as cybersecurity vulnerabilities, ethical concerns, and technological interoperability must be addressed to ensure responsible deployment. As defence forces worldwide continue to adopt and refine these technologies, the synergy of AI, ML, and IoT will play an increasingly pivotal role in strengthening national security and redefining the future of warfare.

References

Ahmed, N. U. (2022). Integrating machine learning in military intelligence process: Study of futuristic approaches towards human-machine collaboration. *NDC e-journal*, *2*(1), 59–89.

Alcántara Suárez, E. J., & Monzon Baeza, V. (2023). Evaluating the role of machine learning in defense applications and industry. *Machine Learning and Knowledge Extraction*, *5*(4), 1557–1569.

Alharbi, S., Attiah, A., & Alghazzawi, D. (2022). Integrating blockchain with artificial intelligence to secure IoT networks: Future trends. *Sustainability*, *14*(23), 16002.

bin Zainuddin, A. A., Sairin, H., Mazlan, I. A., Muslim, N. N. A., & Sabarudin, W. A. S. W. (2024). Enhancing IoT security: A synergy of machine learning, artificial intelligence, and blockchain. *Data Science Insights*, *2*(1), 1–11.

Chandra, A. D. A., & Suresh, L. (2024). Role of Artificial Intelligence on Indigenization in the Indian Defence Industry. *Anvesha*, *16*(1), 1–15.

Chipatiso, E. (2024). Application of GIS and artificial intelligence in military operations: Prospects and challenges. *Space Science Journal*, *1*(2), 01–07.

De Spiegeleire, S., Maas, M., & Sweijs, T. (2017). *Artificial intelligence and the future of defense: strategic implications for small-and medium-sized force providers*. The Hague Centre for Strategic Studies.

Dixit, S., Maurya, M., Jain, V., & Subramaniam, G. (Eds.). (2024). *Artificial Intelligence-Enabled Businesses: How to Develop Strategies for Innovation*. John Wiley & Sons.

Esenogho, E., Djouani, K., & Kurien, A. M. (2022). Integrating artificial intelligence Internet of Things and 5G for next-generation smartgrid: A survey of trends challenges and prospect. *IEEE Access*, *10*, 4794–4831.

Johnson, J. (2019). Artificial intelligence & future warfare: Implications for international security. *Defense & Security Analysis*, *35*(2), 147–169.

Karthikeyan, M., Manimegalai, D., & RajaGopal, K. (2024). Firefly algorithm based WSN-IoT security enhancement with machine learning for intrusion detection. *Scientific Reports*, *14*(1), 231.

Mahmood, M. R., Matin, M. A., Sarigiannidis, P., & Goudos, S. K. (2022). A comprehensive review on artificial intelligence/machine learning algorithms for empowering the future IoT toward 6G era. *IEEE Access*, *10*, 87535–87562.

Mohanta, B. K., Jena, D., Satapathy, U., & Patnaik, S. (2020). Survey on IoT security: Challenges and solution using machine learning, artificial intelligence and blockchain technology. *Internet of Things*, *11*, 100227.

Pasdar, A., Koroniotis, N., Keshk, M., Moustafa, N., & Tari, Z. (2024). Cybersecurity solutions and techniques for Internet of Things integration in combat systems. *IEEE Transactions on Sustainable Computing*, *10*(2), 345–365.

Radanliev, P., De Roure, D., Page, K., Van Kleek, M., Santos, O., Maddox, L. T., & Maple, C. (2020). Design of a dynamic and self-adapting system, supported with artificial intelligence, machine learning and real-time intelligence for predictive cyber risk analytics in extreme environments–cyber risk in the colonisation of Mars. *Safety in Extreme Environments*, *2*, 219–230.

Rani, S., Kumar, N., Srivastva, A., & Sharma, A. (2024, October). Leveraging artificial intelligence and machine learning for enhanced privacy and security. In *2024 IEEE International conference on blockchain and distributed systems security (ICBDS)* (pp. 1–6). IEEE.

Sarker, I. H., Khan, A. I., Abushark, Y. B., & Alsolami, F. (2023). Internet of things (IoT) security intelligence: a comprehensive overview, machine learning solutions and research directions. *Mobile Networks and Applications*, *28*(1), 296–312.

Sharma, P., Jain, S., Gupta, S., & Chamola, V. (2021). Role of machine learning and deep learning in securing 5G-driven industrial IoT applications. *Ad Hoc Networks*, *123*, 102685.

Weng, Y. (2024). Big data and machine learning in defence. *International Journal of Computer Science and Information Technology*, *16*(2), 25–35.

Chapter 14

Future Directions in IoT-Driven Defence Technologies: Opportunities and Challenges

Karuna Sahu[a], *Snehlata Kumari*[b], *Inderjeet Singh*[c] *and R. K. Srivastava*[d]

[a]*Accenture India, India*
[b]*School of Physics, Engineering and Computer Science, University of Hertfordshire, UK*
[c]*Vara Technology, India*
[d]*Department of Computer Science, Dr. Shakuntala Misra National Rehabilitation University, India*

Abstract

The integration of Internet of Things (IoT) technologies into the defence sector is transforming modern military operations by enhancing surveillance, logistics, predictive maintenance (PdM), battlefield management, and autonomous weaponry. IoT enables real-time intelligence gathering, improves decision-making, and optimizes operational efficiency through interconnected sensors, drones, and AI-driven analytics. However, its adoption also introduces critical cybersecurity risks, including vulnerabilities to cyberattacks, state-sponsored threats, and data breaches. Additionally, ethical and legal challenges surrounding autonomous military systems raise concerns about accountability and compliance with international regulations. As defence technologies evolve, the integration of 5G, artificial intelligence (AI), machine learning (ML), and blockchain is expected to enhance security and automation in IoT-enabled defence systems. To fully harness its potential, governments and military organizations must address key challenges related to cybersecurity, interoperability, and ethical governance. This chapter explores the opportunities, risks, and

The Internet of Things in the Defence Industry: Challenges and Solutions for Military Security, 281–306

doi:10.1108/978-1-83549-198-020261015

future directions of IoT in defence, providing strategic insights into its role in modern warfare and national security.

Keywords: IoT in defence; military cybersecurity; autonomous weaponry; real-time intelligence; defence technology integration

1. Introduction

The integration of IoT technologies into defence applications is revolutionizing modern military operations, significantly enhancing capabilities in surveillance, logistics, PdM, battlefield management, and autonomous weaponry. The growing interconnectivity of military assets and real-time data exchange enables defence forces to improve situational awareness, enhance decision-making processes, and optimize operational efficiency (Seet et al., 2024). From smart sensors deployed across battlefields to AI-driven predictive analytics in supply chains, IoT is fostering an era of intelligent, networked defence ecosystems.

One of the most transformative advantages of IoT in defence is its ability to facilitate real-time intelligence gathering and data-driven strategic operations. By leveraging interconnected sensors, drones, and unmanned systems, military forces can effectively monitor adversarial activities, track hostile movements, and automate threat detection with unprecedented accuracy (Konstantellos, 2022). Additionally, IoT-driven logistics and asset management ensure that personnel, weaponry, and critical equipment are maintained, monitored, and deployed efficiently. Autonomous systems, including robotic combat units and AI-powered command centres, are redefining military engagement strategies, improving responsiveness and precision in combat scenarios (Nayak et al., 2023).

Despite its immense potential, the adoption of IoT in defence introduces significant challenges and risks. One of the primary concerns is cybersecurity. As defence infrastructure becomes increasingly interconnected, the risks of cyberattacks, hacking, and data breaches escalate. State-sponsored cyber warfare, sophisticated malware, and advanced persistent threats (APTs) pose critical dangers to IoT-enabled defence networks. Additionally, the ethical and legal implications of autonomous military technologies raise concerns about decision-making in combat, accountability for system failures, and compliance with international laws and conventions (Adil et al., 2024). The vast collection and processing of sensitive defence data further introduce challenges related to privacy, data protection, and information security.

As military technologies continue to evolve, the future of IoT in defence operations is poised for transformative advancements. The integration of 5G, AI, ML, and blockchain into IoT-based defence systems is expected to enhance security, automation, and operational efficiency. However, to fully harness the potential of IoT in defence, governments, military organizations, and defence technology developers must address pressing concerns related to cybersecurity, interoperability, and ethical governance (Verma et al., 2022).

This chapter explores the emerging trends, opportunities, and challenges associated with IoT in the defence sector. By examining the technological, ethical, and operational landscape, we aim to provide strategic insights into how nations can leverage IoT for military superiority while mitigating the associated risks.

2. Emerging Trends in IoT for Defence

The IoT landscape is rapidly evolving, with cutting-edge innovations enabling more efficient and effective defence operations. In particular, defence systems are increasingly incorporating IoT-driven technologies to enhance real-time situational awareness, optimize maintenance routines, and improve battlefield coordination (Verma et al., 2022). The following trends are expected to significantly influence the future of IoT in defence.

2.1. Advanced Sensor Integration

Advanced sensor integration in IoT-driven defence technologies is revolutionizing military operations by providing real-time situational awareness, enhancing decision-making, and enabling autonomous systems. By integrating diverse sensor networks with IoT capabilities, defence systems can leverage real-time data from multiple sources, including environmental, tactical, and operational sensors (Gadekallu et al., 2021). This integration facilitates smarter, more efficient, and more secure military operations. Here's an overview of how advanced sensor integration works in the context of IoT-driven defence technologies.

2.1.1. Key Components of Advanced Sensor Integration in Defence

2.1.1.1. IoT-Enabled Sensor Networks. The backbone of IoT-driven defence systems is the use of a variety of sensors interconnected through wireless networks (Gadekallu et al., 2021). These sensors monitor a broad spectrum of conditions such as environmental data (e.g. temperature, humidity, atmospheric pressure), battlefield information (e.g. troop location, weapon status), and vehicle health (e.g. fuel levels, engine temperature).

Examples of Sensors

- Radar and Sonar: For detecting enemy aircraft, ships, or submarines.
- Infrared (IR) Sensors: To detect heat signatures, useful for detecting enemy vehicles or personnel.
- Seismic Sensors: For detecting underground movements (e.g. tunnels or enemy troops).
- Chemical, Biological, Radiological, and Nuclear (CBRN) Sensors: To detect chemical, biological, or nuclear threats.
- Wearable Sensors: Monitoring soldier health and vital signs in real-time (e.g. heart rate, temperature, motion).

2.1.1.2. Real-Time Data Fusion and Analytics. Advanced data fusion is a critical part of sensor integration in defence IoT systems. Multiple sensors are used to gather diverse data that is then combined to create a coherent, actionable intelligence picture. This allows for better situational awareness and faster decision-making (Gadekallu et al., 2021).

Data Fusion Techniques

- Kalman Filters: Used for tracking and estimating the state of a system based on noisy sensor data (e.g. predicting the position of a moving target).
- Sensor Fusion Algorithms: Combining inputs from cameras, radars, LIDAR, and other sensors to generate a unified view of the environment.
- ML: Algorithms can analyze large sensor datasets to detect patterns, predict outcomes, and provide recommendations for action.

2.1.1.3. Autonomous Platforms and Drones. Autonomous vehicles, unmanned aerial vehicles (UAVs), and drones are becoming integral in defence systems (Suhail et al., 2020). These platforms rely heavily on sensor integration to perform reconnaissance, surveillance, and even targeted strikes autonomously.

Key Technologies

- LIDAR and Computer Vision: Used for obstacle detection and autonomous navigation.
- GPS and IMUs (Inertial Measurement Units): For precise positioning and navigation in both land and aerial vehicles.
- Edge Computing: Processing sensor data on the device (e.g. UAV) itself, allowing for low-latency decision-making.

These platforms use advanced sensor integration to autonomously execute missions such as:

- Surveillance and reconnaissance;
- Monitoring and patrolling borders or sensitive areas;
- Deploying payloads or precision-guided munitions;
- Real-time communication with command centres.

2.1.1.4. PdM & Logistics. PdM is a significant advantage of integrating sensors in military hardware (e.g. aircraft, tanks, and naval vessels). IoT sensors continuously monitor the condition of these assets, transmitting health data to central servers for analysis (Khalil et al., 2022). Predictive analytics then forecast failures, allowing maintenance teams to take proactive action.

Examples

- Vibration sensors monitor engines or mechanical components.
- Temperature sensors detect overheating in critical systems.
- Pressure sensors help monitor hydraulic systems.
- AI-driven models predict failures or service needs before they occur, reducing downtime and ensuring operational readiness.

Logistics operations also benefit from sensor-enabled tracking of equipment, ammunition, and supplies. GPS-enabled sensors track the movement of troops and assets in real time, ensuring optimal resupply routes and improving overall mission efficiency.

2.1.1.5. Cybersecurity and Threat Detection. Advanced sensor networks can also be used to protect military assets from cyber threats (Khalil et al., 2022). By integrating physical and digital security sensors, IoT systems in defence can detect, isolate, and neutralize cyber threats in real-time.

Examples

- Network Intrusion Detection Systems (NIDS): Use sensors to monitor for unusual activity within military communication networks.
- Physical Access Control: Sensors to track the location of sensitive military equipment and personnel.
- Anomaly Detection: AI-powered algorithms to monitor network traffic and detect anomalous behaviour that might indicate a cyberattack.

2.1.1.6. Geospatial Intelligence and Situational Awareness. IoT sensor networks play a critical role in battlefield geospatial intelligence (GEOINT). Data from satellite imagery, UAVs, and ground-based sensors can be combined to produce high-definition maps that support decision-making (Krejčí et al., 2025). This includes:

- Mapping terrain in real-time, factoring in obstacles, weather, and terrain conditions.
- Real-time tracking of enemy troop movements or vehicles.
- Visual and IR data fusion to identify enemy positions or threats.

2.1.1.7. Smart Military Clothing and Wearables. Advanced sensors integrated into military uniforms and equipment provide significant advantages for personnel monitoring. These wearables continuously track the health and status of soldiers, improving safety and operational efficiency.

Examples

- Biometric Sensors: Track vital signs (e.g. heart rate, temperature, fatigue levels) to monitor soldiers' health and prevent heatstroke or exhaustion.
- Exoskeletons: Equipped with sensors to enhance soldier mobility and reduce fatigue, with the additional capability of monitoring physical strain on the body.
- Location Tracking: GPS-enabled wearables can monitor soldiers' location and movements in real time, providing tactical commanders with up-to-date positions.

2.1.1.8. Cognitive and Decision Support Systems. Sensor data can be fed into advanced decision support systems that leverage AI and ML algorithms to assist military personnel in decision-making (Krejčí et al., 2025). These systems analyze incoming data streams from IoT sensors, providing predictive insights and recommendations for actions.

Key Features

- AI-Driven Threat Analysis: Analyzes sensor data to identify potential threats (e.g. unauthorized movements, hostile intent) and suggests appropriate responses.
- Tactical Decision Support: Assists commanders in making informed, real-time decisions based on a comprehensive view of the battlefield.

2.1.2. Key Benefits of Advanced Sensor Integration in Defence

- **Improved Situational Awareness:** Real-time, integrated data from diverse sensors enhances operational visibility, ensuring commanders can make informed decisions with accurate, up-to-date information.
- **Enhanced Operational Efficiency:** IoT sensor networks allow for continuous monitoring of equipment and troops, reducing downtime, improving mission planning, and increasing resource optimization (Tawalbeh et al., 2020).
- **Autonomy and Remote Operations:** Autonomous systems powered by sensor integration reduce the need for human intervention in high-risk areas, allowing for safer, more precise missions.
- **PdM and Readiness:** Predictive models powered by sensor data ensure military assets are always mission-ready, reducing costly repairs and improving logistics efficiency (Chataut et al., 2023).
- **Cybersecurity and Secure Communication:** IoT sensors can monitor network activity for any signs of intrusion, providing proactive defence against cyberattacks that may target critical military infrastructure.
- **Rapid Response and Adaptation:** The fusion of sensor data with real-time AI decision-making ensures that defence forces can rapidly respond to dynamic battlefield conditions, enhancing tactical agility (Tawalbeh et al., 2020).

2.1.3. Challenges and Considerations

- **Data Overload:** Managing and processing large volumes of data from multiple sensor sources in real-time can overwhelm existing infrastructure, requiring advanced computing capabilities and network solutions (Srivastava & Pandey, 2022).
- **Security:** Sensor data in defence systems needs to be encrypted and securely transmitted to prevent unauthorized access or tampering. The IoT infrastructure must be resilient to cyber threats.
- **Interoperability:** Different sensor types (e.g. IR, radar, acoustic) and devices may use different protocols or standards, requiring seamless integration for effective operation.

At the heart of IoT for defence applications lies the integration of advanced sensors. These sensors – ranging from environmental sensors to biometric monitoring tools – are essential for gathering data in real-time and supporting decision-making (Srivastava & Pandey, 2022). Advanced sensors embedded within IoT systems enable soldiers and military equipment to capture vast amounts of data that can be processed for actionable intelligence.

In future military scenarios, sensor integration will likely expand to include a more extensive range of capabilities (Srivastava & Pandey, 2022). For example, next-generation smart helmets could integrate biosensors, providing data on soldiers' physiological conditions while also collecting environmental data (e.g. temperature, air quality). Similarly, autonomous vehicles will use advanced sensors to detect and avoid threats, monitor terrain, and adjust tactics in real time. These sensors will operate seamlessly within larger IoT systems, transmitting data to central command hubs or edge devices for rapid processing.

2.2. Edge Computing for Real-Time Decision-Making

Edge computing for real-time decision-making in IoT-driven defence technologies is transforming how military and defence systems process data, enabling faster, more efficient, and highly responsive operations. By decentralizing computation and bringing it closer to the source of data generation (i.e. the 'edge'), this approach is revolutionizing the ability to make critical decisions in real-time (Reshi & Sholla, 2022). In defence scenarios, where speed, accuracy, and reliability are paramount, edge computing helps overcome the latency and bandwidth limitations that traditional cloud computing models face. This is particularly important when deploying IoT-enabled systems across dynamic, geographically dispersed, and often hostile environments.

2.2.1. Key Concepts of Edge Computing in IoT-Driven Defence Technologies

a. Edge Computing

- Definition: Edge computing involves processing data locally, on devices or edge servers, rather than sending it to centralized cloud servers for analysis. This enables near-instantaneous data processing and decision-making, crucial in time-sensitive military operations (Majid et al., 2022).

Examples: Edge devices could include UAVs, autonomous ground vehicles (AGVs), soldier-worn sensors, tactical communication hubs, or sensors on military hardware (e.g. tanks, aircraft).

b. Real-Time Decision-Making

- The integration of real-time decision-making into military systems through edge computing allows for immediate responses based on sensor inputs, without the delay of transmitting data to a central server. This is essential in situations where split-second decisions can impact mission success or soldier safety (Majid et al., 2022).

c. IoT in Defence

- IoT: IoT involves a network of interconnected devices (such as sensors, vehicles, and wearables) that continuously exchange data. In defence, IoT sensors monitor everything from environmental conditions (e.g. radiation,

temperature) to personnel health and equipment status, enabling smarter, more agile defence systems.
- With IoT-enabled systems, edge computing allows decision-making algorithms to process data from multiple sensor sources quickly, in real-time, improving tactical awareness, mission efficiency, and asset protection.

2.2.2. Benefits of Edge Computing for Real-Time Decision-Making in IoT-Driven Defence

a. Reduced Latency for Mission-Critical Decisions

- Key Challenge: In defence operations, especially on the battlefield, real-time decisions are often required in high-stress, rapidly evolving situations. Delays in processing or transmitting data to distant cloud servers can lead to disastrous consequences (Majid et al., 2022).
- Edge Solution: By processing data on-site, near the source (e.g. drones, tanks, soldier wearables), edge computing dramatically reduces latency, providing military personnel with actionable insights and enabling instantaneous decision-making.

b. Enhanced Situational Awareness

- Data Fusion at the Edge: IoT-enabled devices (e.g. UAVs, sensors, wearable tech) in defence systems produce vast amounts of data. Edge computing allows for local data fusion – combining inputs from different sensors (e.g. IR, radar, GPS, accelerometers) to create a unified picture of the environment (Boudouaia et al., 2024).
- This means soldiers or autonomous systems can react to threats or opportunities faster, based on a comprehensive, real-time understanding of the situation.

c. Autonomy and Self-Sufficiency

- Autonomous Systems: UAVs, unmanned ground vehicles (UGVs), and other autonomous defence platforms rely on edge computing to make autonomous decisions without requiring constant communication with centralized servers (Majid et al., 2022).
- Examples:
    - o A drone can navigate an area, identify targets, and make decisions (e.g. avoid obstacles, change flight path) autonomously based on real-time sensor inputs (e.g. LIDAR, cameras).
    - o Autonomous vehicles (e.g. military trucks, tanks) can assess environmental data and make adjustments to their routes, even in the absence of reliable communication with command centres.

d. Improved Reliability in Disconnected Environments

- Communication Denial: On the battlefield or in remote areas, communication with cloud or central servers might be unreliable due to electronic warfare, jamming, or terrain challenges. Edge computing ensures systems can continue to function independently, even when disconnected from central networks, by allowing critical decisions to be made on the edge (Boudouaia et al., 2024).
- Example: In a military operation in a hostile environment, IoT sensors and edge devices can continue operating, providing data to troops or autonomous platforms for decision-making, without requiring continuous cloud connectivity.

e. Optimized Bandwidth and Resource Efficiency

- Data Reduction: Edge computing minimizes the need for transmitting large volumes of raw data over networks, reducing bandwidth usage and network congestion. Only relevant, processed data or high-priority information is sent to centralized systems, making the entire system more efficient (Boudouaia et al., 2024).
- This is especially important in defence contexts, where bandwidth is often limited and should be reserved for mission-critical communication.

f. Security and Resilience

- Local Data Processing: By processing sensitive data locally at the edge, rather than sending it over potentially vulnerable networks to centralized systems, edge computing enhances security and reduces the risk of cyberattacks (Verma & Prakash, 2020).
- Sensitive information can be encrypted and processed within localized, secure environments, ensuring that even if a communication channel is compromised, critical decisions can still be made independently.

2.2.3. Edge Computing in Specific IoT-Driven Defence Applications

a. Autonomous Vehicles and Drones

- Real-Time Navigation and Collision Avoidance: Edge computing enables drones and AGVs to process data from on-board sensors (e.g. cameras, radar, and LIDAR) to detect obstacles, navigate environments, and make decisions (e.g. take evasive action) without waiting for instructions from a central command.
- Case Study: In a military UAV deployment, edge computing allows the drone to dynamically adjust its flight path in response to changing environmental conditions (e.g. weather, threats) or to detect and avoid enemy radar systems autonomously.

b. Wearable Sensors for Soldier Health Monitoring

- Real-Time Health Monitoring: Edge computing processes data from wearable sensors (e.g. heart rate, body temperature, fatigue levels) worn by soldiers to monitor their physical condition and alert medical teams if a soldier is in distress (e.g. heat stroke, dehydration).

- Tactical Response: Soldiers' wearables can trigger alarms for immediate intervention or suggest nearby safe zones for evacuation, making the response time faster and more efficient.

c. Battlefield Surveillance and Intelligence

- Sensor Networks: IoT-enabled sensors deployed on the battlefield (e.g. seismic, acoustic, IR, motion sensors) provide continuous streams of data. Edge computing enables the local processing and filtering of this data, sending only relevant or critical information to command centres.
- Example: Edge nodes could detect enemy troop movements based on seismic sensors and analyze that data on-site. If a potential threat is detected, the system can send a brief, actionable alert to military personnel in real-time without needing to transmit full sensor data.

d. PdM for Military Assets

- Condition-Based Monitoring: Military assets, such as aircraft, tanks, or ships, are equipped with IoT sensors that monitor their operational health. Edge computing processes this sensor data locally to predict potential failures and alert maintenance crews before critical issues arise.
- Example: If a tank's engine temperature reaches a critical threshold, edge computing systems can trigger maintenance alerts in real-time, allowing the tank to either receive an immediate fix or be taken out of service before it fails in the field.

e. Cybersecurity and Threat Detection

- On-Edge Threat Analysis: Security sensors and software at the edge can detect unusual activity in local networks or devices (e.g. malware, unauthorized access) and take immediate action to mitigate or block threats before they escalate.
- Example: In a military network, an edge device could detect a potential breach attempt, isolate the compromised node, and notify commanders without relying on a centralized server to process the data.

2.2.4. Challenges and Considerations

a. Computational Limitations of Edge Devices

While edge computing enables faster decision-making, edge devices have limited computational power compared to cloud-based systems. This means that algorithms must be optimized for real-time analysis and low-resource environments, which can be challenging for complex tasks.

b. Interoperability

Defence systems often use diverse hardware and software, which may not always be compatible with edge computing platforms. Ensuring seamless integration of various IoT devices (e.g. drones, sensors, wearable devices) and edge computing solutions is critical for maximizing effectiveness.

c. Security

Edge devices in remote or contested environments may be vulnerable to tampering or cyberattacks. Ensuring the security of edge computing nodes, especially when they are operating independently, is paramount.

d. Network Reliability

While edge computing can operate without cloud connectivity, some functions may still require coordination with central systems or other edge nodes. Ensuring reliable communication in remote or challenging environments (e.g. electromagnetic interference [EMI], jamming) is a key concern.

The demand for real-time decision-making in defence operations requires significant computational power at the edge of IoT networks, near the data source, rather than relying solely on cloud computing infrastructure. Edge computing allows IoT devices to process data locally, minimizing latency and bandwidth issues, which is particularly critical in high-stakes combat scenarios.

Edge computing enables military units to analyze incoming sensor data, make quick decisions, and execute commands autonomously, all without relying on a central server. For instance, autonomous drones or robotic ground vehicles could independently assess their environment and adjust their movements or responses based on local data processing. This trend towards edge computing in defence IoT systems is expected to become more prevalent as data needs grow, and as AI-driven decision-making becomes more ingrained in defence operations.

2.3. IoT-Driven PdM in Military Equipment

IoT-driven predictive maintenance in military equipment is revolutionizing how military forces manage the upkeep and readiness of their assets. By integrating IoT sensors and advanced data analytics, PdM systems can anticipate equipment failures before they happen, improving the reliability, availability, and overall performance of military assets. This results in cost savings, enhanced operational efficiency, and the ability to proactively manage the lifecycle of critical military systems.

2.3.1. Key Concepts of IoT-Driven PdM in Military Equipment

a. Predictive Maintenance

- Definition: PdM refers to the use of data-driven techniques to predict when an asset will require maintenance or fail. It allows for timely interventions to repair or replace parts before failure occurs, reducing downtime and preventing costly emergency repairs.
- IoT Integration: IoT devices (sensors, actuators, and communication networks) are embedded in military assets to continuously monitor various

parameters (e.g. temperature, pressure, vibration, and wear) and collect data that is analyzed to forecast potential issues.

b. **Real-Time Monitoring and Data Collection**

- IoT sensors attached to military equipment like tanks, aircraft, ships, and trucks collect continuous data on operational conditions.
- Key Sensors: Vibration sensors, temperature sensors, pressure sensors, fluid sensors, accelerometers, and strain gauges are used to monitor mechanical components, engines, and other critical systems.
- Example: An aircraft's engine might have vibration and temperature sensors to monitor for abnormal conditions such as overheating or excessive vibration, which could indicate imminent failure.

c. **Data Analysis and ML**

- Data Processing: The data collected from IoT sensors is transmitted to either local edge devices or a central cloud platform for analysis. In many cases, this involves sophisticated analytics algorithms that detect patterns and anomalies indicative of wear, fatigue, or degradation.
- ML: Advanced ML models analyze historical data and predict the likelihood of failure based on trends, environmental factors, operational conditions, and usage patterns. The system then generates maintenance alerts or schedules maintenance when certain thresholds are crossed.
- Example: If the vibration pattern of a tank's engine deviates from the historical norm, predictive algorithms will flag this as a potential issue and suggest maintenance before the engine fails.

d. **Communication Infrastructure**

The data collected from IoT sensors on military equipment is transmitted via secure communication networks (e.g. encrypted wireless protocols or dedicated military communication systems). These networks ensure that equipment health data is transmitted in real-time to relevant maintenance teams or command centres.

e. **Edge Computing**

- In some scenarios, edge computing is employed to process and analyze data locally (on the equipment itself or nearby edge devices), reducing the need for constant communication with centralized cloud servers. This is particularly useful for situations where low latency or limited network bandwidth is crucial.
- Example: If a sensor on a military vehicle detects a potential failure (such as an oil pressure drop), the edge device can trigger an immediate local alert, allowing maintenance crews to act before the issue worsens.

2.3.2. Benefits of IoT-Driven PdM for Military Equipment

a. **Increased Equipment Availability and Reliability**

- By identifying problems early, PdM minimizes unscheduled downtime, ensuring that military assets are operational and available when needed.

For example, a combat vehicle that remains in service longer due to timely maintenance can provide sustained tactical support.

- Example: Regular monitoring of helicopter rotor systems might predict a fault before a mission, allowing for repairs during routine downtime rather than in the middle of a critical operation.

b. **Cost Savings**

- PdM reduces the need for expensive emergency repairs and extends the lifespan of military equipment by addressing wear and tear before it leads to catastrophic failures. Preventive repairs are often less costly than reactive repairs.
- Example: By detecting a potential engine failure in a military truck early, the system can prompt a maintenance team to replace a worn-out component before it causes a total engine failure, saving both time and money.

c. **Optimized Maintenance Schedules**

- Traditional maintenance schedules for military equipment often rely on predefined intervals (e.g. based on hours of operation) rather than the actual condition of the equipment. IoT-driven PdM adjusts maintenance schedules based on real-time equipment health data, ensuring maintenance is only done when necessary.
- Example: Instead of performing scheduled maintenance on a vehicle every 500 operating hours, PdM will trigger maintenance only when sensors detect the first signs of wear, such as a hydraulic system losing pressure.

d. **Enhanced Operational Readiness**

- Military operations are highly time-sensitive, and the ability to predict and prevent equipment failures directly impacts mission success. PdM ensures that equipment is always ready for deployment, improving the force's overall operational effectiveness.
- Example: In an emergency situation, a military helicopter that has undergone PdM is less likely to fail mid-flight, ensuring that air support is available when needed.

e. **Data-Driven Decision Making**

- IoT sensors generate large amounts of data, which can be analyzed to identify trends and optimize asset utilization. Military leaders can make data-driven decisions about when and where to deploy assets, considering their maintenance needs and current operational status (Boudouaia et al., 2024).
- Example: Military planners could use PdM data to prioritize the deployment of equipment that has recently undergone servicing, while deferring missions for assets that are near their predicted failure point.

f. **Increased Safety**

- By identifying and addressing potential failures before they occur, PdM ensures that soldiers and personnel are not put in dangerous situations due to faulty or unmaintained equipment (Majid et al., 2022).

- Example: Detecting a brake failure in a military vehicle before it occurs can prevent accidents that could result in personnel injuries or loss of equipment.

2.3.3. Examples of IoT-Driven PdM in Military Equipment

a. Tanks and Armoured Vehicles

- Sensors Used: Vibration sensors, pressure sensors, oil quality sensors, temperature sensors, and GPS.
- PdM: IoT sensors continuously monitor the critical components of tanks, such as engines, suspension systems, and drivetrain, for signs of abnormal wear or failure. If sensors detect increased vibrations in the suspension system or abnormal temperatures in the engine, a PdM system can alert military personnel to schedule repairs before a failure occurs during combat operations.

b. Military Aircraft

- Sensors Used: Fuel pressure sensors, engine temperature sensors, vibration sensors, and cockpit instrumentation.
- PdM: Aircraft, particularly fighter jets and helicopters, are equipped with IoT sensors that monitor engine health, fuel system pressure, and airframe integrity. The data can predict engine wear, fuel system malfunctions, or structural weaknesses, prompting timely maintenance before flight missions (Reshi & Sholla, 2022).

c. Naval Vessels and Submarines

- Sensors Used: Propulsion system sensors, water flow sensors, engine temperature sensors, and corrosion detection sensors.
- PdM: IoT sensors can monitor the propulsion systems of naval vessels, ensuring that critical components such as turbines and motors are functioning optimally. For submarines, sensors can monitor hull integrity for potential breaches or corrosion, prompting maintenance or inspections at the optimal time.

d. Unmanned Aerial Vehicles

- Sensors Used: Battery health sensors, motor temperature sensors, flight control system sensors, and GPS (Chataut et al., 2023; Reshi & Sholla, 2022; Srivastava & Pandey, 2022).
- PdM: UAVs, including drones used for surveillance or targeted strikes, rely on IoT sensors to monitor battery life, motor health, and flight systems. PdM algorithms can forecast when batteries will require replacement or when the motors are showing signs of wear, allowing UAVs to remain operational for extended periods.

e. Military Trucks and Ground Vehicles

- Sensors Used: Engine diagnostics sensors, tire pressure sensors, oil quality sensors, and hydraulic system sensors (Chataut et al., 2023).
- PdM: IoT sensors on military trucks track engine performance, tire health, and oil conditions. If a sensor detects low tire pressure or engine oil

contamination, a PdM alert is generated, reducing the risk of breakdowns during military operations.

2.3.4. Challenges and Considerations

a. Data Security and Privacy

- Military equipment is highly sensitive, and ensuring the security of data generated by IoT devices is critical. Any breach could expose vulnerabilities or compromise mission-critical systems.
- Solution: Implementing robust encryption, secure communication channels, and cybersecurity protocols to safeguard sensor data.

b. Integration with Legacy Systems

- Many military assets are older and may not have IoT sensors built into them. Retrofitting these systems with IoT capabilities can be costly and technically challenging (Srivastava & Pandey, 2022).
- Solution: Developing modular, interoperable IoT sensor kits that can be added to existing military assets without requiring major modifications.

c. Power and Reliability in Harsh Environments

- Military environments are often harsh, with extreme temperatures, vibrations, and exposure to dust or water. IoT sensors must be robust and reliable under these conditions to ensure continuous monitoring.
- Solution: Using rugged, military-grade IoT sensors designed for extreme environments and ensuring redundancy in critical systems.

d. Data Overload

- The sheer volume of data generated by IoT sensors can overwhelm analysis systems, especially in large-scale military operations.
- Solution: Implementing edge computing and real-time analytics to process data locally and only transmit relevant information to central systems.

The PdM of military equipment is another area where IoT technologies are likely to revolutionize defence operations. By embedding IoT sensors in military vehicles, aircraft, and other critical equipment, real-time data about the condition of the systems can be gathered (Awasthi et al., 2025; Verma & Prakash, 2020). This data can be analyzed to predict potential failures before they occur, enabling proactive maintenance and reducing downtime. PdM solutions leverage ML algorithms that process data from IoT sensors to identify patterns and anomalies that may indicate equipment wear or failure. This proactive approach allows defence forces to extend the lifespan of expensive military equipment, reduce repair costs, and increase overall operational efficiency.

3. Potential Opportunities

The future of IoT in defence holds substantial opportunities that can dramatically enhance military capabilities. The following sections explore how IoT technologies could benefit various aspects of defence, from battlefield intelligence to cybersecurity.

3.1. Enhanced Battlefield Awareness and Situational Intelligence

The most significant opportunity IoT presents in defence is the ability to provide real-time battlefield awareness. IoT networks can connect soldiers, vehicles, drones, and sensors in the field, enabling them to share data and coordinate actions instantly. These systems can offer a continuous, panoramic view of the battlefield, allowing commanders to make data-driven decisions based on a comprehensive understanding of the tactical environment (Verma & Prakash, 2020).

IoT-enabled systems, such as wearable devices, smart sensors, and drone-based surveillance, allow for detailed situational intelligence, enabling military forces to track enemy movements, monitor terrain conditions, and analyze strategic options. Additionally, IoT's ability to collect and analyze vast amounts of data from multiple sources allows for predictive analysis, identifying potential threats before they materialize, and improving operational planning.

3.2. Smart Weaponry and Autonomous Defence Systems

The development of smart weaponry and autonomous defence systems is another exciting opportunity enabled by IoT. In future defence operations, IoT-driven technologies will be central to the deployment of autonomous drones, robotic soldiers, and AI-powered weaponry capable of targeting and neutralizing threats with minimal human intervention.

For example, autonomous drones could patrol borders, detect intruders, and respond to threats in real-time using IoT networks. IoT could enable these weapons to receive and transmit data, collaborate with other systems, and adjust tactics on the fly, enhancing both precision and effectiveness. Furthermore, the integration of IoT with robotic defence systems could lead to intelligent military robots capable of navigating complex environments and performing tasks ranging from surveillance to combat operations (Boudouaia et al., 2024; Majid et al., 2022; Reshi & Sholla, 2022; Srivastava & Pandey, 2022).

3.3. Streamlined Military Logistics and Resource Management

Efficient logistics and resource management are critical components of military operations, and IoT technologies offer the potential to streamline these processes. IoT sensors integrated into supply chains, inventories, and equipment can provide continuous monitoring of resources, alerting military logisticians when stock levels are low, when vehicles require maintenance, or when critical supplies are en route.

This level of connectivity improves both operational efficiency and cost-effectiveness, ensuring that military units are properly equipped at all times while minimizing waste. For example, IoT systems can automatically track the movement of supplies, optimize routes for resupply convoys, and predict when additional resources will be required based on real-time demand.

3.4. Strengthening Cybersecurity Through IoT Innovations

As military operations become more connected, cybersecurity becomes an increasingly important concern. IoT technologies offer innovative ways to strengthen military cybersecurity through the monitoring and protection of networks, devices, and critical infrastructure. IoT systems can identify anomalies, detect intrusions, and autonomously initiate countermeasures in the event of a cyberattack (Majid et al., 2022; Reshi & Sholla, 2022; Srivastava & Pandey, 2022).

The integration of blockchain and AI-based cybersecurity tools with IoT systems could offer new methods of ensuring data integrity and security in sensitive military communications. Real-time threat detection, predictive analysis, and automated response mechanisms can significantly enhance the resilience of defence networks against cyber threats.

4. Technological Challenges

The integration of IoT technology into a wide range of applications, from defence to healthcare and industrial systems, has ushered in major advancements. However, IoT systems face significant technological challenges that must be overcome to ensure their efficiency, scalability, and security (Chataut et al., 2023; Majid et al., 2022; Reshi & Sholla, 2022; Srivastava & Pandey, 2022). These challenges become particularly relevant when IoT devices are deployed in critical, high-risk environments like military operations, healthcare, or industrial automation. Below, we delve into four key technological challenges in IoT-driven devices:

4.1. Scalability and Interoperability of IoT Systems

a. Scalability Challenges

Scalability refers to the ability of an IoT system to handle a growing number of connected devices and data flows without compromising performance (Chataut et al., 2023). As IoT applications expand, devices increase, and data volumes grow, systems must remain responsive and efficient.

Challenges

- Data Overload: The more IoT devices are added to a network, the larger the volume of data that needs to be processed, analyzed, and stored. This can lead to data bottlenecks or slowdowns unless the system is capable of scaling effectively.
- Network Infrastructure: In large-scale IoT deployments (e.g. military networks or smart cities), the underlying network must support increased traffic. Legacy networks might struggle with scalability, requiring upgrades to higher-bandwidth solutions or newer technologies like 5G and Low Power Wide Area Networks (LPWANs).
- Edge Computing Versus Centralized Processing: Distributed IoT systems often use edge computing to process data closer to the device (reducing latency). As systems scale, managing distributed devices and data processing efficiently becomes increasingly complex.

Solutions

- Modular Architectures: Modular IoT designs allow for easier addition of new devices without requiring massive overhauls of the system.
- Cloud-Based Solutions: Cloud computing can provide virtually unlimited scalability, allowing for storage and processing of large amounts of data without compromising performance.
- Edge and Fog Computing: By processing data at the edge, these systems can reduce the data load sent to the cloud, making it easier to scale while maintaining performance.

b. Interoperability Challenges

- Definition: Interoperability is the ability of different IoT devices and systems to work together seamlessly, even when they are from different manufacturers or use different communication protocols (Tawalbeh et al., 2020).

Challenges

- Diverse Protocols and Standards: IoT devices may operate on various communication protocols, such as Bluetooth, Zigbee, LoRaWAN, 5G, and Wi-Fi, each with different specifications. This lack of uniformity can create difficulties in achieving interoperability (Boudouaia et al., 2024).
- Proprietary Systems: Manufacturers often develop proprietary IoT solutions, making it difficult to integrate devices from different vendors into a single cohesive system.

Solutions

- Standardization: Encouraging industry-wide standards (e.g. IEEE 802.15.4, 6LoWPAN, MQTT, CoAP) can help improve the interoperability of IoT devices.
- Middleware and Gateways: Middleware software solutions can provide the necessary bridge to enable communication between devices using different protocols. IoT gateways can aggregate data from diverse sources and ensure interoperability between different IoT networks.

4.2. Data Privacy and Cybersecurity Vulnerabilities

Privacy and Security Challenges

IoT devices collect vast amounts of personal, sensitive, or mission-critical data. Protecting this data from unauthorized access or tampering is a major challenge, especially as IoT devices proliferate in both personal and professional environments (Reshi & Sholla, 2022).

Challenges

- Vulnerabilities in Device Software: Many IoT devices are manufactured with weak or outdated security protocols, which can leave them vulnerable to hacking or exploitation.
- Lack of Standardized Security Protocols: IoT security protocols are often not standardized across devices, leaving gaps in security. This makes it difficult to ensure consistent protection across all devices in an IoT ecosystem.
- Data Interception: Since IoT devices often transmit data wirelessly, the data can be intercepted by attackers if proper encryption is not in place. This is a particular risk for devices deployed in military or defence applications where sensitive data may be compromised.
- DDoS Attacks: IoT devices are often targets for Distributed Denial-of-Service (DDoS) attacks, which can overwhelm a network by flooding it with traffic.

Solutions

- Encryption: Strong encryption (e.g. TLS/SSL, AES) ensures that data transmitted between devices is secure and not susceptible to interception or tampering.
- Authentication and Access Control: Implementing multi-factor authentication and strong access controls can prevent unauthorized access to IoT systems.
- Security Standards and Frameworks: Developing and adhering to security standards (e.g. ISO/IEC 27001, NIST Cybersecurity Framework) and frameworks for IoT systems can ensure a baseline of security across devices.
- Regular Firmware Updates: Regularly updating device firmware to patch known vulnerabilities is crucial in defending against cyberattacks.

4.3. Power Consumption and Sustainability of IoT Devices

Energy Efficiency Challenges

IoT devices are often deployed in environments where frequent charging or power replacement is not feasible (e.g. remote military bases, smart agriculture, or remote monitoring systems). Ensuring that these devices can operate efficiently with minimal power consumption is crucial for sustainable operations.

Challenges

- Power-Intensive Sensors: Some IoT devices, particularly those with sensors that require continuous data collection (e.g. cameras, environmental monitors), can drain battery life quickly.
- Energy-Hungry Communication Protocols: Some IoT communication protocols, such as Wi-Fi, require significant power to transmit data, especially over long distances.

- Long Lifespan Requirements: IoT devices in critical applications (e.g. military or remote monitoring) may need to function for long periods without the need for maintenance, which requires highly efficient power management systems.

Solutions

- Low-Power Communication Protocols: Utilizing energy-efficient protocols such as LoRaWAN and NB-IoT can significantly reduce power consumption while maintaining long-range communication.
- Energy Harvesting: IoT devices can incorporate energy harvesting technologies (e.g. solar panels, piezoelectric sensors) to extend operational lifetimes without needing frequent battery replacements.
- Low-Power Sensors and Edge Computing: Deploying sensors that use minimal power and processing data locally at the edge (rather than transmitting everything to the cloud) reduces the energy required for data transmission.

Sustainability Concerns

The increasing number of IoT devices contributes to e-waste, and their energy consumption can exacerbate sustainability challenges (Tawalbeh et al., 2020).

Solutions

- Recyclable Materials: IoT devices can be designed with recyclable or eco-friendly materials to reduce the environmental impact.
- Energy-Efficient Manufacturing: Reducing the energy footprint during manufacturing processes and extending the lifecycle of IoT devices through design improvements.

4.4. Adapting IoT Systems to Extreme Environments

Challenges of Extreme Environments

IoT systems deployed in extreme environments – such as deep-sea exploration, space missions, or military operations in hostile terrains – must withstand harsh physical conditions (e.g. temperature extremes, high humidity, EMI) while maintaining reliable performance (Krejčí et al., 2025).

Challenges

- Environmental Durability: IoT devices must be resistant to temperature fluctuations, moisture, dust, and corrosive environments (e.g. in military or industrial applications).
- Power Supply: In remote or harsh environments, reliable power sources are often unavailable, making it difficult to keep devices running for extended periods.
- Signal Interference: High EMI in areas such as battlefields or industrial settings can disrupt IoT device communication, reducing reliability.

Solutions

- Ruggedized Devices: IoT devices used in extreme environments need to be designed to meet military or industrial standards (e.g. IP67 for water and dust resistance or MIL-STD-810 for military-grade toughness).
- Low-Power, Long-Life Components: Using low-power sensors, energy-efficient communication technologies, and self-sustaining power sources (like solar or kinetic energy harvesting) ensures long operational lifetimes in remote locations.
- Redundant Communication Systems: Implementing multiple communication channels (e.g. satellite, radio, or mesh networks) provides robustness against signal degradation in harsh environments.
- Autonomous Maintenance and Recovery: Some IoT systems in extreme environments are designed to be self-healing or have built-in redundancy to ensure continued operation in case of failure.

IoT-driven devices are reshaping numerous industries, but overcoming the technological challenges associated with scalability, interoperability, cybersecurity, power consumption, and environmental adaptability is crucial for ensuring their success. Addressing these challenges requires a multi-faceted approach, including developing industry standards, leveraging advanced encryption and power management techniques, and designing rugged, energy-efficient devices capable of operating under extreme conditions. As IoT technology continues to evolve, these solutions will be critical to ensuring that IoT systems are both reliable and sustainable in a variety of mission-critical applications (Khalil et al., 2022; Krejčí et al., 2025).

5. Ethical, Legal, and Social Implications (ELSI)

The deployment of IoT technologies in defence raises a host of ethical, legal, and social concerns. As these technologies advance, it is essential to address the potential risks they pose to privacy, autonomy, and human rights.

5.1. Balancing Automation with Human Oversight

One of the most pressing ethical challenges is the need to balance automation with human oversight. Autonomous systems, such as drones and robotic soldiers, have the potential to make military operations more efficient (Majid et al., 2022). However, the ethical dilemma arises when such systems are entrusted with life-and-death decisions without human intervention. Ethical frameworks must be established to ensure that humans remain in control of critical decisions, especially in situations where life-threatening force is involved.

5.2. Privacy Concerns in Military IoT Applications

The integration of IoT in defence often involves the collection of vast amounts of personal and sensitive data, raising significant privacy concerns. Military IoT systems that collect data on soldiers' health, location, and behaviour must be carefully designed to protect individual privacy and prevent unauthorized access. Moreover, surveillance IoT systems deployed in conflict zones must comply with international privacy standards to ensure that civilian rights are not violated (Verma & Prakash, 2020).

5.3. Global Regulations and Standards for IoT in Defence

Given the international nature of modern warfare and defence cooperation, global regulations and standards are necessary to govern the use of IoT in defence applications. These regulations must address issues of data sharing, cybersecurity, and ethical boundaries, ensuring that IoT technologies are used in ways that respect international law and human rights (Chataut et al., 2023). Global governance frameworks are essential to prevent misuse and abuse of powerful IoT technologies.

6. Future Research Directions

The future of IoT-driven defence technologies promises exciting possibilities, but much remains to be explored in terms of innovation, optimization, and ethical considerations. As IoT technologies continue to revolutionize military operations, several key research directions must be pursued to fully harness their potential while addressing emerging challenges. Fig. 14.1 shows the future directions of IoT in defence and other promising possibilities.

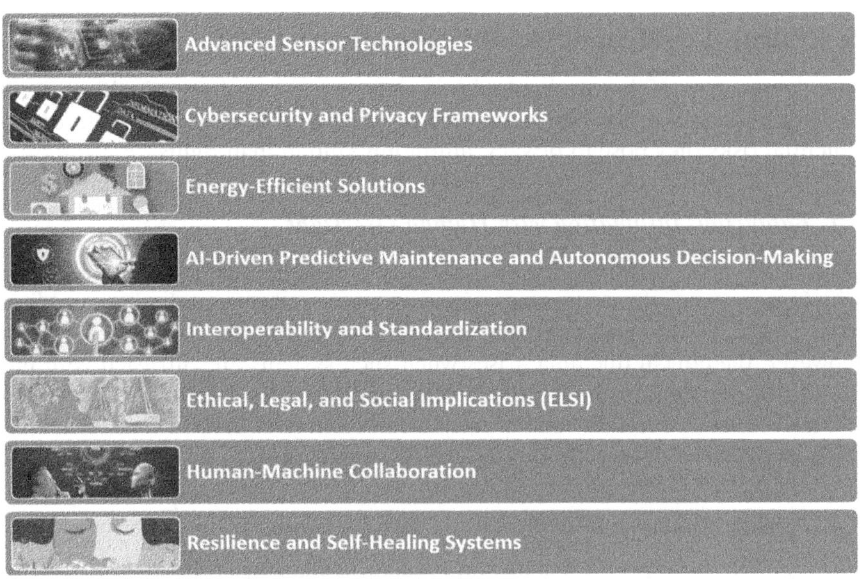

Fig. 14.1. Future Research Directions.

6.1. Advanced Sensor Technologies

Future research will need to prioritize the development of highly sensitive, durable, and adaptive sensor technologies capable of functioning in extreme and dynamic environments. This includes sensors with enhanced precision, longer operational lifespans, and the ability to detect multiple types of threats simultaneously (Chataut et al., 2023; Srivastava & Pandey, 2022). Nanotechnology and bio-inspired sensors could offer breakthroughs in miniaturization and energy efficiency, while self-healing materials could improve the longevity and reliability of sensors in hostile terrains.

6.2. Cybersecurity and Privacy Frameworks

With the increasing interconnectivity of IoT devices in defence systems, cybersecurity will remain a paramount concern. Research should focus on developing lightweight encryption algorithms, secure communication protocols, and decentralized architectures that ensure data integrity and prevent unauthorized access. Blockchain-based security frameworks and zero-trust architectures could offer promising solutions to mitigate cyber threats. Additionally, privacy-preserving techniques such as homomorphic encryption and federated learning will need further exploration to safeguard sensitive mission-critical data.

6.3. Energy-Efficient Solutions

IoT devices in defence applications often operate in remote and resource-constrained environments, making energy efficiency a critical factor. Future studies should explore novel energy harvesting technologies, such as solar, kinetic, and thermal energy, to extend the operational lifespan of IoT devices. Research into low-power communication protocols and energy-aware data transmission methods will also be essential for optimizing the performance of IoT networks (Chataut et al., 2023; Majid et al., 2022; Reshi & Sholla, 2022; Srivastava & Pandey, 2022; Tawalbeh et al., 2020).

6.4. AI-Driven PdM and Autonomous Decision-Making

AI algorithms will play a pivotal role in enhancing the capabilities of IoT-driven defence systems. Research should delve into PdM models that leverage ML techniques to detect anomalies and predict equipment failures before they occur. Autonomous decision-making systems powered by AI will require robust training datasets, explainable AI models, and rigorous testing in real-world scenarios to ensure reliability, safety, and compliance with military protocols.

6.5. Interoperability and Standardization

The lack of standardization among IoT devices poses a significant challenge to seamless integration in defence systems. Future research should focus on developing open standards and interoperable architectures that enable different devices and systems to communicate and collaborate effectively. This will require cross-industry collaborations and the establishment of global standards for IoT in defence.

6.6. Ethical, Legal, and Social Implications

As IoT technologies become more autonomous and pervasive, interdisciplinary research will be essential to address their ELSI. Key issues include the potential for autonomous weapons, data privacy concerns, and the accountability of AI-driven decision-making systems. Collaborative efforts between technologists, policymakers, ethicists, and legal experts will be required to develop regulatory frameworks that uphold human rights, align with international humanitarian law, and foster public trust in these technologies.

6.7. Human–Machine Collaboration

Future IoT-driven defence systems should be designed to augment human decision-making rather than replace it. Research should focus on developing intuitive human–machine interfaces that enhance situational awareness and enable seamless collaboration between human operators and autonomous systems. Augmented reality (AR), virtual reality (VR), and brain-computer interfaces (BCIs) could offer innovative ways to improve the efficiency and effectiveness of human-machine collaboration.

6.8. Resilience and Self-Healing Systems

Ensuring the resilience of IoT systems against physical and cyber threats will be a critical area of future research. Self-healing systems that can automatically detect, isolate, and recover from faults or cyberattacks will be vital for maintaining operational continuity in high-risk environments. Research into biologically inspired algorithms and distributed self-healing architectures will help create more resilient defence systems (Boudouaia et al., 2024; Chataut et al., 2023; Majid et al., 2022; Reshi & Sholla, 2022; Srivastava & Pandey, 2022; Verma & Prakash, 2020).

By addressing these future research directions, IoT-driven defence technologies can become more secure, efficient, and aligned with human values. A multidisciplinary approach involving collaboration between engineers, data scientists, ethicists, policymakers, and military strategists will be key to shaping the next generation of defence technologies in a way that ensures both technological advancement and societal well-being.

7. Conclusion

The future of IoT-driven defence technologies presents a transformative shift in modern military operations, offering unprecedented opportunities to enhance operational efficiency, decision-making, and combat effectiveness. The integration of IoT systems can revolutionize defence infrastructures by enabling autonomous systems, PdM, and real-time situational awareness. These advancements not only bolster strategic capabilities but also contribute to reducing human casualties and optimizing resource utilization. The potential for IoT to improve logistics, supply chain management, and remote monitoring further underscores its critical role in shaping the future of defence ecosystems. However, the rapid proliferation of IoT technologies necessitates a comprehensive approach to address technical, operational, and strategic challenges that may emerge during deployment.

To fully harness the benefits of IoT-driven defence technologies, defence organizations must prioritize investments in robust cybersecurity frameworks, interoperability standards, and ethical governance. Cybersecurity remains a paramount concern, as IoT devices are often vulnerable to cyberattacks that could compromise mission-critical operations. Establishing standardized protocols for data encryption, secure communication, and continuous threat monitoring is essential to safeguarding sensitive information. Additionally, ensuring seamless interoperability between heterogeneous IoT systems across allied forces will require collaborative efforts to define common technical standards. Ethical considerations, particularly regarding autonomous decision-making and data privacy, must also be embedded into the design and deployment of IoT applications. By adopting a holistic approach that balances technological innovation with security, interoperability, and ethical responsibility, defence organizations can unlock the full potential of IoT while adhering to legal, humanitarian, and international regulatory standards.

References

Adil, M., Khan, M. K., Kumar, N., Attique, M., Farouk, A., Guizani, M., & Jin, Z. (2024). Healthcare Internet of Things: Security threats, challenges, and future research directions. *IEEE Internet of Things Journal*, *11*(11), 19046–19069.

Awasthi, A., Krpalkova, L., & Walsh, J. (2025). Bridging the maturity gaps in industrial data science: Navigating challenges in IoT-driven manufacturing. *Technologies*, *13*(1), 22.

Boudouaia, M. A., Ouchani, S., Qaisar, S. M., & Almaktoom, A. T. (2024, January). Supply chain 5.0: Vision, challenges, and perspectives. In *2024 21st learning and technology conference (L&T)* (pp. 203–208). IEEE.

Chataut, R., Phoummalayvane, A., & Akl, R. (2023). Unleashing the power of IoT: A comprehensive review of IoT applications and future prospects in healthcare, agriculture, smart homes, smart cities, and industry 4.0. *Sensors*, *23*(16), 7194.

Gadekallu, T. R., Pham, Q. V., Huynh-The, T., Bhattacharya, S., Maddikunta, P. K. R., & Liyanage, M. (2021). Federated learning for big data: A survey on opportunities, applications, and future directions. *arXiv preprint arXiv:2110.04160*.

Khalil, U., Malik, O. A., Uddin, M., & Chen, C. L. (2022). A comparative analysis on blockchain versus centralized authentication architectures for IoT-enabled smart devices in smart cities: A comprehensive review, recent advances, and future research directions. *Sensors*, *22*(14), 5168.

Konstantellos, A. (2022). An overview of emerging systems-related concepts, approaches and technologies unifying and advancing S&T achievements of the past decades (eg CPS, IoT, I2oT, SoS/E, 5G and Cross-Cutting Decision Making). *CyberPhysical Systems*, 1–98.

Krejčí, J., Babiuch, M., Suder, J., Krys, V., & Bobovský, Z. (2025). Internet of Robotic Things: Current technologies, challenges, applications, and future research topics. *Sensors*, *25*(3), 765.

Majid, M., Habib, S., Javed, A. R., Rizwan, M., Srivastava, G., Gadekallu, T. R., & Lin, J. C. W. (2022). Applications of wireless sensor networks and internet of things frameworks in the industry revolution 4.0: A systematic literature review. *Sensors*, *22*(6), 2087.

Nayak, D., Ganguly, I., Mishra, S., & Anand, K. (2023). Investigation and implication of advanced sensory computing in military and defense applications. In *SCCTT* (pp. 11–25).

Reshi, I. A., & Sholla, S. (2022). Challenges for security in IoT, emerging solutions, and research directions. *International Journal of Computing and Digital Systems*, *12*(1), 1231–1241.

Seet, P. S., Klarin, A., Jones, J., Johnstone, M., Cripps, H., Sharafizad, J., & Marceddo, T. (2024). Opportunities and challenges posed by disruptive and converging information technologies for Australia's future defence capabilities: A horizon scan.

Srivastava, N., & Pandey, P. (2022). Internet of things (IoT): Applications, trends, issues and challenges. *Materials Today: Proceedings*, *69*, 587–591.

Suhail, S., Hussain, R., Khan, A., & Hong, C. S. (2020). On the role of hash-based signatures in quantum-safe internet of things: Current solutions and future directions. *IEEE Internet of Things Journal*, *8*(1), 1–17.

Tawalbeh, L. A., Muheidat, F., Tawalbeh, M., & Quwaider, M. (2020). IoT privacy and security: Challenges and solutions. *Applied Sciences*, *10*(12), 4102.

Verma, A., Bhattacharya, P., Madhani, N., Trivedi, C., Bhushan, B., Tanwar, S., & Sharma, R. (2022). *Blockchain for industry 5.0: Vision, opportunities, key enablers, and future directions*. IEEE Access, *10*, 69160–69199.

Verma, G., & Prakash, S. (2020, June). A comparative study based on different energy saving mechanisms based on green internet of things (GIoT). In *2020 8th International conference on reliability, infocom technologies and optimization (Trends and Future Directions) (ICRITO)* (pp. 659–666). IEEE.

Index

Printed and bound by CPI Group (UK) Ltd, Croydon, CR0 4YY

29/07/2026

14931731-0005